Palgrave Socio-Legal Studies

**Series Editor**
Dave Cowan
School of Law
University of Bristol
Bristol, UK

The Palgrave Socio-Legal Studies series is a developing series of monographs and textbooks featuring cutting edge work which, in the best tradition of socio-legal studies, reach out to a wide international audience.



More information about this series at
http://www.palgrave.com/gp/series/14679

Chris Dietz • Mitchell Travis
Michael Thomson
Editors

# A Jurisprudence of the Body

palgrave
macmillan

*Editors*
Chris Dietz
School of Law
University of Leeds
Leeds, UK

Mitchell Travis
School of Law
University of Leeds
Leeds, UK

Michael Thomson
Faculty of Law
University of Technology Sydney
Sydney, Australia

School of Law
University of Leeds
Leeds, UK

Palgrave Socio-Legal Studies
ISBN 978-3-030-42199-1 ISBN 978-3-030-42200-4 (eBook)
https://doi.org/10.1007/978-3-030-42200-4



Cover illustration: Getty/Gremlin

This Palgrave Macmillan imprint is published by the registered company Springer Nature Switzerland AG.
The registered company address is: Gewerbestrasse 11, 6330 Cham, Switzerland

# Acknowledgements

We would like to express our gratitude to our contributors for giving so freely of their important ideas. Whilst the initial idea for the collection was ours, it is the contributors to this collection who have added so much to this project and made it worthwhile. We have been inspired by their work and we hope this collection goes on to inspire others. We are thankful to the Socio-Legal Studies Association (SLSA) conference convenors in Leeds 2019 for allowing us to convene a *Jurisprudence of the Body* stream. This enabled us to test some of our ideas in the supportive and engaged environment that the SLSA always provides in its conferences and other events. The Leeds conference also helped us to make important connections with people who would go on to be contributors to this collection. We are very grateful for the input of our pool of reviewers: David Griffiths, Marie-Andrée Jacob, Amanda Keeling, Sam Lewis, Stu Marvel, Jose Miola, Craig Purshouse, Sally Sheldon, and Jens Thielen. Each provided the generosity, clarity, and insight that we have come to expect from them over the years. Thanks are also due to the editorial team at Palgrave—David Cowan and Liam Inscoe-Jones—whose assistance has helped us get over the finishing line. Finally, our thanks also go out to our colleagues in the Centre for Law and Social Justice, University of Leeds. This creative and productive space has allowed the ideas that sparked this book to be explored and developed.

# Praise for *A Jurisprudence of the Body*

"Health law offers a key site for rethinking the place of the body in legal systems. With its definitive focus on wellness and vulnerability, death and reproduction, the law's role in producing bodies in all their variety is especially clear. As this timely collection demonstrates, the 'turn to the material' in feminist theory and its concern with social practices of embodiment, offer an opportunity to review the field critically and to take stock of the political contexts and normative implications of health law's many bodies. It also challenges us to consider again what we mean by health law: who are its audiences, who is heard, who is seen, who goes unseen? These challenges are ably taken up in the rich, engaging and coherent set of essays which make up *A Jurisprudence of the Body*."

—John Harrington, *Professor of Global Health Law, Cardiff University*

# Contents

# Notes on Contributors

**Aziza Ahmed** is a Professor at Northeastern University School of Law. Her scholarship examines the legal, regulatory and political environments regarding health in US domestic law, US foreign policy and international law. She was a member of the Technical Advisory Group on HIV and the Law convened by the United Nations Development Programme (UNDP) and has been an expert for many institutions, including the American Bar Association and UNIFEM. Her latest monograph *Feminism's Medicine: Law, Science, Race, and Gender in an Epidemic* is forthcoming with Cambridge University Press.

**Jo Bridgeman** is Professor of Healthcare Law and Feminist Ethics at the University of Sussex where she teaches Perspectives on Healthcare Law, Tort, Gender Equality, Feminism, Law and Society. Her research adopts a critical feminist perspective informed by and developing the feminist ethics of care in consideration of parental, professional and state responsibilities to children. Her work on the medical treatment of children, including the care of children with complex needs, parental responsibility for children undergoing treatment for cancer, withholding/withdrawal of life-sustaining treatment from a child and issues arising from the Bristol Royal Infirmary Inquiry, has been published widely. This chapter develops the conceptual framework advanced in her book, *Parental Responsibility, Young Children and Healthcare Law* (2007). She is working on a book which examines the development of the law governing the medical treatment of children over the past four decades within the changing social, political and legal context.

**Emilie Cloatre** is Professor of Law at the University of Kent. Her research focuses on the relationship between law and 'science in society', and in particular between law and medical practices. She is Principal Investigator on a Wellcome Investigator Award entitled 'Law, Knowledges and the Making of "Modern" Healthcare' (2017–2022).

**John Coggon** is Professor of Law at the University of Bristol Law School, where he is a member of the Centre for Health, Law, and Society. He is also a member of the University's Centre for Public Health and Population Health Science Institute, and an honorary member of the UK Faculty of Public Health. His research interests lie primarily in the areas of mental capacity law and public health ethics and law, and his publications include the monograph, *What Makes Health Public? A Critical Evaluation of Moral, Legal, and Political Claims in Public Health* (2012), and the textbook, co-authored with Keith Syrett and A.M. Viens, *Public Health Law: Ethics, Governance, and Regulation* (2017).

**Chris Dietz** is a Lecturer in Law and Social Justice at the School of Law, University of Leeds. His work considers the regulation of gendered embodiment, with a focus on trans health. He has undertaken visiting fellowships at the Unit of Gender Studies, Linköping University; the Centre for Gender Studies, Karlstad University; and the Centre for Gender Studies, University of Copenhagen.

**Martha Albertson Fineman** is an American jurist, legal theorist, and political philosopher. She is Robert W. Woodruff Professor of Law at Emory University School of Law. Since 2008, Fineman has directed the Vulnerability and Human Condition Initiative at Emory, as well as the Feminism and Legal Theory Project, which she founded at the University of Wisconsin in 1984. Her work considers the legal, social, and political implications of universal dependency and vulnerability, formulating a robust theory of social justice that is an alternative to a rights-based model for determining state or collective responsibility for individual and societal wellbeing.

**Marie Fox** holds the Queen Victoria Chair of Law in the School of Law and Social Justice, University of Liverpool. Her research is concerned with the legal governance of human and animal bodies, legal conceptions of embodiment and regulation of reproduction. Her projects (funded by the Dunhill Medical Trust, Wellcome Trust and Socio-legal Studies Association) focus on pet loss and the place of companion animals in care homes, governance of assisted reproductive technologies, abortion law reform in Northern Ireland

and legal regulation of genital cutting. She is a co-ordinating editor of the journals *Social & Legal Studies* and *Medical Law International*.

**Danielle Fuller** is a Professor in the Department of English and Film Studies at the University of Alberta. Her main areas of research are contemporary cultures of reading and interdisciplinary research methods that combine textual and empirical modes of investigation. Before emigrating to Canada in May 2018, she worked for nearly 21 years at the University of Birmingham, UK. She was the Principle Investigator for 'Death Before Birth' project from its inception to April 2018, and has also led collaborative projects funded by the Arts and Humanities Research Council, Arts Council England and the British Academy.

**Fae Garland** is Lecturer in Law at the University of Manchester where she is a member of both the Centre for Social Ethics and Policy and the Manchester Centre for Regulation and Governance. Her work on gender, sex and law has been widely published in journals such as the *American Journal of Bioethics*, *Edinburgh Law Review*, *Journal of Law and Society*, *Legal Studies* and *New Zealand Law Review*. She has also co-authored a number of national and international governmental reports that explore intersex rights and law and has been PI on a range of empirical projects which consider the impact of law reform on intersex lives. Most recently, she has been awarded funding by the British Academy (with Mitchell Travis) to examine the operation of Maltese legislation which prohibits unnecessary surgeries on intersex infants.

**Claire Horn** holds a BA from McGill University and an MA from New York University. She was awarded her PhD in Law at Birkbeck, University of London, where she was co-supervised by Elena Loizidou and Daniel Monk. Her dissertation "Gestation Beyond Mother/Machine: Legal Frameworks for Artificial Wombs, Abortion, and Care," uses a comparative analysis of the impact of ectogenesis on abortion law in the UK, US and Canada to argue for abortion decriminalization and affirmative protections to abortion access ahead of the development of artificial womb technologies. Horn is a recipient of the Canadian Centennial Scholarship Fund 2018–2019, and is continuing her research on artificial wombs as a Wellcome Postdoctoral Researcher at Birkbeck Law.

**Isabel Karpin** is a Professor at the University of Technology Sydney. She researches on the bioethical implications of laws governing reproductive technologies, genetic testing and disability. She explores the challenge posed by new biotechnological developments on legal understandings of normality, disability, individuality and family.

**Karolina Kuberska** is a medical anthropologist with a special interest in understandings of health, wellbeing, and healthcare. She holds her PhD from the University of St Andrews. Between 2016 and 2018, she was a postdoctoral fellow in the Death Before Birth research team at the University of Birmingham. She is a research associate at THIS Institute at the University of Cambridge where she is involved in a range of projects designed to strengthen the evidence base for improving the quality and safety of healthcare.

**Jeannette Littlemore** is Professor of Applied Linguistics in the Department of English Language and Linguistics at the University of Birmingham. Her research focuses on metaphor and metonymy and explores the facilitative and debilitative role played by metaphor and metonymy in language education and in cross-linguistic and cross-cultural communication more generally. She is interested in the creative use of metaphor and metonymy and in the ways in which figurative meaning is negotiated by speakers with different kinds of background knowledge and different emotional experiences. Her monographs include *Metaphors in the Mind: Sources of Variation in Embodied Metaphor* (2019).

**Sheelagh McGuinness** is Reader in Law at the University of Bristol Law School, where she is Co-Director of the Centre for Health, Law, and Society. Her research focuses on health law and the regulation of reproduction. She is interested in the ways in which law and legal frameworks can shape experience of health care and reproduction and has published across these areas in law, ethics, and health care journals. She was a co-investigator on the Economic and Social Research Council funded (ES-N008359) project "Death Before Birth: Understanding, informing and supporting the choices made by people who have experienced miscarriage, termination and stillbirth".

**Karen O'Connell** is an Associate Professor at the University of Technology Sydney and an expert in discrimination law and biotechnologies of the body. Her research addresses the ways that equality laws might better respond to the experiences of stigmatised groups in society, particularly given emerging neuroscientific and genetic knowledge about the body and disability. She is the recipient of a UTS Chancellor's Postdoctoral Research Fellowship (2010–2015) and an Australia Research Council Discovery Grant (2015–2019).

**Ruth Pearce** is a Research Fellow in the School of Sociology and Social Policy at the University of Leeds, UK. Her research explores issues of inequality, marginalisation, power and political struggle from a trans feminist perspective. Ruth is the author of *Understanding Trans Health* (2018) and editor of *The Emergence of Trans* (2020), with Igi Moon, Kat Gupta, and Deborah Lynn Steinberg. She blogs about her work on http://ruthpearce.net.

**Elizabeth Chloe Romanis** is an Assistant Professor in Biolaw at Durham University and holds an LLB (Hons) in Law and LLM in Healthcare Ethics and Law from the University of Manchester. She is a PhD Candidate at the University of Manchester co-supervised by Alexandra Mullock and Rebecca Bennett. Her PhD is supported by a Wellcome Trust Studentship in Society and Ethics. Her research focuses on the ethical and legal questions arising from the potential use of artificial womb technology as an experimental alternative to neonatal intensive care. Her thesis is entitled: 'Regulating the "Brave New World": Ethico-Legal Implications of the Quest for Ectogenesis.' Her broader research interests include pregnancy and the law, assisted reproduction, innovative reproductive technologies and the legal meaning of birth and life.

**Michael Thomson** is Professor of Health Law at the University of Technology Sydney and the University of Leeds. His research spans health law, children's rights, and legal theory. He has written extensively on non-therapeutic interventions on children and the regulation of reproduction. He is the author of two books, *Reproducing Narrative: Gender, Reproduction & Law* (1998) and *Endowed: Regulating the Male Sexed Body* (2008), and two previous edited collections, *Feminist Perspectives on Healthcare Law* (with Sally Sheldon, 1998) and *Exploring Masculinities: Feminist Legal Theory Reflections* (with Martha Fineman, 2013). His current work explores the place of the body in contemporary theories of social justice and the increasing attention paid to the social environment across the life sciences.

**Mitchell Travis** is an Associate Professor in law at the Centre for Law and Social Justice at the University of Leeds. His work considers the relationships between embodiment, institutions and culture with a primary focus on working with the intersex community. He has worked with the UK Government Equalities Office, the National Health Service and the Norwegian Directorate for Children, Youth and Family Affairs. His continuing work with Fae Garland has been cited by the Office of the United Nations High Commissioner for Human Rights, the Law Society and various intersex organisations.

**Sarah Turner** is a cognitive linguist with a particular interest in the analysis of metaphor and figurative language. She holds her PhD from the University of Birmingham in 2014, then held a teaching position at the University of

Tokyo before taking up a postdoctoral research fellowship at the University of Birmingham on the Death Before Birth project team, 2016–2018. She is Lecturer in English in the School of Humanities at Coventry University. Her research focuses on the analysis of figurative language production to provide insights into physical, psychological and social experiences, with a current focus on the experience of bereavement and grief.

**Nayeli Urquiza-Haas** is a Wellcome Trust Research Associate at the University of Kent, working on the project 'Law, Knowledges and the Making of "Modern" Healthcare' (Wellcome Investigator Award (2017–2022). She holds a PhD from the University of Kent (2015). Her research focuses on vulnerability in feminist legal studies and the regulation of traditional and non-conventional medicines.

**Joshua Warburton** is a researcher and teaching fellow at the School of Law at the University of Leeds. His research interests include health law, consumer law, EU Law, and tort law. He obtained his PhD in Law at the University of Manchester. His projects include studies on medical practice, legal educational reform, and theoretical contract forms.

# 1

# Nobody, Anybody, Somebody, Everybody: A Jurisprudence of the Body

Chris Dietz, Mitchell Travis, and Michael Thomson

## 1 Introduction

Health and embodiment are inextricably linked. How we feel about our bodies has a significant impact upon our health. When we feel healthy, we tend to experience our bodies positively, and vice versa. Similarly, it is difficult to think of an occasion when we experience poor health and yet feel good about our bodies. An unexpected diagnosis can dramatically alter our experience of our bodies, even if we felt fine immediately before we received it. Meanwhile, getting the all-clear from a medical professional following a health test can have unparalleled positive effects upon our general well-being. For this reason, few dispute the centrality of the body within health studies. Yet as we turn our attention to the law, and health law specifically,[1] we note that bodies have not

[1] The sub-discipline of 'health law' covers similar ground to 'health care law' or 'medical law' (though boundaries are contested). Herein, the former is understood as more inclusive than the latter, as it accepts that a subject's 'health' exceeds matters which are dealt with in a medical context (Montgomery 2002: 1–3).

C. Dietz (✉) • M. Travis
School of Law, University of Leeds, Leeds, UK
e-mail: c.p.dietz@leeds.ac.uk; M.Travis@leeds.ac.uk

M. Thomson
Faculty of Law, University of Technology Sydney, Sydney, NSW, Australia

School of Law, University of Leeds, Leeds, UK
e-mail: michael.thomson@uts.edu.au



C. Dietz et al. (eds.), *A Jurisprudence of the Body*, Palgrave Socio-Legal Studies,
https://doi.org/10.1007/978-3-030-42200-4_1

always been considered as seriously as they might have been. Rather than being front and centre in the minds of health law scholars and practitioners, the body has tended to be obscured in various ways. Even when the body has not been masked within health law—for example, in the case of the bodies which have been considered disordered, diseased or disabled, and which have animated many discussions about health—they have tended to be under-theorised. Such bodies have been framed in a manner which fails to address the complexity of embodiment, and the messy instability of bodies.

This collection seeks to uncover and challenge some of the fundamental assumptions that underpin medico-legal knowledge about bodies. In doing so, it raises important questions about how various types of bodies are, and ought to be, regulated. The question of what the body is and how it directs our thinking about law and health is hereby positioned alongside a wider question about how institutions such as law and the healthcare system shape our understanding of bodies. *A Jurisprudence of the Body* brings together a range of theoretical perspectives to consider fundamental questions about health law and the place of the body within it. The collection reflects the shift in feminist thinking 'from an emphasis on the discursive toward the material' (Garland-Thomson 2011: 594), positioning its theoretical focus on the connections between the law and flesh. Some contributors discuss bodies which have been located at the heart of health law debates since the inception of the field. Others consider bodies which remain on the margins. But each contribution addresses the discursive and institutional boundaries of health, and in some cases, seek to dismantle them. This collection is hereby positioned at the intersection of theory, health and law but also at the limits of these spheres—pushing them to breaking point in order to facilitate the possibility of new directions in health care and health justice.

In this introduction, we seek to frame the discussion that will follow. After briefly charting law's (lack of) engagement with the body in the first section (entitled 'Nobody'), we then address the ways in which a de-contextualised conception of bodies has been used to regulate embodiment in the second ('Anybody'). As we explain, such framings inevitably underplay the inherent diversity of human bodies, which will have significant impact upon law and policy, particularly within a health law context. In the third section ('Somebody'), we identify how attempts have been made to re-contextualise bodies in relation to the specific institutions and regulations to which they are subjected in order to better account for this embodied diversity. This improved, but fragmented, understanding of bodies will then be contrasted with the recent return to universality in the fourth section ('Everybody'). In an attempt to move law and policy beyond interrogation of identities, universal approaches—including those developed within vulnerability theory and other embodied theories of justice—have become increasingly pronounced in contemporary legal studies. Intersectional, identarian and post-identarian understandings of bodies are well represented in this collection, as emphasised in the fifth and final section of this introduction.

## 2 Nobody

Traditional jurisprudential approaches have been reluctant to engage with the idea of the body. Positivists have neglected to outline either the impact of law on bodies or the effect of bodies on their relationships with law. Such formulations have failed to consider the body as a determining factor in the attribution of personhood; instead espousing, for example, the view that the person is a legalistic shorthand (Dewey 1926: 655). This view is elaborated by Derham, who writes:

> Just as the concept "one" in arithmetic is essential to the logical system developed and yet is not one something (e.g. apple or orange, etc.), so a legal system (or any system perhaps) must be provided with a basic unit before legal relationships can be devised. The legal person is the unit or entity adopted. For the logic of the system it is just as much a pure "concept" as "one" in arithmetic. It is just as independent from a human being as one is from an "apple". (Derham 1958: 5)

Under this understanding of personhood, the legal person is a unit devised and utilised by law, a container capable of being filled by any entity (such as the doctor or patient of health law). Yet while it may be correct to say that anyone (or anything) can be a legal person, this does not ascribe a basis for *determining* personhood. Nor can it account for the diverse bodies to which personhood has been applied, the injustices it conceals or the bodies that it has privileged and underprivileged. This separation of law and bodies fails to account for the ways in which bodies are shaped, constituted and constructed by the institutions that they are imbricated within. As a result, this disembodied conception of law has been critically described by Grear as 'a socially decontextualized, hyper-rational, wilful individual systematically stripped of embodied particularities in order to appear neutral and, of course, theoretically genderless' (2011: 44).

## 3 Anybody

The lack of emphasis on bodies has given rise to the liberal conception that bodies are largely interchangeable in their interactions with societal institutions, including law and the healthcare system. Liberal framings, such as human rights discourse, have become the dominant language for thinking about law and the body. These tend to be premised upon the supposed universality of the human body. Yet the meaning of humanity, or even biology, is subject to both social and cultural concerns. As Fuss (1996: 1) has claimed: 'the human is a linguistic, cultural, and sociopolitical construct of comparatively recent date'. For Fuss, the concept of the human is more than a simple genetic relation. Instead, it relies upon political and cultural ideology to include and exclude entities from its boundaries at different times. As a consequence, it is unsurprising to find that broader liberal legal considerations have, for the most part, categorised the body 'as an object of analysis rather than as a category of analysis' (Fletcher et al. 2008: 321). This point of focus has failed to account for the value that society places on the living physical body, particularly in terms of our interactions with others and its facilitation of our experience of being in the world (Fletcher et al. 2008: 321). Hyde (1997) notes that the law uses a variety of unsuccessful conceptualisations when dealing with the body, including property, privacy right and machine. Each of these metaphors fails to encapsulate the importance of the body. As Naffine writes, there has been a shift in legal theory from a bodiless conception of law to a particular type of (assumedly interchangeable) body:

> the rational and therefore responsible human legal agent or subject: the classic contractor, the individual who is held personally accountable for his civil and criminal actions. This is the individual who possesses the plenitude of legal rights and responsibilities, the ideal legal actor … he who asserts his will, who grasps and asserts his legal rights. Now there is a discrete possessor of rights. (Naffine 2003: 362)

Principles of liberty, equality and freedom operate to allow individuals the same opportunities for flourishing within Western states. Liberal understandings of meritocracy suggest that anyone can achieve anything—even good health—provided they work hard enough for it. In turn, anti-discrimination law has become prominent in order to prevent people from being unfairly discriminated against on the basis of the particularities of their bodies. In this theoretical tradition, bodies are understood as interchangeable. The 'he' so often used in legislation can be applied to women, while race and disability are not important aspects for the purposes of general (non-specific) legislation. Despite this, indicators such as race, class and disability all have an important effect on outcomes in terms of wealth distribution, educational attainment, criminalisation and health. The interchangeable 'anybody' assumed by liberalism has been shown to privilege a particular type of body. Whiteness, maleness, being able bodied and inheriting wealth are all advantaged by institutions that assume a lack of dependency on the state (Fineman 2004; Brown 2015). Again, as Naffine notes:

> the rational subject must be a fully individuated and integrated physical being before he can begin to assert his will against all other subjects. An explicit biological assumption is therefore that this individual is a rational adult human; a tacit assumption is that this rights-asserting competent legal actor is individuated and therefore sexed (at least in the sense of never pregnant, because this compromises individuation). Individuation and self-containment are essential if the rational subject is to be free to act in ways which affect only his self: if he is to be fully capable of confining and containing the effects of his actions to himself and to no other. (Naffine 2003: 364)

Some individuals are able to 'fit' into society precisely because of their ability to navigate the everyday topography of existence (Garland-Thomson 2011). This liberal legal subject is afforded material anonymity that is available only to individuals who share characteristics of masculinity, whiteness and able-bodiedness. 'Others' are rendered culturally exposed (Travis 2014: 536). This abstraction has led to a focus on rationality and a denial of the importance of the masculine body (Thomson 2008). As a result, 'many feminists have criticised how women, but not men, are defined in corporeal terms' (Fletcher et al. 2008: 331).

We can understand the exclusionary effects of this definition through engaging with Garland-Thomson's (2011) work on the 'misfit'. Garland-Thomson (2011) attempts to explain disability in terms of fitting or misfitting within a given societal context; 'A good enough fit', she explains, 'produces material anonymity' (596). Further, she argues that for white, heterosexual and able bodies, 'fitting is a comfortable and unremarkable majority experience of material anonymity' (Garland-Thomson 2011: 597). This 'material anonymity'—or 'invisibility' (Whitehead 2001)—allows for the white, heterosexual, able-bodied male experience to become standardised and normative. At the same time this normativity allows for this particular group of bodies to remain relatively anonymous. Gatens elaborates on this point, noting that the origins of our political system prevent full engagement from those whose bodies are excluded:

> Since the political body admitted only very specific types of persons to active membership, to abstract from their specific qualities certain minimal common features is to abstract from an abstraction. In other words, the abstract individual, under these lights, appears as a very specific kind of person.... The laws and ethical systems that are likely to develop in this sociopolitical context are going to amount to the encoding of the values and judgments of very specific kinds of person with very specific kinds of interest. There is nothing neutral or disembodied about the abstract liberal individual when viewed from this perspective. (Gatens 1996: 99)

Part of the appeal of accounts of the body which are grounded in theories of embodiment are that they are both able and willing to consider diversity. Grosz (1994) writes about 'alterity', which concerns the articulation of difference in the multiplicity of bodies (209). These differences include race, sex, sexuality, disability and class, as well as cultural specificities. An examination of bodies reveals the diversity of experience, function and identity. Any theorisation of the body which fails to take this into account, therefore, borders on the reductionist. This has had notable consequences in the health law context, as, for example, patient advice and research protocols are often based upon particular normative bodies (Ries and Thomson 2019). Various critiques of this type of reductionism are offered by our contributors to this collection.

## 4 Somebody

All contributions to this collection highlight various ways in which bodies play a vital role in how we understand law and health. Crucially, law and health discourses and practices also fundamentally shape our understandings and experiences of the body. In keeping with developments in feminist legal theory, disability studies and critical race theory, this collection seeks to highlight the importance of the particularities of the body. Thus sex, gender, disability, genetic and chromosomal variations, and illnesses have profound contextual and material aspects that undermine the notion that bodies are interchangeable, equal or equivalent. Health, and more recently health law, has long been animated by discussions of particular bodies; whether they are disordered, diseased or disabled. Each of these are classificatory regimes claiming some knowledge about the body. This collection aims to uncover and challenge the fundamental assumptions that underpin medico-legal knowledge about such bodies.

This interrogation is achieved through a mix of perspectives. A number of contributors look towards embodiment as a perspective that identifies bodies as always shaped by their discursive and institutional contexts (Dietz 2018; Travis 2019; Garland and Travis 2018; Fox and Thomson 2017; Fox and Murphy 2013; Fletcher et al. 2008). Work on embodiment has highlighted the impossibility of separating the material body from its institutional and cultural contexts. Here embodiment is understood as 'a dynamic encounter between flesh and world' (Garland-Thomson 2011: 592). Grosz explains the concept as 'the condition and context through which I am able to have relation to objects' (Grosz 1994: 86). Much of the collection thus draws upon an understanding of embodiment and its subsequent relation to law.

Embodiment theory encourages us to explore the body as a bio-social entanglement (Grabham 2012). It directs us to an examination of the material body and its relationship to its environments and experiences. In the legal sphere, Fletcher, Fox and McCandless (2008) note that 'feminism has shifted from exploring women's rights over their bodies, to analysing how social regulation has gendered the body and embodied experiences' (335). The body becomes central, therefore, in understanding how and where legal phenomena are exacted and the impact that this has on both the individual and groups. This approach presents an alternative analytical focus to traditional feminisms, moving from sexual difference to embodied difference. Such an approach 'helps avoid assumptions that sexual difference will be the primary signifier of embodiment, and allows an intersectional approach to bodily differences' (Fletcher et al. 2008: 334). The term 'embodiment' thus refers to this institutionally constituted, culturally located and material body. Whilst the materiality of the body remains vitally important to such research, for the purposes of this collection, it is located in relation to its discursive and jurisdictional context. This work alerts us to the idea that medical practitioners not only respond to healthcare issues but also create them through their own understandings of 'normality' and 'fixing'. Bodies, as a result, cannot be understood outside of, or as separate to, their medical and legal contexts. Nor can these medical and legal contexts be easily disaggregated when assessing the accessibility of rights or support for such bodies. Instead, the contributors to this collection address the interrelation of these contexts, exploring various power dynamics in the hope of opening them up to challenge.

## 5 Everybody

As well as highlighting various contexts which help us situate bodies, and thus move away from generalisations about 'the' body, a number of contributors to this collection also draw upon, or advocate, theories which re-emphasise the importance of universalism in the regulation of the body. Notably among these is the vulnerability approach pioneered within legal scholarship by Fineman (2008, 2017, this volume). In Fineman's (2017: 143) work, vulnerability is understood to be a universal trait experienced by all humans at all stages in the life course, in both an 'embodied' and socially 'embedded' manner. The vulnerability of the body gives Fineman's theory its normative underpinning and radical potential. Instead of ignoring embodied and embedded vulnerability and leaving individuals to take responsibility for their own health and well-being, we—both as health law scholars and as a society more generally—must do more to build political structures and institutions centred upon providing care for ourselves and other humans.

The starting point of Fineman's approach is shared by Garland-Thomson, who uses the temporality of vulnerability to note that individual bodies are subject to changes in resilience over the course of a lifetime. The human embodied experience is variable and dependent on context. Vulnerability is implicit, therefore, to understanding embodiment, not only between bodies but also over time (Garland-Thomson 2011: 596). Vulnerability thus becomes a perfect starting point for ethical debate; it is through our bodies 'that our finitude and uniqueness are signified to others [...]. Embodiment and ethics are inseparable insofar as we understand human existence in terms of dwelling or spatio-temporal being-in-the-world' (Diprose 2005: 237–238). It is through our embodied individuality that ethics can come to be conceived, and that ethical structures and institutions can then be built and maintained.

The significance of vulnerability theory lies in its examination of embedded vulnerability played out through our relationships with institutions such as health care and law. These institutional relationships are capable of heightening or attenuating our resilience. Vulnerability theory highlights the institutional and generational ways in which resilience is created rightly dismissing political and policy-led notions of 'vulnerable groups' that fail to situate individual bodies in their social contexts. As a consequence, the theory pushes for a more responsive state that is capable of monitoring the ways in which institutions respond to vulnerability and effect resilience (Fineman 2008: 19).

While not all contributors consider vulnerability explicitly, many adopt relational and embodied perspectives of the body to criticise past or present health law, or to propose alternative regulatory frameworks. Some approaches are more universal, while others prefer to maintain focus upon the value of intersectional or identarian approaches that we have previously highlighted. Yet all approaches attempt to go beyond a simplistic understanding of identity and the body in order to demonstrate how the state and its institutions construct the concepts and categories of bodies as well as the social and cultural contexts those bodies are situated within.

## 6 A Jurisprudence of the Body

Asking our contributors to consider the relationship between law and the body in a health context has provoked a range of responses. A number have been animated by the institutional nature of health care as an apparatus for determining bodily outcomes. The first section—'The Body of Health Law'—asks questions about the nature and scope of health care, and how this has changed in recent years. It also addresses several important developments affecting how the body is understood within health law in particular.

Martha Fineman begins by addressing the vulnerable body. In her contribution, 'Reasoning from the Body: Universal Vulnerability and Social Justice', she eschews fragmented conceptions of bodies in favour of a universal understanding of, and response to, human vulnerability. In a similar vein, John Coggon asserts the public nature of health law in 'Studying Public Health Law: Principles, Politics, and Populations as Patients'. Like Fineman, he shifts attention from individualised encounters—such as between the doctor and the patient—and onto the body politic. He shares with Fineman concern regarding institutional arrangements of privilege and responsibility over the familiar academic focus on autonomy and consent. Working at the level of populations allows Coggan to demonstrate the importance of including public health within health law.

In 'Bioinequalities: Rethinking Legal Responses to the Biological and Intergenerational Harm Caused by Inequality', Karen O'Connell and Isabel Karpin draw upon neuroscience and epigenetics to introduce their conception of 'bioinequalities'. Understanding the biological and intergenerational impact of the stress and trauma which arise as a consequence of unequal treatment allows them to reconsider how law should address the embodied effects of various forms of discrimination. The first section ends with 'Healthcare, Wellbeing, and the Regulation of Diversity in Healing', by Emilie Cloatre and Nayeli Urquiza-Haas, which considers how the medical profession differentiates itself, and is differentiated, from other forms of health/care. Drawing upon literatures concerning both vulnerability and care, Cloatre and Urquiza-Haas present an intriguing insight into the regulation of bodies and various forms of more or less alternative therapies in a UK and French context. This analysis raises challenges for the idea of health care as a market and lends further support to the need for the responsive state advocated by Fineman.

Moving away from considerations of the broad scope of health law, other contributors are concerned with the types of bodies that struggle at the margins of the healthcare system. The second section—'Bodies of Health'—teases apart the distinctions and overlaps emerging at the boundaries of health law. It considers how health law shapes and is shaped by the experiences of various types of bodies. These typologies form an important part of the classificatory principles that underpin medicine as science yet may offer alternative and competing conceptions to legal principles. This section also considers the bodies of medical professionals and actors within the system, ensuring that their embodiment is not assumed or taken for granted, but placed at the forefront of theorising about bodies in health law.

The second section begins with 'Temporal Bodies: Emergencies, Emergence, and Intersex Embodiment', in which Fae Garland and Mitchell Travis emphasise the position of bodies in time, and how these are framed by regulation including health laws. By considering the position of intersex people within healthcare systems, Garland and Travis advocate moving away from understanding such forms of embodiment as episodic or constitutive of an emergency. Instead they suggest reframing such bodies by adopting a life-course approach to intersex embodiment. In 'Death Before Birth: Liminal Bodies & Legal Frameworks', Danielle Fuller, Karolina Kuberska, Jeannette Littlemore, Sheelagh McGuinness and Sarah Turner consider the relative framings of the prospective mother's body as well as that of the foetus in the case of pregnancy loss. By engaging with metaphors and the concept of liminality, the authors demonstrate the utility of metaphor analysis to uncover the complex emotional responses to a lost pregnancy. This enables them to identify how the prospective mother and the foetus occupy a liminal space between different types of being in health law as in wider society.

In 'Depathologising Gender: Vulnerability in Trans Health Law', Chris Dietz and Ruth Pearce analyse how trans bodies have been, and could be, framed in attempts to depathologise trans phenomena. While nodding to the apparent successes of human rights activists in states such as Argentina and

Uruguay, they still harbour doubts about the utility of human rights discourse in this context. Instead, they draw upon Fineman's work to suggest that vulnerability theory has much to offer to the trans depathologisation movement. The second section ends with 'Feminist Activism in the Context of Clinical Trials and Drug Roll Out', by Aziza Ahmed, which describes the management of the rollout of the human papillomavirus (HPV) vaccine Gardasil in the United States and India. The differential response to this vaccine in these states offers insights not only into the regulation of pharmaceuticals in both health law systems but also of the different forms of feminist activism in the two countries as well as the way that value is accorded to female bodies along axes of class and race in the global pharmaceutical market.

The remaining contributors are—in part—more speculative, reflecting upon how theory has altered these debates or may contribute to reframing them in the future. This final section—'Reframing Health Law Through Bodies'—offers suggestions for how health law could be reframed to reveal new and important questions about fundamental and taken for granted assumptions of health. Placing the body at the centre of such theorising allows for new directions to be revealed. In 'Establishing Boundaries for Speculation About Artificial Wombs, Ectogenesis, Gender and the Gestating Body', Claire Horn and Elizabeth Chloe Romanis discuss the increasingly widespread assumption that the possibility of gestating an embryo from conception to full term in an artificial womb (full ectogenesis) will be imminently upon us. By insisting that such assumptions must be grounded in existing realities around reproduction and care, Horn and Romanis posit a shift in critical focus away from the pregnant body and onto the institutions which sustain it. In 'A Relational Responsibilities Framework for Children's Healthcare Law', Jo Bridgeman utilises a hypothetical case to illustrate the importance of relational responsibilities in a children's health law context. In contrast to her previous work, Bridgeman focuses less upon the ethical underpinnings of health law in favour of the social and institutional responsibilities demanded by her relational perspective. Finally, in 'Embodied Integrity, Shaping Surgeries, and the Profoundly Disabled Child', Marie Fox, Michael Thomson and Joshua Warburton offer an innovative model of embodied integrity which could protect profoundly disabled children from irreversible non-therapeutic surgical interventions. Again this would require greater consideration of institutional relations—including familial power dynamics—and could radically reshape the legal regulation of disability and health care in the process.

## References

Brown, W. (2015). *Undoing the Demos: Neoliberalism's Stealth Revolution*. New York: Zone Books.

Derham, D. P. (1958). Theories of Legal Personality. In L. Webb (Ed.), *Legal Personality and Political Pluralism* (pp. 1–19). Melbourne: Melbourne University Press.

Dewey, J. (1926). The Historic Background of Corporate Legal Personality. *Yale Law Journal, 35*, 655–673.

Dietz, C. (2018). Governing Legal Embodiment: On the Limits of Self-Declaration. *Feminist Legal Studies, 26*(2), 185–204.

Diprose, R. (2005). A 'Genethics' that Makes Sense: Take Two'. In M. Shildrick & R. Mykitiuk (Eds.), *Ethics of the Body: Postconventional Challenges* (pp. 237–238). London: MIT Press.

Fineman, M. A. (2004). *The Autonomy Myth; A Theory of Dependency*. New York: The New Press.

Fineman, M. A. (2008). The Vulnerable Subject: Anchoring Equality in the Human Condition. *Yale Journal of Law and Feminism, 20*(1), 1–23.

Fineman, M. A. (2017). Vulnerability and Inevitable Inequality. *Oslo Law Review, 4*(3), 133–149.

Fletcher, R., Fox, M., & McCandless, J. (2008). Legal Embodiment: Analysing the Body of Healthcare Law. *Medical Law Review, 16*, 321–345.

Fox, M., & Murphy, T. (2013). The Body, Bodies, Embodiment: Feminist Legal Engagement with Health. In M. Davies & V. Munro (Eds.), *The Ashgate Research Companion to Feminist Legal Theory* (pp. 249–268). Farnham: Ashgate.

Fox, M., & Thomson, M. (2017). Bodily Integrity, Embodiment, and the Regulation of Parental Choice. *Journal of Law and Society, 44*(4), 501–531.

Fuss, D. (1996). *Human, All Too Human*. New York: Routledge.

Garland, F., & Travis, M. (2018). Legislating Intersex Equality: Building the Resilience of Intersex People Through Law. *Legal Studies, 38*(4), 587–606.

Garland-Thomson, R. (2011). Misfits: A Feminist Materialist Disability Concept. *Hypatia, 26*(3), 591–609.

Gatens, M. (1996). *Imaginary Bodies; Ethics, Power and Corporeality*. London: Routledge.

Grabham, E. (2012). Bodily Integrity and the Surgical Management of Intersex. *Body and Society, 18*, 1–26.

Grear, A. (2011). Sexing the Matrix: Embodiment, Disembodiment and the Law – Towards the Re-Gendering of Legal Rationality. In J. Jones, A. Grear, R. A. Fenton, & K. Stevenson (Eds.), *Gender, Sexualities and Law*. Oxon: Routledge.

Grosz, E. (1994). *Volatile Bodies*. Bloomington/Indianapolis: Indiana University Press.

Hyde, A. (1997). *Bodies of Law*. Princeton: Princeton University Press.

Montgomery, J. (2002). *Health Care Law*. Oxford: Oxford University Press.

Naffine, N. (2003). Who Are Law's Persons? From Cheshire Cats to Responsible Subjects. *Modern Law Review, 66*, 346–367.

Ries, N. M., & Thomson, M. (2019). Bioethics and Universal Vulnerability: Exploring the Ethics and Practices of Research Participation. *Medical Law Review*, fwz026. https://doi.org/10.1093/medlaw/fwz026.

Thomson, M. (2008). *Endowed; Regulating the Male Sexed Body*. Oxon: Routledge.

Travis, M. (2014). Non-Normative Bodies, Rationality and Legal Personhood. *Medical Law Review, 22*(4), 526–547.

Travis, M. (2019). The Vulnerability of Heterosexuality: Consent, Gender Deception and Embodiment. *Social & Legal Studies, 28*(3), 303–326.

Whitehead, S. M. (2001). Man: The Invisible Gendered Subject? In S. M. Whitehead & F. J. Barrett (Eds.), *The Masculinities Reader* (pp. 351–368). Oxford: Blackwell.

# Part I

## The Body of Health Law

# 2

# Reasoning from the Body: Universal Vulnerability and Social Justice

Martha Albertson Fineman

## 1 Introduction

What do we mean when we refer to "the body" and speculate about the legal and political significance of "embodiment"? The bodies we typically encounter in critical theory are not uniform or universal, but individualised, modified and defined by certain characteristics that give particularised bodies particular political and legal significance. Bodies are sexed, gendered, aged, raced, abled (or not), displaced, disadvantaged, and so on. The particularity of such bodies (as well as the political and moral implications it is asserted they then acquire) serves as the basis for legal claims against the state, as well as those perceived to be in positions of power and privilege. The perceived social harm done to these particularised bodies (which is typically identified as inappropriate discrimination or exclusion from social benefits enjoyed by others) is the primary focus of most critical thought. Identification of exclusionary harm propels demands for recognition, equality, and inclusion, with an abstract ideal of equality employed to create a space of legal empowerment that allows some individuals and groups to make demands on an otherwise ideally neutral state.

The inevitability of particularity or difference among bodies is implicit in the call for papers that led to this collection. The editors asked if bodies can be understood as outside of, or separate from, medical and legal contexts

M. A. Fineman (✉)
Emory University School of Law, Atlanta, GA, USA
e-mail: MLFINEM@emory.edu



C. Dietz et al. (eds.), *A Jurisprudence of the Body*, Palgrave Socio-Legal Studies,
https://doi.org/10.1007/978-3-030-42200-4_2

(implicitly assuming difference and particularity). For example, they directed attention and enquiry into the *types* of bodies that struggle on the margins of the healthcare system (implicitly referencing discrimination and relative disadvantage). They asked contributors to consider the meaning of a "jurisprudence" of the body, as well as how our understanding of the body affects (presumably, individual) outcomes within health law. I am concerned with the theoretical limitations of considering "the body" as a jurisprudential subject if it has already been conceptually placed within existing or imagined social, legal, or political contexts. If contexts are inevitably tied up with notions of particularity, comparison, and difference, what does that mean for the generation of abstract, general, and universal principles? While some may argue that the idea of universality, even in jurisprudence, is to descend into dreaded "essentialism" and impending subordination, the legal subject is a universal concept. It is the universality or sameness of legal subjects that mandates and justifies their equal treatment in and by law.

Vulnerability theory asserts that the body as a universal concept is where theory should begin. The body is not created, nor should it be confined, by contrived contexts (including ideological and theoretical categories). Critical theory must begin with the body as an ontological entity and consider contexts as conditional, impermanent, indeterminate, and contrived. In this context, I am using "ontological" not to assert the existence of God but to present the material basis for arguing for an ethic of governance built on the recognition of the inevitability and the constancy of human physical dependency and the correspondingly essential, inescapable, and unavoidable role of our dependency on social institutions and relationships.

In both jurisprudence and bioethical discussions, the body should be understood as prior to the social or political, as independent of existing or imagined ethical, or moral social arrangements (although it may be the basis for a critique of them). Social institutions and contexts are necessitated by the ontological body and its needs. The desirability, justness, or appropriateness of existing or proposed social arrangements must be measured against the fundamental reality of this body.

As discussed later in this chapter, beginning with the body exposes the inevitability of dependency. Dependency arises from the body and is manifested by the continuous reliance on social arrangements (or contexts) throughout the life course of each and every individual. This reality is what should guide the ordering of human relationships and institutions, as well as informing the social and political norms we establish and implement in creating regulatory systems, including law, bioethics, and healthcare.

## 2 Theory and Practicality: Step One

Law and bioethics are disciplines concerned with governing human beings and the societies in which they live. As such, they should be grounded in an understanding of what it means to be human. This is an empirical enquiry necessary in defining the subject that is to be of theoretical concern, thus anchoring theory in quantifiable actuality. To a vulnerability theorist, to be human is to be vulnerable. This is a very different place to begin to think about human subjectivity and justice than is typically adopted in legal or political discussions. The individual of theoretical concern in liberal legal and political theory is the venerated holder of "rights," ideally autonomous, independent, and self-sufficient, cherishing individual liberty.

In vulnerability theory, this construct of an autonomous individual is considered to be an ideological construct, which is empirically indefensible, as it bears little relationship to the totality or complexity of the human condition. Law and policy built on this deficient conceptual entity cannot be fully or justly responsive to the totality of human needs. However, while the fiction of an autonomous, independent, and self-sufficient legal subject does not resonate in reality, it is the necessary conceptual foundation for a politics of limited governmental responsibility and state action. This is a politics that serves the interests of the few and powerful who have the resources necessary to evade some implications of vulnerability.

## 3 The Role of Law: Step Two

In discussing how we define the legal subject (the imagined, ordinary being around whom law and policy are formed), it is important to note the role that law and policy play in society in defining the circumstances and conditions of individual lives. Law and policy are not abstractions, but have practical implications. There are two major areas of law that organise individual experience and expectations. Often labelled "private," some laws determine the relationships and consequences between and among individuals interacting within society (these are laws governing things such as contract, tort, crime, family, and employment). These laws recognise that individuals inevitably interact with one another and that such interactions may cause harm, establish expectations or reliance, or warrant the imposition of responsibility or obligation. The law defines both the obligations and duties incorporated into these relationships, as well as establishes the appropriate remedies should they be breached.

Although labelled private, these laws are actually significant manifestations of state or public interest, the products of state action and initiative. Rules and norms of conduct are necessary for a well-ordered and functioning society. This is profoundly evident in the context of social institutions, such as the family, which although deemed private have widely been recognised as having significant public roles. How the legal subject is perceived is certainly relevant to the laws governing the relationship among individuals. We can speculate as to how contract, family, and employment law might change if there were not an autonomous liberal legal subject at their core (Fineman and Fineman 2018).

The second category of laws define the relationship and responsibilities allocated between the institutions of the "state," as well as those who govern the mechanisms of formal authority and power, and the individual as a legal subject (these are laws defining such things as social health and welfare, taxation, governance, and citizenship). These areas of "public" law more directly recognise the state's ongoing relationship with and responsibility to the individual and include constitutional law, administrative law, tax law and criminal law, as well as all procedural law (Marvel 2014; Dinner 2018; Travis 2019). These areas entail the state's obligation to ensure equality before the law, maintain civil and political rights, and facilitate inclusion in society.

This category of law has generated a great deal of critical and political attention. Constitutional law in particular has facilitated vigorous political and legal campaigns over the past several decades leading to far-reaching reforms for elimination of discriminatory or exclusionary treatment of designated "protected" classes based on identity markers such as race, gender, age, ability, and so on. The claim is for the state to actively refrain from and prohibit others from engaging in discriminatory treatment based on these differences among individuals within society. Ideas like human rights and concepts such as equality, liberty, autonomy, and so on come into play in this regard. The objective of state action through law and policy is to eliminate, rectify, or compensate harms resulting from exclusion and discrimination or marginalisation and subordination of protected groups.

Applications of public law concepts have been vigorously developed since the mid-twentieth century under the mantle of equality. The distinction between an ideal of equality and the actuality of discrimination became a paramount lens through which contemporary legal culture assessed the nature and effect of existing public areas of law and determined the desired direction for reform in many private areas as well. An equality/discrimination paradigm still provides the governing logic for both criticism and justification of the status quo. It is appealingly rooted in an understanding of the moral significance of the human being and a belief in our fundamental parity under law

(Fineman 2013a, b). Ultimately, and less sanguinely, the logic of equality also resists rules or practices that might infringe on the liberty of equal individuals or compromise their autonomy, resulting in doctrines that are sceptical of state intervention into the so-called private sphere of life. Also significant is the tendency to view structural problems as fundamentally problems of discrimination, exclusion, and equality of access. We fail to engage in a more comprehensive institutional critique, considering the ways in which institutional structures fail or are flawed indiscriminately.

## 4 Reasoning from the Body: Step Three

A "restrained state" ideology valorising abstracted ideals of equality and liberty currently serves as a basis for policy in both the private and public areas of law. While both areas seemingly address relationships to "the other" (whether individual or state), the individual is ultimately situated as isolated and autonomous (Fineman 2004). The possibility or necessity of individual reliance on the collective (in either its social or governmental form) is thus minimised and formalised. In traditional liberal thought, state or collective action is posited as theoretically antagonistic and inherently problematic for venerated individual liberty. This conception of individual freedom and autonomy, as well as the ideal of restrained state responsibility are only possible when we ignore the realities of the body.

### 4.1 Vulnerability Theory: Embodied Reality

Human beings are embodied beings and therefore neither independent nor self-sufficient. We are vulnerable. Our vulnerability arises from the material and ephemeral nature of the body itself and is constant throughout life. Vulnerability is also universal—it is the human condition.[1] Vulnerability, therefore, is not a characteristic of only some individuals or groups, nor does it differ in quality or degree from one individual or group to another. We are all always vulnerable—there is no position of invulnerability.

[1] When I refer to the human *condition*, I am indicating an empirical reality that shapes human circumstances and experiences and exists across time and space, within cultures and throughout history—the universal. By contrast, to refer to "human *nature*" has normative implications: it is a term often applied to propensities or proclivities of human beings to act in certain ways that can and do vary over time and within societies. Both the tendency toward and socially acceptable nature of responses to the human condition vary and are shaped by things like culture, history, and the interpretations of individual and group experiences. Human nature is a societal conclusion about what is natural or to be anticipated—society's consensus on the inevitability of specific responses to the human condition.

To state the universality of vulnerability is not to ignore that differences exist. However, when and how those differences matter on a theoretical level requires exploration beyond mere assertion of their existence. Typically, critical theorists have been concerned with those differences that distinguish us from one another—demographic differences that are often the basis for injustices. Vulnerability theory, while recognising the importance of and need to address those injustices associated with demographic differences, is also concerned with the deeper structural failure of legal theory to effectively engage with the implications of a second type of difference: developmental difference.

## 4.2 Differences Among Bodies: Demographic Differences

Clearly there are differences among bodies when we look at our societies and assess those characteristics that have salience at any particular time. These are the demographic differences that form the basis for population reports and assessments of policy. They capture a horizontal perspective of society, a snapshot of what are considered relevant or significant differences. The relevant categories currently emphasised in law, policy, and political theory include age, sex, race, sexuality, and ability, as well as measures such as income, geographic area, and education. These demographic differences have formed the basis for successful political critiques of the status quo. Calls to progressive action and laws have been fashioned to address discrimination based on certain demographic differences.

Demographic categories mark individuals who share certain characteristics as different from those who do not share those characteristics, with distinct interests or concerns in need of legal attention. Attention to demographic differences tends to obscure the universal nature of vulnerability and its implications. In fact, critical theory often begins by identifying "vulnerable groups," or asserting some are more or less vulnerable, ignoring vulnerability as inherent in the human condition. In these contexts, the concept of vulnerability is incorrectly used as a synonym for disadvantage, discrimination, or injured.

Such misunderstandings of the theoretical range of the concept results in limiting critical attention to certain variations in embodiment, undermining the possibility of constructing a unitary legal subject and locating the structural possibilities for subordination and exclusion to designated demographic differences. If we looked beyond the fact of exclusion and considered what would be actually gained by inclusion within existing social arrangements, we might perceive justice problems transcending discrimination. In other words, it is important to ask what is actually achieved if the institution to which we gain access is fundamentally flawed and structurally unjust, as are many current employment, political, and financial systems.

Critical theory must be concerned with the fundamental structures of institutions and the need for their transformation, as well as ensuring they are inclusive. A significant question for those concerned with social justice in the twenty-first century has to be whether the equality/antidiscrimination logic that underlies a focus on demographic differences is a sufficient critical tool with which to assess contemporary law and policy. Is there another organising "reality" that should supplement or even replace the discrimination/equality model?

To raise questions about the current effectiveness of the dominant paradigm is not to argue that equality and antidiscrimination are not important or necessary concepts. Identifying and addressing inequality and discrimination were unarguably essential steps in the evolution of a just society. As we know, prior to the mid-twentieth century, formal rules, as well as functioning norms, were built on assertions of fundamental differences among groups defined by gender, race, and other characteristics. These distinctive group categories also established a world of hierarchical legalised identities in which some were susceptible to different, often demeaning treatment. However, formal legal distinctions have now been removed and equal access, at least in theory, has become the norm. While it is undeniably true that more work remains to make equality of access and opportunity a reality, we also should ask whether that goal in and of itself is enough to ensure justice.

Of course, an equality model or nondiscrimination mandate certainly remains the appropriate response in some instances: one person, one vote, and equal pay for equal work are areas where equality seems clearly suitable. It is also warranted when there is residual discrimination in spite of the formal equality rules—discrimination in practice. However, equality is less helpful, and may even be an unjust measure, when applied in situations of inevitable inequality. There are situations where different levels of benefits or burdens are appropriate, even desirable in social arrangements, which are discussed in a subsequent section of this chapter.

The dismantling of *de jure* discrimination has made it apparent that the problems in society often transcend discrimination and exclusion from social institutions. Indeed, there may be substantial problems with existing institutions and their organisation that are obscured by the jurisprudential logic that flows from an equality/antidiscrimination paradigm. Discrimination analysis may fail to adjust for changes in underlying reality. In fact, such analysis may tend to assume change has not happened and the problems are the same as they were 50 years ago.[2]

Most significant, however, is the fact that a continued focus on an equality/discrimination paradigm based on select characteristics has serious limitations in defining just what constitutes harm, as well as the breadth of those who are harmed by current policy and law. A focus on discrimination certainly has failed to develop a strategy for addressing differences in a positive, constructive manner (we tend to get stuck on equality, comparison, and competition). Adherence to equality may even place obstacles on the ability to remedy (or even address) existing inequalities. Further, our conception of equality, tied as it is to the comparative treatment of individuals and groups, may make it difficult to articulate a concept of "social justice" that moves beyond an individual rights framework (Fineman 2019b).

## 4.3 Differences Within the Body: Developmental Difference

Vulnerability theory asks us to look beyond current demographic classifications of difference among individuals existing within society at a particular time. Instead, we consider the theoretical implications of the ontological body and its inevitable susceptibility to change that is at the core of vulnerability theory: "vulnerability reflects our susceptibility to change, both positive and negative, in our physical and social wellbeing over the life course" (Fineman 2019a: 57; Dinner 2018). This understanding of vulnerability as inevitable change over time encompasses, but is not confined to, the possibility of harm or injury. Developmental changes occur as the body matures and are often positive, ushering in new experiences and opening up new possibilities. Developmental changes can indicate increased, as well as decreased, capabilities and capacity over time.

Developmental differences are intrinsic to the body and define the shared human condition. The body progresses through a variety of developmental stages, with implications for capacity, ability, and capability. That reality should be reflected in the construction of a unitary legal subject, as well as being recognised as fundamental to our conception of what it means to be human. Unfortunately, developmental differences and their significance for

[2] We must recognise and incorporate into our critical positions the fact that aspirations have changed, even if there are problems remaining with achievement of those ends. The recognition that discrimination on the basis of characteristics such as race or gender was a major conceptual or theoretical advancement and should give us hope that further advances are possible.

understanding both the human condition and the necessity of constructing a complementary concept of state responsibility are typically obscured, minimised, or ignored in legal theory, whether it be of a critical or liberal bent.[3]

Of course, developmental differences sometimes are recognised in law, particularly when characteristics of specific stages deviate too far from those assigned to the idealised liberal legal subject and cannot be ignored. The tendency in those cases is to create a "special" category of legal or political subjectivity to accommodate the particular nonconforming stage, leaving untouched the paradigmatic "full" legal subject created by the given theoretical perspective. For example, in liberal theory historically children as legal subjects were placed within the confines of the private family. Within the family, the responsibility of the state for and to the child as a distinct legal subject was submerged, a deferral of public responsibility that was facilitated by the creation of the doctrines of parental rights and family privacy.

Within this arrangement, the developmental experiences inherent to childhood, as well as enquiries into what those experiences should mean in defining the nature and extent of state responsibility to the (unitary) legal subject, are obfuscated. Even the legal recognition of the appropriateness of state protection in cases of child abuse and neglect was difficult to achieve and is still problematic in practice. Of course, the child has gained legal status in some quarters. The idea that children have rights exemplified by the United Nation's Convention on the Rights of the Child symbolises the emergence of the child as a distinct legal subject (notably, the United States is the only country that has not ratified the Convention). However, while bringing the child out from under the total coverture of the family found in the common law is viewed as progress, the actual protections or benefits gained from the representation of the child as a separate, individual rights-holder are less clear. The experiences of childhood are not brought into focus, but obscured under the mantle of individual rights.

The assertion that children have rights assumes they can practically, as well as theoretically, occupy a position as a rights-holder vis-à-vis the state and its juridical institutors comparable to adults. However, the problem of rights for children is not just one of lesser capacity or capability. There is also a general problem with the individualistic nature of rights as a concept. The idea of individual rights (whether for children or adults) resonates with conceptual

[3] Vulnerability theory asserts that it is human vulnerability that necessitates the creation of social institutions, be they the family, the community, the nation state, or the international community, as well as providing the bases for the construction of economic, financial, educational, and social welfare systems. These social arrangements arise in response to vulnerability, and their success of failure should be measured by the effectiveness of their responses to the realities of the human (vulnerable) condition.

flaws characteristic of the traditional, limited notions of the legal subject, with its commitment to individual autonomy, liberty, independence, and agency. A rights-based model assumes the individual as a legal subject can be conceived outside of social institutions and relationships (exemplified by Rawl's "veil of ignorance" (Rawls 1971). This leads to ultimately positioning the individual so conceived as perpetually in danger from an abusive and antagonistic state, a view that has affected how those on both left and right of the political spectrum view the potential for state action.

In fact, a rights focus on the individual minimises and obscures the continuous and basic role the state plays in society as a whole, as well as the ways in which it defines the lives of all individuals within it. The whole idea of individual rights tends to assume an ideally restrained or fundamentally distant or disinterested state that may provide some basic services, but is fundamentally detached from and uninvolved in the mundane aspects of individual lives. The idea of individual rights serves as a check on the development of an overly active state (although it is argued rights can also be the basis for positive claims of an economic or social nature—these claims are often in practice, however, unenforceable).

This tension between the view of the individual as independent and the reality of necessary and nurturing or supportive social contexts is starkly visible when it comes to children's rights. No matter how many individual rights are conferred, the developmental stages of childhood mean that the child will be perceived as deficient in terms of the capacity presumed by liberal legal subjectivity. The family is designed as a compensatory institution, allocated primary responsibility for care and control of the child (See also Fox, Thomson and Warburton this volume, Garland and Travis, this volume). This process of designating children as not only rights-holders but also inherently dependent on some mediating social institution has implications for legal theory and the structuring of society. It is not only a "special" (inferior and dependent) legal subjectivity for children (and some of those who are considered disabled or some elderly individuals not deemed to have the ability to be fully independent or self-sufficient) that is created. Also constructed are the expectations, limitations, authority, and nature of the family as an institution, as well as the roles of both parent and child within that family. Significantly, through this process of legal structuring, the state also defines and confines itself.

This deferral (or allocation) by the state of responsibility for individual and social well-being to social institutions created by the state employing law and policy choices is also evident in a less obvious way for those deemed full legal subjects. Markets are supposed to provide economic opportunity, employment provides for health and retirement needs, education is the way to gain opportunity, and so on. These mediating institutions are created and maintained by the state and the reality is that the ways in which they are constructed are dependent on how the legal subject is understood, an insight typically overlooked in legal theory. The pernicious assumption in liberal theory is that an individual can consistently and successfully rely on social institutions, furthering the illusion of independence and autonomy and ignoring the reality of our fundamental dependency on social arrangements. If an individual does not succeed, it can be viewed as an individual, not an institutional, failure.

The fallacy of individual autonomy and independence is not only a problem in legal theory. In political theory, philosophy, economics, and ethics, human beings are consistently presented as ideally independent, fully-functioning adults. An "autonomous-liberal-subject"—a "rational actor," who is liberty-seeking and capable of negotiation, bargaining, and giving informed consent—also informs economics, bioethics, and political theory (Naffine 2009). This subject is not concerned with (in fact does not recognise) his own dependency or the need to consider the general wellbeing of society, let alone the needs of the next generation. This abstracted human subject is taken out of social relationships and freed from social responsibility. This makes it difficult to argue for redistribution of economic resources, affirmative action, or other remedial devices to address existing inequalities. Inequality is understood as an individual, not a social problem.

Vulnerability theory argues that we need a new logic—one that generates and validates different values and norms, responsive to the social and individual implications of ontological vulnerability and inescapable dependency. We need to create a unitary legal subject—one that incorporates all stages of human development and recognises the implications of dependency for the construction of state responsibility. This insistence on recognition of developmental differences and the dependency they reveal underscores the need for law to respond to the totality of the human condition, transforming the legal subject from its current static and unrealistic form into a dynamic, inclusive, and comprehensive model. Such a transformation will mandate serious theoretical engagement on the question of state and individual responsibility.

## 5 Dependency: Step Four

As is apparent from the proceeding section, the concept of dependency is central to vulnerability theory. Dependency is neither contingent, nor deviant. It is also not merely a variation of or euphemism for vulnerability.

Dependency is the individual manifestation of our vulnerability, which also has social dimensions. Our bodies render us inescapably dependent on social relationships and arrangements such as those found in the family, education, finance, employment, and health systems. It is within these social institutions that we must generate the resources or social assets that cumulatively provide "resilience." Significantly, no one is born resilient. Resilience in the form of capabilities, skills, resources, support, a sense of belonging, emotional strength, and so on is gained over the life course, within these social institutions and relationships. Resilience gives us the ability to not only survive, but thrive in the face of our vulnerability.

Like vulnerability, dependency is not a harm or injury, nor is it deviant or exceptional. Dependency, like vulnerability, is intrinsic to the human condition. However, it is important to distinguish between dependency and vulnerability, which are different in important ways. Vulnerability arises from the characteristics and essence of the body (we are embodied beings), while dependency is the term used to describe relationships we have with particular social or institutional arrangements. As embodied beings, we are inevitably embedded in and dependent upon social institutions and relationships.

Dependency, while it is also constant, is best understood as changing and variable. The manifestations of our dependency change over time and we may at various times during the life course be dependent on different institutional and social arrangements. For example, because we begin life as physically unable to care for ourselves, we are inevitably dependent on care from others. Social institutions and relationships are essential to provide that care. This form of dependency, which is located in the body and developmental in nature, I label "inevitable dependency."

Inevitable dependency is most evident in infancy, where the family is the mediating social institution primarily assigned responsibility for caretaking. However, the family does not and cannot bear this burden alone. Healthcare and social welfare systems are designed and justified as necessary to also provide essential resources for caring for the inevitable dependent. These other institutions typically become more prominent than the family in the life of the adult individual when the need for care arises because we are injured, ill, or disabled. Importantly, our dependence on institutions of care persists over the life course, even if the specific social arrangements for that care shift or are episodic, alterable, and individual.

Significantly, there is a second distinct, but related form of dependency that is (or should be) theoretically relevant—a social dependency, which I label "derivative." Derivative dependency in the caretaking context describes the social or institutional consequences that attend assumption of the position or relationship of caretaker. Those who care for the inevitably dependent infant (or otherwise in need of care individual) are themselves structurally dependent on resources, accommodation, and support in order to successfully accomplish that care. These resources can come from within the institution of the family (the spouse's pay cheque or grandmother's childcare). However, supplemental resources also must be provided by social welfare institutions, such as the healthcare system, and governmental systems, such as tax subsidy or public education.

Considering the implications of derivative dependency and the reliance on institutions that it signifies, it is important to realise that social systems, such as the family, the healthcare, and the employment/market systems, operate simultaneously and sequentially. A weakness in one system can be compensated for in another. A strong family can help minimise the impact of a less than sterling educational system. However, successful acquisition of resources in one stage, such as education in childhood, profoundly affects the possibility of success in subsequent social stages, such as in the university or employment.

On a social level, institutions must be designed to work together in interrelated, contiguous, and sequential ways. Institutional arrangements should be thought of as symbiotic. For example, the healthcare system relies on funding from governmental sources but also reflects and adapts to the organisation of educational and professional associations and adjusts to financial systems (including insurance) and regulatory agencies. It must also ultimately be responsive in its design and practice to law and policy. This interdependency profoundly affects the ability of each of these systems to respond and shapes the options and resources available to institutions, as well as for those who perform necessary social roles with them. Focusing on the inherent and inevitable interrelatedness of institutions and the complexity of social arrangements responding to vulnerability and dependency reveals the complexity of the processes and procedures that shaped institutions and the need to be attentive to the way they are constructed, operate, and interact. It also reveals that derivative dependency is not confined to the situation of caretaking. Rather, we are all dependent on social institutions and relationships in order to inhabit and function within the social systems we inevitably occupy.

## 6 Social Identities and Inevitable Inequality: Step Five

Within social institutions we find social relationships, such as that of parent and child. These relationships constitute social identities, defined by the obligations, expectations, responsibilities, and benefits they carry within them.

Social identities are shaped by and conform to the ways that social institutions have been defined. For example, parents have responsibility for the welfare of their children and this social responsibility is complimented by the legal doctrines of parental rights and family privacy. This and other social identities are not natural and inevitable, although they may correspond with natural human impulses and emotions. As legal or social relationships, they are constructed by policy choices in which the state, through law, confers not only responsibility but also power and privilege. Social identities apply to all who occupy the status, regardless of demographic differences. One of the significant theoretical realisations about these universally applicable social identities is that they are typically not equal relationships. Recognition of the inherent inequalities in social relationships further bolsters the need for critical theory to incorporate vulnerability and dependency in addressing the need for social change.

The parent/child relationship is a straightforward example where the need for unequal institutional social identities and conferral of differing levels of authority can be easily justified (although the extent and nature of residual state responsibly is a critical issue). However, it is important to note that social identities reflecting an inherent inequality are the norm, not the exception. Examples of unequal socio-legal relationships in addition to parent/child, include employer/employee (Fineman and Fineman 2018), as well as professional relationships such as doctor/patient and attorney/client, where there is an underlying inequality in knowledge, resources, and access to institutional structures that warrant an asymmetric allocation of responsibility. Law and policy recognises and responds to the related but differing needs of shareholders and consumers (or the community) when it comes to regulating the corporation. Inequality in position, need, and context is also the reality when it comes to intergenerational equalities inherent in considering things like environmental practice and policies, for example. These are situations of "inevitable" or "necessary" inequality from a theoretical perspective, where the social responsibilities and functions are complementary, but different.

While these inherently unequal social relationships or identities represent major areas of life, historically they have conceptually been relegated to the "private" sphere—whether it be designated "family" or "market" and wrongfully perceived as presumptively outside of state action and regulation. Recognising the perpetually active role of the state in the construction and maintenance of these identities and the institutions in which they are located demands a robust response from critical theorists focused on institutional design and the allocation of privilege and benefits. How and why have these relationships and institutions been fashioned in the ways in which they have? What are the justifications for the allocation of unequal privilege and advantage within any given relationship? As an empirical matter, are the justifications supported by the actual functioning of the institutions and relationships within society?

Recognition of the nature and extent of relationships of inescapable and appropriate inequality present major challenges for those structuring, regulating, or monitoring those relationships—for law and ethics. How do we structure essential social relationships of inevitable inequality so that they operate justly and fairly? Asking this question shifts critical enquiry from the characteristics and circumstances of particular individuals or groups to that of universal institutional design and collective social responsibility. Social identities are inclusive and apply to all who occupy them. This does not mean that once established there cannot be discrimination based on demographic differences within the social category, but it does insist that the construction of the category must be considered independent of (and I would assert, prior to) the question of discrimination in order to generate a comprehensive social critique.

If the initial focus of critical theory is on inevitable inequality in the contexts of the function and nature of existing institutional arrangements, it compels an enquiry into the reasons offered to justify the particular choices policymakers have made. This form of critical focus brings to the fore the contrived positions of power and privilege designed for those who are more advantaged within the paired social identities, as well as those who are disadvantaged. Why are policymakers more attentive to the economic risks and needs of the employer vis-à-vis employee? (Fineman and Fineman 2018). How might law and policy more justly balance the corresponding vulnerabilities of these partners in the employment relationship?

Notably, the situation of inevitable inequality found in the employment relationship is handled by imposing a fabricated equivalence between the individuals in the relationship. The fictitious contract that is fabricated in the employment context gives the illusion of equality. This legal fiction not only is an illusion. It also has significant social welfare implications. The idea of an employment contract inappropriately individualises an important and essential social relationship with potentially significant public consequences. It also obscures the responsibility of the state to ensure that this inherently unequal relationship, which is defined and bolstered in employment, labour, and other laws, is nonetheless a just one. An illusory patina of equality is also applied in the construction of autonomy and reliance on "informed consent" to govern the doctor/patient relationship. As already discussed the distinction in the treatment of children compared with adults exemplifies the tactic of positioning individuals differently in order to justify different, unequal legal treatment. In such cases, state responsibility for ensuring equitable treatment for some of these differently positioned individuals (children) is minimised within the overriding framework of equality.

Vulnerability theory allows us to effectively criticise these existing social arrangements, looking beyond the paradigms of equality, rights, and discrimination. Vulnerability theory asks the question: "what is justice?" It incorporates the recognition that justice is often asymmetrical and demands attention to contexts and complexity in a way that simple resort to mantras such as equality may not. It also compels us to grapple with the fact that the state is not and cannot be passive, noninterventionist or restrained. In the normative governing processes of creating and monitoring social institutions and relationships, the state is always active. The question critical theorists should ask is in whose interests and to what ends is the state acting? We cannot merely critique the state, nor can we disavow and abandon it. Critical theory must generate ways to achieve more just ends, actively engaging with the state by not only challenging the results produced within existing social institutional arrangements, but suggesting ways those institutions can be designed to function better.

In addition to clearly defining the roles, purposes, and effects we want institutions and relationships to have, we should be asking fundamental structural questions: what are the distinctive responsibilities and obligations imposed through the creation of social identities for those acting within societal institutions? What are the responsibilities of those who shape and control the rules and practices governing relationships of inevitable inequality? What rules, values, and norms should govern the expectations for the behaviour and practices within relationships of inherent inequality and dependency? What are the ethical and moral, as well as legal, implications of developmental difference and the inevitability of dependency it reveals? What political and legal rules and arrangements should we establish in recognition of vulnerability and dependency?

These and other questions arising from the recognition of inherent inequality present difficult challenges for dominant legal theory, which revolves around the individual and elevates principles such as equality and individual liberty to constitutional mandates in which the human condition with its inevitable dependency and universal vulnerability are ignored or denied.

# 7 Conclusion

Law is both inherently a social endeavour and a primary instrument of accomplishing social justice. Laws establish and regulate duties, obligations, rights, and privileges applicable to all members of a society, as well as defining their relationships with each other and with the state and its institutions. Politicians and philosophers addressing the role and function of law can and do differ when it comes to theories of governance, but there should be a shared recognition of the significance of our understanding of what it means to be human, one that begins with the body.

What it means to be human ultimately shapes the legal relationships and social institutions in which we live our lives, as well as informing what we consider to be justice within those arrangements and institutions. Vulnerability theory challenges the dominant limited and disingenuous vision of legal subjectivity. It advocates for a legal subject demarcated by universal vulnerability and inevitable social dependency, which will more fully reflect the human condition than does a fixation on autonomy, rationality, and liberty. As such, the vulnerable legal subject has the power to disrupt the logic of personal responsibility and individual liberty, rejecting the restrained state of liberal imagination and envisioning a state responsive to the complexities of the human condition.

# References

Dinner, D. (2018). Vulnerability as a Category of Historical Analysis: Initial Thoughts in Tribute to Martha Albertson Fineman. *Emory Law Journal, 67*(6), 1149–1164.

Fineman, M. A. (2004). *The Autonomy Myth*. New York: New Press.

Fineman, M. A. (2013a). Vulnerability, Resilience, and LGBT Youth. *Temple Political & Civil Rights Law Review, 2*, 307–330.

Fineman, M. A. (2013b). Introduction: Vulnerability as Heuristic – An Invitation to Future Exploration. In M. A. Fineman & A. Grear (Eds.), *Vulnerability: Reflections on a New Ethical Foundation for Law and Politics* (pp. 1–12). Farnham: Ashgate.

Fineman, M. A. (2019a). Vulnerability in Law and Bioethics. *Journal of Health Care for the Poor and Underserved, 30*(4), 52–61.

Fineman, M. A. (2019b). Vulnerability and Social Justice. *Valparaiso University Law Review, 53*, 341–369.

Fineman, M. A., & Fineman, J. W. (2018). *Vulnerability and the Legal Organization of Work*. New York: Routledge.

Fox, M., Thomson, M., & Warburton, J. (This Volume).

Garland, F., & Travis, M. (This Volume).

Marvel, S. (2014). The Evolution of Plural Parentage: Applying Vulnerability Theory to Polygamy and Same-Sex Marriage. *Emory Law Journal, 64*, 2047–2088.
Naffine, N. (2009). *Law's Meaning of Life: Philosophy, Religion, Darwin and the Legal Person*. Oxford/Portland: Hart Publishing.
Rawls, J. (1971). *A Theory of Justice*. Cambridge, MA: Harvard University Press.
Travis, M. (2019). The Vulnerability of Heterosexuality: Consent, Gender Deception and Embodiment. *Social and Legal Studies, 28*(3), 303–326.

# 3

# Studying Public Health Law: Principles, Politics, and Populations as Patients

John Coggon

## 1 Introduction

Works in legal scholarship commonly carry a time stamp as a *caveat* to guard against, or at least allow for, future changes. However, the allowance that such a *caveat* might give would be inadequate to capture, or to get past, the profundity of what has happened to perceptions and understandings of public health and law in the short time since this chapter was completed in 2019. Following the outbreak of COVID-19, the world has entered a public health emergency whose scale and impacts are yet unknown, but which has already led to governments instituting extraordinary legal measures in efforts to control the spread of the disease. Within the UK, Parliament has enacted the Coronavirus Act 2020, with provisions designed to limit transmission of the virus and protect healthcare and other services from being fatally overwhelmed. The Act operates alongside other legislative measures, including distinct Regulations to enforce 'lockdown' respectively in England, Northern Ireland, Scotland, and Wales. These public health laws provide (amongst other things) for extraordinary executive powers, extraordinary measures regarding the practice of medicine and other areas of health and social care, and the placing of enormous curbs on individual freedoms. The pandemic starkly demonstrates the depth of our interpersonal, social, and global interconnectedness: how even within framings made by reference to liberal state systems, we exist as "non-individuated individuals" (Coggon 2012a, chapter 10). In underscoring this, the crisis highlights realities whose critical implications are of

J. Coggon (✉)
University of Bristol Law School, Bristol, UK
e-mail: john.coggon@bristol.ac.uk



C. Dietz et al. (eds.), *A Jurisprudence of the Body*, Palgrave Socio-Legal Studies,
https://doi.org/10.1007/978-3-030-42200-4_3

the highest importance for studies in the jurisprudence of the body, in medical jurisprudence, and in questions about the links between social justice and law.

In relation to jurisprudence of the body, public health emergencies, and public health more generally—as explained below—demonstrate how the ostensible physical boundaries of the human body do not straightforwardly track against the boundaries of persons either practically or normatively. At population levels too, global phenomena—including matters such as the spread of infectious disease but also questions such as global trade and its impacts—show how norms based on the idea of impervious or autonomous nation states are similarly not fit alone to serve our conceptual needs in global jurisprudential inquiry (Coggon 2014). The facts of our interconnectedness are marked in terms of how they impact our conceptions of bodily integrity and the nature of society and societies. In relation to medical jurisprudence, the conceptual abstraction of doctor/patient interactions is also challenged. It has long been accepted that, at least within a national healthcare system such as the NHS, 'macro level' questions inevitably bear on the provision of individual health care (Coggon 2016). However, following COVID-19, the vulnerability of the healthcare system and the complexities of the internal functioning of the NHS and its links with wider aspects of social care have much more radically emphasised the need to approach medical jurisprudence with attention to population- and society-level concerns. And this in turn shines sharper light on questions about studies in health law and their relationships with ideas of social justice. The points about interconnectedness make clear how responsibilities for health, within and across nations, cannot be resolved without looking at collective obligations: narrow individualism is just inadequate (cf. Coggon 2012a; Marmot 2015; Venkatapuram 2010). The COVID-19 pandemic is laying bare, within nations as well as across nations, the gross failures in justice that are represented through health inequalities: that is, how health inequalities serve as indicators of points of deep social injustice through compounded, socially-determined disadvantage across multiple values including but stretching far beyond health (and thus matters that require to be addressed outside of the healthcare system).

The importance of understanding law as a determinant of health, as a mechanism for achieving greater social justice, as well as a source of constraint through, for example, human rights protection and adherence to the rule of law, could not be more clearly demonstrated. But we also need to recognise that these problems are not just ones that are limited to instances of public health emergency (see further Gostin et al. 2019). Therefore, beyond editorial constraints that tend against more thoroughgoing amendments, the following text is only lightly edited given the impacts of COVID-19. The pandemic has already radically changed the course of human history globally, and will likely lead to a much greater focus on public health law within university curricula and research agendas. But it is crucial to recognise that public health law is about so much more than control of infectious diseases or the use of law in times of emergency. I would therefore like to see the following arguments stand on their merits in the terms (only lightly further edited) in which I expressed them before public health and law were forced to the front of everyone's minds by COVID-19. An upshot of the current global health emergency, with its overall personal and social implications, as well as those specifically facing healthcare and medical practice, shows, I would argue, the limitations of focusing on medical jurisprudence or questions of jurisprudence of the body without consideration of population-level, social, and political contexts. What follows aims to explain these limitations by looking at contexts that include but span far beyond the coordination of responses to a pandemic.

With those preliminary points made, it is useful to enter analysis of public health law as a field by considering how modern medico-legal studies and practice may be said to have emerged as a response to an absence of law, or at least to a failing in its reach. As the field was delineated, there was profound influence from scholarship in individualistic modes of social philosophy and biomedical ethics (e.g. Illich 1976). These sought to identify the sources and dynamics of power and values within health care, and in particular to evaluate and critique the freedoms of physicians, and the forms of social, political, and legal deference that they enjoyed (see Kennedy 1991). At the heart of modern medical law, conceived both as an academic and as a practical agenda, was a predominant movement to reconfigure the relationships between patient and doctor, with a view to empowering the former and to separating the latter's professional, clinical expertise from her ability to give effect to personal moral or political value judgments.

Although the importance of public health has been a feature of key legal texts on health care for some time now (see e.g. Montgomery 1997), and has come to feature increasingly in newer editions of the leading medico-legal textbooks (contrast e.g. Jackson 2013, 2016; Mason et al. 2002; Mason and Laurie 2006), it has not been treated historically with the depth of attention given to questions such as, for example, an individual patient's informed consent to a remedial clinical intervention. This may be because public health is a truly multi-disciplinary field and—with its reach across sectors too—thus extends far beyond the narrower reach of 'medical' (see Guest et al. 2013). It may just be a question of authors' and tutors' judgments on topic selection, which will necessarily be exclusive given the range of practical areas that might feature in a textbook or teaching syllabus (cf. Jacob 1990). But whatever the reasons or their strengths, the inclusion of public health law within textbooks may generally be represented as a recent phenomenon (Farrell et al. 2017, chapter 1). And taken as a field in its own right, there is only a limited number of such books specifically on public health law (e.g. Gostin and Wiley 2016; Coggon et al. 2017).

At one level, we should be slow in criticising this. One of the defining points about studies in law and health is their rapid expansion and associated pluri-dimensionality. Inevitably, many interesting, important, and relevant points and approaches may—must—be missed within any given text or course curriculum. I will note here three such dimensions. First, because studies in health and law have an ultimate practical focus that is anchored to a particular value—good health, and the viable routes and limits to promoting this value—it invites analyses from across areas *within* law: laws that impact health span private law (including, but not limited to, torts), public law (including, but not limited to, administrative law and human rights), and criminal law (including, but not limited to, criminal regulation of medical malpractice), and they require understandings stratified across domestic, EU, and international legal systems. They also inevitably require understandings of regulation that emanates from non-legal sources (including, but not limited to, the remit of organisations such as the General Medical Council). Second, studies in health and law invite a wealth of critical and evaluative approaches from *without* the law itself. As emphasised in the following discussion, biomedical ethics consistently seems to claim a privileged place here, but it is just one of many methods of framing and analysing (see also Syrett 2019), alongside distinct methods of socio-legal scholarship and empirical bioethics, as well, for example, as different branches of feminist theory, and other areas of jurisprudence and legal philosophy. And to note a final dimension, the nature of the field is such that scholars have generated tremendous depths of expertise in law as applied to very specific individual areas or topics, as varied as dementia, euthanasia, genetics, human reproduction, and organ donation. Given even just these three dimensions and their potential points of intersection, we find a daunting propensity to breadth, depth, and super-specialisation for health law scholars, and it is accordingly easy for any given expert to profess the especial importance of her own research and teaching choices, whilst at the same time of necessity neglecting other, equally significant, areas.

However, whilst we should not be overly critical of omissions of public health from legal curricula and research agendas, there are important reasons to support its inclusion. At an analytical level, the power of law is only partially represented when our focus is on its use as a shield to protect people who are unwell from undue intervention (undue because we see it as unjustifiable medical paternalism (cf *Montgomery* v *Lanarkshire Health Board* [2015]

UKSC 11)) or—with much more limited reach—as a tool to allow them to demand a particular treatment (cf *R (Burke)* v *General Medical Council* [2005] EWCA Civ 1003). Public health law provides a focus on positive states of well-being, the relative enjoyment of health by persons and groups across society, and crucially looks to political (Coggon 2012a, chapter 11) and legal (Gostin et al. 2019) determinants of (ill) health. It thus goes far beyond the medical context, and looks at the whole of our social fabric and how—rightly or wrongly, and for better or worse—this influences our health outcomes and opportunities, balanced alongside other values and goals.

This chapter therefore aims to explain the distinguishing features of public health law and what might be achieved through its featuring in contemporary research and teaching agendas: not to promote its priority *over* other points of interest, but to show what is missed when it is omitted and gained by its incorporation. As a point of biographical more than academic note, it is perhaps worth stating that it was an area that I was initially drawn to because of its analytical distinctiveness; in particular, its natural invitation to critique law through a lens of political philosophy, which I generally find to be more interesting, and more usefully illuminating, than studies focused on law through ethical theories whose normative foundations are limited to unmediated concepts of interpersonal morality (Coggon 2010). The normative questions raised when we consider the public's health are not just a matter of individual right, or of what one person might expect of another: we are interested in what we owe to each other within society but also as members of a shared political community, how these things may be mediated through public institutions. And at a more basic level, it asks what we owe to the state and what it owes to us. We do not simply ask how and whether health ranks as a value alongside others, or focus on theoretically contained individual rights rooted in ethico-legal commitments to bodily integrity; we enter inquiry into the much bigger question 'what makes health public?' (Coggon 2012a). This question then informs the practical social, political, and legal question 'how can health be made public?' (Coggon and Gostin 2020).

Within the established principles—perhaps even dogmas (Dawson 2010)—that circumscribe or pre-analytically charge critical discussions of law and health, public health may be seen as an outlier area (Coggon and Laing 2019). Key concepts such as individual consent often cannot straightforwardly apply (Nuffield Council on Bioethics 2007). Concepts—in particular paternalism—that are treated as normatively loaded in a particular way cannot automatically be taken as they might be in a narrow, clinical context (Wilson 2011). And public health focuses not just on 'downstream' interventions; after the fact responses to remedy ill health. Rather, it looks to 'upstream' conditions within society to protect and promote good health and well-being (contrast Daniels 1985 and 2007). Public health engages questions of social justice and systemic factors that demonstrably impact the public's health (Venkatapuram 2011). It cannot, therefore, be understood or taught (well) with reference simply to principles, theories, frameworks, and approaches that apply to contexts of clinical medicine (Jennings 2003). In this chapter, I accordingly aim to assist understandings of public health law by, first, explaining what public health is about, before outlining the rationale that I and colleagues have taken to systematising the field within legal studies. I then outline briefly how a critical basis to studies in public health law might be founded, allowing consideration of ethical framings drawn from within public health, and offer some conclusions on the value of public health law's incorporation within the body of health-focused jurisprudence.

## 2 Public Health

The term 'public health' is remarkably open and fluid, often being used to mean quite different things even within a single document (including this chapter). Provided we are clear on our meaning in a given instance, this is not a problem. In an earlier conceptual analysis, surveying definitions and inferences that could be drawn given the implications of different uses of 'public health,' I have argued that we can see seven distinct 'faces'—different clusters of ideas—that might be at play when we find the term used:

1. *Public health as a political tool*: in this sense 'public health' is used as an important end, denoting (supposedly) strong or compelling reasons for formulating policy. Here the term may be seen to imply a social mission, a social theory, or a naturally good concept. […]
2. *Public health as government business*: as a function of government, public health may be understood narrowly as relating to the competence or responsibility of specific health agencies, widely as any governmental power that affects health, or somewhere between these extremes.
3. *Public health as the social infrastructure*: in this sense public health is taken to represent society's organisation […] in respect to […] non-State responsibility for health that nevertheless may described as public in character.
4. *Public health as a professional enterprise*: public health refers here to professional approaches […] for example, to the scope of a professional's practical competence […], to the nature of expertise that a professional has, or to his work's being health-related.

5. *Public health as blind benefit/harm*: public health may be used as a qualifier to represent probable benefits or harms within a population [...,] to denote instances of certain harm where the specific identity of those harmed[/benefitted] is unclear [..., or] instances where *ex ante* the ultimate beneficiaries are not known [...].
6. *Public health as conjoined beneficiaries*: here 'the public' has moral, 'solidaristic' connotations [...].
7. *Public health as the population's health*: this [...] refers to the health of a population, either in aggregate or by reference to distribution. [...]. (Coggon 2012a, 46–47)

Each of these faces of public health calls for its own analysis; both conceptual and evaluative (see Coggon 2012a, chapter 3). Ultimately, I would reject calls for attempts to find or adopt *the* meaning of public health. But, as indicated by the above list, it is important when teaching or writing in this area to be clear within a given context about what is being covered, as distinct audiences can draw quite distinct interpretations of what an intended meaning might be. It is useful to begin a discussion of what public health is with this representation of the breadth of meanings that may be attributed to it, as this immediately exposes the ranging concerns and significances that it gives rise to.

However, having acknowledged this breadth and variety, it is of course necessary to gain some focus; again, a matter that whilst essential is inevitably exclusive. Within the context of public health law teaching, it is common to revert to and build on the most practically used and influential definitions of public health and to work from there (see e.g. the framings in Gostin and Wiley 2018, chapter 1). In doing this, two useful points of emphasis may be seen to arise, which can be related directly to the conceptual analysis of philosophers Angus Dawson and Marcel Verweij: the 'public' in 'public health' draws attention to methods of social coordination, both governmental and through alternative social structures; and the reference to 'public' demands a focus on health at a population rather than an individual level (Verweij and Dawson 2009). These two points provide particularly useful 'hooks' for the study of public health law.

There are significant conceptual and practical distinctions to be drawn when we look to collective organised means to protect and promote health and conceive of 'the population as patient' (Gostin 2014). 'Treating' a population raises distinct questions about both rationales for and methods of intervention. Consequently, it also requires distinct analyses of how interventions may be legitimised. Our understanding of how we might properly 'treat' a body of persons will be impacted by analyses of how we may treat a person's body. But our critiques can work in the other direction too and provide a more nuanced understanding of the practical scope and limits, and conceptual bounds, of the body—individually and within a social grouping—in health and law. As noted in the opening words of the introduction, since this chapter was completed and moved into production (towards the end of 2019), the importance of recognising these distinctions has been made stark by the necessity to control the spread of COVID-19; a crisis for people and governments globally. Even with national responses at their early stages, the fundamentality of human and social interconnectedness, the costs that may be carried in terms of individual liberty, and the weight and importance of values other than liberty are clear (see Coggon 2020a). Under and through the Coronavirus Act 2020 and associated and further legislative measures, the UK government and devolved administrations are exercising emergency powers in a way previously unheard of in peacetime. Other liberal democracies are acting similarly, and others again have followed quite different approaches. The questions of legitimacy in these circumstances bring to the fore how vital it is to retain checks on power, assure accountability, proportionality, and protection of human rights, approach public health law with a keen concern for equity, and adhere to a rigorous concept of the rule of law. They also emphasise the vulnerabilities of social institutions and infrastructures. And in relation to medical jurisprudence and medical practice, they show the fragility of assumptions based on analytically abstracted considerations just of an individual patient and doctor. By the time this chapter is published much legal scholarship will have been produced on the COVID-19 pandemic, and for sometime thereafter, crucial developments will emerge. The need for comprehension of public health law in ongoing analysis and practice will be essential.

However, the conceptual and analytical points that I aim to highlight at this stage of the chapter can be demonstrated in brief with reference to a less complex case study in public health ethics: the fluoridation of water supplies (see e.g. Nuffield Council on Bioethics 2007; Coggon and Viens 2017). A fundamental tenet of biomedical ethics and medical law, founded in the principles of respect for bodily integrity and respect for autonomy, provides that medical interventions may not be given to a person who has decision-making capacity, without her consent, if it is just for her own good (i.e. a paternalistic measure, as opposed, say, to a measure to protect others from harm) (see Mental Capacity Act 2005, section 1; *Re T* [1992] 4 All ER 649).[1] This con-

[1] The notable exception to this fundamental of English medical law concerns compulsory treatment authorised under the Mental Health Act 1983. This chapter is not an appropriate place for consideration of that statute or the justifiability of the distinct points of law for mental health care, but for analysis that considers both mental health and public health as 'outlier' areas in health-focused legal studies, and how

sent requirement, if generalisable without qualification, would render water fluoridation illicit in the absence of informed and explicit agreement of everyone who uses the public water supply. At a general level, overall water treatment, through methods such as filtration and chlorination, which *clean* our water and make it drinkable, may be justified because clean drinking water is a basic necessity and water authorities would wrongfully be causing harm if they provided us with untreated water. However, fluoridation is not rationalised by reference to making the water unharmful: it is an additional, *preventive* intervention to promote a health end (reduction of dental caries) that is dissociable from harms that might be caused by the water itself. The key rationales for fluoridating the public water supply is that it is a safe and effective means of preventing ill health and promoting good health across particular populations; in particular, children who are members of more disadvantaged socio-economic groups (Public Health England 2018). However, this treatment is essentially all or nothing: there can be no individual opt-in or opt-out. A decision has to be made, at a policy level, of whether a public as a whole will be treated paternalistically. The 'treatment' requires to be provided through general, coordinated means. Its effect anticipates, rather than reacts to, ill health. And its impact is on persons combined as an aggregate; as a public.

It is of course the case that many population-level health interventions may permit more nuance in their reach, and that rationales other than paternalism may be found for any given measure. For example, some vaccination programmes will be designed purely for the benefit of the individual who may be vaccinated, but others in order to protect third parties from harm or provide a general, 'herd' immunity. Others still will be a combination of these. In terms of implementation, furthermore, vaccination programmes may be unrolled at a general level whilst permitting individual opt-outs. Overall, public health activities span a broad range of functions. These include protection from environmental threats and prevention of the causes of incidence of disease. This may be through, for example, measures to assure food hygiene standards, clean air, refuse collection, a functioning sewerage system, or otherwise provide a sanitary environment. Or it may be through measures to prevent or respond effectively to enormous and imminent threats, such as an influenza pandemic. They also include the promotion of health and well-being through education, and the anticipation of causes of ill health. This may

---

these areas might develop, see Coggon and Laing 2019. There are important questions too, of course, about determinations of incapacity under the Mental Capacity Act 2005, and consequent decision-making (see further the analysis in Coggon 2007, 2016).

be through, for example, sex education, or through obesity reduction strategies to lessen the incidence of disease that is consequent to obesity.

In relation to legal studies, we can bring together the variety and range of public health activities and approaches and create a coherent body of analysis if we unify them through the two 'publics' in 'public health' presented by Verweij and Dawson. To reinforce the point, reflect on what is perhaps the most famous characterisation of public health, published a century ago by Charles-Edward A. Winslow:

> Public health is the science and art of preventing disease, prolonging life, and promoting physical health and efficiency through organized community efforts for the sanitation of the environment, the control of community infections, the education of the individual in principles of personal hygiene, the organization of medical and nursing service for the early diagnosis and preventive treatment of disease, and the development of the social machinery which will ensure to every individual in the community a standard of living adequate for the maintenance of health. (Winslow 1920, p. 30)

Contemporary definitions modify, but clearly draw a great deal from, Winslow's definition (see the definitions reviewed in Verweij and Dawson 2009). Unsurprisingly, 100 years on from his representation of public health, we now see a strong focus on mental as well as physical health (albeit not one that is as well matched in practice as it is in expressed political commitment: Faculty of Public Health and Mental Health Foundation 2016; Coggon and Laing 2019). Equally, scientific understanding has progressed since Winslow's time, leading to an increased understanding of the *social determinants* of health, and the need to consider *health in all policies* if we are to optimise protection and promotion of health and well-being (Davies et al. 2014). Twenty-first-century public health research, practice, and agendas are responsive to identifying different populations with a keener understanding of the causes of compounding or clustering of disadvantage in society (Wolff and De-Shalit 2007) and overall a concern to address, through socially coordinated measures, unfair health inequalities (Marmot 2004, 2015).

Given this, one final practical point about public health bears making, before moving more squarely to the study of public health *law*. Beyond the conceptual and practical dimensions that arise when we 'treat' a population, there are important questions of deciding *which* populations to target. There are, of course, as explored below, challenging questions in political theory, for example, about the role of government in addressing inequalities (e.g. as opposed to asserting without argument that health-related decisions should just be a matter determined by personal responsibility). But at a practical level, we should also in particular be aware of what epidemiologist Geoffrey Rose identified as the 'prevention paradox' (Rose 1985). Rose's analysis explains the differences between looking at, determining causation of, and responding to the manifestation of a disease in the case of an individual patient, and looking at the *incidence* of disease within a whole population and deriving understandings of what causes this and how it might be ameliorated. It is through the latter, for example, that we determine that smoking is a cause of lung cancer. We do not establish the causal link by studying individual cases, but rather by comparing two populations: smokers and non-smokers. Rose arrives at the idea of the 'prevention paradox' because, he explains, to reduce the incidence of disease in society, efforts require to be targeted at *low-risk* populations. In other words, to maximise public health interventions, we often achieve the greatest impact—for example, through measures to reduce salt consumption across a population—by targeting persons whose risk of ill health, taken individually, is low. Whilst for any given person there is low incentive to accept the intervention because of the probability of there being low gain, at a population level, the incidence of disease will be markedly impacted. This manner of complication adds a further challenge to the practical and normative considerations that define the study of public health law, the area to which this chapter now turns.

## 3 Public Health Law

Following the preliminary framings of this chapter, and the discussion of public health in the previous section, we may now consider how *public health law* might be conceived as a field of research and educational interest. The contrasting area of study and practice that I am referring to in this chapter as 'modern medical law' emerged towards the end of the 1970s, and achieved notable velocity following the interest stimulated by Ian Kennedy's Reith lectures *Unmasking Medicine* (Kennedy 1981). As noted in the introduction, in concert with the broad multi-disciplinary field of bioethics within which it sits, early medical law of this era assumed a predominant focus on medical practice, leading to a disregard of the wider features of the healthcare system (including organisational structures) and of the non-physician actors within it (including other healthcare professions such as dentists, midwives, and nurses, and, e.g. managers and administrative decision-makers) (Montgomery 1997). Margaret Brazier and Jonathan Montgomery have recently challenged the wisdom of assuming or accepting the suppositions and framings of 'modern medical law' without regard for a much longer view of its historical context and possible futures (Brazier and Montgomery 2019). However, dominant norms in modern medical law have challenged a medical paternalism that was enshrined in the second half of the last century as a professional ethic, and supported through legal structures developed at common law by a largely deferential judiciary (cf Lord Woolf 2001). Equally, they have provided a partial account of social interactions—the clinical encounter between doctor and patient—and allowed patient autonomy to become a value of such predominant importance that even in wider contexts it is given undue (and often unquestioned) weight (cf Brazier 2006; Coggon 2012b). As a starting point, studies of public health law require attention to the entire social context: any given scholar may *end up* at the view that individual autonomy ought always to triumph over wider questions of welfare or inequalities, but we must *start* with a clean slate rather than inherit the norms of the practically and analytically contained studies of 'modern medical law' (Coggon 2012a).

This question of wider context also invites recognition of the different actors that will be the subjects of analysis. As well as conceiving of persons in society generally, rather than 'patients,' we need to look to relevant institutional actors and the norms that ought to govern their practices: public health laws ultimately impact on individual persons, but we are interested in a collective 'body' (or 'bodies') of persons, and in the roles and responsibilities too of corporate (in particular, but not only, governmental) 'bodies.' This last sense of 'bodies' brings us again to Verweij and Dawson's first idea of 'public' in 'public health': the organised community effort and use of social machinery in order to assure better conditions for the protection and promotion of the public's health. Here we find natural links to the importance of legal studies for public health (Coggon 2018a). This is not least because law necessarily assumes a role as being a *part of* public health. At the 'thicker' end of this, there are governmental responsibilities to protect and promote the public's health, as introduced in England, for example, through sections 11 and 12 of the Health and Social Care Act 2012 (the former relating to the Secretary of State, the latter to Local Authorities as well as the Secretary of State) or as provided under the Public Health (Control of Disease) Act 1984 (and extraordinarily, of course, through powers conferred under the Coronavirus Act 2020). Relevant here are the functions of executive agencies such as Public Health England, as well as organisations such as the NHS and the National Institute for Health and Care Excellence. But this also includes government responsibilities that may not be expressly or obviously designated as relating to 'public health', or exclusively based on policy concerns for the public's health, yet which are nevertheless of relevance to determining how our environments impact our health (e.g. laws governing consumer protection, education, environmental protection, housing, urban planning, taxation). In a perhaps 'thinner' sense, we might also relate this idea of community effort and social machinery to the coordination and governance roles of non-governmental actors that nevertheless serve—or aim to serve—the public's health (e.g. organisations such as the UK Faculty of Public Health). And we should look as well at the impact of powerful private organisations, whose practices may affect health at a population level for better or worse (e.g. supermarkets through their pricing policies on alcoholic drinks or their placing within the shop of sweets) (see further Coggon et al. 2017, chapter 9).

Given the wide reach of public health, as shown in the previous section, and the breadth of legal and governance approaches that are relevant to its proper understanding, delineating the field of public health law risks problems of (what might be perceived to be) overreach (for arguments supportive of such a position, contrast, for example the discussion of delimiting the definitions of 'public health,' respectively, by Richard Epstein (Epstein 2004) and Mark Rothstein (Rothstein 2002)). Nevertheless, Keith Syrett, A.M. Viens, and I have indeed promoted public health law as an area of study that is well characterised by the extensiveness indicated up to this point, characterising it as:

> A field of study and practice that concerns those aspects of law, policy, and regulation that advance or place constraints upon the protection and promotion of the health (howsoever understood) within, between, and across populations. (Coggon et al. 2017, p. 72)

This definition is the product of a review of the nature and scope of contemporary public health agendas, the reach and points of engagement of public health ethics, and an analysis of the history of British law and public health (see Coggon et al. 2017, Part I). In contemporary literatures, we draw in particular from the approaches of UK scholars—especially Robyn Martin and Richard Coker (see e.g. Martin 2006, 2007; Martin and Coker 2006a, b)—and pioneers of public health law in the United States—notably Lawrence Gostin and Lindsay Wiley (see e.g. Gostin and Wiley 2016)—and Australia—in particular Roger Magnusson (see e.g. Magnusson 2007) (Coggon et al. 2017, chapter 4). In developing and explaining our manner of understanding UK public health law, we are keen to emphasise the importance of being open-minded about substantive content, and firmer in our characterisation by reference to regulatory rationales and approaches than limited topics or points of jurisdiction (see also Bennett et al. 2009). That is, rather than delimiting the field by reference, say, to laws that define themselves as concerning 'public health' (e.g. laws about notifiable diseases or specifically designated state powers), or by reference to particular areas of practical concern (e.g. pandemic preparedness or obesity), we look to the broad interrelationships between law, governance, and the impacts of different phenomena—for better or worse—on the public's health. For the reasons summarised in the current chapter, the study and analysis of public health and law would otherwise arbitrarily miss too much.

In Chap. 4 of our textbook, where we present and explain our characterisation of the field, we present in summary form the key points of emphasis to be taken. We write that:

[S]uch a definition provides the different necessary conditions for the study and practice of public health law. Our definition:

- Covers the very broad, but necessary, embrace that is claimed by contemporary public health activity, which includes the provision of a health care system, public health infrastructure, and measures that respond to social determinants of ill health.
- Provides a breadth in its concept of law: we are not simply focussed on 'hard law' measures but look also to social policy broadly conceived to include the governance roles of public and private actors and institutions.
- Embraces different legal and regulatory measures and approaches and reaches across sectors.
- Emphasises the role of law and governance both as means to promote public health agendas and as means to limit what may be done in the name of public health.
- Permits an open interpretation of 'health' allowing analysis of measures that bear not simply on, for example, disease, but also on broader, positive states such as wellbeing.
- Is open to engagement from disciplines outside of legal studies: for example […], the field should be informed by public health ethics. Our definition of public health law is also compatible, for example, with study informed by disciplines such as anthropology, sociology, psychology, history, and economics. (Coggon et al. 2017, 72)

The combination of these points creates the necessary drivers of studies in public health law. But it should be immediately obvious that, barring possibly a degree qualification specifically in the field, a single teaching curriculum will not be able to cover everything that might be included. As such, a defining feature of a given course in public health law will—as in medico-legal studies—be a matter of exclusive selection. In line with the pluri-dimensionality raised in the introduction to this chapter, this applies across points of legal approach and jurisdiction, across critical methods of understanding and analysis, and across possible practical subjects or topics of study. My view is that this is inevitable, and that it should be treated as a strength. There are various reasons for this, but one—which we emphasise in our approach to drafting the more applied, UK and international/global-focused chapters of our textbook (see Coggon et al. 2017, chapters 5–9)—is that a solid aim of public health law is the development of *transferable* understanding (for a wider survey and discussion of rationales for different approaches to framing the study of public health ethics and law in educational contexts, see Syrett and Quick 2009; Dawson and Upshur 2013; Miller 2015; Doudenkova et al. 2017). In the next section of this chapter, I therefore consider it valuable to outline some key *critical* and *analytical* concerns that arise in relation to public health and law, and which can inform the sorts of debates that this volume aims to address.

# 4 Biomedical Ethics, Political Morality, and Social Justice

## 4.1 The Socio-Political Context of Public Health Law

The defining features of public health law, at least as I have presented them in this chapter, by their nature present an area whose paradigms demand a move away from what have become the standardised approaches, framings, and received socio-ethical wisdoms of modern medical law. In public health law, we are not able to abstract individual encounters between doctor and patient from a wider social context and theorise on the basis of that. Like critical medical lawyers, public health law scholars are interested in questions of power imbalances, the proper scope of freedoms, and the contours of our rights in relation to health and welfare. Of necessity, the study of these requires more nuance and variety than that found in 'textbook' clinical encounters (see also Farrell et al. 2017, chapter 3). We find ourselves having to move beyond an apparent assumption that the best way for law to serve an individual is by ensuring that she is adequately informed and by that fact able to decide for herself. Rather than identify just the more powerful and the disempowered party (respectively, the doctor and the patient), we look across society at persons, agencies, and institutions, as well as distinct layers of concentration of power, opportunity, advantage, disempowerment, and disadvantage. When looking at public health, we are raising distinguishable practical questions, including ones focused on promoting positive states of well-being, rather than just the avoidance, remediation, or palliative control of disease. And accordingly, the question of values and (enforceable) obligations is pervasive, rather than focused overwhelmingly on one party (i.e. in modern medical law, the doctor). We look at the responsibilities that everyone does and should owe to each other, and the obligations between persons and communities and institutions of government. These are studied not by reference to the uniform idealisation of the 'autonomous patient' but in a contextualised account of empirical social conditions and structures and real politics. Within public health law, therefore, different (albeit at times overlapping and, in principle, complementary) conceptual and critical approaches and lenses require to be taken to those that are familiar in medical law. These are needed, for example, in order to demonstrate the distinct possibilities for analysis of social inequalities and the consequent contours of social justice. And they lead to distinctive implications for the limits that might be placed on, or qualifications given to, rights and responsibilities, and the presumptive and ultimate conclusion on questions of justifying, for example, interventions that are paternalistic in nature, that call for trade-offs between values across society, or that promote redistribution of resources.

It should be clear from this that our critical focus in public health is properly framed by reference to a political, rather than a purely interpersonal, morality (Coggon 2012a). This insight is not new (see e.g. Jennings 2003; Nuffield Council on Bioethics 2007), but it is something that can get lost in medico-legal scholarship and education that often obscure the places of institutional actors and the relationships between persons as citizens, between persons and the state, and the place, rights, and responsibilities of other (e.g. commercial) organisations. The importance of politics and political context has long been apparent to those working in public health (Mackenbach 2009). But there can be a tendency—given that the same teachers and researchers tend to look at medical law and public health law—to allow paradigms from the former to pervade and even predominate the latter. Within public health research itself, there is an increasing and welcome movement to expose and engage in analyses in political science (see e.g. Bambra et al. 2005; Kickbusch 2013; Bekker et al. 2018). However, a full analysis requires engagement both with the more empirically situated concerns of political science, *and* with the more philosophically oriented inquiry of political philosophy (Coggon 2012a, 2019; Coggon and Gostin 2020). I would encourage colleagues and students to approach their critical understanding of public health law within such framings. Whilst doing so may, in a way that is consistent with the discussions in the previous section, lead to a very broad teaching agenda, some practical 'narrowing' is possible if we focus our points of inquiry around the moral drivers of public health practice.

Although there is legitimate scope for disagreement on how to approach this, one point of critical departure may be the ethics of public health itself. There is something of a consensus that if we look to the ethical agendas espoused within public health, we can identify two 'moral mandates' on which practice—and ultimately interventions—rest (Coggon and Viens 2017). In doing this, we recognise that whatever moral legitimacy public health may claim, at the heart of our inquiry is the use of state power (including through law) to effect public health aims (Thomas et al. 2002). The first mandate that members of the public health community tend to identify is the protection of health, both through preventing ill health and through protecting and promoting good health and well-being; the second is the amelioration of unfair health inequalities. Given these professed ethical imperatives, and the points in the previous paragraphs about framing, the following two subsections of this chapter briefly engage with two heads of critical analysis and inquiry that might accordingly feature in—even underpin—teaching agendas in public health law: first, the question of health improvement and the magnetism of 'nanny state' accusations; and second, the critical focus of redistributive justice.

## 4.2 The First Moral Mandate of Public Health: Promoting Health Under the Shadow of Paternalism Objections

The first, and perhaps most obvious, concern in public health is the prevention of ill health and promotion of good health. This can find itself quickly related to a utilitarian ethic that often (and often too simplistically) becomes associated with public health ethics. By its nature, such imputed association suggests a focus on optimising the aggregate good with little direct regard for persons' rights (or indeed values other than health). Additionally, both within a broad scheme of political morality, and within an area of study that can be beholden to the norms of medical law, we find an ethical reference point that rests on paternalistic ideas and ideals. And as is widely recognised, rightly or wrongly, paternalism has become an automatic indicator of illegitimacy in medico-legal studies.

These sources of tension are a good entry point for critical discussions of the proper role, purpose, and limits of law in the context of population health, and permits tutors to draw from ranging critical perspectives (see Coggon

2012a, chapters 7 and 8; 2018b). Health is a powerful value: whatever a person's political leanings, it is hard to argue that health and well-being are not important. But what can be harder to argue is whether and why these things are a concern of government; a *public* matter. Within the ethico-legal literatures on public health, we find theorists such as Lawrence Gostin (Gostin 2008) and Jennifer Ruger (Ruger 2009), who argue for the special, fundamental importance of health. It is presented as *the* foundational value for political communities. At the other extreme, we find theorists such as Petr Skrabanek (Skrabanek 1994), who espouse a commitment to profound value pluralism, and who shun the idea that health might legitimately stand at all as a value that should direct policy. And there are then many positions that sit in between these extremes, for example, holding that health is important but that government-led public health policies create inefficiencies and conduce overall to poor health outcomes (see e.g. Epstein 2004), or that health is important but as just one of a plurality of basic values (see e.g. Powers and Faden 2008). There are crucial questions for (public) health law students to examine on how health might be the value that motivates and justifies a policy intervention, and how discussions of this may be associated with fundamental characterisations of political morality and legal legitimacy (cf Latham 2015).

Accordingly, the 'hook' provided by the aims of prevention of ill health, protection of good health, and promotion of better health is a strong one. It invites debates about the legitimate aims of legislative and other forms of governance for health. But crucially, it also prompts discussion of *methods* of regulation, with perhaps inevitable reference within this to the 'nanny state' (Coggon 2018b). When exploring different sorts of intervention, it is instructive to evaluate ideas about normative distinctions between 'harder' and 'softer' measures. These include a focus on the vogue of 'nudge' as a (putatively: see Coggon 2020b) benign, or philosophically and politically more straightforward, method of achieving healthier publics (cf Sunstein and Thaler 2003; Thaler and Sunstein 2009; Sunstein 2014, 2016; contrast also the approach and analysis in Davies et al. 2014). Such a focus also allows the analysis of how the legitimacy of interventions might be scrutinised in terms of effectiveness, respect for basic rights and proportionality, equality, and the rule of law, or tempered by reference to the nature of the particular population being targeted (e.g. children; members of particular socio-economic groups) (cf Gostin et al. 2019).

## 4.3 The Second Moral Mandate of Public Health: Addressing Inequalities Under the Shadow of Arguments for Pure Individual Responsibility

The second key normative concern in public health is addressing unfair health inequalities. This clearly is not founded in anything like utilitarian ideas of justice, drawing considerations not just about the aggregate health within a public, but looking as well to distribution. Health inequalities generally are exemplified with reference to statistics concerning systemic causes and distributions of relative health outcomes for different populations but may also be related to the distribution of opportunity to live in good health. It is well recognised that for an inequality to be an inequity, some criterion or principle of fairness is needed. And people of course radically disagree on what is meant by *unfair* inequality. Additionally, public health (ethics) literatures explore how challenging it is to establish how we might index and, through policy, address measures of disadvantage (Braveman and Gruskin 2003; see also Wolff 2009).

Howsoever they may be understood and measured, unfair inequalities in health outcomes and opportunities are directly linked to wider socio-economic inequalities; questions of socio-structural (dis)advantage and (in)opportunity, rather than matters that can in practice just be addressed by persons individually (Marmot 2004, 2015; Venkatapuram 2011). They also require to be addressed by looking across sectors and areas of policy; we cannot just focus on health care (Daniels 2007). As such, when considering public health ethics and law with reference to inequalities, we find ourselves focusing on questions of *redistributive* justice, within a political framing that—with reference to scientific evidence—denies libertarian ideas that people can fairly be held responsible, on their own, for their health.

Amongst the complexities in understanding and evaluating health inequalities as a matter of justice are questions of whether we take health inequalities as themselves to be problematic, or whether we should treat them as indicators of injustice. Furthermore, there is the point that, unlike goods that might be redistributed within a social system (e.g. financial wealth), health itself is not something that can be redistributed (Ashcroft 2015). Within teaching and research agendas concerning public health, we are therefore required to look at and consider distinct theories of social justice (cf Coggon 2012a, chapters 7 and 8). We do this with a view to normative questions of whether and by what means governments might be mandated to redistribute wealth and other goods (e.g. to assure optimal conditions for health in the early years of life), and how governments might be empowered to limit general or commercial freedoms (e.g. through minimum pricing schemes on alcohol) in order to remediate disproportionate health harms amongst less well-off socio-economic groups. Necessarily, we must also do this with a view to evidence bases about how different such measures might practically serve to ameliorate health (and other) inequalities. But in exploring such questions, we should not take it that philosophical debates on competing ideas of justice can be sidelined: health inequalities may be identified through scientific methodologies, but inequities are established by reference to political-philosophical reason.

Within public health discourses, and of course more generally in society, there are plural, competing accounts of how fairness should be understood in relation to health inequalities. A focus on health inequalities, like one on health promotion, allows studies in public health law to engage with divergent practical questions and contexts, elucidating the pulls and drawbacks of different ideas of justice, and overall permitting depth of critical understanding of the possibilities and limitations of law and governance as mechanisms to effect better population health. As discussed in the next section, they do so in a way that can lend fascinating extra dimensions to our understandings of the body in—and of—medical and health jurisprudence.

## 4.4 Public Health Law: Challenging and Enriching the Body in (and of) Biomedical and Health Jurisprudence

A.M. Viens has explained how the 'population approach' of public health challenges theorists to 'tame' the individualism of liberal and republican political theory (Viens 2016; see also the discussions of liberalism, republicanism, individualism, and agency, in the paper to which Viens' paper responds: Weinstock 2016). The influence of such theory, in particular political liberalism, has been marked in the formation of medical law in the UK and beyond. The field's received ethical and jurisprudential wisdoms have been developed by theorists who have espoused individualism, and thus promoted highly individualised concepts of 'the patient.' The atomisation of 'the patient' has led to a heavy emphasis on the presumptive value of individually oriented values: notably, decision-making autonomy, and liberty in the sense of 'negative freedom' from unwanted state interference (including interference by health professionals). Such orientations have meant that even when bioethical works purport to question the reach of liberal individualism's impact from biomedical ethics—for example, the Nuffield Council on Bioethics' report on public health ethics (Nuffield Council on Bioethics 2007)—they have been criticised for producing prescriptions that 'double count' liberty as a value when assessing the legitimacy of mandates for governmental interventions (see e.g. Dawson 2016). Equally, I have criticised that same report, suggesting that the nature of individualism associated with liberal theories can be, and in the Nuffield Council's report was, problematically accepted and overemphasised (Coggon 2008) (see also Baldwin, Brownsword, and Schmidt 2009).

As medical law has expanded through healthcare law to *health law*, ranging critiques of the overinflated value of autonomy have become of increasing salience (Farrell et al. 2017, chapter 3). These include empirical studies that challenge the reductive simplification of a singular and—when informed—empowered patient given that, in reality, we find plural levels of diversity in persons' lived experiences, vulnerabilities, and capabilities, leading to corresponding varieties in what is to be a patient. And they include critical perspectives from, for example, feminist theories, that challenge the normative validity of individual moralities in the face of relational realities.

Studies in public health law bring further challenges in the ways discussed in this chapter: notably, in looking at health opportunities and outcomes by reference to population-level understandings, and by looking at distributions of these opportunities and outcomes in manners that raise questions about social justice. Crucially, this is not just about people as patients, but people in the course of their lives in general. As Sridhar Venkatapuram has forcefully argued, when we are faced with evidence of the health impacts of institutional structures and the forms and effects of how communities are organised, and thereby recognise how an individual's health cannot be determined by the individual on her own, we are faced with evidence that impacts how we think about what makes a fair society. He writes:

> Importantly, social epidemiological research not only explodes outward the classic model of epidemiology, but the research findings also militate against various social consequences of applying the biomedical model. Some of these social consequences include the narrow focus on providing health care and behavior change as the primary avenues to improve health; being inattentive to social group inequalities in health; exaggerating individual volition in health outcomes; and focusing on the material poverty of the most disadvantaged while ignoring psychosocial environments producing ill health in the entire population. (Venkatapuram 2010, p. 124)

Venkatapuram's concerns directly—and very forcefully—undermine excesses of individualism in debates on how we analyse questions about health-related rights, freedoms, obligations, and opportunities. He makes clear how, at both national and global levels, we cannot reduce analysis to individualised models, or limit our practical arena of concern to the sphere of health care.

In the context of 'a jurisprudence of the body,' these challenges offer excellent scope for enhancing our overall critical understandings of law and medicine, and law and health more widely. Public health law approaches can enhance and enrich studies in medical law in its narrower instantiations, as well as throw open the practical social and governmental reach of our inquiry in societal (including legal) engagement with health as a value. Lindsay Wiley has shown well how public health concerns draw together legal understandings with public health science and questions of social justice in a way that significantly challenges legal framings and responses that are rooted in individualistic values (Wiley 2012, 2014). Questions of the scope and limits of concepts such as autonomy and bodily integrity, and the boundaries—physical and in principle—of the body, are thrown into fresh relief when we consider how our social interactions and institutions are determinants of the health that we may—or may not—enjoy. The practical contexts and normative framings of public health outlined in this chapter must be taken seriously, howsoever a critical scholar may ultimately respond to them in terms of normative conclusions on conceptual and analytical questions within jurisprudence. In the ever-burgeoning field of law and health, public health law may be seen to bring particular insights and approaches that radically change our understandings and analyses for the better.

## 5 Conclusions

The importance of law and governance to the achievement of public health goals is not a new insight (Coggon et al. 2017, chapter 3). However, the study of public health law has, for whatever reason, been relatively limited when compared with other areas of health and jurisprudence. Given the inevitable place for law and regulation within public health, and the enormous breadth of socio-political and ethical concerns that are raised by the idea of governance for the public's health, I have sought to show in this chapter how public health law can bring very distinctive, interesting, and important components to health law and to debates on a jurisprudence of the body. Although as a field of study it concerns much more than control of infectious disease, the COVID-19 pandemic and powers such as those granted through the Coronavirus Act 2020 underscore the great significance of public health law. This crisis has also drawn to the fore the social inequities that demand the critical attention of legal scholars, and which are not captured within the analytical framings of 'mainstream' medical law. Studies in public health law put social structures and embedded systems and inequalities into sharp focus. They also provide crucial opportunities for analysis—from many disciplinary perspectives—of the scope, limits, and legitimacy of law and other methods of regulation in achieving fairer societies. By explaining and contextualising public health within and against the wider body of medical and health law, I hope to have shown how inclusion of this often-neglected field can bring a critical dynamism, and broad—potentially global—reach to studies in health and law.

## References


Ashcroft, R. (2015). Ethics and Global Health Inequalities. In J. Coggon & S. Gola (Eds.), *Global Health and International Community—Ethical, Political and Regulatory Challenges*. London: Bloomsbury.

Baldwin, T., Brownsword, R., Schmidt, H. (2009). Stewardship, Paternalism, and Public Health: Further Thoughts. *Public Health Ethics, 2*(1), 113–116.

Bambra, C., Fox, D., & Scott-Samuel, A. (2005). Towards a Politics of Health. *Health Promotion International, 20*(2), 187–193.

Bekker, M. P. M., Greer, S. L., Azzopardi-Muscat, N., & McKee, M. (2018). Public Health and Politics: How Political Science Can Help us Move Forward. *European Journal of Public Health, 28*(S3), 1–2.

Bennett, B., Gostin, L. O., Magnusson, R., & Martin, R. (2009). Health Governance: Law, Regulation and Policy. *Public Health, 123*, 207.

Braveman, P., & Gruskin, S. (2003). Defining Equity in Health. *Journal of Epidemiology and Community Health, 57*(4), 254–258.

Brazier, M. (2006). Do no Harm—Do Patients Have Responsibilities Too? *Cambridge Law Journal, 65*(2), 397–422.

Brazier, M., & Montgomery, J. (2019). Whence and Wither 'Modern Medical Law'? *Northern Ireland Legal Quarterly, 70*(1), 5–30.

Coggon, J. (2007). Varied and Principled Understandings of Autonomy in English Law: Justifiable Inconsistency or Blinkered Moralism? *Health Care Analysis, 15*(3), 235–255.

Coggon, J. (2008). Harmful Rights-Doing? The Perceived Problem of Liberal Paradigms and Public Health. *Journal of Medical Ethics, 34*(11), 798–801.

Coggon, J. (2010). Assisted Dying and the Context of Debate: 'Medical Law' *versus* 'End-of-Life Law'. *Medical Law Review, 18*(4), 541–563.

Coggon, J. (2012a). *What Makes Health Public? A Critical Evaluation of Moral, Legal, and Political Claims in Public Health*. Cambridge: Cambridge University Press.

Coggon, J. (2012b). Would Responsible Medical Lawyers Lose their Patients? *Medical Law Review, 20*(1), 130–149.
Coggon, J. (2014). Global Health, Law, and Ethics: Fragmented Sovereignty and the Limits of Universal Theory. In M. Freeman, S. Hawkes & B. Bennett (Eds.), Law and Global Health. Oxford: Oxford University Press.
Coggon, J. (2016). Mental Capacity Law, Autonomy, and Best Interests: An Argument for Conceptual and Practical Clarity in the Court of Protection. *Medical Law Review, 24*(3), 396–414.
Coggon, J. (2018a). Law. In S. Venkatapuram & J. Bibby (Eds.), *A Recipe for Action: Using Wider Evidence for a Healthier UK: A Collection of Essays Exploring Why We Need Trans-Disciplinary Approaches to Improve the Public's Health*. London: Health Foundation.
Coggon, J. (2018b). *The Nanny State Debate: A Place Where Words don't Do Justice*. London: Faculty of Public Health.
Coggon, J. (2020a). Beyond Liberty: Social Values and Public Health Ethics in Responses to COVID-19. Nuffield Council on Bioethics Blog (26th March, 2020) Available at https://www.nuffieldbioethics.org/blog/beyond-liberty-social-values-and-public-health-ethics-in-responses-to-covid-19, (last accessed 30th March, 2020).
Coggon, J. (2020b). Smoke Free? Public Health Policy, 'Coercive Paternalism', and the Ethics of Long-Game Regulation. *Journal of Law and Society, 47*(1), 121–148.
Coggon, J., & Gostin, L. O. (2020). The Two Most Important Questions for Ethical Public Health. *Journal of Public Health, 42*(1), 198–202.
Coggon, J., & Laing, J. (2019). Exploring New Paradigms in Mental Health and Capacity Law: Persons, Populations, and Parity of Esteem. *Northern Ireland Legal Quarterly, 70*(1), 31–52.
Coggon, J., Syrett, K., & Viens, A. M. (2017). *Public Health Law—Ethics, Governance, and Regulation*. Abingdon: Routledge.
Coggon, J., & Viens, A. M. (2017). *Public Health Ethics in Practice: An Overview of Public Health Ethics for the UK Public Health Skills and Knowledge Framework*. London: Public Health England.
Daniels, N. (1985). *Just Health Care*. Cambridge: Cambridge University Press.
Daniels, N. (2007). *Just Health*. Cambridge: Cambridge University Press.
Davies, S. C., Winpenny, E., Ball, S., Fowler, T., Rubin, J., & Nolte, E. (2014). For Debate: A New Wave in Public Health Improvement. *The Lancet, 384*(9957), 1889–1895.
Dawson, A. (2010). The Future of Bioethics: Three Dogmas and a Cup of Hemlock. *Bioethics, 24*(5), 218–225.
Dawson, A. (2016). Snakes and Ladders: State Interventions and the Place of Liberty in Public Health Policy. *Journal of Medical Ethics, 42*(8), 510–513.
Dawson, A., & Upshur, R. (2013). A Model Curriculum for Public Health Ethics. In D. Strech, I. Hirschberg, & G. Marckmann (Eds.), *Ethics in Public Health and Health Policy: Concepts, Methods, Case Studies*. Dordrecht: Springer.

Doudenkova, V., Bélisle-Pipon, J.-C., Ringuette, L., Ravitsky, V., & Williams-Jones, B. (2017). Ethics Education in Public Health: Where Are we Now and Where Are We Going? *International Journal of Ethics Education, 2*(2), 109–124.

Epstein, R. (2004). In Defense of the 'Old' Public Health. *Brooklyn Law Review, 69*(4), 1421–1470.

Faculty of Public Health and Mental Health Foundation. (2016). *Better Mental Health for all: A Public Health Approach to Mental Health Improvement*. London: Faculty of Public Health and Mental Health Foundation.

Farrell, A.-M., Devereux, J., Karpin, I., & Weller, P. (2017). *Health Law—Frameworks and Context*. Cambridge: Cambridge University Press.

Gostin, L. O. (2008). Meeting Basic Survival Needs of the World's Least Healthy People: Toward a Framework Convention on Global Health. *Georgetown Law Journal, 96*(2), 331–392.

Gostin, L. O. (2014). Public Health: The 'Population' as Patient. In C. DeAngelis (Ed.), *Patient Care and Professionalism*. New York, NY: Oxford University Press.

Gostin, L. O., Monahan, J. T., Kaldor, J., et al. (2019). The Legal Determinants of Health: Harnessing the Power of Law for Global Health and Sustainable Development. *The Lancet, 393*(10183), 1857–1910.

Gostin, L. O., & Wiley, L. F. (2016). *Public Health Law—Power, Duty, Restraint* (3rd ed.). Berkeley: University of California Press.

Gostin, L. O., & Wiley, L. F. (2018). *Public Health Law and Ethics—A Reader* (3rd ed.). Berkeley: University of California Press.

Guest, C., Ricciardi, W., Kawachi, I., & Lang, I. (Eds.). (2013). *The Oxford Handbook of Public Health Practice* (3rd ed.). Oxford: Oxford University Press.

Illich, I. (1976). *Limits to Medicine—Medical Nemesis: The Expropriation of Health*. London: Marion Boyars.

Jackson, E. (2013). *Medical Law—Text, Cases, and Materials* (3rd ed.). Oxford: Oxford University Press.

Jackson, E. (2016). *Medical Law—Text, Cases, and Materials* (4th ed.). Oxford: Oxford University Press.

Jacob, J. (1990). Reviews. *Modern Law Review, 53*(2), 280–282.

Jennings, B. (2003). Frameworks for Ethics in Public Health. *Acta Bioethica, 9*(2), 165–176.

Kennedy, I. (1981). *The Unmasking of Medicine*. London: George Allen and Unwin.

Kennedy, I. (1991). *Treat Me Right: Essays in Medical Law and Ethics*. Oxford: Oxford University Press.

Kickbusch, I. (2013). Foreword: We Need to Build a Health Political Science. In C. Clavier & E. De Leeuw (Eds.), *Health Promotion and the Policy Process*. Oxford, Oxford University Press.

Latham, S. (2015). On some Difficulties for Any Theory of Global Health Justice. In J. Coggon & S. Gola (Eds.), *Global Health and International Community—Ethical, Political and Regulatory Challenges*. London: Bloomsbury.

Mackenbach, J. P. (2009). Politics Is Nothing but Medicine at a Larger Scale: Reflections on Public health's Biggest Idea. *Journal of Epidemiology and Community Health, 63*(3), 181–184.

Magnusson, R. (2007). Mapping the Scope and Opportunities for Public Health Law in Liberal Democracies. *Journal of Law, Medicine and Ethics, 35*(4), 571–587.

Marmot, M. (2004). *Status Syndrome: How Your Social Standing Directly Affects your Health* (Vol. 1, p. 150). London: Bloomsbury.

Marmot, M. (2015). *The Health Gap: The Challenge of an Unequal World*. London: Bloomsbury.

Martin, R. (2006). The Limits of Law in the Protection of Public Health and the Role of Public Health Ethics. *Public Health, 120*(Supp 1), 71–77.

Martin, R. (2007). Law as a Tool in Promoting and Protecting Public Health: Always in our Best Interests? *Public Health, 121*(11), 846–853.

Martin, R., & Coker, R. (2006a). Introduction: The Importance of Law for Public Health Policy and Practice. *Public Health, 120*(Supp 1), 2–7.

Martin, R., & Coker, R. (2006b). Conclusion: Where Next? *Public Health, 120*(Supp 1), 81–87.

Mason, J. K., McCall-Smith, R. A., & Laurie, G. T. (2002). *Law and Medical Ethics* (6th ed.). London: LexisNexis Butterworths.

Mason, J. K., & Laurie, G. T. (2006). *Mason and McCall Smith's Law and Medical Ethics* (7th ed.). Oxford: Oxford University Press.

Miller, F. H. (2015). Teaching Public Health Law: Time for a Status Upgrade. *Journal of Law, Medicine and Ethics JLME, Supplement*, 5–6.

Montgomery, J. (1997). *Health Care Law*. Oxford: Oxford University Press.

Nuffield Council on Bioethics. (2007). *Public Health—Ethical Issues*. London: Nuffield Council on Bioethics.

Powers, M., & Faden, R. (2008). *Social Justice: The Moral Foundations of Public Health and Health Policy*. Oxford: Oxford University Press.

Public Health England. (2018). *Water Fluoridation—Health Monitoring Report for England 2018*. London: Public Health England.

Rose, G. (1985). Sick Individuals and Sick Populations. *International Journal of Epidemiology, 14*(1), 32–38.

Rothstein, M. (2002). Rethinking the Meaning of Public Health. *Journal of Law, Medicine and Ethics, 30*, 144–149.

Ruger, J. P. (2009). *Health and Social Justice*. Oxford: Oxford University Press.

Skrabanek, P. (1994). *The Death of Humane Medicine and the Rise of Coercive Healthism*. London: Social Affairs Unit.

Sunstein, C. (2014). *Why Nudge?* New Haven: Yale University Press.

Sunstein, C. (2016). *The Ethics of Influence: Government in the Age of Behavioral Science*. Cambridge: Cambridge University Press.

Sunstein, C., & Thaler, R. (2003). Libertarian Paternalism Is Not an Oxymoron. *The University of Chicago Law Review, 70*, 1159–1202.

Syrett, K. (2019). Healthcare Resource Allocation in the English Courts: A Systems Theory Perspective. *Northern Ireland Legal Quarterly, 70*(1), 111–130.

Syrett, K., & Quick, O. (2009). Pedagogical Promise and Problems: Teaching Public Health Law. *Public Health, 123*(3), 222–231.

Thaler, R., & Sunstein, C. (2009). *Nudge: Improving Decisions about Health, Wealth, and Happiness*. London: Penguin.

Thomas, J., Sage, M., Dillenberg, J., et al. (2002). Editorial—A Code of Ethics for Public Health. *American Journal of Public Health, 92*(7), 1057–1059.

Venkatapuram, S. (2010). Global Justice and the Social Determinants of Health. *Ethics and International Affairs, 24*(2), 119–130.

Venkatapuram, S. (2011). *Health Justice: An Argument from the Capabilities Approach*. Cambridge: Polity Press.

Verweij, M., & Dawson, A. (2009). The Meaning of 'Public' in 'Public Health'. In A. Dawson & M. Verweij (Eds.), *Ethics, Prevention, and Public Health*. Oxford: Oxford University Press.

Viens, A. M. (2016). Public Health and Political Theory: The Importance of Taming Individualism. *Public Health Ethics, 9*(2), 136–138.

Weinstock, D. (2016). Can Republicanism Tame Public Health? *Public Health Ethics, 9*(2), 123–133.

Wiley, L. F. (2012). Rethinking the New Public Health. *Washington and Lee Law Review, 69*(1), 207–272.

Wiley, L. F. (2014). Health Law as Social Justice. *Cornell Journal of Law and Public Policy, 24*, 47–105.

Wilson, J. (2011). Why it's Time to Stop Worrying About Paternalism in Health Policy. *Public Health Ethics, 4*(3), 269–279.

Winslow, C.-E. A. (1920). The Untilled Fields of Public Health. *Science, 51*(1306), 23–33.

Wolff, J. (2009). Disadvantage, Risk and the Social Determinants of Health. *Public Health Ethics, 2*(3), 213–223.

Wolff, J., & De-Shalit, A. (2007). *Disadvantage*. Oxford: Oxford University Press.

Woolf. (2001). Are the Courts Excessively Deferential to the Medical Profession? *Medical Law Review, 9*(1), 1–16.

# 4

# Bioinequalities: Rethinking Legal Responses to the Biological and Intergenerational Harm Caused by Inequality

Karen O'Connell and Isabel Karpin

## 1 Introduction

Being the subject of unequal treatment is commonly accepted as a stressful psychological experience; however, its physical impact is less well understood. According to recent scientific work in the field of neuroscience and epigenetics, stress and trauma that arise as a consequence of unequal treatment may have a biological as well as psychological impact. Further, those harms may be inherited by future generations. The sources of unequal treatment resulting in stress and trauma that are linked to neurobiological changes and changes in gene expression via epigenetics are diverse. They range from child abuse and domestic violence (Weder et al. 2014; Cordero et al. 2012; Brand et al. 2010; Cecil et al. 2016) to racism, including intersecting identities of LGBTQ-LatinX populations (Kuzawa and Sweet 2009; Goosby and Heidbrick 2013; Singh et al. 2019; Parra and Hastings 2018; Goosby et al. 2018; Aroke et al. 2019), and socio-economic status (SES; McGuinness et al. 2012; McEwen and McEwen 2017; Shields 2017; Kim et al. 2018; McCrory et al. 2019; Tribble and Kim 2019; Giurgescu et al. 2019). These and similar studies claim that such harms can lead to adverse physical outcomes including cardiovascular disease, hypertension, low-birth weight, and psychiatric

K. O'Connell (✉) • I. Karpin (✉)
University of Technology Sydney, Sydney, NSW, Australia
e-mail: Karen.OConnell@uts.edu.au; Isabel.Karpin@uts.edu.au


C. Dietz et al. (eds.), *A Jurisprudence of the Body*, Palgrave Socio-Legal Studies,
https://doi.org/10.1007/978-3-030-42200-4_4

disorders. In this chapter, we argue that law should address the bodily effects of unequal treatment—what we call bioinequalities—and that to do so requires a shift in focus away from an individualised model of harm in favour of a model that understands the harm as shared among individuals, and across communities and generations.

Socially disadvantaged groups have consistently described the stress of unequal treatment as pervasive and cumulative, yet the laws that set out to redress this harm "molecularise" inequality into isolated incidents of discrimination. This tendency to molecularise fails to capture the true impact of inequality and makes it more difficult to prove. Individuals also rarely understand themselves or experience inequality—or privilege—according to the neat and limited identity categories of race, sex,[1] sexuality, age, and disability that form the scaffolding of equality law in Australia and the UK.[2] Finding alternatives to this molecularisation of identity and harm when developing and reforming the law is key to addressing bioinequality across identity categories. Bioinequality is experienced both at the intersection of and embedded within multiple sexed, raced, classed, and disabled (among others) identities (Crenshaw 1989) and is interwoven with the social and material world, and the psychosocial environment (Haraway 1997; Davies 2017; Karpin 2016; O'Connell 2012).

We challenge the individualising orientation of existing laws attempting to redress inequality, calling instead for a legal response that accounts for the intersectional and intergenerational harms of inequality.

## 2 Bioinequalities

We use the term "bioinequalities" to describe the relationship between biology and inequality, as part of a larger project on developing legal responses to newly identified genetic and neurological harms that have their origin in unequal and discriminatory treatment. In revealing the connections between biology and inequality we are drawing on law, in its role as purveyor of justice,

[1] In Australia the federal *Sex Discrimination Act* 1984 (Cth) also covers pregnancy, marital status, family responsibilities, sexual orientation, and gender identity.

[2] Although the UK now has a single *Equality Act* 2010, the categories of discrimination ("protected characteristics") are largely the same: age; gender reassignment; being married or in a civil partnership; being pregnant or on maternity leave; disability; race including colour, nationality, ethnic, or national origin; religion or belief; sex; sexual orientation. The *Equality Act* also prevents genetic information being used in employment decisions (i.e. hiring or firing someone).

to address this link. Our work thus expands the usual narrow meaning of inequality in law to consider bioinequality.

Our use of the concept of bioinequalities originates in our research into legal responses to disability that manifest in challenging behaviour.[3] This research revealed legal and scientific material that linked social inequalities and behavioural disorders. Through this work we identified multiple studies that draw links between social stressors and children subsequently born with behavioural conditions (e.g. Kundakovic and Jaric 2017; Roberts et al. 2013; Babenko et al. 2015). However, we also found that there has been a very limited legal response to this rich body of scientific work emerging in the fields of epigenetics and neuroscience (see Lewis and Thomson 2019, for a recent rare example). Given that these studies show that social stress and trauma associated with unequal treatment has a demonstrable and significant impact on the body, our work considers how this aspect of the harm might be addressed legally.

Research on the physiological harms caused by the stress and trauma of unequal treatment increasingly evidences an intergenerational as well as an individual impact, and the harms identified are not limited to behavioural or cognitive deficits. The mechanisms of in utero and epigenetic inheritance are still being worked out, yet there is strong evidence that social as well as physical trauma can detrimentally change gene expression in individuals and their offspring (Fox Keller 2014; Huang and King 2018; Jablonka 2017), while epigenetic changes through processes such as DNA methylation (e.g., Borghol et al. 2012; Chmurzynska 2010; Jones and Takai 2001; Radtke et al. 2011) can be passed on from one generation to the next. These studies claim that stress in the maternal body can manifest epigenetically through brain effects in offspring such as neurodevelopmental and psychiatric disorders as well as cognitive and intellectual impairment (Babenko et al. 2015; Buss et al. 2010; Kundakovic and Jaric 2017), and in physiological ways such as cardiovascular disease and even allergies. While the science is still contested, with respect to the prenatal environment in particular, Monk, Spicer, and Champagne (2012) reviewed 176 articles that reported findings that the placenta is highly susceptible to maternal distress and is a target of epigenetic dysregulation (See also Lock 2015). Since then, the number of scientific studies in this area has continued to increase exponentially while developing specific lines of inquiry within the broader range of prenatal stress impacts. Sosnowski et al. (2018), for example, review studies on the impact of maternal stress on foetal HPA Axis (stress response receptor) functioning leading to poor post and prenatal

[3] See the research project "The Legal Regulation of Behaviour as a Disability," above n1, as detailed on our website https://bioinequalities.com/

functions, while Flanigan et al. (2018) explore the impact of maternal stress on the prevalence of asthma and allergies in offspring.

Recent neuroscience research similarly suggests that brain effects from childhood disadvantage not only persist over the lifecycle, resulting, for example, in late-life dementia (Radford et al. 2017), but may result in transgenerational, heritable neuro-epigenetic changes to the brain (Bohacek et al. 2013; Sweatt 2013). If these new scientific claims are sustained, epigenetic and neurobiological changes have the effect of amplifying the initial injury of inequality by producing new generations already biologically impacted by past injustices—the biologically unequal.

Legal developments responding to this epigenetic and neuroscientific research would ideally lead to better regulation and improvement in conditions of bioinequality. We trace three ways that the biosciences amplify or entrench inequality and argue that these need to be acknowledged and addressed when developing an effective legal response. These occur, first, where existing inequalities seem invisible to science and so may be further entrenched as bioinequalities; second, where scientific ideas are taken up in social discourse and applied as if neutral, creating new bioinequalities; and third, where the existence of biological traits reinforce essentialist views that form the basis of unequal treatment and bioinequality.

(i) Where existing inequalities seem invisible to science and so may be further entrenched as bioinequalities

The case of sexual and domestic violence, which are typically gendered harms, illustrates the first point. While studies clearly show the epigenetic and neurological impact of social "stressors," such as sexual violence and sex discrimination (Weder et al. 2014; Cordero et al. 2012; Brand et al. 2010; Cecil et al. 2016; Pinto et al. 2010; Radtke et al. 2011), the fact that they stem from systemic gender inequalities can be overlooked in the scientific analysis. The scientific analysis, instead, refers to these gendered harms collectively and neutrally as "stressors" and focuses on their consequences. Significant numbers of scientific studies that examine the impact of stress on the maternal body, for example, view that maternal body as a conduit for stress to harm the foetus or future child in a way that the harm to the mother is overlooked (Karpin 2016). Without the modifying lens to frame the original harm as gendered, the social and legal response may be one that positions the woman, exposed to stress that is also harmful to her offspring, as the responsible agent to mitigate that harm. Loi, Del Savio, and Stupka (2013, 146), for example, referencing studies on the epigenetic effects of low socio-economic status (including one that identified epigenetic evidence of higher methylation in low SES individuals leading to a repression of the senses of smell and taste: Borghol, Suderman and McArdle 2012, 147) drew conclusions about the broader impact of such research. Given that "[e]pigenetics might provide a measureable magnitude of the extent to which environmental insults have, indeed, caused harm in a person's genome," they imagine a future society "in which people can be informed by their family physician of the accumulation of risk due to specific environmental insults, including those arising prenatally and in early childhood for which people cannot be held responsible." Knowledge about prenatal harms, however, impacts potential mothers who are likely to be expected to take on moral if not legal responsibility for avoiding the transfer of those insults to their future children. Where this is described in anodyne terms, as environmental stressors or insults, there is an erasure of the systemic inequalities that underpin low socio-economic status, or a stigmatised racial or ethnic identity, or gendered harms such as violence perpetrated against the mother. The harms to which the woman is subject are overlooked or obscured, and instead the focus shifts to the prevention of transference of that harm to her offspring.

While we are yet to see laws in Australia or the UK that apportion responsibility for epigenetic harm to future children to the woman who gives birth to them, such a response is imaginable given existing laws that prioritise the wellbeing of future children. Both Australia and the UK have laws regulating Assisted Reproductive Technology (ART), which position the welfare of the future child as of paramount consideration in the provision of ART services (see National Health and Medical Research Council 2017; *Assisted Reproductive Treatment Act 2008* (Vic); *Human Reproductive Technology Act 1991* (UK); *Human Fertilisation and Embryology Act 2008* (UK)). Several states in Australia have unborn child protection legislation, including Queensland (*Criminal Code 1899* (QLD) s 313) and Western Australia (*Criminal Code Compilation Act 1913* (WA) s 1(4A)). At least one Australian jurisdiction (the Northern Territory) contemplated introducing legislation that would prosecute or restrain pregnant women if they harmed a foetus due to alcohol consumption but did not introduce the legislation after there was a public outcry (Australian Broadcasting Corporation 2014). For a more concrete sense of what might be enacted, one only has to consider the various foetal protection laws in the USA, which allow women who are suspected of taking drugs or alcohol to be confined while pregnant (e.g. the *Wisconsin Administrative Code*, Chapter 48). Focus on the impact of stress rather than its cause may thus be used to further regulate women as conduits of harm rather than directly protecting them from stressors, including the trauma of gendered violence. In this case, bioinequalities arise in the way that the gendered underpinnings of harm are rendered neutral or invisible, first, when sexual and intimate partner violence are treated as gender-neutral "stressors," and second, when pregnant women, subjected to environmental harms, are framed as no more than vessels transmitting that harm to a foetus.

(ii) Where scientific ideas are taken up in social discourse and applied as if neutral, creating new bioinequalities

Other bioinequalities arise where seemingly neutral scientific concepts are applied in ways that work to reinforce existing social assumptions. For example, the idea of "plasticity," which has arisen primarily in the context of neuroscience but also more recently in the context of epigenetics, has produced new scientific knowledge and much cultural interest in the capacity of brains and genes to change over time.

While brain plasticity is discussed in generally positive terms for children and adults without disability, with a focus on the brain's capacities to learn and regenerate in ideal ways under targeted stimuli, the concept has been applied to differently abled individuals in ways that absorb and sometimes amplify existing social values around disability and responsibility. Fein (2011) traces the emergence of two kinds of neuroscientific self in a study of children with autism spectrum disorder (ASD) and children with mental illness that is characterised as "emotional dysregulation" (ED):

> [T]he notion that mental conditions can be divided into those that are 'neurochemical' – malleable, fluid, discovered by a psychiatry deeply reliant on psychopharmacology and amenable to its interventions – and those that are 'neurostructural' – fixed and "unfixable," intrinsic to personhood – seems to be taking powerful hold. (48)

The consequences of this division into two categories of neurological selfhood "unpredictable but responsive in one case, compliant but socially estranged on the other" (Fein 2011, 48) are complex and sometimes beneficial—such as when presumptions about a lack of agency meant that children with ASD in the study were seen as not morally culpable for misbehaviour, which was attributed to "stress." However, they can also work to reinforce existing inequalities, such as when children with ED, whose disabled selfhood is characterised as "malleable," are seen as more morally culpable for similar behaviour, even if their problems arose from socially disadvantaged backgrounds.

With respect to epigenetic plasticity, one of the early claims about the impact of epigenetic changes was their reversibility. If environment could trigger epigenetic changes that turned some genes off and others on, then it was argued that changes to the environment—both psychosocial and physical—could reverse the process and inhibit intergenerational consequences of epigenetic expression. Plasticity then, in this context, is meant to challenge the view of the gene as a fixed entity and instead reconceptualise it "as more 'plastic' and 'reactive' to its various environments than originally depicted" (Dupras et al. 2019).

Dupras and Ravitsky (2016) discuss the wide spectrum of plasticity among epigenetic variants. They suggest that understanding:

> levels of epigenetic plasticity among variants is a prerequisite to assigning moral epigenetic responsibilities, since it is a necessary criterion for identifying the actual 'capacity to act' on epigenetic health by some specific actors in society (citizens, parents, healthcare professionals, scientists, public health agencies, corporations, governments or international organisations). Depending on the epigenetic variant and disease at stake, different actors might be assigned novel (or enhanced) moral responsibility. (Dupras and Ravitsky 2016)

Plasticity could, on this account, give rise to a cooperative view of evolution where responsibility for poor evolutionary outcomes is identified as a social responsibility. The problem here, as with neuroscientific plasticity, is that without a comprehensive account of bioinequality which addresses the existing social context as one already laden with gendered, raced, and other identity-based biases, those groups who are already vulnerable to scrutiny and intervention may be targeted as responsible for mitigating social and environmental harms.

Thus, it is not possible to view talk of neurochemical "plasticity" or "epigenetic plasticity" as a merely neutral scientific description of how bodies and brains are made. Instead plasticity, in its application to specific groups, carries moral and legal weight that is tied to the different characteristics attributed to those groups and their alignment with social norms (O'Connell 2016).

(iii) Where the existence of biological traits reinforce essentialist views that form the basis of unequal treatment and bioinequality

A third aspect of bioinequalities concerns the way that emerging science can be used to identify biological traits that then become the basis for an equality claim. For example, the federal Disability Discrimination Act prohibits discrimination where a person is treated less favourably because they have or are imputed to have a genetic predisposition to a disability (*Disability Discrimination Act* 1992 (Cth), section 4).[4] It is likely that this would also include what might be called "epigenetic discrimination," where epigenetic information might provide complementary information about a disease risk profile that could be adversely used by third parties to discriminate against an individual, for example, in the provision of insurance (Dupras et al. 2018). Equality laws such as anti-discrimination legislation typically rely on a version of essentialism to identify individuals as among a class of people who are different and, furthermore, disadvantaged by that difference. Given that the aim of equality laws is to protect the human rights of those who are subject to discrimination, it is reasonable to see this essentialist turn as a strategic one, in the sense in which the term was coined by Gayatri Spivak in the 1980s (Spivak 1988). She argued that essentialism could be used strategically to enable a marginalised group that is identified by a shared trait to act collectively to demand social justice, where the trait is the basis of differential and degrading treatment. The risk of strategic essentialism is that the people who have identified themselves politically around the trait they share are then subject to prejudice in relation to that trait, and where that trait is biological, they may be subject to deterministic and reductive thinking. The group may be defined by the trait and denied the right to make claims that speak to their heterogeneity and intersectionality.

Warin, Kowal, and Meloni explore the use of what they call strategic *biological* essentialism by indigenous Australians who draw on the language of environmental epigenetics to provide an account of shared intergenerational harm derived from a history of discrimination and trauma. The harm they identify is one that is not just situated in individuals but is a shared indigenous experience of "biosocial injury" (Warin et al. 2019). However, Warin et al. caution that:

"[e]nacting forms of citizenship through identification with biosocial deprivation may not only lead to intensified biopolitical attention from the state but also consolidate quasi essentialist notions of specific biological difference among certain populations seen as epigenetically different" (2019, p. 4). They go on to say the risk of "strategic biological essentialism" is that it may also justify "heightened biopolitical governance" (2019, 16). This becomes further complicated when the person who has been biologically harmed by

[4] Notably both the USA and Canada have standalone genetic antidiscrimination legislation. See the US Genetic Information Non Discrimination Act (GINA) and the Canadian Genetic Non Discrimination Act (GNDA).

prior discriminatory treatment is again disadvantaged as a result of the biological harms that have resulted from the original deprivation. In this case they might be viewed as being subject to a form of bioinequality.

We recognise that there is a risk in identifying a class of people who have been subjected to a history of discrimination and abuse as biologically and physically altered by that foundational inequality. However, the fact that the harm may be transferred intergenerationally and that the psychosocial life experience of harmed individuals has scientific significance, can also have positive effects, opening a space for fundamental legal change to redress the harm. That change involves a move away from individualising harm and responsibility towards a remedy that takes account of the impact of the psychosocial environment of inequality on the harmed group.

## 3 The Gender and Race of Bioinequalities

Having identified these three kinds of "bioinequality" as instances where the biosciences may amplify existing inequalities or create new ones, we turn to some specific examples where the biosciences are interacting with inequality in novel ways. We contend that the science is culturally and socially embedded and therefore permeated by the same gendered and raced assumptions that underlie the unequal treatment that precipitates the harm being studied. This does not mean that the science is of no value. To the contrary, if we approach these new scientific accounts of human selfhood with a critical eye that is attentive to the moments where race and gender are deployed politically, we can obtain more benefit from the science and create laws that work to undo unfair outcomes.

### 3.1 Gender and Maternity in the Construction of Stress

It is clear that the way that stress is understood is subject to gendered and raced assumptions and biases, among others. In addition, stress studies can ignore the structural contributors to experiences of stress. For example, the disproportionate focus on the maternal body as a site of stress and potential for epigenetic and neurological harm transference is a function of gendered assumptions about the more significant role of the maternal in child development. It is common to read in Developmental Origins of Health and Disease (DoHAD) research that the higher exposure of women to social and environmental stressors such as poverty or pollution can translate epigenetically into their future child's vulnerability to disease (Shields 2017). These impacts also, it is argued, cascade down generations. Yet these scientific accounts are often posited as if they are simple factual accounts of cause and effect. The fact that there is a disproportionate focus on women and the maternal in the study of DoHAD and epigenetic effects is, however, driven by gendered assumptions around cause and effect. There are significantly fewer peer-reviewed articles on "paternal stress" compared to "maternal stress."[5]

Furthermore, the association of women with stress itself is also gendered. Studies consistently indicate that women have higher prevalence rates of anxiety disorders (e.g. McLean et al. 2011) and a greater likelihood of expressing emotions verbally (e.g. Deng et al. 2016), which may contribute to their increased vulnerability to emotional distress and related disorders (Bangasser and Valentino 2014).

This approach locates the gender differential in the individual rather than the environment, making it susceptible to biologisation. For example, in scientific studies, public speaking is used as an exemplar of a presumptively and universally stressful event. Yet, the experience of public speaking occurs in an unequal context where women and racial minorities are more likely to be negatively interrupted and less likely to be treated as authoritative speakers (Richards 2016; Hancock and Rubin 2014). At the same time, daily activities such as taking a walk are used in scientific studies as a baseline for a non-stressful stimulus, yet we know that women taking a walk can involve negotiating unsafe spaces and street harassment. If this context goes unrecognised in scientific studies, the "source" of the stress is more likely to be attributed to the biological sex of the individual rather than their sex discriminatory environment. Where neuroscientific studies fail to see that structural discrimination can be the source of stress, these differences in mood and mental health disorders may be attributed to individual differences in brain characteristics rather than arising at least in part from gender-biased environments. Differences in the brain will not be traced back to environmental triggers no matter how carefully controlled the "environment" of the study if the differently gendered worlds are invisible (e.g. Platt et al. 2016).

Further, even when gendered stressors are correctly identified as environmental, the attribution of responsibility and the regulatory response to that

[5] In 2018, we conducted a search on the University of Technology, Sydney, Library's Primo Central Index using the search terms "maternal stress" and "paternal stress" and restricting the range to titles of peer-reviewed articles. The Primo Central Index is a centralized index of articles and other information sources. It covers all subject and discipline areas and includes articles and other publications from major academic publishers. Among the "peer reviewed" journal articles there were 11,126 with "maternal stress" in the title and just 468 with "paternal stress" in the title on March 18, 2018.

harm can be shaped by unequal social standards. Karpin (2016) discusses this in the context of social and environmental epigenetics, demonstrating that where environmental or social stressors are identified as impacting future generations, there is a tendency to focus on the responsibility of pregnant and potentially pregnant women to be aware of and mitigate those harms. Where a woman may be exposed, for example, to partner violence, the stress that she experiences may be written on to her body epigenetically and passed on to her future child (Pinto et al. 2010; Cordero et al. 2012; Radtke et al. 2011). It is already, of course, well accepted that domestic violence is a social ill and should be stopped, and where it is not stopped, its perpetrators should be punished and their victims provided with social supports. There is also a significant body of literature that explores the way in which these harms have a psychological impact that may lead to child victims repeating the abuse on their own children (see e.g. UNICEF 2006; World Health Organisation 2007). However, new research adds an ongoing and physical dimension suggesting that the intergenerational impact may include biological harms that are transmitted to future generations through bodily changes brought about by parental exposure to violence. Scientific research that identifies this intergenerational effect, however, tends (as noted above) to focus disproportionately on the pregnant or potentially pregnant woman, who is seen as a conduit of social and environmental harms to the future children (Sharp et al. 2019; Soubry 2018). Only a small body of new research is looking at the role that men play in the transmission of epigenetic harms, and it seems that this research bias is unjustified. Research being undertaken at Tufts University recently demonstrated that early trauma in males also might lead to epigenetic changes in sperm miRNA, resulting in poor mental and physical health of their offspring (Feig 2018). While women remain the primary focus, however, of scientific studies, it is likely that they will be viewed as one of the "set of moral agents," which Dupras and Ravitsky (2016) argue are made responsible for preventing the intergenerational transmission of that harm. In this way, the gendered assumptions underpinning the scientific research deflect and distract from appropriate identification of social responsibility for the harm.

## 3.2 Race and Entrenched Disadvantage

With regard to the biological processes through which the stress of social inequality is inscribed on the body, Goosby et al. write that "the environment in the womb mirrors maternal stress-related factors, preparing the child for the mother's social environment" (2018). The genomic burden of social experiences is therefore disproportionately shouldered by those experiencing disadvantage. For example, as Goosby argues, the stress of being chronically subject to interpersonal racism can moderate epigenetic processes over the life course (Goosby et al. 2018).

However, even where it can be shown "scientifically" that racial trauma and racial discrimination can be linked to intergenerational consequences of poor health for racially oppressed communities, these scientific "facts" can be deployed politically in ways that further perpetuates disadvantage. This is particularly likely where the claim for restitution is made by a group that is systemically maltreated and disadvantaged. Warin, Kowal, and Meloni make just such an argument in the context of their study of indigenous researchers and policy makers in Australia. They state:

> [A]n epigenetic biopolitics may lead to a condemnation of one's condition if the accumulated effects of historical burden have made their cause irredeemable. Although the responsiveness of the epigenetic body to the environment is appealing to some Indigenous people, bodies that are deeply permeable to outside forces are no less vulnerable to forms of vigilance and disciplinary practices than bodies that are seen as stable and permanent. (Warin et al. 2019, p. 15)

It is against this background—of the tendency for gendered and raced environmental harms to be shifted back to the unequal individual—that we turn to the problems and potential of equality laws in dealing with the intergenerational transmission of the harm that comes from the stress of race and gender inequality.

## 4 Problems with Equality Law

In considering the capacity of current laws to respond to intergenerational biological harms, there are already well-documented weaknesses in legal responses to inequality. Australia has a weak human rights system, with no constitutional equality guarantee, no federal statutory bill of rights, and no direct incorporation of international human rights laws into domestic law. This means that any attempt to argue for new rights—such as a right to bio-equality—has little political appeal and no legal scaffolding on which to hang. Australia's equality laws, primarily expressed in anti-discrimination laws that are shaped around key equality conventions, such as CEDAW CERD and the CRPD, are our primary means of guaranteeing equality rights. Yet the problematic relationship of discrimination law to widespread social inequality has long been noted. Early scholars of Australian discrimination law drew attention to the slipperiness of the promise of equality it offered. Thornton (1990), in *The Liberal Promise*, points out the inherent conflict in a system that seems to offer equality without setting out any means of effecting the significant transfer of social and economic power this would entail. The mode of redress they set up overwhelmingly relies on individual complaints.

Individual and singular approaches to discrimination also mean that when discrimination is experienced across multiple and compound attributes, rather than being easier to prove, it is harder. While a single act can constitute discrimination, it is often in their compound and cumulative effect that their true harm is visible. This is particularly the case where the harm from discrimination manifests biologically having a detrimental physical impact that is passed on to future generations.

Discrimination being framed as an "occasional error in a neutral context" (Gaze 2002) is one of the key reasons that current laws do little to instate social equality. The federal anti-discrimination acts ignore the underpinning fact that the context of discrimination is not neutral; that incidents of race discrimination, for example, take place against a backdrop of pervasive, systemic racism, both historical and contemporary. The woman who experiences sexual harassment likely makes that claim—if indeed she is one of the mere 17 per cent of those who reports at all (Australian Human Rights Commission 2018)—as someone who has lived through a myriad of other gendered experiences from street harassment to unequal pay. Law fails to acknowledge that discrimination can, and commonly does, accrue over time, and across multiple identity categories. Women who are discriminated against at work end up in positions where they are more likely to experience further disadvantage.

> [P]olicy frameworks have commonly focused on gender inequality as individual incidents of discrimination, each separate from the other. But in doing so, we have failed to recognize the cumulative impact of each of these individual events.... One instance of sex discrimination will often position a woman to be more vulnerable to another instance. (Broderick 2009)[6]

[6] In our study of legal responses to behavioural disabilities we found a number of cases where women with personality disorders who were claiming workers compensation for bullying and harassment at work were found to be only eligible for compensation for the aggravation of their pre-existing personality disorder and for a limited period of time. Moreover, the personality disorders were often attributed to a early incident of sexual or physical abuse. See Karpin, I. and O'Connell, K. (forthcoming) Disability, Gender and the Institution of Justice: An examination of Australian case law involving personality disorders. In Spivakovsky, C., Steele, L. and Weller, P. (Eds.), *The Legacies of Institutionalisation: Disability, law and policy in the 'deinstitutionalised' community.*

These cumulative experiences create discriminatory or hostile environments and have troubling bodily and health effects. For instance, the general context of racial intolerance creates a discriminatory environment that results in harmful psychological effects. Mental health organisation Beyond Blue found that 21 per cent of people surveyed would move away if an indigenous person sat near them, or "watch" them out of suspicion that they might steal something if they were in a shop (Beyond Blue 2014a). This led to their "The Invisible Discriminator" campaign, highlighting the mental health effects of subtle forms of racism (Beyond Blue 2014b).

The presumption that already stigmatised individuals experience discrimination as "blank slates" not only fails to capture the full bodily and psychic harm of discrimination, but shifts the responsibility away from social institutions that otherwise might be called to account. For example, with respect to the history of maltreatment of Australia's first people, Thornton notes:

> The perennial attempt to slough off historical and social context is a convenient way of depoliticising law and representing it as neutral and innocent, as though it had not played a significant role in constructing Aboriginal people as Other to its paradigmatic legal person, as well as authorising acts of violence and dispossession. (Thornton 2010, p. 144)

The neutrality approach of discrimination law treats individuals, unmarked by histories, including their own, as encountering anomalous acts of mistreatment as they navigate otherwise benign public institutions. As Thornton describes it:

> 'Strict legalism' seems to mean self-referentialism, which enables the judges to slough off not only all knowledge of discrimination as a social phenomenon, but interdisciplinary perspectives and the non-discrimination aims of the legislation as well. Erasure of the problem means that they then have no obligation to devise a remedy. (Thornton 2009, p. 21)

The stark reality of structural and systemic inequality where people in fact encounter institutions that are structured in the image of—and therefore for the benefit of—privileged social groups is overlooked. Discrimination law further ignores intergenerational disadvantage, in which people are born into already stigmatised groups within families marked by experiences of inequality.

Research into intergenerational disadvantage also tends to focus only on relationships between parents and children in a supposedly linear transmission of disadvantage.

> The majority of research examining social mobility and intergenerational disadvantage has done so at an individual level or family level of parent-child associations (e.g. the role of parent education on outcomes in childhood and beyond). These associations can be extrapolated to describe the cyclical nature of intergenerational disadvantage, where parents directly affect their offspring in the same way that they themselves were affected by their own parents. (Hancock et al. 2015)

Hancock, Zubrick, and Mitrou (2015) go on to point out that a cyclical approach does not provide the whole picture because more complex multi-generational influences, such as grandparents' relationships with grandchildren, are ignored. We know that social disadvantage also gets communicated by these relational practices within families, for example, through parents teaching children to lower expectations or behave in ways that will protect them from racism or gendered violence. Increasingly, however, we also know, through developments in social and developmental health science scholarship, that the harm is also passed on biologically as well as through recent scholarship on epigenetics, neuroscience, and inequality.

## 5 Bioinequalities: Promises and Dangers for Equality Laws

### 5.1 What Are the Embodied Harms of Bioinequalities?

Epigenetic findings on the transmission of social inequality sit within a broader body of scientific and health literature examining the link between discrimination and poor health outcomes. Empirical public health data, for example, increasingly links inequality and discrimination to health detriments (Krieger 2014), including physical harms such as deficiencies in blood pressure and cardiovascular health (Brondolo et al. 2011; Cuffee et al. 2012; Dunlay et al. 2017; Paradies et al. 2015). In 2014, Krieger identified over 500 empirical studies on discrimination and health in the public health literature, a significant increase from the 20 studies that had existed when she first surveyed the field in 1999. While this research has largely focused on individual rather than systemic sources of harm, it can be read alongside research in other fields that shows the significance of society-wide inequalities for health outcomes. Research on the social determinants of health (SDOH), for example, explores the impact of social factors on the health of individuals and communities, and research on the developmental origins of health and disease

(DOHaD) adds an important temporal element, demonstrating how preconception and in-utero experiences impact the health of individuals and their relations over the lifecycle (Monk et al. 2012; Rubin 2016; Wadhwa et al. 2009).

Together, these fields of research provide a powerful account of how broad-based social inequality may result in embodied harm, individually, socially, and intergenerationally.

## 5.2 How Law Can Respond to the Embodied Harm of Inequality?

If law is to seriously address inequality, as it sets out to do, it needs to take the psychological and biological harms of discrimination seriously, recognising a form of bioinequality. It is also necessary to shift its focus away from the individual and towards institutional and society-wide responsibility for harm. Here the biosciences offer a new perspective.

First, the ability to point to material harm within the body helps to make visible, and potentially measurable, the stress and trauma of a range of experiences, including discrimination, that have previously been diminished or overlooked. As Van der Kolk writes, "the body keeps the score" (Van der Kolk 2014). These measurable harms cut across identity categories to *experience* categories, making the experience of stress or trauma the locus of the harm, rather than the identity of the person. The biosciences add a crucial corrective here.

Second, the biosciences make very clear that inequality is not only experienced through individual acts but transmitted through hostile social environments. The biosciences evidence the impact of broad-based and historical harms. Current equality law frameworks are inadequate to deal with the kinds of systemic inequality that might be passed on to future generations. Nevertheless, legal recognition of the bodily effects of race, sex, and socio-economic disadvantage is key to ensuring long-term resolution of persistent health deficits in vulnerable groups. Recalibrating or rewriting equality laws so that they respond to the health consequences of systemic race and gender-based harms can prevent material injuries to the affected groups as well as the generations to follow.

Despite these promises that the biosciences hold out in rethinking and recalibrating equality law to take bodily and systemic harms seriously, there are also some important dangers to note.

As we argue above, the biosciences themselves can unwittingly perpetuate or even amplify inequality. Wherever you put a system that is, for example, purportedly gender-neutral in a sexist context, without sensitivity to how gender bias works, that system can operate to further inequality (see e.g. Craido Perez 2019).

Given the way that neuroscience and epigenetics deal in damage to the brain and genome over time, there is also a danger that these claims of material harm will be used against the groups appealing for equality. Warin et al. write:

> To use suffering to legitimate human rights ... is a political tactic that can provide certain types of leverage. In the case of Indigenous epigenetics, this tactic leverages a biopolitics of hope and is gaining visibility for new ways to address Indigenous ill-health, healing and reparation. But through this strategic biological essentialism, the environment may become essentialized, enfolded into a powerful language of damage that justifies heightened biopolitical governance. (2016, p. 16)

For those of us hoping that epigenetic and other bioscientific knowledge might be used to better address inequality, there is also a very real threat that the same knowledge might be applied to opposite effect. The long history of eugenics and other racist (and sexist) strands of science has relied on an idea that certain groups are biologically lesser than others. There is a danger that epigenetics and neuroscience can be used to argue that particular groups, due to their exposure to environmental stressors, including in utero or through intergenerational exposure, are born already damaged. This would amplify and biologise inequality in ways that are dangerous and unjust.

It is arguable, then, that the biosciences need to engage with theories of inequality as urgently as law needs material evidence of biological and systemic harm. Much work has been done by critical scholars of science, such as Haraway (1991, 1997) and Fox Keller (2014), to embed science in a broader politics. However, law and legal research have too often been absent from these scholarly engagements. As knowledge of the health effects of discrimination proliferates, the need for legal responses takes on new urgency. What has not been considered is the legal response that would mitigate against these systemic and intergenerational inequalities.

## 6 Legal Responses to the Science of Intergenerational Inequalities

At this critical point in our developing knowledge of the impact that inequality has on bodies over time, we need a legal framework that can recognise and respond to the harms newly identified by these scientific findings. A first step in this process is building a body of scholarship that draws connections between emerging bioscientific knowledge on inequality and those areas of law that are best able to respond. A legal approach that recognises the bodily and intergenerational effects of inequalities—a harm of bioinequality—would be transformative, targeting the intransigent problem of perpetual social disadvantage for particular vulnerable groups. Laws directed at these systemic and intergenerational harms would be beneficial, not just for individual health but also for the health of future generations.

The connections currently being made in epigenetic research between biological and social stressors have brought together science and social science—but not law—in new collaborations (see Geronimus 2013; Landecker and Panofsky 2013; Meloni 2015; Rutter 2012; Sullivan 2013; Warin et al. 2016). This intersection between biological and structural factors rarely draws on the growing legal literature (see Rothstein et al. 2009 for a singular and quite dated exception that is sometimes cited in the scientific and social-scientific literature. For examples of legal responses, see Lewis and Thomson 2019; O'Connell 2016 and Karpin 2018). The law should, however, be an essential component. Epigenetic changes in the body are mutable and so can potentially be rehabilitated in ways that genetic inheritance cannot (Landecker and Panofsky 2013, p. 334). This presents a significant opportunity for legal intervention in the transgenerational transmission of harm.

In developing a legal response to bioinequalities, there are particular areas of resonance between the scientific findings on bodily and intergenerational effects of inequality and areas of potential law reform. While, as noted above, Australia has not embraced large-scale national human rights protections for equality, there is significant potential for change through more local but less abstract measures. Addressing bioinequalities by building on group, regulatory, and environmental approaches to inequality at the local and institutional level can create meaningful change.

First, given the issues with an individual complaints-based model in responding to inequality, we suggest that responding to broad social and intergenerational inequality effects requires a regulatory approach, alongside existing individual complaints mechanisms. One example of a regulatory approach is seen in South Australia, where the *Public Health Act 2011* now includes an Equity Principle which requires that decisions and actions made under the Act, do not "as far as is reasonably practicable, unduly or unfairly disadvantage individuals or communities." In the UK, efforts to respond to health inequalities include a "Guidance for NHS Commissioners on Equality and Health Inequalities," which sets out legal duties to take account of equality issues when making decisions and setting policies in the context of the provision of health services. Epigenetic and other bioscientific work makes it patently clear that such broad-based social and legal responses are required to tackle entrenched inequalities that are so embedded over time.

Second, there has long been a turn in discrimination scholarship, championed in particular by Fredman, to make "positive duties" the focus of a response to discrimination (2008). Where there is a reliance on already socially disadvantaged individuals to bring their own complaints and be their own advocates, this is clearly a recipe for further injustice. Broad-based approaches such as "positive duties" on employers to ensure greater workplace equality in the UK Equality Act (*Equality Act 2010* (UK), s. 149; Fredman 2008) can be further developed to account for a positive health-related duty on governments, institutions, and private actors. Most recently, Smith, Schleiger, and Elphick (2019) have argued that one effective way of addressing sexual harassment—a form of sex discrimination—in the Australian context is to deploy the workplace health and safety regulatory system to prevent the psychological harms of harassment. It would be one step further to argue that workplace environments need to take a harm-prevention approach to bioinequalities more broadly.

A third area is in bringing evidence about bioinequalities into litigation. This can be used, for example, to offset the tendency of damages in cases involving discrimination to overlook the scale of the impact of the stress and trauma of inequality on the body (O'Connell 2019). The biosciences can offer material evidence of this to provide individuals with more appropriate compensation, as well as being an impetus to law makers to take serious account of the scope of the response that is needed. A new legal right to bio-equality could also be developed as both a public legal claim and an individual legal claim for what we are calling socio-environmental harms. Socio-environmental harms are public harms that are attributable to living in an environment that is socially and psychologically damaging.

To ensure that remedies are appropriate and have a lasting impact an effective legal response to the social and intergenerational impact of inequality must be addressed beyond the individual. The approach that we suggest would insert the concept of bioinequalities, and the combined scientific and legal knowledge of how the biosciences impact inequality, into a range of practical regulatory, group, and individual measures to provide new forms of justice over time.

## 7 Conclusion

There is growing recognition that laws need to focus on regulating socio-environments and institutions rather than individuals. Legal and regulatory interventions from the local to the international have attempted to tackle inequality but have done so in piecemeal ways. Those who come before the law do not do so as neutral actors but as unequal subjects within a web of political, social, psychological, and material relationships, which may further entrench disadvantage. These relationships—between individuals, between people and their environment, and within individual bodies—are mediated by social institutions including law that ultimately determine a person's capacity to function well and be "well" both now and for generations to come. Epigenetics and neuroscience provide an account of social inequality that gives scientific weight to first-person narratives of the bodily and systemic harms caused by discrimination. In this chapter, we have argued for a more complex, legal response to both the psychological and biological impact of unequal treatment that takes account of the social, environmental, and cumulative effects of treatment that creates not just social inequality but bioinequality.

## References

Aroke, E. N., Joseph, P. V., Roy, A., Overstreet, D. S., Tollefsbol, T. O., Vance, D. E., & Goodin, B. R. (2019). Could Epigenetics Help Explain Racial Disparities in Chronic Pain? *Journal of Pain Research, 12*, 701–710.

*Assisted Reproductive Treatment Act* 2008 (Vic).

Australian Broadcasting Corporation. (2014, March 14). Drinking Alcohol During Pregnancy Targeted as NT Government Considers Rights of Unborn Child. *ABC News Online.* https://www.abc.net.au/news/2014-03-14/nt-government-considering-rights-of-unborn-child/5320016. Accessed 6 Sept 2019.

Australian Human Rights Commission. (2018). *Everyone's Business: Fourth National Survey on Sexual Harassment in Australian Workplaces.* https://www.humanrights.gov.au/our-work/sex-discrimination/publications/everyones-business-fourth-national-survey-sexual. Accessed 10 Dec 2019.

Babenko, O., Kovalchuk, I., & Metz, G. A. (2015). Stress-Induced Perinatal and Transgenerational Epigenetic Programming of Brain Development and Mental Health. *Neuroscience and Biobehavioural Reviews, 48*, 70–91.

Bangasser, D. A., & Valentino, R. J. (2014). Sex Differences in Stress-Related Psychiatric Disorders: Neurobiological Perspectives. *Front Neuroendocrinal, 35*(5), 303–319.

Beyond Blue. (2014a). *Discrimination Against Indigenous Australians: A Snapshot of the Views of Non-Indigenous People Aged 25–44*. Resource document. https://www.beyondblue.org.au/docs/default-source/research-project-files/bl1337-report%2D%2D-tns-discrimination-against-indigenous-australians.pdf?sfvrsn=2. Accessed 24 July 2019.

Beyond Blue. (2014b). *The Invisible Discriminator*. Campaign webpage. https://www.beyondblue.org.au/who-does-it-affect/stop-think-respect-home/the-invisible-discriminator. Accessed 24 July 2019.

Bohacek, J., Gapp, K., Saab, B. J., & Mansuy, I. M. (2013). Transgenerational Epigenetic Effects on Brain Functions. *Biological Psychiatry, 73*(4), 313–320.

Borghol, N., Suderman, M., McAdrle, W., Racine, A., Hallet, M., Pembrey, M., Hertzman, C., Power, C., & Szyf, M. (2012). Associations with Early-Life Socio-Economic Position in Adult DNA Methylation. *International Journal of Epidemiology, 41*(1), 62–74.

Brand, S. R., Brennan, P. A., Newport, D. J., Smith, A. K., Weiss, T., & Stowe, Z. N. (2010). The impact of maternal childhood abuse on maternal and infant HPA axis function in the postpartum period. *Psychoneuroendocrinology, 35*(5), 686–693. https://doi.org/10.1016/j.psyneuen.2009.10.009

Broderick, E. (2009). *Lifelines: Sex Discrimination Over the Lifecycle*. Speech delivered at the National Museum of Australia, Canberra on 2 October 2009. Australian Human Rights Commission. https://www.humanrights.gov.au/about/news/speeches/lifelines-sex-discrimination-over-lifecycle-2009. Accessed 24 July 2019.

Brondolo, E., Love, E. E., Pencille, M., Schoenthaler, A., & Ogedegbe, G. (2011). Racism and Hypertension: A Review of the Empirical Evidence and Implications for Clinical Practice. *American Journal of Hypertension, 24*(5), 518–529.

Buss, C., Davis, E. P., Muftuler, L. T., Head, K., & Sandman, C. A. (2010). High Pregnancy Anxiety During Mid-Gestation Is Associated with Decreased Gray Matter Density in 6-9 Year-Old-Children. *Psychoneuroendocrinology, 35*(1), 141–153.

Cecil, C. A. M., Smith, R. G., Walton, E., Mill, J., McCrory, E. J., & Viding, E. (2016). Epigenetic Signatures of Childhood Abuse and Neglect: Implications for Psychiatric Vulnerability. *Journal of Psychiatric Research, 83*, 184–194.

Chmurzynska, A. (2010). Fetal Programming: Link Between Early Nutrition, DNA Methylation, and Complex Diseases. *Nutrition Reviews, 68*, 87–98.

Cordero, M. I., Poirier, G. L., Marquez, C., Veenit, V., Fontana, X., Salehi, B., Ansermet, F., & Sandi, C. (2012). Evidence for Biological Roots in the Transgenerational Transmission of Intimate Partner Violence. *Translational Psychiatry, 2*(4), 1–06.

Craido Perez, C. (2019). *Invisible Women: Exposing Data Bias in a World Designed for Men*. New York City: Vintage Publishing.

Crenshaw, K. (1989). Demarginalizing the Intersection of Race and Sex: A Black Feminist Critique of Antidiscrimination Doctrine, Feminist Theory and Antiracist Politics. *University of Chicago Legal Forum, 1989*(1), art 8.

*Criminal Code* 1899 (QLD).
*Criminal Code Compilation Act* 1913 (WA).
Cuffee, Y. L., Hargraves, J. L., & Allison, J. (2012). Exploring the Association Between Reported Discrimination and Hypertension Among African Americans: A Systematic Review. *Ethnicity & Disease, 22*(4), 422–431.
Davies, M. (2017). *Law Unlimited: Materialism, Pluralism and Legal Theory*. Milton Park: Taylor & Francis Group.
Deng, Y., Chang, L., Yang, M., Huo, M., & Zhou, R. (2016). Gender Differences in Emotional Response: Inconsistency Between Experience and Expressivity. *PLOS One, 11*(6), e0158666.
Dunlay, S. M., Lippmann, S. J., Greiner, M. A., O'Brien, E. C., Chamberlain, A. M., Mentz, R. J., & Sims, M. (2017). Perceived Discrimination and Cardiovascular Outcomes in Older African Americans: Insights from the Jackson Heart Study. *Mayo Clinic Proceedings, 92*(5), 699–709.
Dupras, C., & Ravitsky, V. (2016). The Ambiguous Nature of Epigenetic Responsibility. *Journal of Medical Ethics, 42*, 532–541.
Dupras, C., Song, L., Saulnier, K. M., & Joly, Y. (2018). Epigenetic Discrimination: Emerging Applications of Epigenetics Pointing to Limitations of Policies Against Genetic Discrimination. *Frontiers in Genetics, 9*, 202.
Dupras, C., Saulnier, K. M., & Joly, Y. (2019). Epigenetics, Ethics, Law and Society: A Multidisciplinary Review of Descriptive Instrumental, Dialectical and Reflexive Analyses. *Social Studies of Science, 49*, 1–26.
*Equality Act 2010* (UK).
Feig, L. A. (2018). Reduced Levels of miRNAs 449 and 34 in Sperm of Mice and Men Exposed to Early Life Stress. *Translational Psychiatry, 8*(1), 101.
Fein, E. (2011). Innocent Machines: Asperger's Syndrome and the Neurostructural Self. In M. Pickersgill & I. Van Keulan (Eds.), *Sociological Reflections on the Neurosciences* (pp. 29–34). Bingley: Emerald Group Publishing.
Flanigan, C., Sheikh, A., DunnGalvin, A., Brew, B. K., Almqvist, C., & Nwaru, B. I. (2018). Prenatal Maternal Psychosocial Stress and Offspring's Asthma and Allergic Disease: A Systematic Review and Meta-Analysis. *Journal of Clinical and Experimental Allergy, 48*(4), 403–414.
Fox Keller, E. (2014). From Gene Action to Reactive Genomes. *The Journal of Physiology, 592*(11), 2423–2429.
Fredman, S. (2008). *Human Rights Transformed: Positive Rights and Positive Duties*. Oxford: Oxford University Press.
Gaze, B. (2002). Context and Interpretation in Anti-Discrimination Law. *Melbourne University Law Review, 26*(2), 325.
Geronimus, A. (2013). Deep Integration: Letting the Epigenome Out of the Bottle Without Losing Sight of the Structural Origins of Population Health. *American Journal of Public Health, 103*(S1), S56–S63.
Giurgescu, C., Nowak, A. L., Gillespie, S., Nolan, T. S., Anderson, C. M., Ford, J. L., et al. (2019). Neighborhood Environment and DNA Methylation:

Implications for Cardiovascular Disease Risk. *Journal of Urban Health: Bulletin of the New York Academy of Medicine*. https://doi.org/10.1007/s11524-018-00341-1.
Goosby, B., & Heidbrick, C. (2013). The Transgenerational Consequences of Discrimination on African American Health Outcomes. *Sociology Companion, 7*(8), 630–643.
Goosby, B., Cheadle, J. E., & Mitchell, C. (2018). Stress-Related Biosocial Mechanisms of Discrimination and African American Health Inequities. *Annual Review of Sociology, 44*, 319–340.
Hancock, A. B., & Rubin, A. B. (2014). Influence of Communication Partner's Gender on Language. *Journal of Language and Social Psychology, 34*(1), 46–64.
Hancock, K., Zubrick, S., & Mitrou, F. (2015). *Multigenerational Disadvantage in Australia*. Resource document, Telethon Kids Institute. https://www.telethonkids.org.au/our-research/brain-and-behaviour/mental-health-and-youth/human-capability/lcc-projects/multigenerational-disadvantage-in-australia/. Accessed 24 July 2019.
Haraway, D. (1991). *Simians, Cyborgs and Women: The Reinvention of Nature*. New York: Routledge.
Haraway, D. (1997). *Modest_Witness@Second_Millennium.FemaleMan©Meets_OncoMouse™: Feminism and Technoscience*. New York: Routledge.
Huang, J. Y., & King, N. B. (2018). Epigenetics Changes Nothing: What a New Scientific Field Does and Does Not Mean for Ethics and Social Justice. *Public Health Ethics, 11*(1), 69–81.
*Human Fertilisation and Embryology Act 2008* (UK).
*Human Reproductive Technology Act 1991* (UK).
Jablonka, E. (2017). The Evolutionary Implications of Epigenetic Inheritance. *Interface Focus*. https://doi.org/10.1098/rsfs.2016.0135.
Jones, P. A., & Takai, D. (2001). The Role of DNA Methylation in Mammalian Epigenetics. *Science, 293*(5532), 1068–1070.
Karpin, I. (2016). Regulatory Responses to the Gendering of Transgenerational Harm. *Australian Feminist Studies, 31*(88), 139–153.
Karpin, I. (2018). Vulnerability and the Intergenerational Transmission of Pyschosocial Harm. *Emory Law Journal, 67*, 1115–1134.
Kim, P., Evans, G. W., Chen, E., Miller, G., & Seeman, T. (2018). How Socioeconomic Disadvantages Get Under the Skin and into the Brain to Influence Health Development Across the Lifespan. In N. Halfon, C. B. Forrest, R. M. Lerner, & E. M. Faustman (Eds.), *Handbook of Life Course Health Development* (pp. 463–497). New York: Springer.
Krieger, N. (2014). Discrimination and Health Inequities. *International Journal of Health Services, 44*(4), 643–710.
Kundakovic, M., & Jaric, I. (2017). The Epigenetic Link Between Prenatal Adverse Environments and Neurodevelopmental Disorders. *Genes, 8*(3), 104.

Kuzawa, C., & Sweet, E. (2009). Epigenetics and The Embodiment of Race: Developmental Origins of US Racial Disparity in Cardio Vascular Health. *American Journal of Human Biology, 21*(1), 212–215.

Landecker, H., & Panofsky, A. (2013). From Social Structure to Gene Regulation and Back: A Critical Introduction to Environmental Epigenetics for Sociology. *Annual Review of Sociology, 39*, 333–357.

Lewis, S., & Thomson, M. (2019). Social Bodies and Social Justice. *International Journal of Law in Context., 15*(3), 344–361.

Lock, M. (2015). Comprehending the Body in the Era of the Epigenome. *Current Anthropology, 56*(2), 151–177.

Loi, M., Del Savio, L., & Stupka, E. (2013). Social Epigenetics and Equality of Opportunity. *Public Health Ethics, 6*(2), 142–153.

McCrory, C., Fiorito, G., Ni Cheallaigh, C., Polidoro, S., Karisola, P., Alenius, H., et al. (2019). How Does Socio-Economic Position (SEP) Get Biologically Embedded? A Comparison of Allostatic Load and the Epigenetic Clock(s). *Psychoneuroendocrinology, 104*, 64–73.

McEwen, C., & McEwen, B. S. (2017). *Social Structure, Adversity, Toxic Stress, and Intergenerational Poverty: An Early Childhood Model* (SSRN Scholarly Paper No. ID 3018063). Retrieved from Social Science Research Network website: https://papers.ssrn.com/abstract=3018063

McGuinness, D., McGlynn, L. M., Johnson, P. C., MacIntyre, A., Batty, G. D., Burns, H., Cavanagh, J., Deans, K. A., Ford, I., McConnachie, A., McGinty, A., McLean, J. S., Millar, K., Packard, C. J., Sattar, N. A., Tannahill, C., Velupillai, Y. N., & Shiels, P. G. (2012). Socio-Economic Status Is Associated with Epigenetic Differences in the pSoBid Cohort. *International Journal of Epidemiology, 41*(1), 151–160.

McLean, C., Asnaani, A., Litz, B., & Hofman, S. (2011). Gender Differences in Anxiety Disorders: Prevalence, Course of Illness, Comorbidity and Burden of Illness. *Journal of Psychiatric Research, 45*(8), 1027–1035.

Meloni, M. (2015). Heredity 2.0: The Epigenetics Effect. *New Genetics and Society, 34*(2), 117–124.

Monk, C., Spicer, J., & Champagne, F. (2012). Linking Prenatal Maternal Adversity to Developmental Outcomes in Infants: The Role of Epigenetic Pathways. *Developmental Psychopathology, 24*(4), 1361–1376.

National Health and Medical Research Council. (2017). *Ethical Guidelines on the Use of Assisted Reproductive Technology in Clinical Practice and Research*. Guidelines, NHMRC. https://www.nhmrc.gov.au/about-us/publications/ethical-guidelines-use-assisted-reproductive-technology#block-views-block-file-attachments-content-block-1. Accessed 25 Aug 2019.

O'Connell, K. (2012). "A Plural Thing": Inventing a Feminist Brain-Based Subject of Law. *Australian Feminist Law Journal, 37*, 15–32.

O'Connell, K. (2016). Unequal Brains: Disability Discrimination Laws and Children with Challenging Behaviour. *Medical Law Review, 24*(1), 76–98.

O'Connell, K. (2019, May 10). Rush Gets $850,000, But What of the Victims of Sexual Harassment? *The Australian*, p. 28.

Paradies, Y., Ben, J., Denson, N., Elias, A., Priest, N., Pieterse, A., Gupta, A., Kelaher, M., & Gee, G. (2015). Racism as a Determinant of Health: A Systematic Review and Meta-Analysis. *PLoS One, 10*(9), e0138511. https://doi.org/10.1371/journal.pone.0138511.

Parra, L. A., & Hastings, P. D. (2018). Integrating the Neurobiology of Minority Stress with an Intersectionality Framework for LGBTQ-Latinx Populations. *New Directions for Child and Adolescent Development, 2018*(161), 91–108.

Pinto, L. A., Sullivan, E. L., Rosenbaum, A., Wyngarden, N., Umhau, J. C., Miller, M. W., & Taft, C. T. (2010). Biological Correlates of Intimate Partner Violence Perpetration. *Aggression and Violent Behavior, 15*(5), 387–398.

Platt, J., Prins, S., Bates, L., & Keyes, K. (2016). Unequal Depression for Equal Work? How the Wage Gap Explains Gendered Disparities in Mood Disorders. *Social Science & Medicine*. https://doi.org/10.1016/j.socscimed.2015.11.056.

*Public Health Act* 2011 (SA).

Radford, K., Delbaere, K., Draper, B., Mack, H. A., Daylight, G., Cumming, R., Chalkley, S., Minogue, C., & Broe, G. A. (2017). Childhood Stress and Adversity Is Associated with Late-Life Dementia in Aboriginal Australians. *The American Journal of Geriatric Psychiatry, 25*(10), 1097–1106.

Radtke, K. M., Ruf, M., Gunter, H. M., Dohrmann, K., Schauer, M., Meyer, A., & Elbert, T. (2011). Transgenerational Impact of Intimate Partner Violence on Methylation in the Promoter of the Glucocorticoid Receptor. *Translational Psychiatry, 1*(7), e21.

Richards, J. (2016). Let Her Finish: Gender and Deliberative Participation in Australian Senate Estimates Hearings (2006–2015). https://doi.org/10.13140/RG.2.2.34505.75368

Roberts, A. L., Lyall, K., Rich-Edwards, J. W., Ascherio, A., & Weisskopf, M. G. (2013). Association of Maternal Exposure to Childhood Abuse with Elevated Risk for Autism in Offspring. *JAMA Psychiatry, 70*(5), 508–515.

Rothstein, M. A., Cai, Y., & Marchant, G. E. (2009). The Ghost in Our Genes: Legal and Ethical Implications of Epigenetics. *Health Matrix, 19*(1), 1–62.

Rubin, L. P. (2016). Maternal and Pediatric Health and Disease: Integrating Biopsychosocial Models and Epigenetics. *Pediatric Research, 79*(1–2), 127–135.

Rutter, M. (2012). Gene-Environment Interdependence. *European Journal of Developmental Psychology, 9*(4), 391–412.

*Sex Discrimination Act* 1986 (Cth).

Sharp, G., Schellhas, L., Richardson, S., & Lawlor, D. (2019). Time to Cut the Cord: Recognizing and Addressing the Imbalance of DOHaD Research Towards the Study of Maternal Pregnancy Exposures. *Journal of Developmental Origins of Health and Disease, 10*, 1–4.

Shields, A. (2017). Epigenetic Signals of How Social Disadvantage "Gets Under the Skin": A Challenge to the Public Health Community. *Epigenomics, 9*(3), 223–229.

Singh, G., Morrison, J., & Hoy, W. (2019). DOHaD in Indigenous Populations: DOHaD, Epigenetics, Equity and Race. *Journal of Developmental Origins of Health and Disease, 10*(1), 63–64.

Smith, B., Schleiger, M., Elphick, L. (2019). Preventing Sexual Harassment in Work: Exploring the Promise of Work Health and Safety Laws. Australian Journal of Labour Law, 32, 219–249. https://papers.ssrn.com/sol3/papers.cfm?abstract_id=3299784

Sosnowski, D. W., Booth, C., York, T. P., Amstadter, A. B., & Kliewer, W. (2018). Maternal Prenatal Stress and Infant DNA Methylation: A Systematic Review. *Developmental Psychobiology, 60*(2), 127–139. https://doi.org/10.1002/dev.21604.

Soubry, A. (2018). Epigenetics as a Driver of Developmental Origins of Health and Disease: Did We Forget the Fathers? *BioEssays, 40*, 1700113.

Spivak, G. (1988). Can the Subaltern Speak. In C. Nelson & L. Grossberg (Eds.), *Marxism and the Interpretation of Culture*. Bassingstoke: Macmillan Education.

Sullivan, S. (2013). Inheriting Racist Disparities in Health: Epigenetics and the Transgenerational Effects of White Racism. *Critical Philosophy of Race, 1*(2), 190–218.

Sweatt, J. D. (2013). The Emerging Field of Neuroepigenetics. *Neuron, 80*(3), 624–632.

Thornton, M. (1990). *The Liberal Promise: Anti-Discrimination Legislation in Australia*. Melbourne: Oxford University Press.

Thornton, M. (2009). Disabling Discrimination Legislation: The High Court and Judicial Activism. *Australian Journal of Human Rights, 15*(1), 1–28.

Thornton, M. (2010). The Racial State as a Legal Person. *Australian Journal of Legal Philosophy, 35*, 140–146.

Tribble, R., & Kim, P. (2019). Intergenerational Transmission of Poverty: How Low Socioeconomic Status Impacts the Neurobiology of Two Generations. In A. W. Harrist & B. C. Gardner (Eds.), *Biobehavioral Markers in Risk and Resilience Research* (pp. 49–67). Springer International Publishing, New York City.

UNICEF. (2006). *Behind Closed Doors: The Impact of Domestic Violence on Children*. https://www.unicef.org/protection/files/BehindClosedDoors.pdf. Accessed 6 Sept 2019.

Van der Kolk, B. (2014). *The Body Keeps the Score: Brain, Mind, and Body in the Healing of Trauma*. New York: Penguin Books.

Wadhwa, P. D., Buss, C., Entringer, S., & Swanson, J. M. (2009). Developmental Origins of Health and Disease: Brief History of the Approach and Current Focus on Epigenetic Mechanisms. *Seminars in Reproductive Medicine, 27*(5), 358–368.

Warin, M., Moore, V., Davies, M., & Ulijaszek, S. (2016). Epigenetics and Obesity: The Reproduction of Habitus Through Intracellular and Social Environments. *Body & Society, 22*(4), 53–78.

Warin, M., Kowal, E., & Meloni, M. (2019). Indigenous Knowledge in a Postgenomic Landscape: The Politics of Epigenetic Hope and Reparation in Australia. Science, Technology, & Human Values, 0162243919831077. https://doi.org/10.1177/0162243919831077

Weder, N., Zhang, H., Jensen, K., Yang, B., Simen, A., Jackowski, A., Lipschitz, D., Douglas-Palumberi, H., Ge, M., Perepletchikova, F., O'Laughlin, K., Hudziak, J., Gelernter, J., & Kaufman, J. (2014). Child Abuse, Depression and Methylation in Genes Involved with Stress, Neural Plasticity and Brain Circuitry. *Journal of the American Academy of Child and Adolescent Psychiatry, 53*(4), 417–434.

*Wisconsin Administrative Code*, Chapter 48.

World Health Organisation. (2007). *The Cycles of Violence: The Relationship Between Childhood Maltreatment and the Risk of Later Becoming a Victim or Perpetrator of Violence*. Violence and Injury Prevention Programme, World Health Organisation. http://www.euro.who.int/__data/assets/pdf_file/0008/98783/E90619.pdf. Accessed 6 Sept 2019.

# 5

# Healthcare, Well-being, and the Regulation of Diversity in Healing

Emilie Cloatre and Nayeli Urquiza-Haas

## 1 Introduction

Patients in Europe today can be faced with an array of options when it comes to well-being. Taking the UK as an example, someone suffering from chronic headaches may start by visiting their GP, who may prescribe painkillers and/or advise them on lifestyle changes. The patient however may grow unconvinced by the efficacy of the treatment, or indeed be unwilling to rely on pills to deal with everyday pain. Others may not have visited their doctor in the first place, preferring other routes, maybe less clinical, more spiritual or more 'natural'. One quick online search will offer plenty of suggestions on how else they could approach their pain. From acupuncture to select medicinal plants, traditional Chinese medicine, osteopathy, meditation or homeopathy, they will find a whole marketplace of solutions, some available through their pharmacy and to some extent through the NHS (though that will be dependent on sympathetic doctors and local health authorities, and likely to include only some select solutions that are closer to their own logics of care), but others in health stores and through private providers. They may also remember hearing about the old energy-healer from their village, who some say has made miracles with their touch and prayers. Or, in a very different register, they may turn instead

The original version of this chapter was revised. A correction to this chapter is available at https://doi.org/10.1007/978-3-030-42200-4_13

E. Cloatre (✉) • N. Urquiza-Haas (✉)
University of Kent, Canterbury, UK
e-mail: E.Cloatre@kent.ac.uk; N.Haas@kent.ac.uk


C. Dietz et al. (eds.), *A Jurisprudence of the Body*, Palgrave Socio-Legal Studies,
https://doi.org/10.1007/978-3-030-42200-4_5

to a high-end, futuristic-sounding, clinic on Harley Street that offers expensive, but unique and, it claims, 'revolutionary' treatment. Maybe a friend has mentioned their own healer there, and claims that he has cured what all doctors had told them could not be curable, with his radically new understanding of biology and the human body: water treatment and the right diet can do miracles, he says, where biomedicine would only cause more pain and discomfort, all for the benefits of pharmaceutical companies. Because biomedicine is not to be trusted, their friend has not actually been checked by a doctor for a while, but feels better, and their healer is confident that they are on the mend.

Along with illustrations of some of the many forms that healing offerings can take today, the examples above hint at a few of the dichotomies that tend to be superimposed over the field: between health and 'well-being'; between biomedicine and 'alternative' healing; between state-backed institutions (e.g. GPs or hospitals) and a market of healing; and maybe between practices deemed safe and dangerous; 'honest' and deceptive; care and abuse; and, some would say, between healers and 'quacks'. However, the drawing of such boundaries is contested: different institutions and agents would draw these lines in their own ways.

Although diversity of practices in healing, and debates about the value of particular practices, are nothing new, the controversies triggered by non-conventional medicines seem to have been intensifying over the past few years, or at least re-emerging to unsettle the few 'non-biomedical practices' that had for the previous decades negotiated a place within 'mainstream' healthcare. A campaign called 'NoFakeMed' has grown in France, mobilising (mostly young white male) doctors against what they consider unproven therapies (notably homeopathy and acupuncture); the NHS has largely defunded those same therapies; herbalists have both seen the introduction of new regulations they are sceptical about in relation to herbs, and continued to push against their own illegality of practice in France. But such push back against complementary and alternative medicines (CAM) is also riddled with ambivalence. For example, the biomedical institution has opened its door to practices that may at first sight seem even further from its understanding of medicine: social prescribing is enabling the NHS to delegate some of its treatments to a broad-range of community and well-being practices—from yoga, to meditation, to broadly defined 'well-being' sessions offered to students and academics alike (Yoga in Healthcare Alliance 2019). Hypnosis has been integrated in medical practice in France after being for a long time considered a new-age deviance. Patients also continue to propose their own understandings of health, turning to self-prescribed treatments, the internet or non-medical therapists for their everyday care. While this is often seen as a private issue, sites of friction between public health and individual choices are growing, as illustrated lately by the increasing pull of the antivaccination movement, often feeding onto shared 'anti or non-medical' discourses, and the recent measles outbreaks (Pym 2019).

In these events, biomedicine is being challenged, either giving ground, or reasserting its own position (and sometimes doing a bit of both): alternative ways of imagining health are being deployed, sometimes resting on very long-standing thoughts system (e.g. Chinese medicine), sometimes on much newer and contested theories, or even problematic pseudo-healers. Finally, those questions are also affected by contemporary austerity politics and the increasing encroaching of neoliberal logics onto healthcare: as the space for publicly funded healthcare is reduced, new decisions need to be made about what continues to deserve funding or not, and indeed what funded interactions may look like. While some non-biomedical practices may be favoured (e.g. through social prescribing), they may be proposed instead of other forms of care (e.g. access to mental healthcare) rather than as an additional option, reducing instead of expanding the possibilities offered to patients within publicly funded care. Patients who seek different types of interactions, different types of caring or different ways of healing are directed to an ever-growing market place from which, as we return to, the state is markedly absent.

We approach this field with a particular interest in regulation, and how states can organise practices in such a messy field as contemporary healthcare and well-being, particularly where it doesn't fit the borders of institutional biomedicine. Regulators, on the one hand, may be keen to offer patients a degree of freedom and choice over how they heal their own body. While this may enable a welcome accommodation of diversity in healing cultures, it is also part of a neoliberal approach to healthcare: the neoliberal patient is also one that is in charge of their own health and often has to make market-based decisions. At the same time, and while freedom of choice should be accommodated, illness generates vulnerabilities and reduces resilience, and it seems reasonable to expect states to protect patients from the dangers that unscrupulous healers, or indeed some deceptive claims to healing, may represent. Similarly, when public health is at risk from questionable claims—such as some of those of antivaccination movements—regulators may wish to intervene to protect a broader public. State authorities and institutions therefore partake in the process of defining who and what sort of care should be provided 'legally'—which herbs, which practice, which therapist is allowed to act under which conditions—and which they should pay for or subsidise. However, if medical law has proven how complex it can be to adjudicate and draw lines of legitimacy where scientific practice is concerned, the task becomes even more complex in fields where the nature of 'knowledge' or evidence is loaded with cultural assumptions, a history of dominance of some forms of (colonial and gendered) knowledge over others, and is entangled in institutional systems that have themselves been developed mostly with biomedicine in mind.

The analysis that follows sets out a core dilemma that we have been wrestling with in our questioning of how alternative medicines are, and could be, regulated, and suggests some ways of thinking about, or 'thinking with' (Haraway 2003) these issues. Contemporary regulation tends to rely on a core difference between proven and unproven therapies to adjudicate questions of authorisations and funding. Yet its registers of proof are predominantly to be found in scientific logics. But scientific logics cannot answer questions posed by other ontological worlds, including those that some patients or some communities may inhabit. 'Other' medicines tend to rely on ways of knowing and doing operate on their own systems of thought, even if some elements could be fitted into a scientific logic. However, regulators, at least in Western Europe, have not fully developed alternative ways of thinking about hierarchies and effectiveness in healing practices. This creates at least two problems for the regulation of alternative healing: on the one hand, a difficulty in apprehending if and under what conditions some non-biomedical therapies could contribute to the delivery of care; on the other, the withdrawal from regulating those privately funded practices, and the risk of aggravating the vulnerability of their users. Our analysis is therefore led by a main question: how can we move beyond the dead-end that regulation finds itself in, and imagine new ways to apprehend healing that are not based exclusively on biomedical paradigms? We propose that approaching the problem as one of cosmopolitics, where universes aren't always compatible, helps frame the issue at stake in regulating, and the need to move the debate to registers that are not primarily about scientific evidence. We suggest that scholarship on vulnerability and care, in turn, can help us reimagine how questions of regulation and ordering could be approached differently. The chapter is organised in three parts: first, we return in more details to how scientific paradigms participate in drawing regulatory boundaries, and the shortcomings of their contributions; second, we propose a reframing of the field as one of coexisting ontologies; and third, we turn to scholarship on vulnerability and care to suggest some starting points in reimagining how the field could be ordered otherwise.

## 2 Diversity in Practices and the Hegemony of Biomedical Understandings of the Body

The regulation of legitimate healthcare and its boundaries in Europe is best understood against the historical landscape of the rise of biomedicine. For a long time, medical practices in Europe were best characterised as a 'marketplace of healthcare', in which healers of various kinds coexisted with emergent biomedicine, and few relied on anything that resembled a state-sponsored healthcare system (Porter 1999). As biomedicine made its way towards its 'golden age', in the nineteenth and twentieth centuries, it progressively pushed aside other ways of knowing and healing, or at least organised a hierarchy of distribution and access (Green 1997; Griggs 1997). Such rise always had political undertones and implications: where folk knowledge had been distributed across social classes and communities, and was often held by women, the experts of biomedicine were for a long time exclusively educated white males (Ehrenreich and English 2010). The persistence of patterns of beliefs, or as we propose to think them here, of contrasting ontologies, are also to be read as the coexistence of worlds across which healing practices had to be distributed.

The rise of biomedicine was, of course, in part, triggered by some of its breakthroughs: medical milestones from vaccinations to antibiotics came to produce small revolutions of knowledge and practice, which would mark biomedicine as a science of hope. But the story of the institutional rise of biomedicine, more relevant to our purpose here, cannot be reduced to one of the establishing of the superiority of one type of knowledge over others. Indeed, the rise of biomedicine within state institutions predates its most significant discoveries, and if today the significance of biomedical knowledge to improving health in populations is well-recognised, historians have long pointed to the fact that its emergence has always been as much about politics as it has been about the raw discovery of natural and objective truths (Cook 1990; MacLennan and Pendry 2011; Porter 1999). If nowadays only a minority contests the overall value of biomedicine, contemporary medical practices, and the institutional and economic make-up in which they are inscribed, continue to be the subject of some controversies, such as scandals around drugs or medical devices, built-in inequalities (e.g. gendered or racial), and the limits of the 'all clinical'.

Partly (though by no means only) because of such controversies and limitations, even since it became more established and gained a particularly central place within healthcare systems, biomedicine has never entirely pushed away other ways of imagining health. However, one of the most visible and long-standing impacts of biomedicine has been its embedding into an institutional apparatus that has been unequalled by those of any other therapeutic practices, at least in Europe: biomedicine has successfully established itself as occupying a particular space in state decisions surrounding healthcare in terms of institutions as well as laws. A significant state apparatus has come to not only embed, but also depend on, the inner logics of biomedicine in its everyday functioning. Centrally for this chapter, this has meant that legal regimes have adopted and been built around the understanding of bodies proposed by biomedicine, embracing its ontology of bodies as the only one able to reflect a universal reality.

## 2.1 Law, Biomedicine and the Neoliberal Organisation of Care

Indeed, the institutionalisation of biomedicine came with, and fed into, legal logics, that continue to be influential today. When determining which professions should be able to heal bodies, and under which conditions, or how those should be organised against one another, the hierarchies and assumptions of biomedicine itself are essential (and the place of relevant associations in organising and regulating professions is significant) (Lunstroth 2006; Sibbritt et al. 2018). Similarly, determining how products (including herbal medicines) should be approved as health products, along with the conditions of their sale and distribution, has come to rely on systems of proofs derived from biomedicine itself. Sites considered as spaces of healthcare, and their regulatory framing, or in fact how navigating in and out of particular spaces may affect the type of care that a patient may be entitled to, are also dependent on a set of rationales derived from particular understandings of bodily care. Finally, how care is to be financed, and what care is to be financed, is regulated through systems of evidence mostly derived from biomedicine (NHS England 2017; Meakin and Jackson-Main 2018).

The particular ways in which such systems are organised, and such rationalities expressed, varies from jurisdiction to jurisdiction even within Europe (CAMDOC Alliance 2010). In our research, we have predominantly, as far as the European context is concerned, focused on the regulatory systems laid out by France and the UK. Those provide usefully contrasting examples, nevertheless both sharing a particular approach to evidence-making. A key difference between the regulation of therapeutic practices in France and the UK is their use of il/legality. France, leaning on a Republican reliance on central-state law as a primary regulatory tool, draws explicit lines between therapists (and, though less directly, therapeutic practices) considered legal or illegal. Therapists that do not hold biomedical qualifications are ringfenced into the latter, while health professionals are provided with some degree of flexibility in using techniques and therapies of their choosing (including non-biomedical) to provide care to their patients. Therefore, doctors or midwives are able to provide acupuncture or homeopathy, but no pathways are offered to others to provide such therapies. The UK appears, at first sight, as more accommodating. In practice, however, it operates a clear distinction between practices that will be maintained within the free national healthcare system, and those that will be left to a less regulated market of healing, open to those who can afford to purchase such therapies as a particular type of consumer good. The latter will mostly be organised through a mixture of voluntary regulation and the general principles of criminal law where harm and abusive practices are concerned. Though law is not used explicitly as a tool to squeeze out alternative therapies or practitioners, other forms of regulatory managerial logics are embedded within the healthcare system, which results in their gentle nudging to the edges of legitimate care.

In spite of those differences, the two systems heavily rely on mechanisms of proof that help determine the conditions of access to different treatments and their potential funding by the state. Treatments, products and practitioners seeking state endorsement find themselves having to demonstrate their efficacy. Where they fail, the effects are regulatory as well as socio-political: they are pushed to the edge of the system of healthcare, but have also been increasingly attacked by medical and scientific lobbies that are quick to describe treatments for which they see no evidence of efficacy as fake (Meakin and Jackson-Main 2018). At one level, this seems commonsensical: it seems fair that treatments that the state is paying for should be held to some form of standards of proof, and of knowledge, or indeed that its users can be assured that what they have been offered 'works'. At the same time, what comes to be considered as evidence is, within the regulatory system and beyond, of a very particular nature, resting on the idea of universal science that other ontologies, as we return to, may simply not see as relevant to their own workings (Lin and Law 2019).

## 2.2 Proving Through Science and Biomedicine

Although scientific medicine has progressively expanded, as well as questioned, the range of evidence that it considers as valid, it continues to rely primarily on scientific tests and logics. Importantly, for our purpose, regulatory systems also tend to borrow from these systems of proof to adjudicate what therapy is considered as legitimate and valuable or not. Two particular mechanisms can be taken as illustration of such disconnect, and of the tensions between universal scientific standards and the multiple ontologies of healing that we return to below: the idea of 'blindness' in clinical trials, and the expectations that proof should be of efficacy 'beyond the placebo effect' (Martin et al. 2015; Mol 2003).

The idea that tests for efficacy should be conducted blindly is now well-embedded in biomedical research, and by extension in research on all other healing systems (Jin 2010; Adams 2002). Relying on the logics of science, the assumption here is that the efficacy of a treatment should not be altered by the conditions of its administration—notably whether the person receiving it is aware of what they are being offered. In order to make blind clinical trials operate, it is important that patients are all treated under the same conditions, so that they cannot deduce from how or by whom a treatment is administered whether what they are offered is the product being tested, or something else. If such systems fit the logics of biomedicine, that assumes that the body should produce a consistent and mechanical response to a particular treatment, anthropologists have long pointed out that it is ill-adapted to other ways of thinking and practicing medicine. For example, some medical systems put such emphasis on the relationship between therapist and patients, and the interaction during the treatment itself, that it cannot be translated into the clinical and homogenised form of testing that blindness requires (Adams et al. 2005; Pollock 2014). For other traditions, context is so significant to the holistic working of a treatment that seeking to eliminate it is likely to drain it from any potential efficacy.

A second key principle in evidence-making in medicine is that treatments should be able to prove themselves beyond the 'placebo' effect. Here, the assumption is that a treatment should have an inherent physical effect that can be isolated from what the patient may expect from it, or believe it will do. In other words, a treatment should be able to respect the principle (established in biomedicine but questionable under numerous other systems) that belief and bodily mechanics, or body and mind, can be neatly separated in therapeutic practice. Readings of the 'placebo effect' within regulatory practice and beyond tend to understand it as being equivalent to 'non-effective'. As a consequence, the defunding of certain CAM practices by states, or some of their attacks across traditional and social media, have often been justified on the basis that the practice had not been able to prove itself beyond the placebo effect. However, critiques have pointed out that alternative understandings of the meaning of placebos in the making of knowledge could be proposed, or at least layered over current perceptions (Harrington 1999; Friesen 2019). For example, within an ontological frame in which beliefs and healing are not entirely separated, a product working only under particular conditions may be read as much as showing the effectiveness of belief or of the value of the relationships that surround therapeutic practice (and may be dependent on the use of a particular product, but not purely stem from it).

In these key mechanisms, evidence as understood in both biomedical practice and, by extension, regulatory decision-making, has limitations as far as other ways of knowing are concerned: by definition, science can only help us decipher what is scientifically proven or not.

## 2.3 What of the 'Unproven'?

Before we turn to this, it is worth emphasising, of course, that when things are not proven under the terms of biomedicine, and/or consequently not recognised by state regulators or relevant health institutions, they do not stop existing. They may continue to seek to be recognised through science, looking for evidence that can translate some of their contributions in terms more aligned with those of science and regulation, in spite of the difficulties this poses. Indeed, as we mentioned, some non-biomedical practices have been integrated into medical practice—though which and how has varied over the years. But where that does not succeed, in the UK at least, they are displaced onto the market and private providers. Even where products, practitioners or practices are technically 'illegal' agents, like in France, unregulated products or healers rarely disappear. Instead, the unregulated continues to exist within the spectrum of practices that patients seek to access and providers will continue to offer. In fact, the law is not particularly suited to interrupt what are often relatively discreet, everyday practices. Instead, legal boundaries simply displace unregulated healers and products from visible to less visible spaces (such as private healers on high-streets, home practices, or even online therapy sessions), or affect their conditions of practice (e.g. how much those using particular therapies will report it to their doctor; how much regulatory checks will be placed onto practitioners or products). This is a significant dilemma for regulators, or when thinking about law and medical pluralism: where things are not proven (in scientific terms), they are often not 'recognised' as relevant to healthcare, or as being about 'medicine', and folded instead into categories such as 'wellness' or 'well-being'. But such lack of recognition may effectively result in those practices operating outside of any formal system of care and therefore outside of the regulations and checks and controls that would normally be applied to healthcare. For example, while the UK has sought to set standards for the conduct of unregulated practitioners through voluntary self-regulation schemes for professional associations, overseen by the Professional Standards Authority (Professional Standards Authority 2017), some of these associations argue that healers who don't abide by standards of practice will continue to do so. This is because since their professions are not recognised by law as legitimate healthcare professions in the same way biomedical professions are, the use of their title is not protected nor associated to particular training standards (Interview 16.11.2019). The paradox or dilemma is one of balancing recognition and regulation: disproving or dismissing practices may be at the cost of ensuring the safety of those who will continue to use them, and find value in them. If the state is to care for all citizens equally, we may need to find new ways to engage and organise practices that do not 'fit', or cannot be proven (or indeed disproven) through science. In what follows we propose to reframe and displace some of these conversations in an attempt to imagine what a different type of regulatory debate might look like.

# 3 Multiplicity, Ontologies and Medical Pluralism

In this section, we argue that a core challenge facing regulators is that the multiple healing systems that patients may encounter are based on contrasting ontologies that limit the relevance of scientific evidence as an arbiter of legitimacy. STS scholarship has long emphasised that medical and bodily practices rely on a multiplicity of ontologies. Annemarie Mol (2003), in her exploration of atherosclerosis, concluded that the disease itself that doctors, patients and lab analysts all seek to deal with is simply not the same for all those involved. In the same way, bodies in general are not simply being perceived, or read, or experienced, in a different way by each of the actors involved, but constitute a different 'thing' altogether for each of them. Since then, attention has turned to how contrasting ontologies can coexist within biomedical practices, or within the circuits of state-provided healthcare (Pickersgill 2013). As well as providing richer descriptions of the knowledge-making (and contesting) processes at play in medical practices, the turn to acknowledging multiple ontologies has sought to bring back the political into some of the claims of biomedicine. Whereas body normativity erases all differences by reducing biological facts to mere givens, as if they were self-contained universal truths, feminist, disability and critical race studies, among others, have often pointed out the power relations embedded into body discourses which take an idealised version of masculine bodies as the measuring model, including those that pathologise and disempower feminine, maternal, ill, and disabled bodies, marking them as abnormal deviations from the norm (Goffman 2006; Subramaniam 2009). Margrit Shildrick suggests vulnerable bodies are monstrous insofar as they represent an excess that shatters the fiction of the 'proper' individual of liberalism (2001). Acknowledging these critiques and the coexistence of bodily ontologies can also help us move to a new type of understanding of what is at stake in healing practices moving in and out of biomedicine, by bringing experience, subjectivities, and politics back into the realm of regulating healthcare.

Although inspired by different roots, philosophical rather than sociological, the concept of cosmopolitics can help us engage further with some of the tensions that underpin the field of healing. Thinking through cosmopolitics is partly about defining who can contribute to a common world, and under what conditions (Stengers 2005). Starting from the assumption that there is no single truth, and no single set of material realities, on which perspectives can be confronted, opens up the possibility for the complexity of the world(s) to be reassessed. It also opens up new ways of thinking about the place of non-human entities in the worlds that we inhabit—and indeed how bodies coexist with them. Here, we propose that it may, for example, enable us to imagine the multiplicity of healing worlds, including in law, on their own terms rather than in reference to biomedicine. One particular contribution of cosmopolitics is to enable us to move away from what Blaser (2013) calls the 'problem of reasonable politics' and reframe conflicts over realities as ontological rather than cultural. In an area such as healing, it opens up the possibility to critically re-approach the position of science as the only mediator of an objective truth, a perspective dominating the make-up both of 'real' medicine and of bodily ontologies. Debates around healing practices can potentially be moved to a terrain that is social and ontological rather than settled only through an appeal for the rules that science, and biomedicine, may rest upon. Although this does not need to result in the abandonment of any hope for a common world, it requires a shift of starting and end points: rather than assuming a single factuality of which one reading will be faithful, and others 'deviant', we could accept that multiple factualities coexist and can be understood through a multiplicity of faithful and valuable descriptions, whilst also recognising the institutional and political legitimacy and consequent privileging afforded to some of these factualities.

Therapies on offer to patients in contemporary Europe (and, of course, beyond) rest on a variety of conceptions of the body, and on different cosmopolitics. The point is most strikingly illustrated if looking at practices that rest on a long-standing and highly documented set of theories that carefully articulate and illustrate their understanding of healing, such as Chinese or Tibetan medicines (Adams 2002; Janes 1999). Here we can only briefly sketch some of the key differences between such systems and biomedicine, but these can illustrate why contrasts are best understood as ontological and why for regulatory purposes they are not solvable through science only. First, while biomedicine has tended to understand bodies and disease through a segmented approach—where organs, diseases, dysfunctions are often considered within a limited set of internal relationships—other traditions have promoted more holistic understanding of bodily functions, where circulation both across bodies and between bodies, souls and environments is fundamental to well-being. Second, biomedical bodies are 'mechanical': they operate according to a set of principles grounded in scientific evidence, carefully separated from beliefs or faith. For example, their response to either disease or cure is not understood as depending on anything other than internal physical responses, and it is disconnected from spirituality. In other systems, the relations between mind, body and faith are much more entangled, and the connections between bodies and spirituality understood as an integral part of healing and health. Similarly, those differences hint at the potential place that nature and cosmologies can play in bodily realities: while biomedicine tends to adopt an internal view of bodily health, where external factors can occasionally cause internal disruptions, other systems perceive bodies as more intimately connected to an outside world. Energies and their circulation may be prevalent in some systems of thought, while they will only figure in biomedicine where and if they can be explained through more mechanical explanations: as an illustration, understandings of acupuncture in traditional Chinese medicine—where the introduction of needles is seen as a way to trigger energy circulation—differ from those deployed in some of its more 'Western science'-based understandings, where the introduction of needles is seen as relevant only to its more immediate site. Overall, the separation between mind and body operated by biomedicine also has political implications in how biomedicine and institutions that surround it have come to relate to other therapeutic systems. In particular, biomedicine's grounding into mechanical understandings and explanations of the body, and its reliance on science, has meant that it has posited itself as being about 'reason', where others' reliance on faith and philosophy has been interpreted as producing a lesser form of knowledge. Finally, such understandings of bodies as 'mechanical' are illustrative of a final element worth pointing out here: those contrasting bodily ontologies also impact on conceptions of treatment. Biomedicine is characterised by its reliance on medicines as 'magic bullets': healing can be devolved to targeted interventions—drugs or surgery—that individually will 'fix' bodily dysfunctions. On the other hand, systems adopting a more holistic understanding of bodies will typically associate treatments with a view to target not only a specific symptom but also the broader imbalances that underlie it, including the wider social, environmental and spiritual context. Said otherwise, the source of illness, nor healing, cannot be circumscribed within the imagined impermeable borders of the body; instead, bodies are conceived in more dynamic terms as material entities embedded in complex assemblages of 'naturecultures' (Haraway 2000, 105).

It is worth, finally, pointing to the relation between different ontologies of bodies and healing, and their social and institutional implications. Some understandings of the body, including biomedical, may be able to organise and institutionalise healthcare as a standalone social and professional practice, delegated to particular spaces or individuals (the clinic and professionalised medicine). Others may be better suited or indistinguishable from a more diffused set of community practices, where prayers, food and ethics all contribute to being physically healthy. Whether illness is conceptualised as the result of a bodily response to external or internal disease-trigger, a disruption to the homeostatic order of the body's physiology (Mukherjee 2018), or as (e.g.) the poor circulation of vital energies, or the manifestation of unwelcome spirits (Bivins 2007), it will affect the determinations of who should be able and entitled to 'fixing' just the sick person. Contrasting understandings of the body, therefore, also have social and institutional ramifications.

Arguably, such reading can also be applied to practices that have a longer Western history and have sustained different experiences alongside biomedicine, as well as different social makings: for example, not only folk herbal medicine or faith healing but also the contemporary 'witchcraft' of our country-sides or that reclaimed by contemporary urban feminist witches (Sigal 2018). But those movements also reflect a different form of political challenge, enacted through the contestation of biomedical ontologies. Taking the example of mesmerism, Darnton (1986) demonstrates how the rise of the therapeutic movement in France was deeply entangled into revolutionary and post-revolutionary politics. Proposing a new way of understanding and dealing with bodies was also a way to push against the established socio-political order, and the role of science within it. Contemporary movements seeking to return to more 'natural' ways of healing can similarly be read as entangled with particular politics that seek to propose alternative worldings in which bodies, nature, and industries are rearranged.

Overall, looking at both the context of medical pluralism today and its long-standing history involves considering the coexistence of contrasting ways of living through and with bodies, and of imagining the world. Such differences are important to acknowledge in order to understand the gap between those seeking to appeal to patients' 'reason' by waving science-based arguments, and users of alternative therapies with whom those arguments may not echo: cosmopolitical tensions cannot be solved by 'politics of reason'. They are also important in understanding the depth of the regulatory limitations of scientific evidence. Instead of focusing primarily on scientific evidence produced, for example, through clinical trials, turning to other resources where vulnerability and care are brought back to the centre of the dilemma may be more productive. Feminist scholarship has often remarked how law has functioned symbolically, historically and normatively as a socio-political tool deployed to order and shape social worlds (Hunter 2017). Despite the appearance of universality, the law has been underpinned by a set of beliefs held largely by a white, male, politico-economic elite in Europe (including, as we have seen, in the context of medicine). By making visible the plurality of actors' histories and genealogies, social justice movements in the twentieth century have pushed the boundaries of traditional notions of law and justice, or of factuality and universal experience.

## 4 Vulnerability and Care Beyond Scientific Paradigms

But if the field of healing is about multiple ontologies, and coexisting worlds, it is also riddled with vulnerability. This is where the core dilemma we are continuing to work through is situated: illness, or the search for its prevention, highlights the complex nature of vulnerability in the relationships that patients experience. Some have argued that it creates an ontological shift of its own, a 'Cosmopolitics of illness' (Schillmaeir 2014). Similarly, it would be naïve to read the field of alternative healing as only being about multiple ontologies: to some extent, its multiplicity also makes it easier for unscrupulous or dangerous pseudo-healers to sustain their own claims as they create their own unfounded theories. If science is insufficient to separate the legitimate from the problematic, because it is not shared by all as a meaningful point of reference, a risk is to see some imitate ontological difference, or mimic new cosmopolitics, in order to build an image of legitimacy. Over the years, fraudulent healers have been found to cause significant harm to patients, and at times prosecuted for financial and physical abuses, as well as for infringing rules more specific to medical practice (medical malpractice and/or unauthorised medical practice) (Lavorgna and Di Ronco 2019). Scandals in healthcare contexts have increased the pressure on regulators to minimise abuse (Professional Standards Authority 2015; Ijaz et al. 2016). If such fraudulent healers cannot be taken as the norm of alternative healing, they illustrate one of the dangers of introducing too much relativism into scientific proof, and into law, and a helpful reminder of why critique of science as the arbiter of legitimacy in regulatory processes, and a turn to the relativism suggested by the multiple ontologies of healing, is not sufficient in itself. To illustrate this, one might think of pseudo-healers offering 'gay conversion therapy' or marketing their own 'radical' claims to newly discovered theories that require significant financial, physical (abandoning other treatments, extreme fasting, etc.) or personal sacrifices (e.g. cutting off family and community ties; renouncing biomedical offerings) from their clients with no external validation of their techniques, other than through their own telling. In recent years, fake cancer treatments that have resulted in patients' death where conventional treatment could have cured them have been a particular focus of attention from the media, as well as the judicial system (Lavorgna and Bishop 2019).

In stories of such abuse, a common feature is the surrendering to the narratives of healers who claim to have an unmediated access to a different kind of truth that requires the cutting of pre-existing ties in order to be accessed by others. This is often incentivised by claims to redefine entire fields of truth, promising healing through self-discovered techniques that would also challenge all pre-existing practices, and often borrow from both scientific languages and alternative philosophies to construct an illusion of credibility. If we were to simply acknowledge the coexistence of ontologies as something that law needs to account for, and argue for the withdrawal of 'reasonable politics' without other safeguards, we may be at a loss when distinguishing what belongs to alternative worlds and cosmopolitics, and what constitutes only their shadow. This is particularly so because such fraudulent practitioners often carefully imitate certain features of both biomedicine and long-standing traditional practices—borrowing languages and titles from the former, for example, and connections to faith or an interdependence of body and mind from the latter. Such patterns of rewriting, translating, mimicking and reclaiming highlight the embeddedness of vulnerabilities and impact on people's resilience, going beyond issues of genuine coexistence of multiple ontologies. They raise matters of ethics, or matters of care, that require us to think more carefully about the various systems at play. While thinking in terms of cosmopolitics may help us understand the stakes of fitting traditional Chinese medicine or Tibetan medicine into contemporary healthcare systems, it would probably give too much credit to some of the self-proclaimed 'heroes' of alternative healing, whose so-called discoveries primarily result (often knowingly) in harm rather than care. In order to explore how to work around this dilemma, and how to move beyond (or aside) science while maintaining some boundaries in care, we turn to the concepts of vulnerability and care.

Vulnerability is a ubiquitous and yet ambiguous term that is often associated with the potential of injurability. In the legal context, it also denotes situations where a person's naivety or other personal characteristics, such as disability, illness or even gender, create or aggravate power imbalances in a relationship. While metonimically associated with risk, harm, fragility, injurability and wounding, feminist and queer scholarship sought to re-appropriate it and deploy it as a call for a return to ethics beyond identity politics. Others, like Karen Barad and Anna Lowenhaupt Tsing, draw on vulnerability to describe deeply entangled worlds that inevitably 'cross-contaminate' (Dolphijn and Van der Tuin 2012; Lowenhaupt Tsing 2015). One of the greatest conceits emerging out of liberal capitalism is that of individualism. Of course, some legal entities may act as individuals, as if they can survive alone, and deny that their survival depends on making profit out of exploiting human and non-human beings. Rather than being a characteristic of identity, vulnerability marks unexpected and un-defined encounters where 'the self and the other are mutually engaged, and yet are irreducible the one to the other' (Shildrick 2001, 78). This view holds in sight the uniqueness of each world and accounts for collaborative and transformative entanglements between these worlds, without erasing their historical and material differences. While vulnerability entails working or moving through 'incommensurable layers of power and emotion' (ibid.) represented in both antagonist and agonistic encounters, it holds into account this ambivalence.

In legal studies, Martha Fineman opened up the field of inquiry by replacing the disembodied rational legal person with an embodied vulnerable person whilst holding on to the idea that state and law can rectify injustice (Fineman 2008; Wall 2008). Others, like Judith Butler and Isabell Lorey, have questioned the faith in the state and public institutions as 'protectors'. Indeed, they remind us that the state and other public authorities have been a source of precarity, understood as the differential allocation of injurability across socio-political categories, including gender, race, and class (Lorey 2015; Butler 2009). In other words, precarity is not simply a form of violence inflicted by a single powerful actor, but it is inflicted because of the unequal distribution of relationality and care on different groups, and implemented by more discrete actors who have been historically allowed to wield violence and domination over others, or who exert power through subtle or even 'benign' disciplinary technologies. As Ann V. Murphy argues, vulnerability's ambivalence resides in the fact that it signposts both the potential of care and violence (2012). In the context of alternative medicine, considerations of vulnerability may untangle the monopoly of biomedicine over body onto epistemologies (Barad 2007), without falling into a situation where harms may be subsumed by stale debates about cultural relativism. As regulators seek to confront the coexistence of worlds other than those of biomedicine, these critiques offer important insights into how some may fall out of its hands, while helping us refocus on what is at stake in them remaining, nonetheless, in the care of the state (Fineman 2019).

In the sections that follow, we propose that in order to progress in this contested field, we need to move beyond the search for scientific evidence and confront more thoroughly relational vulnerabilities. We seek to do this by turning our attention to practices of care. Following the double movement of recent scholarship on care (Puig de la Bellacasa 2011; Martin et al. 2015; Murphy 2011), we argue that care is both a useful guide to how alternative healing can be approached (i.e. as a way to care for the field, and stay with its trouble), and to what some of its core problematic is about (i.e. relational practices of care that surround and produce knowledges). This is a way to acknowledge and engage the vulnerabilities that define fields of healthcare practices, and to put the question of regulation back to the task of approaching the relations that foster such vulnerabilities, including market relations.

To a degree, healing is irremediably bound with care, insofar as the distress from illnesses calls for an action to be remedied. But restoring health, often understood as eliminating disease through effective and safe drugs, is not the same as 'good care'. As Annemarie Mol argues, as public accountability for healthcare converged in the mid-twentieth century with evidence based on clinical trials, other forms of care, particularly everyday care practices, have been neglected by public authorities (Mol 2006). Effectively, 'health-care' lost part of its meaning by turning scientific evidence in the laboratory as its synonym, and more importantly, it effaced the social dimension of embodied care. The effect on the ground is not only that people come to distrust biomedical solutions because they are partial but also that inadequate solutions are deployed for monitoring the field of alternative therapies. Rather than looking at situations where care has been denied or relationship of trust between a carer and a patient has been broken, policy and regulation may fetishise biomedical data as a marker for accountability in the context of healthcare. In that sense, we suggest reading 'care' as a way to disentangle the multiple cosmopolitics of healing from a straightforward regulatory solution.

In recent years, feminist STS scholarship has taken renewed interest in the notion of care (Martin et al. 2015). If the idea of caring has a range of everyday meanings, this work has largely been about reclaiming the complexity of the term 'care', a notion that can, but does not have to, build onto positive sentiments or affect. Care does not necessarily materialise either into healing, but as noted by Donna Haraway, caring confers caretakers with the power to objectify bodies (Haraway 2003). The relation of caring is one that is made up through social ties that run beyond the relationship of cared for and carer, and depends on the positionality of each in a broader kinship. At the same time, care has the potential to generate both healing and abuse, well-being and pain. Bearing this in mind, we can turn to the sharp edges of care and vulnerability in alternative medicine, and open up the space to consider multiple ontologies without falling into the traps of extremes, such as the distrust towards caring because it can be a mask of domination, nor an uncritical belief in the ethical power of the concepts of vulnerability and care. For example, Laura Foster notes the remnants of colonial narratives in the advertisements of traditional herbal products, showing the continuity of exploitative relations transposed to the global 'well-being' market (Foster 2016). Heeding to the ambiguity underpinning vulnerability, the later can be regarded as the departure point for care but not necessarily its destination (Murphy 2012). For this reason, we keep in mind Maria Puig de la Bellacasa's instigation to problematise 'the neglect of caring relationalities in an assemblage' (2011, p. 94), as well as the multiple standpoints that potentially hold together 'more sustainable caring relationalities and life conditions in an aching world' (ibid, p.100). Care is at the same time an object of study and a reminder of the need to engage the complex layering of relationships.

Turning to the multiple ways in which healers 'care for', vulnerable bodies may open a way to produce the form of triage that is inevitable in the context of healthcare between layers of practices more or less supported by the state, without stumbling into the circular trap of biomedicines' hierarchy over alternative medicines, nor allowing the excesses by impersonators to breed more general distrust and repression against traditional and alternative medicine practices. As austerity politics continue to squeeze the resources available within the public provision of health, broadening at the same time the marketplace of healing, 'care' is often the thing that disappears. As feminist and disability scholars have noted, wherever there is a gap of care, other actors will fill it out. In the absence of formal state structures of social and health safety, family members, often female, fulfil the role of social carers. But there are also opportunistic actors, from lone healers to corporate entrepreneurs, who prowl and scout for new markets in a deeply interconnected and highly profitable globalised world. Turning to care is not suggested here as a naïve search of the 'good' or benevolent healer over the 'bad' or harmful one. Instead, our interest is in care as a slippery notion, one that can be mobilised in contradictory ways, yet remains defined by relationships, and to some extent the response they provide to vulnerability. If focusing on care does one thing clearly, however, it is to remind us that scientific evidence is only one part of the complex puzzle that surrounds patients' bodies as they are healed or seek to be healed. While clinical trials can tell us about efficacy, for example, they are not able to engage with caring relationships: those cannot be tested blindly. Some would argue that this does not matter precisely because what we should be looking for in ordering and regulating practices is hard, objective evidence of bodily responses. Even if care and healing relationships matter, one could argue that they do not need to matter to the definition of which practices make it in and out of the health system, public or market-based. We suggest, however, that focusing away from efficacy (or rather from efficacy only) and towards relationships of care can help regulators confront the challenge of cosmopolitics in healthcare provision in at least two ways.

First, it enables us to 'remain with the trouble' (Haraway 2016). For sure, focusing away from science, or science only, takes us into murky territory: whether something is sufficiently proven or not is, after all, one straightforward way to settle answers about what practices can do to and for bodies. In spite of the limitations and imperfections that we highlighted above, it remains the easiest shortcut to worthiness that regulators can turn to where they need to 'side' with defenders or opponents of a particular practice. But in the everyday practice of healthcare, or as we may rephrase it, in seeking to redress vulnerabilities or build resilient bodies, softer processes are at play. Minding, caring, soothing and reassuring can all play a part in helping distraught bodies heal and improve, or preventing their vulnerabilities from becoming exposed. But harming, controlling and disempowering can also be part of the practice of care. Turning to care, however, is also about seeking to engage a different form of relationality and suggests a different problematisation of the debate. It reminds of the importance of thinking of things otherwise, of embracing their complexity, of gathering the affects and interests that surround and constitute practices, of the need to sketch out the vulnerabilities that they address or create or to pay attention to the agents involved without denying their voices or confronting them to a universal bodily experience. Engaging in careful mapping out of the field of healing and of what is at stake is also about dealing with the uncomfortable, and the relationality of healing, which cannot be resolved only through the workings of labs and chemicals. Instead of seeking to reduce complexity, to provide straightforward answers, it aims to negotiate with a relationality that is never only about 'reason'.

By recalibrating attention away from individual bodies and towards their relational vulnerability and healing, may also open other ways of looking for answers in how to order or regulate and decentre the idea of evidence from one of pure rationale. Patients' voices, in all their subjectivity, are more relevant to an analysis of healing as caring (whether gently or violently) than as one where healing is only about curing (whether it is efficacious or not). As resources continue to be limited by austerity politics, favouring proof of efficacy around relationality, approaches that seek to stay with the trouble can at least show that some choices are partly political, rather than purely reasonable. For example, deciding that herbal medicine should or should not be funded under the NHS can be presented not only as a response to the efficacy of herbal medicine but also as a judgement on the effectiveness of the type of consultations herbalists offer—smells, touch, talks as well as biological properties. Because care is more 'slippery' (Martin et al. 2015) than scientific proof, it reminds us that resolution is likely to be partial in any regulatory mapping, and that boundary-drawing involves playing through multiple registers and criteria, and re-evaluating whose voices are relevant.

Second, focusing on care may enable us to rethink normative boundaries, even if it doesn't in itself give us ready-made normative answers. In other words, it may give a way to argue for the state to remain involved, in a lighter touch, and through other paradigms, where science (or lack thereof) cannot justify interventions. As we have highlighted, a danger with embracing the multiplicity of bodily ontology, and of healing ontologies, is to renounce any form of judgement over the legitimacy of particular practices. But we may still want to draw lines between, for example, systems of indigenous or traditional healing that are derived from long-standing and communal views of bodily health, and the preaching of proponents of gay conversion therapy, or of healers who claim radical pseudo-scientific and entirely self-referential 'new theories' and may even use them to abuse, physically or financially, their own 'patients' or effectively drive them away from proven medical treatments that could have improved their health outcomes. Fundamental differences exist between these scenarios, however, that provide social markers that may be used to define the legitimate from the illegitimate. If care is one factor in shaping vulnerability, agreeing on common principles of care may also be more possible where unreconcilable ontologies are at play, thus offering a way to agree on norms of care rather than needing an external single truth to mediate these relationships. We do not wish here to make overbearing claims on what 'good' and 'bad' care can look like, and our interest is in seeking a starting point rather than a concluding one. But by shifting away from 'matters of fact' to 'matters of care', debates around healing and how to regulate it could benefit from the development of shared principles on how to care for vulnerable bodies not only within the formal state system of health but also beyond: caring could involve acknowledging roots rather than individual power; it may involve caring for a shared idea of justice in which identities are not disrupted, challenged, or sought to be rewritten; protecting social ties, or family ties, rather than seeking to undo them; or it may require a mutual respect for the very same multiplicity of ontologies that enabled the unproven to remain (including that of biomedicine). Focusing on care rather than truth would pave the way towards a different type of decision-making and valuing as far as healing practices are concerned. Where the state has so far disengaged, leaving aside the difficult questions of how to organise the marketplace of non-biomedical healing, we may instead want it to find new ways of dealing with the multiple ontologies that underlie this field. If care cannot in itself provide us with normative answers, it can open new ways of negotiating normative boundaries. Drawing on these fragile and cross-contaminated 'onto-epistemologies' loosens the hold of biomedicine and the law over the body, drawing attention to how 'practices of knowing and being' are thoroughly intertwined in 'material practices'(Barad 2007, 379). Attentiveness to practices of care rather than claims to care (Martin et al. 2015) could shift the attention to the ways in which care is an assemblage of people rather than the individualistic and 'heroic' act of a guru with the 'power' to heal.

## 5 Conclusion

Our purpose in this chapter has been to explore the regulation of alternative and traditional medicine through a new lens in order to both grapple with the dilemma it raises and propose some (modest) ways forward. We have started from the observation that law is at a loss with the cosmopolitics of healing and their diversity. Similarly, the multiplicity of bodily ontologies that have continued to become visible and to be claimed in the past decades have created ongoing pressures for the regulation of healthcare. Rather than approaching those purely through 'reasonable politics', as regulators have tended to do, a turn to a critical and relational approach to care may open some ways forward in apprehending the dilemmas at play. Imposing biomedical understandings of therapeutic care as being the only valid viewpoints, or the only ones worth explicitly engaging with, because they are the only 'proven' ones, has too often resulted in the shutting down of alternative ontologies, and their silencing (rather than disappearance). At the same time, recognising such multiplicity runs the risk of entirely doing away with both notions of proof and standards of care, which dangerously opens the door to a form of relativism in practice that can feed onto vulnerabilities and enable abusive practices. The dilemma becomes one of acknowledging multiple ontologies in care while drawing new lines of practice that enable vulnerabilities to remain accounted for. In this chapter, we have proposed that turning to feminist understandings of care and vulnerability, and focusing on networks of relationships rather than primarily on 'efficacy' can give us some ways forwards both in understanding the dilemmas faced by regulators and in side-stepping some of the dead-ends that they have encountered.

## References


Adams, V. (2002). Randomized Controlled Crime: Postcolonial Sciences in Alternative Medicine Research. *Social Studies of Science, 32*(5), 659–690.

Adams, V., Miller, S., Craig, S., Nyima, S., Droyoung, L., & Varner, M. (2005). The Challenge of Cross-Cultural Clinical Trials Research: Case Report from the Tibetan Autonomous Region, People's Republic of China. *Medical Anthropology Quarterly, 19*(3), 267–289.

Barad, K. (2007). *Meeting the Universe Halfway: Quantum Physics and the Entanglement of Matter and Meaning*. Durham: Duke University Press.

Bivins, R. (2007). *Alternative Medicine: A History*. Oxford: Oxford University Press.

Blaser, M. (2013). Is Another Cosmopolitics Possible? *Cultural Anthropology, 31*(4), 545–570. https://doi.org/10.14506/ca31.4.05.

Butler, J. (2009). *Frames of War: When Is Life Grievable*. London: Verso.

CAMDOC Alliance. (2010). *The Regulatory Status of Complementary and Alternative Medicine for Medical Doctors in Europe*. Brussels.

Cook, H. J. (1990). The Rose Case Reconsidered: Physicians, Apothecaries, and the Law in Augustan England. *The Journal of History of Medicine and Alied Sciences, 45*(November), 527–555. https://doi.org/10.1093/jhmas/45.4.527.

Darnton, R. (1986). *Mesmerism and the End of the Enlightenment in France*. Harvard: Harvard University Press.

Dolphijn, Rick, & Van der Tuin, Iris. (2012). 'Matter Feels, Converses, Suffers, Desires, Yearns and Remembers' Interview with Karen Barad. In *New Materialism: Interviews & Cartographies*. Hosted by MPublishing: Open Humanities Press. http://quod.lib.umich.edu/o/ohp/11515701.0001.001/1:4.3/%2D%2Dnew-materialism-interviews-cartographies?rgn=div2;view=fulltext#note_1

Ehrenreich, B., & English, D. (2010). *Witches, Midwives, & Nurses: A History of Women Healers*. New York: Feminist Press.

Fineman, M. A. (2008). The Vulnerable Subject: Anchoring Equality in the Human Condition. *Yale Journal of Law and Feminism, 20*, 1–23.

Fineman, M. A. (2019) "Vulnerability in Law and Bioethics." Journal of health care for the poor and underserved *30*(5): 52–61.

Foster, L. A. (2016). Decolonizing Patent Law: Postcolonial Technoscience and Decolonizing Patent Law: Postcolonial Technoscience and Indigenous Knowledge in South Africa. *Feminist Formations, 28*(3), 148–173.

Friesen, P (2019) "Mesmer, the placebo effect, and the efficacy paradox: Lessons for evidence based medicine and complementary and alternative medicine." *Critical Public Health, 29*(4): 435–447.

Goffman, E. (2006). Selections Froms Stigma. *The Disability Studies Reader*, 131–140.

Green, M. (1997). Witchcraft Suppression Practices and Movements: Public Politics and the Logic of Purification. *Comparative Studies in Society and History, 39*(02), 319–345. https://doi.org/10.1017/S0010417500020648.

Griggs, B. (1997). *Green Pharmacy: A History of Herbal Medicine*. Rochester: Healing Arts Press.

Harrington, A (1999) "Introduction". In *The placebo effect: An interdisciplinary exploration, edited by Anne Harrington* Cambridge and London: Harvard University Press.

Haraway, D. (2000). *How Like a Leaf: An Interview with Thyrza Nichols Goodeve*. New York: Routledge.

Haraway, D. (2003). Situated Knowledges: The Science Question in Feminism and the Privilege of Partial Perspective. In Y. S. Lincoln & N. K. Denzin (Eds.), *Turning Points in Qualitative Research: Tying Knots in a Handkerchief* (pp. 21–46). Walnut Creek: Altamira Press.

Haraway, D. (2016). *Staying with the Trouble: Making Kin in the Chthulucene*. Durham: Duke University Press.

Hunter, Rosemary. (2017). The Implementation of Feminist Law Reforms: The Case of Post-Provocation Sentencing. https://doi.org/10.1177/0964663916666628.

Ijaz, N., Boon, H., Muzzin, L., & Welsh, S. (2016). State Risk Discourse and the Regulatory Preservation of Traditional Medicine Knowledge: The Case of Acupuncture in Ontario, Canada. *Social Science & Medicine, 170*, 97–105. https://doi.org/10.1016/j.socscimed.2016.08.037.

Janes, Craig R. (1999) "The health transition, global modernity and the crisis of traditional medicine: the Tibetan case." *Social Science & Medicine, 48*(12): 1803–1820.

Jin, L. (2010). From Mainstream to Marginal? Trends in the Use of Chinese Medicine in China from 1991 to 2004. *Social Science & Medicine, 71*(6), 1063–1067. https://doi.org/10.1016/j.socscimed.2010.06.019.

Lavorgna, A., & Bishop, F. L. (2019). Framing of CAM-Adjacent Health Scams in the UK Media. In *Medical Misinformation and Social Harm in Non-Science Based Health Practices: A Multidisciplinary Perspective* (pp. 147–161). London: Routledge.

Lavorgna, A., & Di Ronco, A. (2019). Introduction. In A. Lavorgna & A. Di Ronco (Eds.), *Medical Misinformation and Social Harm in Non-Science Based Health Practices: A Multidisciplinary Perspective* (pp. 1–6). London: Routledge.

Lin, W.-y., & Law, J. (2019). A Correlative STS: Lessons from a Chinese Medical Practice a Correlative STS: Lessons from a Chinese Medical Practice. *Social Studies of Science, 44*(6), 801–824.

Lorey, I. (2015). In A. Derieg (Ed.), *State of Insecurity: Government of the Precarious*. London: Verso.

Lowenhaupt Tsing, A. (2015). *The Mushroom at the End of the World: On the Possibility of Life in Capitalis Ruins*. Princeton/Oxford: Princeton University Press.

Lunstroth, J. (2006). Voluntary Self-Regulation of Complementary and Alternative Medicine Practitioners. *Albany Law Review, 70*(1932), 209–302.

MacLennan, E., & Pendry, B. A. (2011). The Evolution of Herbal Medicine as an Unorthodox Branch of British Medicine: The Role of English Legislation from 1914 to the Present Day. *Journal of Herbal Medicine, 1*(2), 35–41. https://doi.org/10.1016/j.hermed.2011.08.002.

Martin, A., Myers, N., Viseu, A., & Myers, N. (2015). The Politics of Care in Technoscience. *Social Studies of Science, 45*(5), 625–641. https://doi.org/10.1177/0306312715603249.

Meakin, R., & Jackson-Main, P. (2018). Plus Ca Change? The Case for Complementary and Alternative Medicine Charities. *The Charity Law & Practice Review, 20*, 1–24.

Mol, A. (2003). *The Body Multiple: Ontology in Medical Practice*. Durham: Duke University Press.

Mol, A. (2006). Proving or Improving: On Health Care Research as a Form of Self-Reflection. *Qualitative Health Research, 16*(3), 405–414. https://doi.org/10.1177/1049732305285856.

Mukherjee, Siddhartha. (2018, July). My Father's Body, at Rest and in Motion. *The New Yorker*. https://www.newyorker.com/magazine/2018/01/08/my-fathers-body-at-rest-and-in-motion

Murphy, A. V. (2011). Corporeal Vulnerability and the New Humanism. *Hypatia, 26*(3), 575–590. https://doi.org/10.1111/j.1527-2001.2011.01202.x.

Murphy, A. V. (2012). *Violence and the Philosophical Imaginary*. Albany: State University of New York Press.

NHS England. (2017). *Items Which Should Not Be Routinely Prescribed in Primary Care: A Consultation on Guidance for CCGs*. London. https://www.engage.england.nhs.uk/consultation/items-routinely-prescribed/

Pickersgill, M. (2013). Sociotechnical Innovation in Mental Health: Articulating Complexity. In M. L. Flear, A. Farrell, T. K. Hervey, & T. Murphy (Eds.), *European Law and New Health Technologies* (pp. 323–342). Oxford: Oxford University Press.

Pollock, A. (2014). Places of Pharmaceutical Knowledge-Making: Global Health, Postcolonial Science and Hope in South African Drug Discovery. *Social Studies of Science, 44*(6), 848–873. https://doi.org/10.1177/0306312714543285.

Porter, Roy. (1999). *The Greatest Benefit to Mankind: A Medical History of Humanity from Antiquity to the Present*. Paperback. London: Fontana Press.

Professional Standards Authority. (2015). *The Role of Risk in Regulatory Policy*.

Professional Standards Authority. (2017). *Untapped Resources: Accredited Registers in the Wider Workforce*. https://www.professionalstandards.org.uk/docs/default-source/publications/untapped-resources%2D%2D-accredited-registers-in-the-wider-workforce-november-2017.pdf?sfvrsn=0

Puig de la Bellacasa, M. (2011). Matters of Care in Technoscience: Assembling Neglected Things. *Social Studies of Science, 41*(1), 85–106. https://doi.org/10.1177/0306312710380301.

Pym, Hugh. (2019). Minister Targets Anti-Vaccination Websites. *BBC*. https://www.bbc.co.uk/news/health-47699791

Schillmaeir, M. (2014). *Eventful Bodies: The Cosmopolitics of Illness*. Oxon: Ashgate Publishing.

Shildrick, M. (2001). *Embodying the Monster: Encounters with the Vulnerable Self*. London: Sage.

Sibbritt, D., Kaye, M., Millbank, J., Stuhmcke, A., Wardle, J., & Karpin, I. (2018). How Are Complementary Health Professions Regulated in Australia? An Examination of Complementary Health Professions in the National Registration and Accreditation Scheme. *Complementary Therapies in Medicine, 37*(January), 6–12. https://doi.org/10.1016/j.ctim.2017.12.012.

Sigal, Samuel. (2018, November). The Witches of Baltimore. *The Atlantic*. https://www.theatlantic.com/international/archive/2018/11/black-millennials-african-witchcraft-christianity/574393/

Stengers, I. (2005) "The Cosmopolitical Proposal." In *Making Things Public: Atmospheres of Democracy*, edited by Bruno Latour and Peter Weibel. 994–1004. Cambridge, MA: MIT Press.

Subramaniam, B. (2009). Metamorphoses: A Retrospective Essay on Feminist Science Studies. *Signs: Journal of Women in Culture and Society, 34*(4), 951–980.

Wall, I. R. (2008). On Pain and the Sense of Human Rights. *Australian Feminist Law Journal, 29*, 53–76.

Yoga in Healthcare Alliance. (2019). *Yoga on Social Prescription*. https://yogainhealthcarealliance.com/yoga-on-social-prescription/

# Part II

## Bodies of Health

# 6

# Temporal Bodies: Emergencies, Emergence, and Intersex Embodiment

Fae Garland and Mitchell Travis

## 1 Introduction

Intersex people include a wide range of physical variations that at the gonadal, hormonal, or chromosomal level gives the individual a combination of masculine and feminine characteristics. Some intersex variations are present at birth where the child's genitalia appear 'ambiguous' in terms of sex. In these cases, the medical profession presents parents with the dilemma of whether the child should undergo gender-normalising surgery and, if so, when (Groveman 1998; Chase 1998). While this decision must be made in the child's best interests, there is widespread concern that healthcare is inappropriately framing intersex embodiment as an emergency requiring action and intervention in order to 'fix' the child and subsequently end the emergency. Troublingly, even within healthcare literature and guidelines, the main emergency that medical professionals are responding to is not the intersex variations themselves (which are routinely benign—Zillén et al. 2017) but are instead aimed at managing societal and familial reactions to intersex variations. Surgical interventions to 'correct' the intersex variation are, in the

F. Garland (✉)
University of Manchester, Manchester, UK
e-mail: fae.garland@manchester.ac.uk

M. Travis
School of Law, University of Leeds, Leeds, UK
e-mail: M.Travis@leeds.ac.uk



C. Dietz et al. (eds.), *A Jurisprudence of the Body*, Palgrave Socio-Legal Studies,
https://doi.org/10.1007/978-3-030-42200-4_6

majority of circumstances, therefore medically unnecessary. Moreover, research has demonstrated that these procedures are harmful, and consequently, in the absence of the individual's consent, these medical interventions have been declared to be manifest breaches of human rights by both the academy and International Human Rights Bodies. Nevertheless, States are failing to prohibit such practice and healthcare continues to routinely offer bio-medical 'solutions' in the form of 'normalising' genital surgeries to 'fix' social emergencies. Indeed, in the English and Welsh context at present, juridical and clinical assessments of best interests have done little to afford intersex embodied infants any real protections from these gender-normalising interventions. This chapter is, therefore, part of a broader project by the authors to explore the systemic reasons as to why States are failing to disrupt medical power/knowledge in this area and consider how States can be compelled to act.

In particular, this chapter reflects on the way in which the medical profession uses time, or rather temporality, to prevent threats to its power/knowledge in this area. Time is a measurement through which we measure change or duration and is usually measured as progression into the future while present events are continuously relegated to the past. In contrast, temporality refers to the way in which time is experienced or constructed. Bodies are, consequently, always temporal. Institutions, such as healthcare, the law, or the family, in which bodies are continuously embedded and dependent, generate multiple modes of temporality that are crucial to the ways that bodies are understood within society. These institutional temporalities have an important effect on the distribution of resources and responsibilities as they dictate how the state responds to these issues. Whilst some public health responses, for example, are understood in terms of 'crises,' and thus deserving of immediate financial investment, other issues that could be the subject of public health interventions are constructed as 'normality' and thus less deserving of financial aid (Lewis and Thomson 2019). As a consequence, it is vital to understand institutional temporalities as political acts rather than as 'natural' or 'inevitable.' Using this temporal lens, this chapter argues that the medical profession uses temporality and particularly the concept of emergency to further evade present and future processes of external scrutiny that challenges its medical power/knowledge. Whilst intersex variations are congenital and thus lifelong, they are often treated within the institution of healthcare as episodic, occurring at different points of the life course for acute and discrete periods of time. As a result, healthcare has been able to frame intersex variations as emergencies to create a sense of immediacy that does not just justify but *necessitates* medical intervention typically before the child is 12 months old (Lee et al. 2006).

Our purpose for this chapter, therefore, is more than mere intellectual inquiry. Rather we intend our analysis to have practical effect on the way in which the State and healthcare approach intersex embodiment. By revealing the responsibility gap created through healthcare's use of temporality, we argue that the temporal shift from emergency to emergence must be State-led, specifically through legislation. Highlighting the ways in which healthcare institutions construct temporality allows us to rethink the inevitability of clinical decision making in this area. For instance, the chronic (lifelong) nature of intersex variances demands an understanding of the intersex body throughout the life course. Such a focus allows for consideration of the child as emergent rather than an isolated and discrete temporal event somehow divorced from adulthood. An approach attentive to these issues of temporality is capable of considering solutions to social emergencies through the monitoring and adjustment of institutions—not through the alteration of children's bodies. Whilst acknowledging the plurality of different experiences of medical temporality, we argue that a psychosocial understanding of temporality in the context of healthcare is more in keeping with this temporal reframing as it is better able to consider the life course of the person. Furthermore, recent legislative shifts that are attentive to temporality such as Malta's Gender Identity, Gender Expression and Sex Characteristics Act 2015 may offer examples of best practice to policy makers whilst supporting psychosocial approaches. Building on this, this chapter offers the concept of deferability as an important new aspect in determining clinical and juridical best interests assessments. Whilst deferability has been discussed in some case law, its application has been ad-hoc and primarily arisen where there has been a dispute between parents or between parents and healthcare professionals. In this chapter we outline deferability as an important new tool capable of assessing institutional accounts of temporality allowing for delineation between emergencies and non-emergencies. As such, deferability offers legal theorists a way in which to monitor and evaluate the temporal constructions of societal institutions significantly adding to best interests assessments. Furthermore, this chapter offers guidance on how States should respond to and alter these institutional responses by highlighting the need for them to reconsider their role in temporal constructions of the body.

## 2 Temporality

Whilst culturally, it is acknowledged that time can go slowly or quickly, thicken, or even seem to stop, this malleability of temporality is something that is rarely acknowledged within law or healthcare. Humans are unusual amongst animals in the sense that their understandings of time are dictated through objects (seen as objective measures) and institutions rather than relying solely on the environment (Birth 2012: 2). As Greenhouse notes, "As new institutional forms developed—industrial workshops, the state, contracts and courts—different forms of time multiplied as they were juxtaposed in contiguous social fields" (1989: 1636). Temporality, or the ways in which time is experienced and mediated through these institutions, has been an under-explored variable in the shaping of clinical and juridical judgement. Recently, temporality has received a renewed invigoration of interest from legal philosophers (Valverde 2009, 2015; Grabham 2011, 2014, 2017; Harrington 2016; McNeilly 2018; Gordon-Bouvier 2019). For these scholars time plays an important part in the ways in which law is understood; time is not linear, self-sufficient, nor objective. In different contexts, spaces, and jurisdictions, time can be understood in quite different and sometimes competing ways.

Liberal approaches to time have tended to emphasise the universality, objectivity, and linearity of time. Key to this construction has been the idea of "progress" through time that connect past societies to future ideals (Greenhouse 1989: 1638). Drawing upon Fitzpatrick, Harrington argues that the project of liberal legalism represents time "spatially as a series of discrete containers, helping to realize the positivist goal of sharply distinguishing law from its wider social environment" (Harrington 2016: 74; Fitzpatrick 2001: 93). This 'liberal' conception of time is similarly reproduced in healthcare and will be examined in more detail in the following section. Liberal understandings of time as 'discrete containers' has led to a lack of juridical focus on the life course. Instead, law has tended to catalogue its subjects through categories such as age with a concomitant understanding of events as distinct and singular. More often than not, therefore, law fails to identify the power relations that are played out in the political constructions of temporality. As Emily Grabham notes, "Time is expressed, and lived out, through an imminent sense of the forthcoming, but it is also the subject of power relations through which agents' engagement with the field can be directed or shaped" (Grabham 2011: 113). Temporality therefore is expressly political in state determinations of resources and responsibility. This leads Greenhouse to conclude that "If linear time dominates our public lives it is because its primary efficacy is in the construction and management of dominant social institutions, not because it is the only "kind" of time that is culturally available" (1989: 1637).

Temporality is always constructed through our relations with the social—and must, consequently, be understood in terms of its political utility. Whilst the state has maintained monopolies over the construction of 'universal time' (Greenhouse 1989) even within the state, temporality cannot be understood as singular or monolithic as different aspects of the assemblage of the state compete over the governance and meanings of time. Similarly, different institutions—also seeking to govern their own jurisdictions—will construct temporality in different and competing ways. As such, temporality must be understood as multiple and can be seen as a process of 'sorting' "through which human and non-human actors create the temporalities that structure legal and policy landscapes" (Grabham 2014: 69). Focusing on the temporal aspects of law can help us to understand the reasons behind the internal inconsistencies within a number of policy developments or legal judgements. Such investigations help to uncover situations in which struggles over time can conceal "basic ethical and political values" (Harrington 2016: 71) as well as illuminate the "normative underpinnings of apparently loosely related governmental projects" (Grabham 2011: 122). Moreover, such approaches push the temporal to the forefront of political and legal analysis acknowledging that temporality is "a co-product of action, or action itself, not a background for action" (Grabham 2014: 73). Importantly for this chapter, temporality can be understood as playing a central function in the justification of institutional responsibilities. Where previous work demonstrated how medical nomenclature enabled the State to avoid responsibility for intersex by deferring to an arbitrary medical jurisdiction (Garland and Travis 2020), this chapter argues that bio-medical power/knowledge has been further strengthened by healthcare's temporal framing of intersex. Temporality, it seems, is being used not only to justify non-therapeutic medical interventions on intersex infants but also to abrogate the responsibility of the medical profession in the face of mounting external scrutiny. The next two sections set out the problematic ways in which healthcare has framed intersex embodiment as an emergency.

## 3 Emergency

As medical technology advanced throughout the course of the twentieth century, the medical profession increasingly expanded its jurisdictional remit to include intersex variations, reframing them as 'diseases' or 'disorders' of sex development, which necessitate 'fixing' through medical interventions (Griffiths 2018a, b; Fausto-Sterling 2000). In many ways, the medical timeframes of intersex embodiment remain reliant on the early work of John Money, who claimed that "age eighteen months was the temporal limit for deciding which gender a child would be raised, since during this period gender identity and role should be stabilized" (Meoded Danon 2018: 91). The first 18 months of childhood remain the medical professions' ideal time for these surgeries to take place (Lee et al. 2006). This medical co-opting of intersex has meant that this type of embodiment has become understood as temporal—depicted by key medical professionals (notably endocrinologists, surgeons, and urologists) as a discrete state of emergency in childhood that becomes apparent upon the discovery of an intersex variation. Whilst we acknowledge this state of emergency is co-produced through the social anxieties of parents, as we will discuss further in this chapter, there are alternate approaches to intersex embodiment that might serve to de-escalate the anxieties of parents. Healthcare professionals and their framing of intersex embodiment serve as the dominant actors in the temporal construction of the body. This medical framing powerfully serves to justify the 'gender assignment in newborns' as a necessity arising from the intersex variance in question. As Meoded Danon notes, "the diagnostic timeframe for intersex bodies … aims to speed treatment decisions and medical interventions for intersex babies and children in order to assign their bodies to a particular gender" (2018, 90). The 'hows and whens' of medical intervention serve to illustrate their inevitability even where 'the child' and family members are involved in the decision-making process. This viewpoint is typical of a dominant bio-medical narrative that understands intersex embodiment as a state of emergency solely located in childhood (Fausto-Sterling 2000) or as an exception to professional standards around bodily integrity, cosmetic surgery, and consent (Davis and Murphy 2013; Harrington 2016).

However, much recent work around intersex and non-therapeutic medical intervention has sought to disentangle immediate and deferrable interventions (Monro et al. 2017; Amnesty International 2017; Garland et al. 2019; Horowicz 2017; Zillén et al. 2017; Garland and Slokenberga 2018) particularly given that nearly all intersex variations do not threaten the life or health of the individual, but may render the genitals as 'atypical.' Congenital adrenal hyperplasia (CAH), for example, is one of the most common forms of intersex variation, and the treatment protocols developed for it have had wide-ranging implications for the clinical management of other intersex variations (Newbould 2017). CAH is a variance wherein some of the hormones (cortisol and aldosterone) within the adrenal cortex are absent. The consequence of this can be life-threatening in that the individual cannot retain salt and thus requires immediate life-saving hormonal treatment. In addition, CAH can lead to the overproduction of testosterone, which causes the infant to have ambiguous genitalia. Thus, when an infant is born with ambiguous genitalia, it *may* be an indicator of CAH and therefore necessitates immediate tests to ensure that the infant does not have salt-wasting CAH. However, the ambiguous genitalia are not—themselves—life-threatening. Nevertheless, there has been a medical reluctance to distinguish between the CAH emergency and the CAH resulting in genital ambiguity (Newbould 2017). This has meant that historically treatments to correct life-threatening salt-wasting have been done in conjunction with the cosmetic construction of the genitals. 'Fixing' the genital ambiguity has been depicted as part and parcel of 'fixing' CAH. Yet, even while some intersex variations are accompanied by a certain level of medical emergency, it is still possible to distinguish between immediate and deferrable interventions. Clearly, we can see a distinction between the necessity of life-saving surgery and the deferability of surgery conducted for aesthetic or social reasons. Whilst salt-wasting is an inherent material issue that requires medical support in order to live, the need to 'normalise' ambiguous genitalia is profoundly shaped by the embedded cultural and societal contexts in which intersex embodied people find themselves.

Healthcare professionals' claims of emergency are thus exposed as social rather than medical. Nonetheless, the construction of emergency has important legal effects on law. In negligence cases, for example, it is easier for a defendant to show that they acted reasonably and met the standard of care in an emergency situation.[1] Whilst international consensus statements have favoured the idea of deferring surgical intervention, healthcare practitioners continue to believe that these surgeries relieve parental anxieties and so routinely practise these surgeries (Liao et al. 2019). The focus on familial anxiety highlights these issues as social rather than arising from the intersex variation itself. Emily Grabham highlights two medical temporalities that undergird these 'emergencies'; the "cascading time of sex development" and the "time of repair and retrieval" (2012: 7). In the cascading time of sex development, sex differentiation is constructed as a linear development—clearly definable, traceable, and mappable. As Grabham writes "sex is produced through a sequencing effect, where hormonal, gonadal and morphological stages follow on from each other" (Grabham 2012: 8). These medical explanations are presented as 'natural' and deviations from this linearity as 'disordered' and in

[1] See *Ng Chun Pui v Lee Chuen Tat* [1988] RTR 298, 302 per Lord Griffiths and *Wilsher v Essex AHA* [1987] QB 730, 749 per Mustill LJ.

need of intervention in order to alleviate the social anxieties caused by such atypicality. Here, it is useful to reflect on the term 'order' referring to the arrangements of events in time. 'Disorder,' in turn, is used as a temporal judgement meaning to 'disturb the order of.'[2] The temporal roots of order and disorder then are useful for reflecting on the 'inevitable' and 'natural' progression of events that healthcare practitioners assume. Grabham notes how these temporal constructions of biological (foetal) development reinforce heteronormative and patriarchal understandings of sexuality and the passive feminine subject even at the hormonal and chromosomal levels (2012: 9–10).[3] These temporal constructions of disordered sexual development are used to justify the concept of 'medical emergency' as a 'reordering' in the present. Thus, whilst medical emergency harbours an innate governing logic of presentism it is based within a medical understanding of abnormality anchored to past failures of the body to develop along 'normal' lines.

This maps onto the second of Grabham's medical temporalities, which she refers to as the "time of repair and retrieval" (2012: 7). In relation to intersex embodiment, retrieval forms one of the underlying rationalities for surgery through the "refashioning [of] developmental time lines" (Grabham 2012: 12). Thus, retrieval is reliant upon a nostalgic temporality that harks back to a developmental stage where the child was not intersex (Morland 2006; Griffiths 2020). Whilst such a stage never existed, it certainly cannot be retrieved, and yet this logic continues to lie beneath medical justifications in this area, lending further weight to the logic of medical emergency. The governing rationality of repair contains similar problems of temporality. Grabham highlights three particular problems with repair: incrementalism, follow-up surgeries, and medical learning curves (Grabham 2012). Incrementalism pertains to a medical conceptual logic that considers surgeries as singular and isolated considering "one body part at a time" (Roen 2008: 52; Creighton et al. 2001; See also Fox et al. 2020). This type of medical approach fails to consider the cumulative effects that such surgeries have on the intersex embodied child as the temporal logic of emergency presents these interventions as isolated and discrete events. This is bound up with the second point, that of repeat surgeries. Unplanned follow-up medical interventions after the initial non-therapeutic surgical/medical interventions on children are exceedingly common and range from vaginal dilation to dependency on hormones after the removal of gonads and to repeat surgical procedures. One study found, for

---

[2] We are grateful to David Griffiths for this point.

[3] Grabham highlights how popular accounts of the ovum are often represented as passive when in fact that are highly active and discrimianting in choosing the sperm cells that they envelop (2012: 9–10).

example, that 89% of genitoplasties (planned as one-stage procedures) required at least one further major surgery (Creighton et al. 2001). In part, the high frequency of these follow-ups is because of the young ages of the 'patient' and because of the (often) experimental nature of the techniques utilised. As Grabham notes:

> Going back is a linear reversal or detour, the object of which is a moment in the past which is temporally different from present action.... In fact, locating the problem in the past enables what would otherwise be classed as 'new' procedures and provides a justifying context for the associated risks of those procedures. (Grabham 2012: 13)

Here, the understanding of intersex variations as episodic enables the 'fixing' mentality that characterises the medical profession's approach to intersex embodiment—even where the harms in need of repair have been caused by initial medical interventions. The final medical temporality that Grabham identifies is that of the learning curve. In this temporality, the justification for intervention is placed in the future—at an undefined time where treatments are improved. For Grabham, this allows "relatively unpracticed procedures to take place in the present, which may later become the object of 'repair' surgeries" (Grabham 2012: 13–14). A recent study has confirmed the presence of these beliefs within the medical professional with participants "maintaining a high level of professional confidence in preserving clitoral sensitivity while normalising genital appearance" (Liao et al. 2019: 4). Poor results in surgeries are either attributed to older techniques or as unique to other teams (Liao et al. 2019: 4; Meoded Danon 2018: 91). Ultimately, this leads to a situation where "parents' and patients' decisions are not being guided by realistic risk information" (Liao et al. 2019: 5). Intersex variations are still being constructed as something that can be 'fixed' even where these medical interventions ultimately harm intersex people.

Similarly located in an imagined future, as a justification of their position, some surgeons have made reference to social rather than medical concerns (or emergencies) such as "the locker room test"—referring to the idea that children may be bullied at school if their genitalia are revealed to their peer group (Griffiths 2020; Fausto-Sterling 2000; Meoded Danon 2018). In the largest study of medical professionals working with intersex children, Liao et al. found that none of the participants had come across instances of children being bullied for their genital appearance (2019: 3). Nonetheless, "unmanageable negative psycho-social consequences were generally assumed" (Liao et al. 2019: 3). Such justifications ignore the very real and immediate harms wrought through surgery on the child in the present in favour of focusing on imagined harms that locate the intersex person in a state of perpetual adolescence (in the locker room, at the urinal, dating, having sex) (for similar arguments in the context of disability see Fox et al. 2020).

At the same time, we can identify a competing temporal logic whereby both medical practitioners and parents (who are often important drivers of such surgeries) fail to engage with the very real concerns around sexual pleasure (or even infertility) of intersex embodied people post-surgery. Whilst in the preceding paragraph the spectre of sex was used to justify surgery—form of the genitalia seems to be prioritised over the pleasure of the intersex person. Reconstructive surgeries often leave the individual with 'functional genitalia' but with very little sensitivity due to the removal of nerve endings and excess scar tissue. These disparities highlight the normative underpinnings of these interventions—both justifications conceal a medical concern with the preservation of the gender binary and heteronormativity being played out through constructions of temporality. Temporal aspects of medical conceptions that perpetuate the infantilisation of the intersex person through episodic accounts of intersex variances thus have an important function in continuing to privilege the power/knowledge of the medical practitioner over and above the experiences of the patient, child, or intersex person. These surgeries, rather than helping to improve the lives of individuals actually serve to create lifelong negative physical consequences, lead to dependency on the medical profession and serve to damage the individual's relationships with core institutions such as the family and education (Garland and Travis 2020; Meoded Danon 2018). Moreover, Meoded Danon notes the non-linear haunting effect of these medical interventions, where "early irreversible surgeries … are not necessarily forgotten over time, but rather remembered and present in various somatic responses" (2018: 89). This non-linearity also highlights that medical knowledge and constructions of time in this area are neither singular nor monolithic.

Notably, the medical conceptualisation of intersex as an emergency not only diminishes the resilience of intersex embodied persons but also serves as a mechanism through which the medical profession creates a future-proof jurisdiction that is (largely) free from external scrutiny (Garland and Travis 2020). At the time of decision-making, the medical profession has been able to avoid legal analysis of whether gender-normalising surgery is within the child's best interests and potentially prevent the intervention from taking place. Best interests assessments are used in health and child law to inform the decisions made on behalf of people who are unable to give consent either through mental capacity, or unconsciousness, or childhood. Many of the cases concerning the assessment of best interests occur because of a clash between families and healthcare practitioners and their views about treatment (or its withdrawal) on patients who cannot consent. As Holman J. notes in *An NHS Trust v MB* [2006] EWHC 507, "Best interests are used in the widest sense and include every kind of consideration capable of impacting on the decision. These include, non-exhaustively, medical, emotional, sensory (pleasure, pain and suffering) and instinctive (the human instinct to survive) considerations." This is reflected in section 1(3) of the Children Act 1989, which focuses on the risk of any harm, emotional and educational, as well as the physical needs of the child, and any of the characteristics of the child which the court considers pertinent. Given the amount of evidence being produced regarding the harmful consequences of gender-normalising surgeries, a strong case could certainly be made to demonstrate how these medical interventions are not in the child's best interests. While decisions regarding genital-normalising surgery on infants ultimately fall to the parents,[4] they must still be made in the best interest of that child.[5] However, litigation essentially relies on parental disagreement with medical practice, which is unlikely given that healthcare's temporal construction of the body leaves little time or space for parents to question such practice or to receive psychosocial support with regard to the social anxieties that arise in relation to parenting an intersex child.[6]

Accordingly, the medical profession can avoid external scrutiny, while it plans and performs surgical interventions. This is not to claim that the court's application of best interests would necessarily produce favourable outcomes for the intersex child. Certainly, academics have demonstrated how the courts have often over-emphasised family integrity and parental well-being at the expense of the child's own interests (Horowicz 2017; Fox and Thompson 2005). Indeed, in the case of circumcision, the court has actually entrenched male-genital cutting as a legitimate choice for parents (Fox and Thompson 2005). Accordingly, the medical profession (and parents) may be able to manipulate the best interest test through this logic of emergency depicting gender-normalising surgeries as necessary to 'correct' intersex children and thus to avoid psychosocial 'harm' (Horowicz 2017: 199). Nevertheless, the fact that decisions relating to gender-normalising surgeries are even yet to be considered by the courts is problematic and allows the medical profession to maintain control over intersex bodies. These issues raise two important

[4] Or those with parental authority as defined by s 3 Children Act 1989.

[5] Parents are bound by the same assessments as the courts. See e.g. *Gillick v West Norfolk and Wishbech AHA* [1986] AC 112 [184] per Lord Scarman.

[6] Cases that have come to court have revolved primarily around parental disagreement. See, for example, *Re J (Child's Religious Upbringing and Circumcision)* [2000] 1 FCR 307.

propositions. First, doctors are not interpreting best interests properly as they are failing to consider the adult the child will become or the child's interests over their life course. Second, when making judicial best interests assessments, deferability must always (rather than rarely) be taken into account.

In the context of healthcare, external scrutiny and perceptions of malpractice are a significant threat in terms of its own economic and reputational security. Where the profession faces legal action for past interventions, it potentially faces financial penalties that will result from litigation and/or out-of-court settlements as well as potential criminal prosecution if an intervention was found not to be in the best interests of the child.[7] At the same time, reputational threats to medical power/knowledge challenge the jurisdiction of the medical profession itself and could detrimentally impact upon the way the NHS is publically funded and the social status of medicine more broadly. This is particularly pertinent given that the NHS "is subject to reform, cost-cutting and political compromise" (Fenton 2013: 139). With this backdrop, we consider how the medical profession's focus on temporality depoliticises the issues involved.

Given the increasing volume of evidence of the harms of these practices, the choice to not view intersex embodiment over the whole life course must be viewed as strategic institutional preference to 'future-proof' its jurisdictional claims. The consequences of this strategy are revealed where medical professionals are directly challenged by intersex adults on the interventions that were performed upon them. Medical practitioners are able to distance themselves from these early events in two ways; first, by suggesting that practice has changed, and, second, by highlighting that they, as individuals, were not involved in these historic events. These strategies allow the medical profession to claim that 'time has moved on,' 'that was then and this is now,' and 'practice has changed,' creating a temporal gap between the knowledge of the intersex adult and current medical practice. A recent example can be drawn from an article published in *European Urology* that responds to the Council of Europe Human Rights Commissioner's Issue Paper on Human Rights and Intersex People. In this article, the authors contend that the Human Rights Commissioner "does not recognise what has changed nor what is now widely understood as best practice in the field" (Cools et al. 2016: 408). They go on to add that, "What the paper calls "current medical approaches" is to a large extent inconsistent with recently published data and current medical practice" (Cools et al. 2016: 408). Similar examples can be found in Norway where physicians wrote an open letter to a national newspaper maintaining that

[7] This would mean that the parents did not have the authority to consent to practice.

medical practice had changed and intersex activists were not fully informed (Wæhre et al. 2017). Medical professionals and the institution of healthcare are accordingly able to avoid taking responsibility for the continuing harms of non-therapeutic medical interventions whilst simultaneously further disempowering intersex voices by challenging the individual's knowledge base. Nonetheless, the issues raised by the intersex community are not dependent on the improvement of technique but the dangers inherent to non-consensual, non-therapeutic medical interventions.

This temporal disconnect presents intersex adults as uninformed and lacking the current knowledge to be able to make a justifiable evaluation of ongoing medical practice. This method of distancing and discrediting allows the medical profession to raise doubts about the individual's reliability and whether the institutional harms actually occur in the manner the individual claims. As such, intersex activists must rely on the academy to 'objectively' account for their experiences. These challenges to intersex knowledge continue despite evidence demonstrating that practice has changed very little over time (Monro et al. 2017; Roen 2019; Creighton et al. 2014). Consequently, where doctors are performing interventions in the present on intersex infants as research demonstrates still occurs (Monro et al. 2017; Creighton et al. 2014; Liao et al. 2019), it will remain possible for the medical profession to employ similar strategies if and when they are challenged in the future by the adult that intersex child becomes. Consequently, it becomes possible to see how logics of emergency and surgical/medical progression are used to delimit professional knowledge and prevent external scrutiny. The discrete event of 'fixing' that happened in the individual's childhood is disconnected from their current lived adult experience. This disconnect is bolstered by the fragmentation of the medical profession into specialties and sub-specialties that continue to see medical interventions as discrete issues—particularly in adulthood where access to Multi-disciplinary Teams specialised in intersex variations is less common.

Moreover, the episodic nature of the emergency has prevented attempts to reconsider professional best practice in this area and protected current iterations of best practice from serious scrutiny. Here, the temporal framing of an emergency enables the bio-medical narrative of intersex to maintain its authority in these matters and deflect criticism from other actors such as parents and/or other healthcare professionals. In these cases, "clinical imperatives can set temporal horizons to the process of legal decision making itself" (Harrington 2016: 80). Both Harrington (2016) and Davis and Murphy (2013) have highlighted medicine's ability to act as a 'state of exception' within law. As Davis writes:

> Constructing intersex as a medical emergency allows doctors to circumvent professional medical ethics that would normally prevent them from performing swift, irreversible, and medically unnecessary surgeries on children's bodies.... Although doctors tend to claim that they are merely information providers, it is important to keep in mind that they make treatment recommendations from a position of power and authority over the intersex "emergency" they create. (Davis 2015: 118).

Understanding the temporalities involved in determining these states of exception allow us to see how legal standards are "subordinated to a clinical understanding of the public good" (Harrington 2016: 82). Constructions of intersex variances as 'fixable' play a significant role in altering the application of institutional standards away from the (supposedly) universal and abstract temporality of human rights and towards an individual and immediate clinical understanding of 'best practice' (which may fail to consider the long-term psychosocial and health outcomes of the intersex embodied person). Such cases are marked by "A loss of reason [that is] central to the legal and medical construction of the emergency" (Harrington 2016: 82). The immediate focus of best interest creates a lack of recognition of the adult that 'the child' will become. Whilst medical guidelines pay lip-service to the way these interventions may impact into adulthood, these rarely factor into clinical decision making. Conversely the spectre of the 'disordered' intersex adult (who has not undergone surgery) continues to haunt the imagination of medical professionals. As a consequence, the construction of intersex embodiment as an emergency solely located in childhood prevents proper discussion around the deferment of medical interventions.

Certainly, such temporalities have informed the discourse around intersex embodiment constructed through the concept of 'medical emergency' (Davis 2015) and the immediacy that such a term inspires. As we have seen, in these contexts, it is the healthcare professionals' anxieties around normative bodies that dictate the temporality rather than the intersex variance. Emergencies require action with medical logics determining that to do otherwise would be neglectful and risk legal challenge. Moreover, the concept of emergency strengthens bio-medical hierarchies through its dictation of the order in which professionals are introduced into healthcare management (as well as the resources allocated to them). As we have seen, the logic of emergency demands a level of immediacy, which prevents not only practitioners from really reflecting on the ethical nature of their actions but also parents from being given an appropriate timeframe (or psychosocial support) for making decisions that may have lifelong implications for their child. The ways in which options are framed, therefore, becomes crucial to the decisions that parents make (Streuli et al. 2013). For example, in a recent study by Garland, Thomson, Travis, and Warburton it was found that in some NHS trusts, paediatric surgeons would be present at the initial meeting with parents to discuss their options (forthcoming). Surgeons are a key component in portraying intersex issues as episodic and immediately 'fixable' through medical intervention. Furthermore, international research in this area found that psychologists were only available for face-to-face discussions with parents in 53% of centres (Kyriakou et al. 2016). Such research highlights the shaping effect that the make-up of the medical team can have on parental decision making. This temporal framing thus reifies the idea that the child's intersex variation is an emergency to parents. Temporality is a crucial element, therefore, in the privileging of clinical judgement and the protection of medical professionals from serious scrutiny. The view presented so far roughly characterises the dominant understandings of intersex care espoused by endocrinologists, urologists, and surgeons. However, there have been calls, particularly in the psychological literature, to shift to a psychosocial model of care for intersex people that offers a distinctly different understanding of intersex temporality.

## 4 Emergence

This section argues for a shift in healthcare away from 'fixing' intersex variances and towards having the institutional support systems in place that will enable intersex embodied people to flourish. In part, this need for care over the life course has been recognised in leading medical guidelines on intersex variations. In the 2006 intersex consensus statement, for example, psychosocial care provided by mental health practitioners was seen as a key part of managing intersex variations (Lee et al. 2006: E492). When the consensus was updated ten years later, it was emphasised that "education and psychological support was needed … to [allow individuals to] make sense of the condition, relate to their community and establish relationships" (Lee et al. 2016: 170). Notably, psychosocial support is considered crucial both for the child *and* for their family to ensure that they are capable of making appropriate and informed decisions in relation to their own healthcare management. Indeed, one of the leading providers of intersex healthcare in the UK was criticised recently for failures to provide psychological support to patients (Kirkland 2017). However, this lack of focus on care over the life course is not an isolated practice; in a recent study with parents of intersex children, Bennecke et al. (2015) found that only half of the parents who identified a need for psychological support received 'adequate' provision. This is problematic, as the birth of a child with an intersex variance can often be a time of immense distress for parents. Moreover, along with the usual complications, emotions, and exhaustions of parenthood, they are also faced with a need to understand information relating to complex medical and genetic variations, stigma, ambiguity regarding gonadal tumour risk, a lack of certainty about future gender identity, and uncertainty regarding fertility potential (Ernst et al. 2018: 1). Psychosocial care, therefore, forms a key component of supporting intersex people over the life course. It is vital for both intersex individuals and the familial institutions in which they find themselves.

Offering alternative care pathways to children and families should be an important feature of the Multi-disciplinary Team that deals with intersex people, as they are particularly capable of reframing temporal logics of the body from emergency to a perspective capable of considering the adult the child will become. Consideration of psychological well-being over the life course is necessary for fully appreciating best interests assessments. This shift in temporality is in keeping with recent legal work on bodily and embodied integrity that understands the child as emergent (Fox and Thomson 2017; Fox et al. 2020). This work seeks to integrate "physical and psychological dimensions of integrity in recognition of the child's emerging legal subjectivity" (Fox and Thomson 2017: 503). Such reconceptualisations of the body help to unpack its complexity by acknowledging it as both physical and psychological, dependent and embedded in a web of institutional and societal relationships. Helpfully, however, these relational accounts do not simply collapse into a veneer for prioritising the will of the family (Fox and Thomson 2017: 523); instead, it shifts integrity to the core value of best interests decision making (Fox and Thomson 2017: 524). In seeing the body as emergent it places emphasis on the ways in which embodied integrity allows the conditions for "self-determination that enable the individuated self, and contrasts sharply with the static, propertied, and bounded notion often envisioned in legal discussions of conventional integrity" (Fox and Thomson 2017: 529). We would add that these views also seem to characterise dominant medical thinking in the field of intersex healthcare management. An approach grounded in embodied integrity, therefore, is much more suited to considerations of the body over the life course. Such an approach is attentive to the "memory of the flesh and the ways in which bodies remember" (Meoded Danon 2018: 95). We would therefore support a shift from the current endocrinologist/urologist-based model to a psychosocial model with "psychological health care [being] the foundation upon which other kinds of health care may be built as needed" (Roen 2019: 517).[8] Such an approach is in keeping with a wider understanding of best interests that encompasses multiple approaches and contexts. This is evidenced in *Aintree v James* [2013] UKSC 67 where Lady Hale highlighted that psychosocial concerns would be paramount in best interests assessments. As law and psychology are increasingly brought into contact in their determinations of 'selfhood,' this embodied understanding may represent a progressively more important (and mutually constitutive) co-production of bodies.

Where psychosocial care has been offered as a key aspect of intersex healthcare management, there are growing concerns about *when* this care is introduced (Chadwick et al. 2014; Garland et al. forthcoming), highlighting the battles for the construction of temporality that exist within institutions. If a psychosocial care model does become dominant, it leaves the current 'emergency based' endocrinologist dominated model open to criticism. As a result, as Liao et al. note, although "multi-disciplinary care pathways for ... DSDs often allude to the importance of psychological interventions, [they] ... are usually set up without due consideration of them" (Liao et al. 2014: 131). As previously mentioned, the presence of a surgeon at the initial discussions with parents around their choices means they are well placed to influence the parents' decision-making process before parents come into contact with any form of psychosocial support (Garland et al. forthcoming). Thus, while Liao notes, "it is obvious that parents affected by DSD first and foremost require sustained psychological support ... this does not seem to be the central focus in paediatric management" (Liao et al. 2010: 86). This approach would require a shift in institutional thinking away from intersex variances as episodic towards supporting intersex embodiment over the whole of the life course.

Yet, without state intervention, the medical profession has been reluctant to change and instead psychosocial care has been an afterthought, subject to complex internal hierarchies and claims of territory within the medical profession. As Liao and Simmonds note, "the risk for psychological services of being an emotional repository without any capacity to influence the overall service ethos is relatively high" (2014). Offering alternative care pathways has not been the case under the current endocrinologist-dominated model where clear hierarchies between healthcare professionals remain persistent (Liao et al. 2010, 2015). Rather the temporal strategies being employed by the medical profession are designed to shield them from criticism, instead of

[8] We note here that we feel a tentative pang of concern around re-embedding psychology into every aspect of state response. We would highlight, however, the shifts within psychology from its origins as a disciplinary regime focused on norms to its current emphasis on care. Whilst these shifts warrant broader consideration, unfortunately, this current chapter does not have the space.

acting in the best interests of intersex people. In the wake of these internal problems, reform led by the medical profession may not be appropriate and thus action must be State-led and focus on institutional reform. The State must also take responsibility for the resources that are available (Fenton 2013: 139) to ensure that healthcare institutions can afford practitioners who are adequately trained to provide psychosocial support from the outset. Moreover, reform must consider the ways in which the medical profession interacts with other societal institutions and ensure that they appropriately support intersex embodied individuals.

# 5 Deferability

Thus far, this chapter has demonstrated the need for a temporal shift in medicine that frames intersex variations in terms of emergence rather than emergency. Depicting such variations as an emergency has led to harmful and non-therapeutic medical interventions being performed on intersex individuals before they are able to consent. In this section we engage with Helen Stalford's contention that "in reality best interests assessments are unnervingly instinctive and highly contingent on the subjective assessment and value framework of the decision-maker" (2017: 43). This chapter adds to this by focusing on the ways in which temporality dominates the framing of best interests assessments. In this section we offer the concept of 'deferability' as a way of countering this temporal dominance by testing whether clinical practices that interfere with a subject's embodied integrity can be understood as emergencies. Put simply, such a test asks whether medical interventions can be deferred. If they cannot be deferred, the situation is an emergency. If the practice can be deferred, then it will be in the child's best interests to wait until the child is old enough to give consent or until the intervention can no longer be deferred. Deferability, therefore, is presented as an important new component of best interests assessments that assess institutional accounts of temporality allowing for delineation between emergencies and non-emergencies without relying upon more loaded and ambiguous terms such as 'necessity.'

Malta can perhaps be seen as the first state to engage with intersex issues in this temporal manner. Section 14 Gender Identity Gender Expression and Sex Characteristic Act 2015 (Malta) states:

> It shall be unlawful for medical practitioners or other professionals to conduct any sex assignment treatment and/or surgical intervention on the sex

> characteristics of a minor which treatment and/or intervention can be deferred until the person to be treated can provide informed consent.

Malta's legal provisions in this area draw upon nascent understandings of embodied integrity postponing interventions until the child can provide informed consent or until such time as the interventions become no longer deferrable. Intersex activists have described this legislation as the 'gold standard' of legal recognition (Garland and Travis 2018). By placing bodily integrity at the centre of reforms, commentators and critiques have commended Malta for enacting real protections for the intersex community, which recognise the legitimacy of the corporeal experiences of intersex individuals (Garland and Travis 2018; Ní Mhuirthile 2018). Decoupling legal regulation from the medical narrative of intersex enables individuals to more fully integrate and participate in society. It places decisions surrounding surgery and gender identity in the hands of the individual rather than in the hands of parents or medical professionals. This approach draws attention to the manner in which "the value of embodied integrity lies precisely in how it underpins the child's emergent subjectivity, meaning that her needs are never synonymous with those of others, or merely an extension of them" (Fox and Thomson 2017: 523). Such an account powerfully challenges the privilege of the medical profession in determining the temporality of intersex experience and allows for new biographical narratives to flourish.

The temporal notion of 'deferability' also fits neatly with a best interests assessment that places embodied integrity as its core legal value (Fox and Thomson 2017). While s1(3) Children Act 1989 offers a number of factors to be taken into account, *Re A (medical treatment: male sterilisation)* [2000] 1 F.C.R. 193 demonstrates how ultimately best interests assessments are a balancing act. Thorpe L.J. stated that:

> Pending the enactment of a checklist or other statutory direction it seems to me that the first instance judge with the responsibility to make an evaluation of the best interests of a claimant lacking capacity should draw up a balance sheet. The first entry should be of any factor or factors of actual benefit.... Then on the other sheet the judge should write any counterbalancing dis-benefits to the applicant.... Then the judge should enter on each sheet the potential gains and losses in each instance making some estimate of the extent of the possibility that the gain or loss might accrue. At the end of that exercise the judge should be better placed to strike a balance between the sum of the certain and possible gains against the sum of certain and possible losses. Obviously only if the account is in relatively significant credit will the judge conclude that the application is likely to advance the best interests of the claimant.

We would note that whilst there may be some benefits to non-therapeutic medical interventions, asking whether they are deferrable (i.e. the benefits could still be accrued if the intervention was postponed) significantly enhances the use of best interests. A focus on the deferability of interventions allows them to be seen as valuable but also recognises that they can be postponed enhancing the autonomy of the intersex person. By using deferability, judges and clinicians can bring together two important values that may (and, indeed, often have) otherwise been in conflict. This approach is not unprecedented within English courts. In *Re D* [1976] 1 All ER 326, for example, Heilbron J held that sterilisation was not in the interests of an 11-year-old girl with Soto Syndrome at least at that time as she might develop so as to be able to make her own choices later in her minority or in adulthood. The mother, concerned about her daughter's growing sexual awareness, wanted her sterilised to prevent pregnancy. Heilbron J recognised the procedure was neither medically necessary nor indicated and concerned that D would later understand its implications:

> where the evidence shows that her mental and physical condition and attainments have already improved, and where her future prospects are as yet unpredictable, where the evidence also shows that she is unable as yet to understand and appreciate the implications of this operation and could not give a valid or informed consent, but the likelihood is that in later years she will be able to make her own choice, where, I believe, the frustration and resentment of realising (as she would one day) what had happened could be devastating, an operation of this nature is, in my view, contra-indicated.

More recently, the court in *Re L and B (Children: Specific Issues: Temporary Leave to Remove from the Jurisdiction: Circumcision)* [2016] EWHC 849 (Fam) settled a disagreement between parents over whether two boys should undergo circumcision based on the father's religious beliefs. Here the court chose to:

> defe[r] that decision to the point where each of the boys themselves will make their individual choices once they have the maturity and insight to appreciate the consequences and longer term effects of the decisions which they reach. Per Roberts J at [143]

Both of these cases demonstrate the benefits that deferability can bring. While neither court denied the value of either procedure, they were able to use something akin to deferability to separate child welfare concerns from social and familial anxieties and distil the necessary from the unnecessary. However, while deferability as a concept is not wholly alien to judicial reasoning, cases using this approach are few and far between, and many cases concerning unnecessary medical procedures have failed to disentangle parental interests from best interests assessments (Horowicz 2017; Fox and Thompson 2005). Consequently, we argue that deferability needs to be built in to juridical decision-making tools.

Moreover, the benefits of this temporal dimension are further supported in the leading case of *Re F (mental patient sterilisation)* [1990] 2 A. C. 1. Here Lord Goff considered in detail the link between best interests and emergency. For him, emergency may give rise to the notion of necessary treatment potentially suspending the need for consent. However, he also notes that emergencies cannot be permanent. As he writes:

> Furthermore, in the case of a … stroke victim, the permanent state of affairs calls for a wider range of care than may be requisite in an emergency which arises from accidental injury. When the state of affairs is permanent, or semi-permanent, action properly taken to preserve the life, health or well-being of the assisted person may well transcend such measures as surgical operation or substantial medical treatment and may extend to such humdrum matters as routine medical or dental treatment, even simple care such as dressing and undressing and putting to bed.

For our purposes, this distinction echoes our own delineation between emergency and emergence. Emergence requires support from a range of different social institutions—in this chapter we have concentrated primarily on psychosocial care, but this could be added to by, for example, law, social care and education. Here Lord Goff considers the life course rather than just the immediacy of the issues dictated through the temporality of emergency. Law is capable, therefore, of disrupting the temporalities offered by the medical profession. Whilst Lord Goff does not consider the concept of deferability, it is easy to see how such an approach could bolster the existing understanding of best interests.[9] Building on this, the concept of deferability allows an incremental approach to intersex health to be undertaken. Deferability, in this context, does not mean simple postponement—as Lord Goff notes in his discussion of the stroke victim, it actually requires higher levels of assessment. Monitoring for cancer symptoms in intersex people, for example, would become prioritised over and above the removal of tissue on the basis of

[9] Note that if faced with two options that are equally good the courts should select the least invasive (contained in Mental Capacity Act 2005 but reflects statements at common law in sterilisation cases prior to the Act coming into force).

perceived cancer risks. Whilst this could be argued to increase the focus on already over-surveilled bodies, emphasis on deferability following an embodied integrity approach allows us to give precedence to non-invasive forms of care (Fox and Thomson 2017). This need for regular and consistent health checks means that deferability encourages institutional support over the life course to assess potential sources of harm. Such an account recognises the potential for intersex bodies to have increased cancer risks but also contextualises them against cancer risks in general and the ways in which these are managed. This attentiveness to intersex embodiment over the life course stands in stark contrast to the 'fixable' child's body but is in keeping with emergent health law perspectives we have identified (Fox and Thomson 2017; Fox et al. 2020).

This shift in focus from intervention to monitoring requires engagement from the state, the medical profession, and the law. Indeed, the resource implications stemming from the preceding discussion necessitate some level of state involvement. Despite the benefits of a legal engagement with deferability, we do not believe that meaningful change can occur without the serious engagement of the medical profession with these issues. Blanket legislative prohibitions that do not engage with the medical profession will undoubtedly fail to improve standards in this area. Such legislation will not contain the nuanced level of detail required on this complex issue to ensure that intersex individuals are really protected within clinical settings (Garland et al. 2019).

In order to carefully map out recommendations for updated guidelines in this difficult field, expertise in medicine, ethics, and law, as well as the intersex community are needed to ensure the emergent body of the intersex embodied child is respected. Part of this will involve providing specific funding to ensure that healthcare services have adequate resources to provide psychosocial care. However, as we have seen, the failure to sufficiently provide psychosocial support may not just be due to a lack of resources but may be due to complex medical hierarchies and a temporal depiction of intersex that paints immediate surgical treatment of intersex bodies as necessary. The State must find a way of reframing conceptions of temporality within medicine, and we offer the example of Maltese legislation as one potentially fruitful avenue of exploration.

Legislation, similar to that in Malta, along with a broader shift in the clinical management of intersex care towards deferability and monitoring through psychosocial care may begin to provide adequate state support to intersex embodied people. It is in this context that healthcare must be transformed to ensure a psychosocial approach to care that focuses on the emergent body. It is clear that in its current form the systemic hierarchies and internal problems within healthcare mean that the institution is not best placed to self-regulate on these issues. The lip-service that has been paid to psychosocial care and the failure to truly incorporate alternate pathways to care thus far is testimony to its inability to self-govern in this area. While it is commendable that the NHS has developed a specialised commissioning group looking specifically at intersex variations, to date no healthcare service has engaged with the necessary temporal shift in understandings of intersex without State intervention. Thus, reform must be State led, and this will require a reconceptualisation of responsibility as, historically, the UK government has characterised these issues as solely the responsibility of the NHS (Garland and Travis 2020).[10] While there is a greater shift by the UK government towards politically recognising the medical treatment of intersex persons (having recently issued a Call of Evidence (2019) on this matter), an effective State will need to ensure that not only are greater resources provided to healthcare to ensure adequate funding is provided for psychosocial support, but the State will also need to address systemic inequalities that pervade other social institutions (Garland and Travis 2018).

Consequently, we offer the concept of deferability as a key component of ensuring embodied integrity. In particular, deferability can be seen as a legal tool that assesses institutional accounts of temporality allowing for delineation between emergencies and non-emergencies. Clinical and juridical decision making, we would argue, must include deferability in its accounts of best interests decision making. This will allow for institutional accounts of temporality to be appropriately evaluated. More speculatively, we also posit that deferability may have some purchase in other areas where temporality is relied upon. Assessment of 'national emergencies,' for example, and their subsequent derogations from human rights law might usefully be seen through this framework. Moreover, this framework could be applied to policy making more generally. Assessment of the threat of climate change, for example, might also be understood through a lens of deferability and emergency.

[10] See the UK's response to criticism from the 72nd Session of the UN Committee on the Rights of the Child 23 May 2016, at http://stop.genitalmutilation.org/post/UK-Questioned-over-Intersex-Genital-Mutilations-by-UN-Committee-on-the-Rights-of-the-Child

## 6 Conclusions

This chapter has demonstrated how the logic of emergency is being used by the medical profession to justify non-therapeutic and harmful interventions on intersex infants. These emergencies are not medical but are in fact social emergencies and produce harmful lifelong negative consequences for intersex embodied people. Medical practice must shift its temporal understanding of intersex to focus on the emergent body. This reframing will enable care pathways to better conceptualise the life course of the individual and is more in keeping with best interests and children's rights. The notion of emergency not only justifies early interventions but also operates in a way that prevents external scrutiny over practice. Medical professionals can circumvent ethical issues and hinder discussions about best practice grounded in human rights frameworks or best interests assessments. Entrenched hierarchies that place biomedicine at their apex prevent healthcare from meaningfully incorporating psychosocial support within care pathways. Moreover, emergency logics and the episodic construction of intersex enable medics to deflect criticism received from the intersex adult that the child becomes. Ultimately, it is the State who must intervene and reconsider its role in the construction of time. Utilising psychosocial care and legal conceptions of deferability will allow individuals greater voice in the choices made about their bodies. It will prevent non-therapeutic interventions being performed without the individual's consent, whilst still allowing the possibility for the individual to choose to consent to such procedures once they are able to meaningfully partake in the decision-making process.

Moreover, this chapter has sought to highlight the role of temporality in the construction of bodies within healthcare. Such an approach can highlight the plurality of temporality that can exist within healthcare approaches—the differences in understanding of issues between, for example, endocrinologists and psychologists can be traced, to some extent, to their reliance upon different temporal registers. In addition, we have demonstrated the ways in which temporality can be used to depoliticise issues—subtly shifting the ways in which claims of harm or abuse are framed. Such an approach may have wider appeal when examining the ways in which the body interacts with healthcare and the state more broadly. Bodies are constituted through temporal frameworks, and the way these are constructed is always a political act. As such, legal and legislative responses to healthcare must also be understood as temporally and politically loaded. Careful attention to temporality is thus required to ensure that state and legal approaches to the body are in keeping with the notions of social justice. This chapter also offered deferability as an important new component of clinical and juridical accounts of best interests assessments. Deferability, as we present it, proposes a significant tool for assessing institutional accounts of temporality, allowing for greater delineation between emergencies and non-emergencies. In doing so, deferability builds upon and adds to the prominence of embodied integrity as a key component of legal and medical practice whilst also potentially adding to areas as diverse as human rights derogations and climate change. While case law has demonstrated the utility of this approach, its use has been sparing and ad hoc, thus, we argue that it should be built in to both clinical and judicial decision making.

Reflecting on our own experience of time we also note that this chapter advocates a linear notion of political progression and perhaps falls into the 'liberal' understanding of time that we highlighted at the outset. Whilst we recognise this, we must also acknowledge our place within the intersex community with its own political agenda and motivations. The intersex community's desire for an end to non-therapeutic medical interventions itself denotes a clear and unambiguous temporal register and sense of direction. As a result, we have allowed our political loyalties to the intersex movement to shape our own understandings of time. Following this, the true social emergency is around medical standards and, following the twitter hashtag popularised by intersex activists in the wake of the #metoo movement, #timesup.

## References


Amnesty International. (2017). *First, Do No Harm: Ensuring the Rights of Children with Variations of Sex Characteristics in Denmark and Germany*. Report. https://www.amnesty.org/download/Documents/EUR0160862017ENGLISH.PDF. Accessed 2 Aug 2019.

Bennecke, E., Werner-Rosen, K., Thyen, U., et al. (2015). Subjective Need for Psychological Support (PsySupp) in Parents of Children and Adolescents with Disorders of Sex Development (DSD). *European Journal of Pediatrics, 174*(10), 1287–1297.

Birth, K. (2012). *Objects of Time: How Things Shape Temporality*. New York: Palgrave.

Chadwick, P. M., Smyth, A., & Liao, L. M. (2014). Improving Self-Esteem in Women Diagnosed with Turner Syndrome: Results of a Pilot Intervention. *Journal of Pediatric and Adolescent Gynecology, 27*, 129–132.

Chase, C. (1998). Surgical Progress Is Not the Answer to Intersexuality. *Journal of Clinical Ethics, 9*, 385–392.

Cools, M., Simmonds, M., Elford, S., Gorter, J., Ahmed, F., D'Alberton, F., Springer, A., & Hiort, O. (2016). Response to the Council of Europe Human Rights

Commissioner's Issue Paper on Human Rights and Intersex People. *European Urology, 70*, 407–409.
Creighton, S., Minto, C. L., & Steele, S. J. (2001). Objective Cosmetic and Anatomical Outcomes at Adolescence of Feminising Surgery for Ambiguous Genitalia Done in Childhood. *The Lancet, 358*, 124–125.
Creighton, S., Michala, L., Mushtaq, I., & Yaron, M. (2014). Childhood Surgery for Ambiguous Genitalia: Glimpses of Practice Changes or More of the Same? *Psychology and Sexuality, 5*(1), 34–43.
Davis, G. (2015). *Contesting Intersex: The Dubious Diagnosis*. New York: New York University Press.
Davis, G., & Murphy, E. (2013). Intersex Bodies as States of Exception: An Empirical Explanation for Unnecessary Surgical Modification. *Feminist Formations, 25*(2), 129–152.
Ernst, M. M., Liao, L.-M., Baratz, A. B., et al. (2018). Disorders of Sex Development/Intersex: Gaps in Psychosocial Care for Children. *Pediatrics, 142*(2), 1–4.
Fausto-Sterling, A. (2000). *Sexing the Body: Gender Politics and the Construction of Sexuality*. New York: Basic Books.
Fenton, R. (2013). Assisted Reproductive Technology Provision and the Vulnerability Thesis. In M. Fineman & A. Grear (Eds.), *Vulnerability: Reflections on a New Ethical Foundation for Law and Politics* (pp. 125–146). Farnham: Ashgate.
Fitzpatrick, P. (2001). Modernism and the Grounds of Law. Cambridge: Cambridge University Press.
Fox, M. & Thompson, M. (2005). Cutting it: Surgical Interventions and the Sexing of Children. *Cardozo Journal of Law and Gender*, 12, 81–98.
Fox, M., & Thomson, M. (2017). Bodily Integrity, Embodiment, and the Regulation of Parental Choice. *Journal of Law and Society, 44*(4), 501–531.
Fox, M., Thomson, M., & Warburton, J. (2020). Embodied Integrity, Shaping Surgeries and the Profoundly Disabled Child. In C. Dietz, M. Travis, & M. Thomson (Eds.), *A Jurisprudence of the Body*. London: Palgrave.
Garland, J., & Slokenberga, S. (2018). "Minorities Within Their Own Families" Protection of the Rights of Children with "Intersex Conditions" in Europe. *Medical Law Review, 27*(3), 482–508.
Garland, F., & Travis, M. (2018). Legislating Intersex Equality: Building the Resilience of Intersex People Through Law. *Legal Studies, 38*(4), 587–606.
Garland, F., & Travis, M. (2020). Making the State Responsible: Intersex Embodiment, Medical Jurisdiction and State Responsibility. *Journal of Law and Society, 48*.
Garland, F., Samuelsen, N., & Travis, M. (2019). *Law and Intersex in Norway: Challenges and Opportunities*. Report. https://pdfs.semanticscholar.org/e3d0/1b8a91c05d9c29f628cc8ccc13b820f4fbf9.pdf. Accessed 2 Aug 2019.
Garland, F., Thomson, M., & Travis, M., Warburton, J. (forthcoming). Children Born with 'Disorders of Sex Development' and Medical Practice: Results from a Freedom of Information Exercise. *Bioethics*.

Gordon-Bouvier, E. (2019). Crossing the Boundaries of the Home: A Chronotopical Analysis of the Legal Status of women's Domestic Work. *International Journal of Law in Context, 15*, 479. https://doi.org/10.1017/S1744552319000326.

Government Equalities Office. (2019). *Variations in Sex Characteristics: A Call for Evidence*. Call for Evidence. https://www.gov.uk/government/consultations/variations-in-sex-characteristics-call-for-evidence. Accessed 2 Aug 2019.

Grabham, E. (2011). Doing Things with Time: Flexibility, Adaptability, and Elasticity in UK Equality Cases. *Canadian Journal of Law and Society, 26*, 485–508.

Grabham, E. (2012). Bodily Integrity and the Surgical Management of Intersex. *Body & Society, 18*, 1–26.

Grabham, E. (2014). Legal Form and Temporal Rationalities in UK Work-Life Balance Law. *Australian Feminist Studies, 29*, 67–84.

Grabham, E. (2017). Time and Technique: The Legal Lives of the 26-Week Qualifying Period. *Economy and Society, 45*, 379–406.

Greenhouse, C. (1989). Just in Time: Temporality and the Cultural Legitimation of Law. *The Yale Law Journal, 98*(8), 1631–1651.

Griffiths, D. (2018a). Diagnosing Sex: Intersex Surgery and 'Sex Change' in Britain 1930–1955. *Sexualities, 21*(3), 476–495.

Griffiths, D. (2018b). Shifting Syndromes: Sex Chromosome Variations and Intersex Classifications. *Social Studies of Science, 48*(1), 125–148.

Griffiths, D. (2020). Queering the Moment of Hypospadias "Repair". *GLQ*.

Groveman, A. (1998). The Hanukkah Bush: Ethical Implications in the Clinical Management of Intersex. *Journal of Clinical Ethics, 9*, 356–359.

Harrington, J. (2016). *Towards a Rhetoric of Medical Law*. New York: Routledge.

Horowicz, E. (2017). Intersex Children: Who are we really Treating?. *Medical Law International, 17*, 183–218.

Kirkland, F. (2017). Great Ormond Street Hospital Failing Intersex Children. *Newspaper Article*. https://www.bbc.co.uk/news/uk-41593914. Accessed 15 Aug 2019.

Kyriakou, A., Dessens, A., Bryce, J., et al. (2016). Current Models of Care for Disorders of Sex Development – Results from an International Survey of Specialist Centres. *Orphanet Journal of Rare Diseases, 11*, 155–165.

Lee, P. A., Houk, C. P., Ahmed, S. F., & Hughes, I. A., in collaboration with the participants in the International Consensus Conference on Intersex organized by the Lawson Wilkins Pediatric Endocrine Society and the European Society for Paediatric Endocrinology. (2006). Consensus Statement on the Management of Intersex Disorders. *Paediatrics, 118*(2), e488–e500.

Lee, P. A., Nordenström, A., Houk, C. P., et al. (2016). Global Disorders of Sex Development Update Since 2006: Perceptions, Approach and Care. *Hormone Research in Pædiatrics, 85*, 158–180.

Lewis, S., & Thomson, M. (2019). Social Bodies and Social Justice. *International Journal of Law in Context., 15*, 344–361.

Liao, L.-M., & Simmonds, M. (2014). A Values-Driven and Evidence-Based Health Care Psychology for Diverse Sex Development. *Psychology and Sexuality, 5*(1), 83–101.

Liao, L.-M., Tacconelli, E., Wood, D., Conway, G., & Creighton, S. M. (2010). Adolescent Girls with Disorders of Sex Development: A Needs Analysis of Transitional Care. *Journal of Pediatric Urology, 6*, 609–613.

Liao, L.-M., Wood, D., & Creighton, S. M. (2015). Parental Choice on Normalising Cosmetic Genital Surgery: Between a Rock and a Hard Place. *BMJ Editorial.* https://www.bmj.com/content/351/bmj.h5124?casa_token=HZYVIXoRd2gA-AAAA:uICdeFK0VGZl2ZEKp09C3pf969HeSrl1vmZnFqu9gHhVtEihebpWH3ptQbWq_o0KLL_1hrlUJus. Accessed 15 Aug 2019.

Liao, L.-M., Hegarty, P., Creighton, S., et al. (2019). Clitoral Surgery on Minors: An Interview Study with Clinical Experts of Differences of Sex Development. *BMJ Open, 9*, e025821. https://doi.org/10.1136/bmjopen-2018-025821.

McNeilly, K. (2018). Are Rights Out of Time? International Human Rights Law, Temporality, and Radical Social Change. *Social & Legal* Studies, 1–22. https://doi.org/10.1177/0964663918815729.

Meoded Danon, L. (2018).Time matters for intersex bodies: Between socio-medical time and somatic time. *Social Science and Medicine*, 208, 89–97.

Monro, S., Yeadon-Lee, T., Crocetti, D., Garland, F., & Travis, M. (2017). *Intersex, Variations of Sex Characteristics, and DSD: The Need for Change*. Huddersfield: University of Huddersfield Press.

Morland, I. (2006). The Glans Opens Like a Book' Writing and Reading the Intersexed Body. *Continuum: Journal of Media and Cultural Studies, 19*(3), 335–348.

Newbould, M. (2017). When Parents Choose Gender: Intersex, Children and the Law. *Medical Law Review, 24*(4), 474–496.

Ní Mhuirthile, T. (2018). The Legal Status of Intersex Persons in Malta. In J. Scherpe, A. Dutta, & T. Helms (Eds.), *The Legal Status of Intersex Persons* (pp. 357–368). Cambridge: Intersentia.

Roen, K. (2008). 'But we have to do something': Surgical `correction' of atypical genitalia. *Body and Society, 14*, 47–66.

Roen, K. (2019). Intersex or Diverse Sex Development: Critical Review of Psychosocial Health Care Research and Indications for Practice. *Journal of Sex Research, 56*(4–5), 511–528.

Streuli, J. C., Vayena, E., Cavicchia-Balmer, Y., & Huber, J. (2013). Shaping Parents: Impact of Contrasting Professional Counseling on Parents' Decision Making for Children with Disorders of Sex Development. *The Journal of Sexual Medicine, 10*(8), 1953–1960.

Travis, M. (2019). The Vulnerability of Heterosexuality: Consent, Gender Deception and Embodiment. *Social and Legal Studies, 28*(3), 303–326.

Valverde, M. (2009). Jurisdiction and Scale: Legal 'Technicalities' as Resources for Theory. *Social and Legal Studies, 18*(2), 139–157.

Valverde, M. (2015). *Chronotopes of Law: Jurisdiction, Scale and Governance*. New York: Routledge.

Wæhre, A., Diseth, T.H., Bjørdalen, H., Lund, A., & Ræder, H. (2017). The Treatment of the Model Hanne Is Not Representative. *Dagbladet* https://www.dagbladet.no/kultur/behandlingen-av-modellen-hanne-er-ikke-representativ/67014633. Accessed 15 Aug 2019.

Zillén, K., Garland, J., & Slokenberger, S. (2017). *The Rights of Children in Biomedicine: Challenges Posed by Scientific Advances and Uncertainties (2017) Committee on Bioethics of the Council of Europe Report*. http://www.diva-portal.org/smash/get/diva2:1065442/FULLTEXT01.pdf. Accessed 15 Aug 2019.

# 7

# Death Before Birth: Liminal Bodies and Legal Frameworks

Karolina Kuberska, Danielle Fuller, Jeannette Littlemore, Sheelagh McGuinness, and Sarah Turner

## 1 Introduction

It is estimated that approximately 1 in 5 known pregnancies end in miscarriage, approximately 1 in every 200 births is a stillbirth and roughly 2000 terminations for reasons of fetal anomaly are performed in the UK each year (NHS 2018; Tommy's 2019). Following a pregnancy loss, both the woman's body and that of the fetus have somewhat uncertain statuses; both occupy a

K. Kuberska
THIS Institute, University of Cambridge, Cambridge, UK
e-mail: karolina.kuberska@thisinstitute.cam.ac.uk

D. Fuller
Faculty of Arts, University of Alberta, Edmonton, AB, Canada
e-mail: dfuller@ualberta.ca

J. Littlemore
Department of English Language and Linguistics, University of Birmingham, Birmingham, UK
e-mail: j.m.littlemore@bham.ac.uk

S. McGuinness (✉)
University of Bristol Law School, Bristol, UK
e-mail: sheelagh.mcguinness@bristol.ac.uk

S. Turner
School of Humanities, Coventry University, Coventry, UK
e-mail: ad0091@coventry.ac.uk


C. Dietz et al. (eds.), *A Jurisprudence of the Body*, Palgrave Socio-Legal Studies,
https://doi.org/10.1007/978-3-030-42200-4_7

liminal space between different states of being. The woman has begun to develop an identity as a mother but cannot perform this identity with this particular child in the way she had expected. Her body may still look pregnant but she has lost something that was physically part of her but that was also on track to become a person in their own right. The experience of pregnancy loss is thus a disruption to the expected linear reproductive experience and can result in a woman not being recognized as the parent she may feel she is. The fetus, too, occupies a liminal space in that it lies somewhere between a baby and 'human tissue' (Squier 2004); it is at once part of the mother and a separate entity, and, in many cases, it embodies an imagined future that will never be. Pregnancy loss can be distinguished from other forms of bereavement due to the liminal status of what is lost and its close involvement with the body; a death has occurred inside the woman's body. This form of highly embodied bereavement engenders complex emotions that are difficult to articulate, and that may also be contradictory (Layne 2003).

The liminal status of the fetus raises interesting challenges for the law surrounding pregnancy loss. Fetal remains are lawfully the tissue of the pregnant woman, but socially and culturally they have a far more complex and nuanced status as being potentially representative of an absent child or a lost life (Austin and McGuinness 2019). As such, experiences of reproductive loss and the liminal status of the woman's body and the fetal remains are challenging, unsettling normal fixed categories in health law. These challenges have consequences for those affected, who often lack knowledge of the legal options for the disposal and memorialization of the remains available to them, and may find that the legal options available to them do not reflect their lived experiences.

This chapter has two connected aims. First, it shows how metaphor analysis can be used to inform socio-legal understanding of pregnancy loss with a particular focus on its status as a liminal, embodied experience. This new understanding can inform researching and teaching on the body by showing how metaphor can be used as a socio-legal method. Second, it contributes to the increased interest in, and value of, liminality in health law scholarship (Laurie 2017).

Feminist research focusing on the place of law in social, political, economic and cultural life has highlighted the gendered way in which law and legal concepts are constructed, with the normative body of the law focusing on the male, and paying insufficient attention to the female, pregnant and fetal forms (Bordo 1993; Morgan 1997; Young 1990). This chapter aims to address this, furthering our knowledge and understanding of the socio-legal and theoretical approaches to understanding bodies and embodiment in law (Fox and Thomson 2017). We provide an overview of the legal framework that governs reproductive loss in England and Wales. We also give an overview of the law on miscarriage and stillbirth and how that shapes experience of reproductive loss and also practices for disposal of fetal remains. In doing so, we critically assess the legal frameworks that regulate and contain bodies and bodily material. Brazier (2009) has questioned whether bodily integrity constitutes the 'core legal value' in contemporary health law. This chapter takes up Brazier's question by critically assessing the conceptual limits of bodily integrity in law given its reliance on a normative account of the body that is often male and always singular (Naffine 2003). This normative account is challenged in the case of pregnancy, where the body is not one but not two, and in the case of pregnancy loss—more challenging again—where the body never progresses beyond this liminal position before returning to being just one (Karpin 1992). As such, this chapter provides a critique of the conceptual limits of bodily integrity, and our analysis is grounded in a feminist epistemological framework that emphasizes the importance of respecting lived experience as a form of knowledge (Smith 1987).

We begin our chapter by providing an in-depth account of the conceptual and methodological framing for our approach. We discuss liminality, embodiment and metaphor, and show how they inform our understandings of the socio-legal relationship between law and pregnancy loss. We then use some of the findings from our ESRC-funded interdisciplinary project 'Death before Birth',[1] which investigated the accounts of women who had experienced some form of pregnancy loss, to illustrate the ways in which a metaphor analysis can provide insights into the ways in which people communicate their lived experience. We use these findings to critique the legal framework which governs reproductive loss. Our analysis focuses primarily on the experience of pre-24-week loss (miscarriage) and considers (i) the relationship between the formerly pregnant person and fetal remains and (ii) disposal of the remains and associated ceremonial practices (see also Austin and McGuinness 2019; Kuberska 2020). We focus on the individual and socially constructed character of the liminal nature of the fetus and of the woman's body as well as the implications that these have for those involved. This chapter follows the line of reasoning presented by Fletcher and colleagues who state that:

> [l]aw's conventional approach to regulating bodily interventions has been to consider the body as an object of analysis rather than as a category of analysis. In our view, legal analysis could offer a richer understanding of law's engagement with bodies and bodily materials if it adopted a thicker conception of embodiment. (Fletcher et al. 2008, p. 321)

[1] Economic and Social Research Council (ESRC) grant identifier: ES-N008359, https://deathbeforebirthproject.org

## 2 Conceptual Framings: Liminality, Embodiment

In this section we provide further detail on how the concepts of liminality and embodiment can work together to shed light on the experience of pregnancy loss which is at once highly private but at the same time subject to public scrutiny. We suggest that a recuperation of our understanding of bodily integrity in law is necessary if legal frameworks are to be sufficient to accommodate those who experience reproductive loss, or indeed any understandings of bodily integrity that deviate from traditional normative understanding. Our analysis follows the recent approach advocated for by Fox and Thomson who argue that:

> the concept should be reframed in a way that reflects the theoretical shift from physical bodies to embodiment [...], and that is grounded in the lived experience of embodied beings. This would understand bodies both as a constitutive part of human identity and as existing at the intersection of the material, the institutional and the symbolic. (2017, p. 521)

The 'Death Before Birth' project had the overall aim of examining the law surrounding the disposal of the remains of pregnancy and the ways in which it is interpreted, and to examine the narratives of women and those who support them, focusing on metaphor as a commonly used resource for expressing the inexpressible. Our research examined questions ranging from the status of fetal material to an examination of how law can legitimatize or stigmatize certain sorts of pregnancy loss and bereavement. Through a detailed analysis of interviews with a range of stakeholders and bereaved individuals, we uncovered the way in which law shapes experiences of pregnancy loss and bereavement. In this project, our legal interpretation of the issues surrounding pregnancy loss was informed by an analysis of the ways in which women who have experienced pregnancy loss employed metaphor to describe and frame their experience. Our use of mixed methods in our research design and our analytic focus on metaphor allowed us to reach a fuller understanding of their responses to the liminal embodied nature of their experiences, and the ways in which they were affected by the law. Our approach aligned broadly with studies in legal consciousness in that we avoided a 'law-first' approach (Silbey 2005) and instead adopted a narrative interview method eliciting participant 'stories' about their experiences of reproductive loss (Squire et al. 2014). We then analyzed the metaphors used in these 'stories' to outline the nature of the legal framework which shaped and defined these experiences. Our findings highlight the limitations in how legal frameworks accurately reflect experiences of reproductive loss.

## 2.1 Liminality as a Theoretical Frame for Analyzing Health Law Concept

Liminality, a concept from anthropology, has become a popular lens for socio-legal healthcare research (see e.g. Laurie 2017). We do not attempt here to provide a comprehensive overview of the anthropological work that has been done on liminality. Instead, we will provide a basic account of what liminality means and how it is useful for the purposes of health law and our understanding of experiences of pregnancy loss. In his ground-breaking work *The Rites of Passage*, Arnold van Gennep outlined three key stages in rites of passage, with liminality occurring at the middle stage ([1909] 2004). This understanding was then applied and nuanced in anthropological work by Victor Turner (1967, 1969, 1974). For Turner, the middle stage, or liminality, is the point of being 'betwixt and between' or 'on the threshold' (1967). As a conceptual lens then, liminality sheds light on the ways in which entities or things can be unlike both what came before and what comes after; as such, liminal entities have a *sui generis* quality.

Legal analysis and legal concepts, particularly with regard to the human body and human material, have often been reliant on binary constructions of persons and property or persons and things (Hyde 1997). Human relations are often bound in such constructions, and legal relations are often defined by this process of categorization. However, when we identify one thing as like the others, we are not merely classifying the world; we are investing particular classifications with consequences and positioning ourselves in relation to those meanings. As such, it is mistaken to assume that the categories we use for analysis just exist and simply sort our experiences, perceptions and problems through them (Minow 1990).

Liminality is useful when considering experiences of pregnancy loss and also of disposal of pregnancy remains. Pregnancy has often been understood as a liminal phase, between woman and mother, not one but not two (Karpin 1992; Kukla 2005). While in the womb, the fetus exists in a liminal space, on a threshold:

> betwixt-and-between the moral, day-to-day cultural and social stages and processes of getting and spending, preserving law and order, and registering social status. (Turner 1979, p. 465)[2]

When a fetus is expelled early from the womb, its liminality has the power to destabilize or disrupt legal categories, and such disruption often demands a regulatory response (Fox and McGuinness 2016). The regulation of 'bodies situated at the margins of humanity reveal[s] much about what law values in terms of embodiment' (Fletcher et al. 2008, p. 325). The boundaries of these legal categorizations, or the gray area in between, are often unclear and ambiguous:

> Liminal entities are neither here nor there; they are betwixt and between the positions assigned and arrayed by law, custom, convention, and ceremonial. (Turner 1969, p. 95)

There is a rich body of academic critique that has explored liminality in depth and that has normalized it as one of possible ontological statuses for all kinds of beings (see e.g. Han et al. 2018; Kaufman and Morgan 2005; Kilshaw 2017; Squier 2004). In other words, liminality as an ontological status does not need resolving into a more permanent condition in order to be understood and accepted. However, as this chapter elucidates, the liminality *of the fetus* is problematic when considered in the context of the law. Legal structures tend to require unambiguity as a condition to function. Pregnancy and the fetus as liminal concepts need not be problematic all the while a pregnancy is progressing in an expected fashion, as pregnant women have a range of broadly shared social scripts which legitimize and contain the liminal complexities. However, a pregnancy loss disrupts these well-known patterns. In seeking to achieve order over acknowledging complexity, the legal imaginary risks overlooking lived embodied experiences, which are complex in their liminal status.

## 2.2 Pregnancy Loss as an Embodied Experience

Embodied cognition holds that people's experiences of the world are mediated by their bodies and the ways in which they interact with the world through their bodies (Gibbs 2006a, b). Pregnancy and pregnancy loss thus have significant effects on individuals' experiences of the world, due to their

---

[2] See also Squier (2004), especially Chapter 1.

status as important and transformatic life events. Not only does pregnancy have the power to change social and legal identities (through conferring the status of 'parent'), it also effects significant changes in the body. Pregnancy can thus be considered transformative, not just in terms of producing a new person, but also transformative of the self of the pregnant woman (see Thompson 2005; Côté-Arsenault et al. 2009). Young describes the embodied nature of pregnant experience, the shifting boundaries of bodily integrity and the liminal status of the body as follows:

> [A pregnant woman] experiences her body as herself and not herself. Its inner movements belong to another being, yet they are not other, because her body boundaries shift and because her bodily self-location is focused on her trunk in addition to her head. (1990, p. 161)

In law, bodily integrity has often been reduced to respect for autonomy reliant on individual and fixed understandings of corporeality. This contrasts with anthropological and feminist critique of the mind–body dualism where there has been an increased understanding of the complex interplay and connection between the physical and mental aspects of bodily integrity, both of which form part of our ontology and are constitutive of self (see Bendelow and Williams 1998; Fox and Thomson 2017; Grosz 1994; Herring and Wall 2017; Scheper-Hughes and Lock 1987). Authors like Drucilla Cornell have long argued that it is not possible to disentangle the mind from the body—key for Cornell is the capacity for self-imagination and integration (1995). This approach can easily be applied to pregnancy, as the pregnant body is not fixed and is constantly subject to change (Young 1990). This is summarized well in the following passage from Iris Marion Young:

> As my pregnancy begins, I experience it as a change in my body, I become different from what I have been. My nipples become reddened and tender, my belly swells into a pear. I feel this elastic around my waist, itching, this round, hard middle replacing the doughy belly with which I still identify. Then I feel a little tickle, a little gurgle in my belly, it is my feeling, my insides, and it feels somewhat like a gas bubble, but it is not, it is different, in another place, belonging to another, another that is nevertheless my body. (1990, p. 163)

The pregnant woman, her body and the fetus challenge traditional legal understanding which see the body as fixed and bounded. As such we need a reimagination of bodily understandings in law in order to accommodate women's perceptions of themselves and their relationship to their fetus. In the opening to *Mass Hysteria: Medicine, Culture, and Mothers' Bodies*, Rebecca Kukla states that:

> the fetus and, with it, the pregnant woman are not objects that come with ready-made stable boundaries. … [T]he maternal body incarnates one human being at the beginning of pregnancy and two at the end of it, and it is by no means clear how to tell a coherent story of this passage. (2005, p. 4)

For those who experience reproductive loss, particularly prior to 24 weeks, this lack of coherence continues, or indeed can be exacerbated, once the pregnancy ends in a way which disrupts the standard perceptions of reproduction as a linear process that results in a live born child (Reiheld 2015; Murphy 2012). When reproductive loss is mediated through the cultural taboo surrounding it, the experience can be made worse through lack of recognition or acknowledgment, both socially and legally, of what the person has been through. The disruptive nature of reproductive loss is important not just in terms of ruptures to sense of self but also practically in terms of how it shapes (legal) decision-making at this time.

## 3 Metaphor as an Interpretative Tool for Socio-Legal Analysis

In order to better understand the experience of pregnancy loss, and the implications that this has for health law, we need to develop a stronger understanding of the liminal status of the woman's body and that of the fetus, and to more fully appreciate the ways in which pregnancy loss is an *embodied* experience. One obvious way to improve our understanding of pregnancy loss is to ask women about their experiences and to analyze the narratives that they produce. However, simply looking at what they say may not be enough. It is also important to look at *how* they say it. One analytical tool that is useful in this endeavor is metaphor. The ways in which people use metaphor to describe their experiences can provide rich insights that may not be accessed via more superficial analyses of the content of what they say. Metaphor (where one thing is described in terms of another) is very good at describing experiences that are not widely shared or that are otherwise difficult to express (Semino 2010, 2011). Furthermore, when people describe intense emotional experiences, they tend to make use of creative metaphor (Gibbs and Franks 2002). More importantly, with reference to liminality and the embodied nature of pregnancy loss, metaphor allows us to say two things at once as it always works on at least two levels (i.e. the concept being described and the concept being drawn upon to describe it). It thus allows people to express the corporeal and the incorporeal elements of a lived experience at the same time, in the same phrase. People may therefore reach for metaphors in response to liminality. Finally, metaphor has been shown to be a useful mechanism for exploring experiences that are not widely shared and provides an insight into experiences which may not otherwise be accessible (Littlemore and Turner 2019a, b). Metaphor is thus particularly useful in talking about the experience of reproductive loss, which is just as common as it is a social taboo (Layne 2003).

We understood the tension that can arise between the law around the disposal of remains and the interpretation of that law by clinical practitioners, support agencies and bereaved parents as both a social problem and an intellectual challenge. In designing our interdisciplinary investigation into the choices and decisions that people make about how to dispose of fetal remains after a pregnancy loss, we wanted to respect the ways in which all parties understood and experienced the law, while exploring how options and choices about disposal might be better communicated. We were also keenly aware that public discussion about what happens to remains after pregnancy loss is often limited to 'scandals' about disposal that are reported (often somewhat sensationally) in the mass media.[3]

Metaphor is a useful mechanism for exploring experiences that are not widely shared as it frequently involves the use of something that is familiar, tangible or common to describe something that is abstract, emotional or unfamiliar (Littlemore 2019). Unlike a more conventional content analysis, a metaphor analysis permits an in-depth exploration of the ways in which people conceptualize emotional experiences and the underlying attitudes and assumptions that inform the way they describe them. As such, rather than relying on an explicit articulation of how participants' experiences are shaped by law, a metaphor analysis provides insights into experiences that can then be situated within broader legal frameworks.

At this point, it is useful to define what we mean by metaphor. Metaphor is a device by which one concept, experience or object is defined or described in terms of another (Cameron 2003). For example, people sometimes talk about the need for a 'level playing field' in the workplace to refer to the idea that there should be equal opportunities for all in areas such as career progression. There is no actual playing field involved here, but the workplace is construed metaphorically as if it were a football game or some other sports game that requires a level terrain so that one of the teams does not have an unfair

[3] See for example 'Dispatches—Exposing Hospital Heartache', Channel 4, 2014.

advantage over the other. While traditionally considered solely a literary or creative device, contemporary views of metaphor consider it to be a fundamental element of human language and thought, and an important device that we use to understand, conceptualize and express our experiences (Lakoff and Johnson 1980). Metaphor allows us to express abstract content and emotional experiences in very physical, bodily based terms. For example, we talk (and think) about affection as warmth (e.g. 'he has such a warm personality'), importance as size (e.g. 'we have a big day coming up') and difficulties as burdens (e.g. 'that's a weight off my shoulders') (Lakoff and Johnson 1999). In each of these cases, an abstract concept or experience is understood and expressed in more concrete, physical terms, via metaphor.

Although people employ metaphors such as these all the time, they are particularly prevalent when people are talking about complex, difficult or emotionally charged experiences. As such, metaphor analysis has been shown to offer important insights into health experiences, for example, depression (Charteris-Black 2012), illness (Sontag 1979), cancer (Gibbs and Franks 2002), addiction (Shinebourne and Smith 2010), mental health post-trauma (Wilson and Lindy 2013) and end-of-life care (Semino et al. 2017). The reason for this is that metaphors provide a tool to understand and describe these abstract, personal experiences by relating them to more concrete, universal ones. Metaphors highlight some aspects of an experience while downplaying others (Lakoff and Johnson 1980), and it is often necessary to employ more than one metaphor to capture the richness and conflicting facets of an experience, as evidenced in many of the papers written by Raymond Gibbs (e.g. 2016). Thus, by examining the metaphors that people use when talking about their lived experiences, we gain insights into the ways in which they highlight some aspects of these experiences while downplaying others. Metaphor analysis is therefore a useful method for gaining insight into real life experiences and how legal frameworks shape such experiences. Because metaphor analysis is effective in showing the complexities, tensions and ambiguities of emotionally charged experiences, it is a useful tool for exploring the experience of pregnancy loss as well as the legal categorizations and frameworks that structure it. The analysis of metaphorical language can provide deeper and more nuanced insights into the lived experience of embodied liminality that characterizes pregnancy loss.

# 4 The 'Death Before Birth' Project

## 4.1 Data Gathering

In order to investigate the experience of pregnancy loss, we gathered qualitative and textual data that spanned a range of institutional, professional and experiential points of view, including those of our project partner organizations the MA, ARC and SANDS.[4] We designed five stages of research investigation. Of these, two are pertinent to the current discussion. Stage two consisted of semi-structured interviews with bereavement care providers in hospitals within NHS England and with professionals in the funerary industry (five funeral directors, eight bereavement service managers and two officers at national funeral care institutions). These interviews enquired about practitioners' knowledge, use of and opinions about the Human Tissue Authority's 'Guidance on the disposal of pregnancy remains following pregnancy loss or termination'. In the fourth research stage, we conducted 31 qualitative interviews with women who had experienced a pregnancy loss, that is, miscarriage (n = 11), termination due to fetal anomaly (n = 11) or stillbirth (n = 9). Since we wanted interviewees to talk about the aspects of their experience in a style that felt comfortable to them, we used a form of narrative elicitation adapted from narrative methods, and restricted our prompts to phrases like 'can you tell me how that felt?' (Riessman 2008). We encouraged reflection on the emotional responses to pregnancy loss and decision-making about what to do with fetal remains and how or if to mark the death of their fetus or baby as we wished to honor the experiences of loss as fully embodied and affective realities for the women involved. Phase four of the research also involved interviewing a small sample of partners and friends who had supported a parent through a miscarriage, termination for fetal anomaly or stillbirth (n = 5).

As the above description of our project methods suggests, we were committed to examining how the people who are most intimately involved in making choices and decisions about the disposal of fetal remains understand the law, the guidance about disposal and, where applicable, their own experiences of loss. Our methods of data gathering and data analysis were therefore informed by feminist epistemology, especially standpoint theory which emphasizes the

[4] Miscarriage Association (MA) supports people with experiences of miscarriage (MA 2019). Antenatal Results and Choices (ARC) helps parents and healthcare professionals through antenatal testing and its consequences (ARC 2019). Stillbirth and Neonatal Death Charity (Sands) works to reduce the number of babies dying and to better understand the causes of baby deaths and to provide bereavement support services at a local and national level (Sands 2019).

importance of respecting lived experience as a form of knowledge (Harding 1991; Smith 1987). An advantage of employing such a methodology in a project that tackles socio-legal issues such as the liminality of the fetus or of fetal remains is that feminist standpoint theory recognizes all knowledge as partial and situated (Haraway 1988). In other words, there is no 'objective' or 'omniscient' viewpoint from which the issue of liminality regarding the disposal of fetal remains can be understood. There are multiple viewpoints and multiple knowledges, regardless of what the law of a nation-state might demand of its citizens in terms of definitions, actions and limits. For example, when a doctor uses the legal term 'fetal remains', people who have experienced a miscarriage might react by balking at that term if they understand their loss to involve a baby (i.e. a human being) who requires a funeral ceremony. In evidence here are several forms of knowledge: common sense knowledge legitimated by culturally valent ideas about miscarriages as a form of baby loss, medical knowledge about pregnancy loss and knowledge of legal definitions of the pregnancy remains as the mother's tissue. Some of these areas of knowledge are the result of professional training, while others are acquired more informally as the result of everyday experience that is, in turn, informed by people's situation within specific socio-economic, political, legal and cultural contexts. Researchers employing methods such as the ones we designed and combined must therefore also attend to the structures (e.g. legal parameters, institutional regulations and practices), ideologies, discourses and power differences that shape people's relationship to their experiences.

## 4.2 Metaphor Identification and Analysis

The interviews were transcribed and the transcripts were coded for metaphor in NVivo. We employed an adapted version of the PRAGGLEJAZ Group (2007) Metaphor Identification Procedure, which we combined with Cameron's (2003) vehicle identification procedure to identify metaphors at the level of the phrase. We then categorized the metaphors into at least one semantic category. These included, for example, space, darkness and light, movement, growth, ascent and descent, and containment. For example, the metaphor 'I was in quite a dark place there' was categorized as 'lightness and darkness', 'location' and 'container'. Through an iterative process, we identified 71 topics that these metaphors were being used to talk about. These included, for example, 'the diagnosis', 'memory-making', 'decision-making' and 'recovery'. Each metaphorical chunk of language was assigned to at least one topic. The coding schemes that we used for the identification of the topics and the metaphor categories were developed by three coders through joint analyses of the first five transcripts. Subsequent transcripts were then coded individually. Each transcript was checked by a second coder, and marginal cases were discussed until agreement was reached (see Littlemore and Turner 2019b).

We used our metaphor analysis to explore the different ways in which the women were experiencing their loss. In this chapter we focus on the metaphors that were used to describe aspects of the experience that affected the decision-making process for the disposal of the remains of pregnancy, including decisions that were made about memorialization and funeral arrangements. In our analysis, we also considered metonymy. Metonymy is a much more subtle form of figurative language than metaphor and, as such, is harder to identify in a systematic manner (Littlemore 2015). Unlike metaphor, where one thing is described or experienced in terms of another unrelated entity, metonymy involves the use of one entity to refer to another that is closely related or even something that it forms part of, so we might for example use the term 9/11 to refer to the terrorist attack that took place in New York on that day in 2001. Metonymy is often more nuanced than metaphor; it allows the analyst to gauge which aspects of a situation are most salient in the speaker's mind, and how the ways in which the speaker chooses to frame a situation can change. Therefore, like metaphor, it is a useful tool for examining liminal experiences. Our analysis of metonymy was not as systematic as our analysis of metaphor, and did not attempt to identify every use of metonymy in the dataset. Rather, we identified and then conducted in-depth analyses of salient uses of metonymy that related directly to embodiment and liminality.

## 5 Liminal Bodies, Legal Frameworks and Metaphorical Insights

In England and Wales, the Births and Deaths Registration Act 1953 section 41 (as amended by the Stillbirth (Definition) Act 1992 section 1(1)) defines stillbirth as 'a child which has issued forth from its mother after the 24th week of pregnancy and which did not at any time after being expelled from its mother breathe or show any other signs of life'.[5] When a stillbirth occurs, a Medical Certificate of Stillbirth is issued, which must then be taken to the register office within a specified period in order to register the stillbirth. Upon

[5] Similar legislation governing this distinction also applies to Northern Ireland and Scotland.

registration, the parents will be issued with a stillbirth certificate and also a certificate which permits burial or cremation. Some of our participants would have preferred to receive both a birth and death certificate in recognition of their experience and their child's existence (Fuller et al. 2018). Women who have had a stillbirth are entitled to maternity leave and benefits.

Pregnancy losses that occur prior to 24 weeks' gestation are considered a miscarriage and legally the remains are considered the woman's tissue (Human Tissue Act 2004). There is no legal possibility to formally register a miscarriage, although many hospitals will provide the woman with an informal certificate and many crematoria keep non-statutory registers. Our research evidenced a range of opinions from women who had experienced pregnancy loss about the registration of births pre-24 weeks' gestation. Some were content with an informal certificate of loss that they had been offered by the hospital; others wished for the opportunity to formally register their baby's birth or death in recognition of their experience (Fuller et al. 2018). Burial, cremation and sensitive incineration of pre-24-week remains are all permissible (HTA 2015). Our findings show that the legal rules on disposal of remains before 24 weeks' gestation are ambiguous and poorly understood (McGuinness and Kuberska 2017). Finally, there is no formal entitlement to leave or benefits following a miscarriage other than statutory sick leave.

In what follows we present three areas where the women's use of metaphor provides insights into the lived experience of pregnancy loss and how this is shaped by law. These insights provide an understanding of the embodied, liminal nature of this experience and reveal limits of, and tensions in, legal frameworks with regard to three key aspects of pregnancy loss: pregnant embodiment, the disposal of fetal remains and the use of ceremonial practices which often follow reproductive loss. Our analysis shows how law has the capacity to legitimatize and stigmatize different experiences of pregnancy loss and bereavement.

## 5.1 Pregnant Embodiment and the Divided Self

Isabel Karpin has influentially argued for the importance of reconceptualizing the maternal–fetal relationship in law to counter narratives that frame the pregnant person in opposition to the fetal subject (Karpin 1992). Using the frame of 'not one but not two', she suggests we recuperate the maternal–fetal connection:

> to place the woman in control of her body/self and the fetus and not, as she was constructed in the pre-technological era, as subject to her body nor, as she might otherwise be constructed in the age of technology, as subject to the fetus. (1992, p. 330)

Recent work on bodily integrity has emphasized the importance of adopting an integral approach to the understanding of self and body (Fox and Thomson 2017). Our findings show how such approaches are important in order to accommodate the variety of ways in which body and self are fractured by experiences of pregnancy loss.

The embodied nature of pregnancy loss was found to manifest in metaphors where the women blended the physical and emotional experience of loss. Here is a comment from a woman who had opted for a termination following a diagnosis of fetal abnormality:

> I feel a lot stronger 'cos not many people go through this. … It's not like losing a parent … I've lost grandparents and even friends that have died but it's NOT like that because *it's part of you and is a part of me.* It's like *I lost myself for a long, long time and then you have to try and rebuild yourself,* and your confidence, and everything. (WP4-T11-FA-3, our emphasis) [6]

The physicality is extremely strong in this quote, and she uses it to distinguish her experience from other forms of bereavement.

The disruptive nature of reproductive loss is important not just in terms of ruptures to the sense of self but also practically in terms of how it shapes legal decision-making. Many of the women we spoke to used bodily based metaphors to describe feelings of confusion and an inability to think coherently. Here are two accounts, both from women who experienced miscarriages:

> I think it's quite hard because you have that massive shock … *and your brain shuts down* … and I couldn't process it. (WP4-T4-M-3, our emphasis)

> And then as soon as it [became] a real thing … I had to say the words 'I've had a miscarriage' … that's when I just felt like *everything had just fallen out of the world* and like I just failed and that … there was no control there was … nothing and I just felt so *empty* and … confused. (WP4-T9-M-8, our emphasis)

The use of metaphor in these accounts links to the liminal status of the pregnancy, the fetus and the loss as discussed by Young (1990). In the second quote, the woman feels empty because what has been lost is an embodied part of her. Her confusion comes from how her bodily boundaries have shifted, and she has lost something that was part of her but also had the potential to

[6] Some of the quotations in this paper have been edited to ensure they are intelligible to the reader. These edits have been minimal and have not impacted the substance of the quotations.

be a person in their own right. Her body has expanded literally and metaphorically to include another being, and when that being is no longer there, this is an attack on both her body and her identity. She has been violently returned to her pre-liminal state rather than moving to the post liminal state in which she would have been transformed into a mother, had the pregnancy progressed to term (Côté-Arsenault et al. 2009). This can be exacerbated through the lack of formal legal recognition of her experience.

In our analysis we also came across many 'divided self' metaphors (they constituted the eighth most used metaphor category overall) as evidence of the ways in which women tried to manage and control these transformations. This suggests that some acknowledgment of this need to split oneself into separate 'parts' may be beneficial for those who experience reproductive loss. One of our participants, who had made the decision to terminate following diagnosis of fetal abnormality, recognized her own ambivalence, commenting:

> I took that decision to end it… Because, you know. I didn't want to do that part…the *mother part of me didn't want to do that at all.* I wanted to carry him and have him. (WP4-T11-FA-3, our emphasis)

Such acknowledgment might not only help people to distance themselves from difficult decisions, it might also enable them to incorporate their identity as parents in their decision-making processes. Although the idea of dividing one's identity into different roles is a fairly conventional one, here we see that the woman has already acquired a new role, that of the mother, and that this role is in conflict with the reality of the situation, where she is ending her pregnancy.

The recognition or validation of self in the wake of pregnancy loss is a recognized challenge. Samantha Murphy states 'by creating this foetus, this unborn child as a social being, we turn this woman into "its mother"—defining her in terms of the foetus' (Murphy 2012, p. 118). Yet, in situations of reproductive loss, where there is no living child existing in the world:

> the very people who have encouraged the mother-in-the-making to take on this role and may have participated with her in the social construction of her 'baby' often withdraw their support for these interrelated projects and act as if nothing of any significance took place. (Layne 2003, p. 17)

One of our project participants who had themselves experienced reproductive loss and now supported others in this situation describes the situation as follows:

> There's only me that knew that I was ever pregnant. You know. There's only me that knows I ever had a baby. Well obviously my family knows but there is nothing to say that she existed. Okay, she never made it into this world but she existed. (WP3-05/2017)

Dividing oneself and compartmentalizing one's emotions can become an important mechanism for coping with loss. Some of our participants reported that mentally they were not really 'there' throughout the process, as we can see in this comment from a woman who had opted for a termination following a diagnosis of fetal abnormality:

> It was almost like at the time *we were on autopilot* ... and if I was to say to someone in retrospect, I don't think we, I certainly didn't, deal with it properly at the time ... and I think that's why I sort of struggled with it last year, because I think *it all just sort of slapped me with it sort of out of the blue.* (WP4-T1-FA-1, our emphasis)

These metaphors evidence varying degrees of agency and show how our participants distanced themselves from the situation they were in.

Pregnancy loss disrupts social scripts and leaves bereaved parents at a loss as to what they are expected to do. When establishing her identity after pregnancy loss, a woman has to negotiate a set of interacting clines: from a state in which she sees herself as one, to a state in which she sees herself as two; from a state in which her pregnancy is something that she is experiencing, to a state in which she *is* her pregnancy (Cornell 1995; Karpin 1992); from a state in which she claims identity as a mother, to a state in which she does not. Such clines are not binary states; people move along them in both directions and can find themselves at different points depending on where they are in the process. These clines interact with one another, and, as we will see in the following section, with the different ways in which the mother perceives the pregnancy. The liminality of this experience gives rise to a number of potentially conflicting identities which are not easily reconciled. These identities are temporary fixed states that we naturally gravitate toward within a complex system. Within a Western European tradition of thinking about ontology, the desire to fix our identity is understandable since the notion of a coherent self informs not only lawmaking and healthcare provision, but also cultural ideas about what it means to be well and thriving as a 'whole' person. Following a pregnancy loss, however, achieving a sense of fixed identity becomes very difficult.

## 5.2 Maternal/Fetal Bodily Relations

Much attention has been paid to the social life of the living fetus (Lupton 2013). Technologies allowing visualization of the inside of the womb have increased the likelihood that the fetus be considered a person (Taylor 2008). In the social and cultural imagination, the fetus is accelerated through the liminal phase to the position of child (see Layne 2003). On the other hand, less attention has been paid to dead fetuses (although see Hardacre 1997; Morgan 2009). Analyses of dead fetuses to date have tended to treat them as an object of analysis and regulation, often overlooking what our social relation to dead fetuses can tell us about legal and kinship relations. The living fetus exists on a cline betwixt and between legal personhood and non-personhood (Petchesky 1987). This has implications for how the dead fetus is perceived; as it had the potential to move between these two states when it was viable, so too it can have the potential to move between these different states in the minds of the people grieving it after its death. Our study revealed this in a wide variety of reactions to the loss and consequential attitudes toward the remains, all of which will have a bearing on the decisions that are ultimately made regarding disposal (Fuller et al. 2018).

In 2014, following a number of 'scandals' and in particular the airing of a Dispatches documentary on incineration of fetal material, the Human Tissue Authority was tasked with creating guidance for disposal of pregnancy remains (Browne 2017). Prior to 24 weeks' gestation, the remains are treated as the person's tissue or, in the language of the Human Tissue Act 2004, 'relevant material' (Human Tissue Act 2004, s. 53). Disposal of 'relevant material' does not normally fall within the remit of the Human Tissue Authority that, instead, has the statutory authority to regulate its removal, storage or use (Human Tissue Act 2004). Notwithstanding this, the Human Tissue Authority Code of Practice did recognize that fetal material could be considered more sensitive than other tissue in the new 'Guidance on the disposal of pregnancy remains following pregnancy loss or termination' published in 2015 (HTA 2015). It included the following options for disposal: cremation (shared or individual), burial (shared or individual), sensitive incineration (incineration separate to other clinical waste), burial at home or at some other site subject to certain limitations and as such endorsed existing approaches that existed in professional codes of practice (HTA 2015; ICCM 2015; RCN 2018; see also Sands 2016). One of the key points of tension in the development of the Guidance was the question of whether 'sensitive incineration' should continue to be seen as permissible. Ultimately, it was decided that it should.

Our findings endorse this approach, and we found that each option was important to different parents for different reasons (see Austin and McGuinness 2019). Some parents wanted to dispose of the remains without ceremony, whereas others wanted to organize some kind of funeral in order to help them come to terms with the loss and honor their baby. In some cases, differing attitudes toward the status of the fetus can be seen in the language that is used to talk about it. Consider the following narrative by a woman who, after having experienced a miscarriage, was really upset that she had not been informed about what the miscarriage would be like and how she might preserve the remains:

> And I didn't know what to do. I didn't know how to cope with what was happening. I was in pain. So – it sounds awful but – the baby ended up falling into the toilet. And I couldn't stay in the bathroom so I went back into the bedroom and my husband, who was in the bathroom with me the whole time and helping me to pass the baby, he had a look at the baby and tried to get it out of the toilet so that we could do something with the body. But [when] he came back in the bedroom a couple of minutes later, [he] just said the baby had sort of disintegrated. The body'd split apart and there was nothing much he could do about getting it out of the toilet. [A]nd then we had a terribly awful practical talk about what did we do next, so we ended up flushing the toilet. (WP4-T24-M-11)

In her commentary, the interviewee shifts back and forth between 'baby' and 'body' twice, and then moves away from referring to the remains at all by talking about 'what did we do next': a sentence in which the plural 'we' clearly signifies the woman and her partner but does not include the 'baby' ('so we ended up flushing the toilet').

In the following example, the woman is surprised at being offered cremation as a form of disposal following a miscarriage:

> So [my pregnancy] stopped growing at six weeks but I was twelve to thirteen weeks pregnant 'cos my body hadn't realised that nothing was happening. So [the doctor] said your only option is a cremation and that has to be on site and it's up to you whether you want to be there or not … but the remains have to remain on site. And I was like: right, okay, that makes no sense bothering to… I just thought: oh, why wouldn't it just go in with general clinical waste – if they're not deeming it as a thing? So it sort of made no sense. I was like: is it a thing? 'Cos one minute it is a thing and the next it's not a thing? (WP4-T9-M-8)

These accounts, both from women bereaved through miscarriage, evidence different relationships with fetal remains. The latter example also highlights the symbolic significance attached to particular disposal options, and the fact that this makes those options feel inappropriate for some women. The final sentence uttered by this participant emphasizes the ambiguity that is often experienced and the liminal nature of the fetus: 'one minute it is a thing and the next it's not a thing'.

In addition to heterogeneous perceptions of the remains, it is also the case that attitudes toward the baby may change dramatically over the course of the loss, as is shown in the next two extracts from our interviews with a woman who had experienced a stillbirth. This woman's commentary shows that even when a baby is lost at term, there is some ambiguity surrounding their status. In the first extract, the woman had been asked if she would want to hold her baby when it was born. The second excerpt talks more generally about her attitude toward her stillborn child:

> I don't think it should be a pre-asked question … I think that's the biggest thing [because] they asked me this question on the Thursday, the day before I actually had him. And at the time, he was a problem. He was a dead baby inside of me … he was a problem … But because they'd asked me the question I had that doubt in my head of: do I want to hold him? Would I want to hold him? Will I look at that baby and want to hold that baby? It's a dead baby. And it was only [because] me and my husband spoke and said we can't not hold him. We've got to hold him. But I think that if I was asked after I had him and a midwife had been holding him and said here's your baby. Do you want to hold your son? That, to me, would be really different thing. (WP4-T28-S-7)

> It's okay to have these experiences with your child because that is your son … it's not a dead baby. It's your son. It's your daughter. And that's the way you will view them going forward. You won't view them as being *this problem, this stillbirth, this death that's happened, this process...* That's how it's dealt with at the time but you will view them in the future as being your son. Your daughter. And then you'll look back and regret not treating them that way. (WP4-T28-S-7, our emphasis)

These examples from our interviews show that during the loss, and in its aftermath, a baby can change from being a (biomedical) problem to be solved, to a baby to be mourned. We can identify another cline at work here between the idea of the fetus as a baby and, more broadly speaking, as not a baby. This underscores the importance of giving parents time to consider the options around disposal carefully and to make the choice that is best for them. They also evidence the strange space that the fetus occupies in the social and legal imaginary (Kuberska and Turner 2019). By describing the baby metonymically as a 'problem', a 'stillbirth', a 'death' or a 'process', the woman is focusing attention away from the baby itself and drawing attention to different aspects of its existence, all reported from the perspective of the adults involved, thus putting a certain amount of distance between her and the baby. Perhaps even more than metaphor, metonymy provides the opportunity to frame a particular situation, to focus on some aspects of an experience while downplaying others and to represent it from different angles (Littlemore 2015). All of this may help people to cope with different aspects of the situation at a time. Once the 'problem' acquires personhood, attention can be paid to how it is mourned. The current legal framework attempts to attach significance to fetal remains within frameworks underpinned by binary understandings of property/person or person/thing (Deckha 2012). Pregnancy remains/fetal remains exist as both subject and object depending on the situation and, in doing so, they contain the dual capacity of being both person and thing.

## 5.3 Funerals for Fetuses

Professionals working in the funerary industry in England are guided in their practice by the law and professional guidance.[7] Best practice is also disseminated through official training for funerary professionals which is generally organized and delivered by these organizations (see e.g. Malt et al. 2019). Funeral professionals also often perform social rituals or ceremonies alongside these disposal practices. As mentioned above, legal disposal of pre-24-week fetal remains does not require a funeral ceremony but, as the previous section demonstrated, people may experience pregnancy loss as bereavement and understand 'the remains' to represent not only their own hopes and dreams as a prospective parent, but also to operate metonymically as the stand-in for their child and the life that their baby might have lived. Metonymic links such as the following, made by a woman who had experienced a miscarriage, are found between the ashes and the idea of a living baby:

> We were going to scatter his ashes on his due date but I don't feel ready to let him go. I just like knowing he's in the house. I just–I just don't want to let him go right now. And I don't know if I ever will, I just–we don't have a special urn or anything. He really is just stashed away in a sideboard but I just like knowing he's at home with us. (WP4-T20-M-10)

[7] HTA Guidance on the Disposal of Pregnancy Remains (2015); ICCM (2015) the Federation of Burial and Cremation Authorities (FBCA); or the National Association of Funeral Directors (NAFD).

In this excerpt, the metonymy is found in how the ashes stand for the baby, reinforced by the use of the personal pronouns 'his', 'him' and 'he'. There is a further metonymic relationship which shades into metaphor, in that literally scattering the ashes (metonymically standing for the baby) equates to metaphorically letting go of the baby.

With this in mind, the examples and discussion contained in this section detail how ceremonial practices that accompany disposal are informed by socio-cultural understandings of fetal personhood. We will also see how the ceremonies attached to shared cremations reproduce and normalize those notions of personhood, and we will discuss why in some cases that normalization may be problematic,[8] given how often they assume an objective reality and a fixed identity for the fetus that others may not share. We will identify some alternative ways in which 'the remains' are treated and viewed by those who experience pregnancy loss as a further illustration of their complex liminal status within English society. The anthropologist Victor Turner famously defined ceremonies as 'confirmatory' and rituals as 'transformative' (1967, p. 95). Rather than simply marking the transition from life to death, these ceremonies for fetal remains appear to confirm their complex liminal status as not-quite-babies but more than 'the mother's tissue'.

Most of the funeral directors and bereavement service managers we interviewed in our study agreed that all pregnancy losses, irrespective of the stage of gestation, deserve the same care and dignity as the remains of a person who has lived and died. Such an approach is influenced by the notion—explicitly articulated in, for example, the HTA (2015) Guidance—that 'sensitivity' toward both families and the remains should be foregrounded. The equivalence drawn here between a life that has not been lived and one that has illustrates the intermediary role that funerary practitioners play in the disposal of the remains of pregnancy. Not only are they operating at the interface between legal requirements and parents' choices about what should occur, but also they are mediating between different conceptualizations of life and personhood.

The funeral-like ceremonies or services that often accompany the cremation or burial of fetal remains can also be understood as part of a sensitive professional practice. However, there is another way in which fetal personhood is recognized within the funerary profession because the ceremonies have much in common with those performed for people who have lived and died (Kuberska 2020). Several types of ceremonies were described in the documents that we collected from the NHS trusts and in the interviews we held with funerary industry professionals (see McGuinness and Kuberska 2017).

[8] See Morgan and Michaels, Eds. (1999).

For example, pregnancy remains are placed in coffins or coffin-like containers and are transported to the cemetery or crematorium chapel either by a funeral director or a designated member of the bereavement team in an appropriate vehicle. A short service is often held and typically features elements like music, a short reading (e.g. a poem) and a few words spoken by a funeral director or perhaps a hospital chaplain. The coffin or coffins (if the cremation or burial is shared) are placed on a catafalque during the service which is followed by an act of committal (closing of the curtain around the coffin(s) or slight lowering of the coffin(s) into the catafalque). Often these services include explicitly Christian elements such as Biblical readings, blessings and prayers. Thus, not only are many ceremonies religious in tone, but they are also specifically Judeo-Christian in practice—an aspect of the ceremonies that is potentially problematic in a multi-faith society. By incorporating activities like prayers and blessings into ceremonies, funerary professionals overlay the notion of fetal personhood that is inferred in the performance of a service that is usually inspired by a life lived, with a more specifically Christian ideal of life's value and of death as a passage into an afterlife with the deity.

A key difference between these funeral-like ceremonies for fetal remains and those performed for people who have lived is that families may not be in attendance. Indeed, the parents in our research sample were not always informed that there would be any type of ceremony when the remains of pregnancy loss were to form part of a shared cremation arranged by the hospital. Similarly, many of the trusts whose documentation we examined held general services of remembrance on a monthly, biannual or annual basis, yet families were often unaware of this practice. These various types of 'unwitnessed ceremonies' introduce a note of ambiguity into the ways in which fetal remains are being perceived by the professionals conducting them: rather than straightforwardly granting the personhood that is implied in the construction and enactment of a funeral-like service, the unwitnessed ceremony destabilizes that process, further amplifying the liminal status of the fetus (Kuberska 2020).

As Kuberska has demonstrated in her longer reflection on this data, such ceremonies result 'in the normalization of a very specific social order where funerals for pre-24-week pregnancy losses come to be expected' (2020, p. 207). In other words, when specific values, activities and attitudes become the norm or default, other ways of thinking and being may be excluded. Kuberska writes:

> Normalizing unwitnessed ceremonies accompanying shared cremations as proper funerals can become a double-edged sword. On the one hand, it helps to

> reiterate the idea that mourning a pregnancy loss can be more than justified. On the other hand, it obscures situations in which no special significance is accorded to pregnancy remains, suggesting that such stances are less 'respectful' because they are unaccompanied by ritualized disposal. (2020, p. 225)

For example, not all the women in our study who had experienced a miscarriage viewed their experience as the loss of a baby. Furthermore, not everyone we talked to wanted a funeral or funeral-like service conducted by professionals. Some women did not want any kind of service or memorialization, as we can see in this comment from a woman who had opted for termination following diagnosis of fetal abnormality:

> I don't want to go to a memorial garden, I don't want to go to a little bit of green at the hospital and remember my baby, that's not how I want to do it, so it's not something that interests me at all. And they, apparently, have sort of services at the hospital in the in the chapel in there, but again that's not something I want to go to. (WP4-T1-FA-1)

Several people preferred more personalized and private rituals like planting a tree or flower in a domestic garden. Such rituals may produce different metaphorical meanings for those who perform them, but the association of 'the remains' with nature suggests that what is being represented through the planting is an organic and cyclical notion of life that is not restricted to human experience. Here the same woman describes her engagement with a funeral professional:

> He was really good. 'Cos he'd lost a baby through a miscarriage, so I'd said: the first baby that we lost [around] Easter time, so I want something that flowers sort of Easterish … so it's the right time. And, so they had a planting programme, but they didn't have any trees available that they planted that would flower at Easter. So he changed all the planting programme for me, he got this tree that was some sort of cherry blossom. And I said: I want it near the playground, because I want to be able to take my little girl, and then say to her: *that's my tree, or that's our tree, although … she doesn't know why we've got a tree.* (WP4-T1-FA-1, our emphasis)

In such instances, rather than taking fetal personhood for granted, the bereaved parents could be understood as articulating the liminal status of their unborn baby by substituting a tree, plant or flower for 'the remains'. This is a clear example of how metaphorical thinking can help people come to terms with the experience of pregnancy loss. The loss is understood as part of the wider life cycle and the cherry blossom tree, which is in bloom for a very short time every Easter, is a metaphor for the 'short but beautiful' life of her baby girl.

## 6 Conclusion

In this chapter we have provided an overview of how a consideration of liminality, embodiment and metaphor can help us to develop a better grasp of the socio-legal relationship between pregnancy loss and law from the point of view of those who have experienced it. This includes both the physical and the emotional aspects of the experience, as well as the different choices they make and the feelings that motivate them.

Our analysis has shown pregnancy to be an embodied liminal experience. This affects how the baby and the mother are conceptualized, and consequently how the loss is conceptualized, how this affects the decisions that are taken following a loss and how we can critique conventional memorialization practices in light of this. These practices are designed to construct a framework around something that is otherwise understood to be chaotic.

> Locating personhood in fetal biology is consistent with a conception of personhood as a quality that accrues quickly and is fixed at a particular point in the gestational cycle. Fetal development is considered to be a natural biological process that, once set in motion, proceeds largely of its own accord. A person can be created out of a minimal social interaction. Within a Western European context, we usually ascribe personhood to beings that have engaged in some sort of social interaction. When personhood is understood to be ascribed by non-social factors, it cannot be readily rescinded, attenuated or truncated by social action. Western persons, once established, are not easily undone. (Conklin and Morgan, 1996, p. 665)

We have shown how metaphor provides a useful lens for exploring the experience of pregnancy loss and its status as an embodied liminal phenomenon. We have also provided insights into the transformative nature of this lived experience, demonstrating how identities shift along distinct yet interacting clines. The interaction between the chaos of the experience and the set legal framework within which it is situated represents a site of conflict that challenges and disrupts accepted classifications and boundaries. We have demonstrated that the fetus exists in a liminal state and that when this liminality is not resolved into a live birth, neither social nor legal scripts are able to accommodate it in a satisfactory way.

## References

ARC. (2019). *Home|ARC Supports Parents Throughout Antenatal Testing and Its Consequences*. Retrieved November 21, 2019, from https://www.arc-uk.org/

Austin, L., & McGuinness, S. (2019). Reproductive Loss and Disposal of Pregnancy Remains. *Northern Ireland Legal Quarterly, 70*(1), 131–153. Retrieved from https://nilq.qub.ac.uk/index.php/nilq/article/view/31.

Bendelow, G., & Williams, S. J. (1998). *Emotions in Social Life: Critical Themes and Contemporary Issues* (S. J. Williams & G. Bendelow, Eds.). London: Routledge.

Bordo, S. (1993). *Unbearable Weight: Feminism, Western Culture, and the Body*. Berkeley/Los Angeles: University of California Press.

Brazier, M. (2009). Introduction – Being Human: Of Liberty and Privilege. In S. W. Smith & R. Deazley (Eds.), *The Legal, Medical and Cultural Regulation of the Body: Transformation and Transgression* (pp. 11–22). https://doi.org/10.4324/9781315556192-7.

Browne, C. (2017). Foreword. In S. McGuinness & K. Kuberska (Eds.), *Report to the Human Tissue Authority on Disposal of Pregnancy Remains (Less than 24 Weeks' Gestational Stage)* (pp. 3–5). Retrieved from https://testprojectwebsiteblog.files.wordpress.com/2017/09/death-before-birth-hta-report-2017.pdf.

Cameron, L. (2003). *Metaphor in Educational Discourse*. London: Continuum.

Charteris-Black, J. (2012). Shattering the Bell Jar: Metaphor, Gender, and Depression. *Metaphor and Symbol, 27*(3), 199–216. https://doi.org/10.1080/10926488.2012.665796.

Conklin, B. A., & Lynn M. Morgan, L. M. (1996). Babies, Bodies, and the Production of Personhood in North America and a Native Amazonian society. *Ethos, 24*, 657–694.

Cornell, D. (1995). *The Imaginary Domain: Abortion, Pornography & Sexual Harassment*. New York: Routledge.

Côté-Arsenault, D., Brody, D., & Dombeck, M.-T. (2009). Pregnancy as a Rite of Passage: Liminality, Rituals & Communitas. *Journal of Prenatal & Perinatal Psychology & Health, 24*(2), 69–87. Retrieved from https://www.questia.com/library/journal/1P3-2113516821/pregnancy-as-a-rite-of-passage-liminality-rituals.

Deckha, M. (2012). Legislating Respect: A pro-Choice Feminist Analysis of Embryo Research Restrictions in Canada. *McGill Law Journal, 58*(2), 199–236. https://doi.org/10.7202/1013389ar.

Fletcher, R., Fox, M., & McCandless, J. (2008). Legal Embodiment: Analysing the Body of Healthcare Law. *Medical Law Review, 16*(3), 321–345. https://doi.org/10.1093/medlaw/fwn017.

Fox, M., & McGuinness, S. (2016). The Science of Muddling Through: Categorising Embryos. In C. Stanton, S. Devaney, A.-M. Farrell, & A. Mullock (Eds.), *Pioneering Healthcare Law: Essays in Honour of Margaret Brazier* (pp. 199–210). London: Routledge.

Fox, M., & Thomson, M. (2017). Bodily Integrity, Embodiment, and the Regulation of Parental Choice. *Journal of Law and Society, 44*(4), 501–531. https://doi.org/10.1111/jols.12056.

Fuller, D., Littlemore, J., McGuinness, S., Kuberska, K., & Turner, S. (2018). *Preliminary Project Findings for Meeting with Representatives of the Department of Health and Social Care.* Bristol: Birmingham.

Gibbs, R. W. (2006a). *Embodiment and Cognitive Science.* New York: Cambridge University Press.

Gibbs, R. W. (2006b). Metaphor Interpretation as Embodied Simulation. *Mind & Language, 21*, 434–458.

Gibbs, R. W. (2016). Introduction. In R. W. Gibbs (Ed.), *Mixing Metaphor* (pp. vii–xiv). Amsterdam: John Benjamins Publishing Company.

Gibbs, R. W., & Franks, H. (2002). Embodied Metaphor in Women's Narratives About Their Experiences with Cancer. *Health Communication, 14*(2), 139–165. https://doi.org/10.1207/S15327027HC1402_1.

Grosz, E. (1994). *Volatile Bodies: Toward a Corporeal Feminism.* Bloomington: Indiana University Press.

Han, S., Betsinger, T. K., & Scott, A. B. (2018). *The Anthropology of the Fetus : Biology, Culture, and Society* (S. Han, T. K. Betsinger, & A. B. Scott, Eds.). New York: Berghahn.

Haraway, D. (1988). Situated Knowledges: The Science Question in Feminism and the Privilege of Partial Perspective. *Feminist Studies, 14*(3), 575–599. https://doi.org/10.2307/3178066.

Hardacre, H. (1997). *Marketing the Menacing Fetus in Japan.* Berkeley/Los Angeles/London: University of California Press.

Harding, S. G. (1991). *Whose Science? Whose Knowledge? Thinking from Women's Lives.* Ithaca: Cornell University Press.

Herring, J., & Wall, J. (2017). The Nature and Significance of the Right to Bodily Integrity. *Cambridge Law Journal, 76*(3), 566–588. https://doi.org/10.1017/S0008197317000605.

HTA. (2015). *Guidance on the Disposal of Pregnancy Remains Following Pregnancy Loss or Termination.* Retrieved from http://www.rcn.org.uk/__data/assets/pdf_file/0020/78500/001248.pdf

Human Tissue Act 2004. (2004). *Human Tissue Act 2004.*

Hyde, A. (1997). *Bodies of Law.* Princeton: Princeton University Press.

ICCM. (2015). *The Sensitive Disposal of Fetal Remains: Policy and Guidance for Burial and Cremation Authorities and Companies.* London: ICCM.

Karpin, I. (1992). Legislating the Female Body: Reproductive Technology and the Reconstructed Woman. *Columbia Journal of Gender and Law, 3*(1), 325–350.

Kaufman, S. R., & Morgan, L. M. (2005). The Anthropology of the Beginnings and Ends of Life. *Annual Review of Anthropology, 34*, 317–341. https://doi.org/10.1146/annurev.anthro.34.081804.120452.

Kilshaw, S. (2017). Birds, Meat, and Babies: The Multiple Realities of Fetuses in Qatar. *Anthropology & Medicine, 24*(2), 189–204. https://doi.org/10.1080/13648470.2017.1324617.

Kuberska, K. (2020). Unwitnessed Ceremonies: Funeral Services for Pre-24-Week Pregnancy Losses in England. In S. Kilshaw & K. Borg (Eds.), *Navigating Miscarriage: Social, Medical and Conceptual Perspectives* (pp. 206–232). New York/Oxford: Berghahn.

Kuberska, K., & Turner, S. (2019). The Presence of Absence: Tensions and Frictions of Pregnancy Losses – An Introduction. *Women's Studies International Forum, 74*, 91–93. https://doi.org/10.1016/j.wsif.2019.03.009.

Kukla, R. (2005). *Mass Hysteria: Medicine, Culture, and Mothers' Bodies.* Oxford: Rowman & Littlefield Publishers, Inc.

Lakoff, G., & Johnson, M. (1980). *Metaphors We Live By*. Chicago: University of Chicago Press.

Lakoff, G., & Johnson, M. (1999). *Philosophy in the Flesh: The Embodied Mind and Its Challenge to Western Thought*. New York: Basic Books.

Laurie, G. (2017). Liminality and the Limits of Law in Health Research Regulation: What Are We Missing in the Spaces in-Between? *Medical Law Review, 25*(1), 47–72. https://doi.org/10.1093/medlaw/fww029.

Layne, L. L. (2003). *Motherhood Lost: A Feminist Account of Pregnancy Loss in America*. New York: Routledge.

Littlemore, J. (2015). *Metonymy: Hidden Shortcuts in Language, Thought and Communication*. Cambridge: Cambridge University Press.

Littlemore, J. (2019). *Metaphors in the Mind: Sources of Variation in Embodied Metaphor*. Cambridge: Cambridge University Press.

Littlemore, J., & Turner, S. (2019a). Metaphors in Communication About Pregnancy Loss. *Metaphor and the Social World, 10*(1), 45–74. https://doi.org/10.1075/msw.18030.lit

Littlemore, J., & Turner, S. (2019b). What Can Metaphor Tell Us About Experiences of Pregnancy Loss and How Are These Experiences Reflected in Midwife Practice? *Frontiers in Communication, 4*, 1–17. https://doi.org/10.3389/fcomm.2019.00042.

Lupton, D. (2013). *The Social Worlds of the Unborn*. Basingstoke: Palgrave Macmillan.

MA. (2019). *The Miscarriage Association: Pregnancy Loss Information and Support*. Retrieved November 21, 2019, from https://www.miscarriageassociation.org.uk/

Malt, O., Littlemore, J., & McGuinness, S. (2019). Supporting Funerals Following Miscarriage or Stillbirth. *SAIF Insight*, 22–24. Retrieved from https://saifinsight.co.uk/wp-content/uploads/2019/09/GC-SAIF-Insight-September-2019-1.pdf

McGuinness, S., & Kuberska, K. (2017). *Report to the Human Tissue Authority on Disposal of Pregnancy Remains (Less than 24 Weeks' Gestational Stage)*. Retrieved from https://testprojectwebsiteblog.files.wordpress.com/2017/09/death-before-birth-hta-report-2017.pdf

Minow, M. (1990). *Making All the Difference: Inclusion, Exclusion, and American Law*. Ithaca/London: Cornell University Press.

Morgan, L. M. (1997). Imagining the Unborn in the Ecuadoran Andes. *Feminist Studies, 23*(2), 322. https://doi.org/10.2307/3178403.

Morgan, L. M. (2009). *Icons of Life: A Cultural History of Human Embryos*. Berkeley/Los Angeles/London: University of California Press.

Morgan, L. M., & Michaels, M. W. (1999). *Fetal Subjects, Feminist Positions* (L. M. Morgan & M. W. Michaels, Eds.). Philadelphia: University of Pennsylvania Press.

Murphy, S. (2012). Bereaved Parents: A Contradiction in Terms? In S. Earle, C. Komaromy, & L. Layne (Eds.), *Understanding Reproductive Loss: Perspectives on Life, Death and Fertility* (pp. 117–128). Retrieved from http://oro.open.ac.uk/34723/.

Naffine, N. (2003). Who Are Law's Persons? From Cheshire Cats to Responsible Subjects. *Modern Law Review, 66*(3), 346–367. https://doi.org/10.1111/1468-2230.6603002.

NHS. (2018). *Stillbirth: Overview*. Retrieved November 20, 2019, from https://www.nhs.uk/conditions/stillbirth/

Petchesky, R. P. (1987). Fetal Images: The Power of Visual Culture in the Politics of Reproduction. *Feminist Studies, 13*(2), 263–292. https://doi.org/10.2307/3177802.

PRAGGLEJAZ Group. (2007). MIP: A Method for Identifying Metaphorically Used Words in Discourse. *Metaphor and Symbol, 22*(1), 1–39. https://doi.org/10.1080/10926480709336752.

RCN. (2018). *Managing the Disposal of Pregnancy Remains: RCN Guidance for Nursing and Midwifery Practice*. London: RCN.

Reiheld, A. (2015). 'The Event that Was Nothing': Miscarriage as a Liminal Event. *Journal of Social Philosophy, 46*(1), 9–26. https://doi.org/10.1111/josp.12084.

Riessman, C. K. (2008). *Narrative Methods for the Human Sciences*. Thousand Oaks: Sage Publications.

Sands. (2016). *Pregnancy Loss and the Death of a Baby: Guidelines for Professionals death Charity* (4th ed.). Coventry: Tantamount.

Sands. (2019). *About Sands | Sands – Stillbirth and Neonatal Death Charity*. Retrieved November 21, 2019, from https://www.sands.org.uk/about-sands

Scheper-Hughes, N., & Lock, M. M. (1987). The Mindful Body: A Prolegomenon to Future Work in Medical Anthropology. *Medical Anthropology Quarterly, 1*(1), 6–41.

Semino, E. (2010). Descriptions of Pain, Metaphor, and Embodied Simulation. *Metaphor and Symbol, 25*(4), 205–226. https://doi.org/10.1080/10926488.2010.510926.

Semino, E. (2011). Metaphor, Creativity and the Experience of Pain Across Genres. In J. Swann, R. Carter, & R. Pope (Eds.), *Creativity in Language and Literature: The State of the Art* (pp. 83–102). https://doi.org/10.1007/978-1-349-92482-0_6.

Semino, E., Demjén, Z., Hardi, A., Payne, S., & Rayson, P. (2017). *Metaphor, Cancer and the End of Life: A Corpus-Based Study*. London: Routledge.

Shinebourne, P., & Smith, J. A. (2010). The Communicative Power of Metaphors: An Analysis and Interpretation of Metaphors in Accounts of the Experience of Addiction. *Psychology and Psychotherapy: Theory, Research and Practice, 83*(1), 59–73. https://doi.org/10.1348/147608309X468077.

Silbey, S. S. (2005). After Legal Consciousness. *Annual Review of Law and Social Science, 1*(1), 323–368. https://doi.org/10.1146/annurev.lawsocsci.1.041604.115938.

Smith, D. E. (1987). *The Everyday World as Problematic: A Feminist Sociology*. Toronto: University of Toronto Press.

Sontag, S. (1979). *Illness as Metaphor*. London: Allen Lane.

Squier, S. M. (2004). *Liminal Lives: Imagining the Human at the Frontiers of Biomedicine*. Durham: Duke University Press.

Squire, C., et al. (2014). *What Is Narrative Research?* London: Bloomsbury.

Taylor, J. S. (2008). *The Public Life of the Fetal Sonogram: Technology, Consumption, and the Politics of Reproduction*. London: Rutgers University Press.

Thompson, C. (2005). *Making Parents: The Ontological Choreography of Reproductive Technologies*. Cambridge, MA: The MIT Press.

Tommy's. (2019). *Miscarriage Statistics| Tommy's*. Retrieved November 26, 2019, from https://www.tommys.org/our-organisation/charity-research/pregnancy-statistics/miscarriage

Turner, V. W. (1967). *The Forest of Symbols: Aspects of Ndembu Ritual*. Ithaca/London: Cornell University Press.

Turner, V. W. (1969). *The Ritual Process: Structure and Anti-Structure*. New York: Routledge.

Turner, V. W. (1974). Liminal to Liminoid, in Play, Flow, and Ritual: An Essay in Comparative Symbology. *Rice University Studies, 60*(3), 53–92.

Turner, V. W. (1979). Frame, Flow and Reflection: Ritual and Drama as Public Liminality. *Japanese Journal of Religious Studies, 6*(4), 465–499.

van Gennep, A. ([1909] 2004). *The Rites of Passage* (M. B. Vizedom, & G. L. Caffee, Trans.). London: Routledge.

Wilson, J. P., & Lindy, J. D. (2013). *Trauma, Culture, and Metaphor: Pathways of Transformation and Integration*. New York: Routledge.

Young, I. M. (1990). *Throwing Like a Girl and Other Essays in Feminist Philosophy and Social Theory*. Bloomington: Indiana University Press.

# 8

# Depathologising Gender: Vulnerability in Trans Health Law

Chris Dietz and Ruth Pearce

## 1 Introduction

This chapter challenges how gender has been positioned under the control of health professionals in the regulation of trans bodies.[1] Trans people have formed complex relationships with health professionals, whose influence is often crucial in determining access to body modification treatments including hormones and surgeries. We have previously argued that this constitutes an overreach of medical jurisdiction, particularly where this intersects with legal gender recognition processes or the accessibility of health care provision (Pearce 2018; Dietz 2020). This chapter is more forward-looking, assessing the potential of a human right to depathologisation. After deciding that latent risks in this strategy might outweigh potential benefits, we propose an alternative agenda which understands trans bodies, and the institutions which regulate their access to health care, as vulnerable. This change of emphasis offers

[1] We use the term 'trans' here to refer to people who do not identify with the gender that they were assigned at birth and take active steps to make some form of social and/or medical transition away from that assigned gender.

C. Dietz (✉)
School of Law, University of Leeds, Leeds, UK
e-mail: c.p.dietz@leeds.ac.uk

R. Pearce
School of Sociology and Social Policy, University of Leeds, Leeds, UK



C. Dietz et al. (eds.), *A Jurisprudence of the Body*, Palgrave Socio-Legal Studies,
https://doi.org/10.1007/978-3-030-42200-4_8

key insights which could benefit the activists and scholars engaged in the 'trans depathologisation movement' (Davy et al. 2018: 15).

Like other contributions to this collection, this chapter identifies a body that has been under-theorised in health law. This is one result of trans phenomena being medicalised in various ways since the start of the twentieth century. Trans issues have, over time, become more commonly discussed within legal studies, but this has mostly been due to research conducted by scholars drawing on human rights and anti-discrimination perspectives (Whittle 2002; Dunne 2017; Sharpe 2010, 2018). Yet empirical research indicates that the positive impact of human rights reforms, including gender recognition legislation, may be undermined where they fail to address access to health care (Dietz 2018). Trans health has been well-researched in sociology (Davy 2011; Pearce 2018; Vincent 2020) and history (Meyerowitz 2002; Gill-Peterson 2018). Though trans issues have become more prominent within health law (Sørlie 2018; Dietz 2020), they are yet to become an established topic of study in this field.[2] Drawing upon developments in Argentina, Denmark, Uruguay, and the UK, this chapter seeks to address this deficit, developing a new research agenda for trans health law.

Once psychiatric terms enter everyday use, the boundaries between what is considered normal and pathological 'begin to blur' (Lane 2010: 105). When such terms are imported into law—for example, in requiring trans people to have been granted a psychiatric diagnosis in order to become eligible for gender recognition—authoritative norms establish the boundaries of acceptable gendered practice. These might relate to what names people have, how they dress and behave at home and in the workplace, how their body looks, and what kind of medical interventions they have (or haven't) had to modify their bodies. Trans people, and others, are then judged in relation to these norms. Yet 'medicolegal' understandings of trans phenomena (Butler 1993; Davy 2010) are not static. Since the later decades of the twentieth century, the standards which maintain the boundaries of acceptable gendered embodiment have been subjected to near-constant scrutiny and challenge. Courts and legislatures have responded by creating a diverse body of 'reform jurisprudence' (Sharpe 2010: 99), with trans people now regulated in a patchwork fashion, depending upon where in the world they reside. While some states offer no form of gender recognition, others require people to undergo compulsory sterilisation in order to be granted recognition (Honkasalo 2020). A growing number permit subjects to self-declare legal gender status, and have this

[2] Trans issues are not considered in most medical law textbooks, including Jackson (2016) and Brazier and Cave (2016). In Herring (2018), they are considered in relation to resource allocation.

recognised without further pre-condition (Castro-Peraza et al. 2019). This chapter will not present a comparative review of different forms of legal gender recognition available within different states (see ibid). It seeks to address the policy concerns of states towards the latter end of the scale instead.

At the time of its enactment, the UK Gender Recognition Act (GRA) 2004 was considered a 'groundbreaking reform' (Cowan 2009: 247). It dispensed, ostensibly, with a 'biological approach' (Sharpe 2010) which understood gender to be 'fixed at birth' (*Corbett v Corbett* [1970] 2 All ER 33 [1971] P 83, 104). It was the first European law not to require sterilisation (such as through the removal of reproductive organs) as a pre-condition for recognition (Dunne 2017). Yet the GRA 2004 still 'pathologises' trans phenomena—treating them as indicative of a mental disorder—by requiring applicants to provide supporting evidence from specialist health professionals that they have received a diagnosis of 'gender dysphoria' (GRA 2004, s. 2(1)(a)). This contrasts with legislation based upon the principle of self-declaration, which is said to constitute 'the optimal gender recognition model' (Dunne 2015: 539). The foremost example of self-declaration, the Argentinian Gender Identity Law (*Ley de Identidad de Genero 26.743*) (LIG) 2012, responds to critiques of previous gender recognition laws by permitting trans people to make a formal declaration of their gender status and have this recognised in civil registration systems without further pre-requisites. This enacts a shift away from the pathologisation of trans bodies.

Following the enactment of the LIG 2012, critiques of the pathologisation of trans identities have gained momentum at national and international levels. Such critiques have recently been re-framed as arguments in favour of the 'depathologisation' of trans phenomena (Davy et al. 2018). This might reflect a desire among activists and scholars to reformulate their critical stance into a more affirmative policy proposal, akin to those seen in calls for universal design in both bioethics (Ries and Thomson 2019) and disability law and policy (Lawson 2008). The demand for depathologisation of trans phenomena is increasingly talked about as a right, and in some cases a human right (Cabral et al. 2016). It is at this point that we wish to enter the debate. While we acknowledge the challenges faced by the activists and scholars advocating depathologisation in this and other areas, we are also cautious about latent risks associated with the uncritical employment of human rights language. If such languages are left to reflect theoretically limited understandings of embodiment, this could end up reducing the potential scope and impact of depathologisation. In calling for a stronger dialogue between health law and trans studies, this chapter proposes some directions of travel for such collaboration. It argues that human rights interventions in this area would benefit from being guided by vulnerability theory, as developed by Fineman (including in this collection). By engaging vulnerability to analyse trans issues at the intersection of law and medicine, we offer a more realistic framing of trans bodies. Beyond its ontological intervention, which emphasises our bodily materiality, vulnerability theory demands a more considered policy offering from states, which must respond to, rather than withdraw from, the complexity of human embodiment. It also allows scholars to consider the vulnerability of institutions, including professional medical regulators and national health care systems—in a manner which has yet to be fully explored in the existing vulnerability literature.

The chapter is structured in three parts. The first discusses how gender has been pathologised, and recounts some of the ways in which pathologisation has been criticised. After reviewing the thrust and objectives of these critiques, we discuss what trans people stand to gain from a prospective depathologisation of their identities. The second part turns to depathologisation, identifying how the literature in this area has developed from the negative to the affirmative in recent years. Having identified a tendency to move towards the adoption of human rights language, we discuss some pitfalls that might be associated with this strategy, before identifying what the impact of this might be for the trans people who supposedly stand to benefit. In the third and final section of the chapter, we propose an alternative. With reference to Fineman's vulnerability theory, we evaluate the advantages of acknowledging vulnerability when seeking to depathologise trans identities. This identifies potential avenues for future research at the intersection of human rights, health law, trans studies, and vulnerability theory. The chapter contributes to human rights and health law literatures by asserting the utility of considering the vulnerability of trans patients. It also deepens the vulnerability theory literature by considering the vulnerability of institutions, in this instance addressing that of professional medical regulators and other organisations within national health care systems.

## 2 Diagnosing Gender

The international context has changed significantly since the enactment of the GRA 2004 put the UK in 'pole position' in terms of gender recognition legislation, in Europe and the wider world (Sharpe 2009: 242). Before then, the UK was one of four Council of Europe states which offered no option to amend legal gender status (*Goodwin v UK* App no 28957/95, ECtHR, 11 July 2002, para 55). At present, most European states offer some form of gender recognition, and many have abolished requirements for compulsory sterilisation as a pre-requisite to recognition (Castro-Peraza et al. 2019).[3] Though the European Court of Human Rights (ECtHR) has shied away from finding that a requirement to undergo some form of medical treatment violates the Article 8 right to a private life (Cannoot 2019: 22), criticism of gender recognition legislation which pathologises trans identities is increasingly prevalent at national and international levels. In the UK, this targets the GRA 2004, which requires applicants for gender recognition to be in receipt of a diagnosis of 'gender dysphoria' before they can be granted a gender recognition certificate (GRA 2004, s2(1)(a)). The diagnosis of gender dysphoria is currently defined in the fifth edition American Psychiatric Association's (APA) (2013) *Diagnostic and Statistical Manual of Mental Disorders* (*DSM-5*). This manual has come under sustained critique within various fields, including disability studies (Bartlett and Sandland 2014: 1–8). It stands accused of enacting 'diagnostic bracket creep' (Lane 2010: 105, citing Kramer 1997: 15) or 'diagnostic imperialism' (Rose 2019: 7), whereby psychiatry expands to cover increasing areas of human behaviour since the first edition of the *DSM* was published in 1968.

In the *DSM-5*, gender dysphoria is defined as a 'marked incongruence between one's experienced/expressed gender and assigned gender' (American Psychiatric Association 2013: 452) which is associated with 'clinically significant distress or impairment in social, occupational, or other important areas of functioning' (ibid: 453). It is said to last for at least six months, and is indicated by at least two of the following:

1. A marked incongruence between one's experienced/expressed gender and primary and/or secondary sex characteristics [...].
2. A strong desire to be rid of one's primary and/or secondary sex characteristics because of a marked incongruence with one's experienced/expressed gender [...].
3. A strong desire for the primary and/or secondary sex characteristics of the other gender.
4. A strong desire to be of the other gender (or some alternative gender different from one's assigned gender).
5. A strong desire to be treated as the other gender (or some alternative gender different from one's assigned gender).

[3] The ECtHR has found that requiring sterilisation as a pre-condition for gender recognition violates Article 8 of the European Convention on Human Rights; *AP, Garçon, and Nicot v France* App nos 79885/12, 52471/13, and 52596/13 (ECtHR, 6 April 2017).

6. A strong conviction that one has the typical feelings and reactions of the other gender (or some alternative gender different from one's assigned gender). (ibid: 452)

Psychiatrists' authority over trans people is institutionalised through medical protocols and legislation, but also individualised through the relationships that exist between patients and practitioners. As Davy and Toze (2018) have observed, gender dysphoria is interpreted and operationalised in a highly inconsistent manner within the medical and psychiatric literatures. This reflects the diversity of professional opinions and approaches, which in practice mean that quite different demands can be made of trans patients depending on the clinic they attend, and the individual attitudes held by the practitioners responsible for diagnosing them and providing referrals for treatment. In the UK, while some trans patients find that they are supported in exploring and expressing their gender regardless of how normative or non-normative it might be, others report being refused treatment or support in accessing gender recognition through the GRA 2004 if they do not conform to gender stereotypes or intend to undergo particular medical interventions such as genital surgery (Pearce 2018). They might go on to self-medicate with hormones or undergo surgeries overseas (if they have the financial means). The risks involved in both routes indicate that the employment of the gender dysphoria diagnosis could constitute another example of pathologisation working against people's health needs (Davis 2010), impacting upon trans people's health more generally.

While the concept of gender dysphoria may have been new to the law in 2004, it has informed medical discourse in relation to transsexualism since the early 1970s (Hines 2010). This reflects a long and complicated historical relationship between the law, trans people, and health professionals. Norms have been developed through an on-going interaction between the two latter groups, before being imported into law by legislation such as the GRA 2004 (Pearce 2018; Riggs et al. 2019). Doctors have both helped and hindered trans people in their search for access to body modification technologies—usually in the form of hormones and surgeries—and assisted reproduction. Sexologists such as Harry Benjamin gained fame through treating, and publishing research about, trans patients. Psychiatrists continue to play an important gatekeeping role, not only in determining trans people's access to body modification technologies, but also in facilitating or blocking access to legal gender recognition in states including the UK (Pearce 2018). By judging trans embodiment with reference to a range of subjective standards, psychiatrists maintain norms which legitimate some trans people while at the same time excluding others. This places them in an authoritative position at the intersection of medical and legal regulation of gender.

Sociological and socio-legal literature on the GRA 2004 has long been critical of the exclusionary effects of pathologising trans identities in the health care system and in statutory legislation (Cowan 2009; Davy 2010; Hines 2010). Such critiques have recently begun to gain wider traction. As the UK Government Equalities Office (2018: 15) stated in its consultation document on reforming the GRA 2004: 'The Government's view is clear: being trans is not a mental illness. It is a simple fact of everyday life and human diversity'. While such a statement constitutes an interesting development, its impact will be negligible unless it is backed up by reforms to the GRA 2004 that would enable this statement to become reflective of legal and medical practice. To date, these have not been forthcoming. Similar critiques could be made of states such as Denmark, where a law purporting to prohibit the treatment of trans phenomena as constitutive of a mental illness was passed in May 2016 (B7 Bill to debate removing transsexualism from the diagnosis code (*Forslag til folketingsbeslutning om fjernelse af transseksualisme fra sygdomsliste*)). Having adopted self-declaration two years earlier (L 182 Law amending the Act on the Central Person Registry (11 June 2014) (*L 182 Lov om ændring af lov om Det Centrale Personregister*)), one might assume that trans people in Denmark would be able to access health care and gender recognition without a psychiatric diagnosis. Yet on a formal level, 'transsexualism', as defined in the tenth edition of the World Health Organization's (WHO) (1992) *International Statistical Classification of Diseases and Related Health Problems* (*ICD-10*), is retained in the Danish national diagnosis code (albeit in its own distinct section). And in practice, trans people are still granted or denied access to body modification technologies by psychiatrists using diagnostic manuals including those of the WHO and the APA (Dietz 2018).

Following the lead of the sociological literature and international advocacy groups such as Global Action for Trans∗ Equality (GATE), critiques of pathologisation have become more embedded in the international human rights literature (Theilen 2014; Cannoot 2019; Gonzalez-Salzberg 2019). Pathologisation is now considered not only as an exclusionary method for distinguishing between 'true' trans people and others, but also as a stigmatising process even for those who are granted a diagnosis of 'gender dysphoria'—in the light of the assessments which they are expected to undergo, and the information that they are required to disclose, within the clinical setting (Dietz 2018: 190). Concerns may be raised as to how far the argument that trans people are not mentally ill does justice for those trans people who do have mental illnesses, disabilities, or neurological differences (as in the context of asexuality, discussed by Kim 2010). But critiques of pathologisation have been raised in the disability context (Bartlett and Sandland 2014: 1–8; Rose 2019), including from proponents of the social model of disability (Lawson and Priestley 2017). Alliances between trans activists and disability activists have also been mooted in the trans studies literature (Krieg 2013). In any case, abolishing pathologisation does appear to hold significant appeal among trans activists and scholars alike. Critiques of pathologisation have, in conversation with international activism, developed into calls for the 'depathologisation' of trans phenomena. We turn to the trans depathologisation movement in the next section, examining how it is being formulated, how its demands are being implemented, and what potential limitations it might encounter in practice.

## 3 Depathologisation and Its Limitations

As critiques of gender recognition law shift from concerns about the absence of recognition, to physical pre-requisites (such as sterilisation), and now on to psychiatric requirements, the human rights law and health sociology literatures have begun to converge around the strategic importance of depathologising trans phenomena. As we have noted, we understand this as a shift in strategy from the oppositional to the propositional. No longer does the literature merely criticise the pathologisation of trans identities, it also proposes mechanisms to ensure that states and medical authorities actively cease to do so. Even greater convergence between the legal and sociological literature is evidenced in recent attempts to re-formulate the demand to depathologise as a right, or even a human right (Theilen 2014; Cabral et al. 2016; Davy et al. 2018; Castro-Peraza et al. 2019).

The language of human rights has become an established lens through which to consider trans issues. Human rights perspectives have been mobilised to challenge the ways in which gender is regulated in various nation states, as inadequate legislative provisions have created, or at least contributed to, problems for those who do not identify with the sex/gender that they were assigned at birth. The first wave of these critiques lamented the absence of gender recognition laws across the world, the effect of which was to prevent trans people from amending their legal gender from that which they were assigned at birth. As the establishment of gender recognition processes became more common, a second wave of human rights interventions trained their lens upon the pre-conditions involved in those laws. In both instances, the basic language of human rights was well-suited to being mobilised to challenge these laws and establish new legislation in their place—identifying, as they did, an individual trans person or group of trans people whose life, body, and autonomy were being (more or less) forcibly interfered with or ignored to meet the authoritative demands of an illiberal nation state. Yet questions can be asked as to how effective human rights concepts can be when it comes to countering more subtle medical norms than compulsory sterilisation.

Whether as 'reference points', or 'as part of an argumentation strategy', the increasing significance of human rights principles within the depathologisation movement—including 'human dignity', 'bodily integrity', and 'self-determination'—has been noted (Davy et al. 2018: 27). Theilen (2014: 332) adds 'human freedom' and 'personal autonomy' to the list of values which 'cannot be reconciled with trans pathologisation'. Each of these concepts is, without exception, borrowed from the human rights literature. Drawing upon a classical liberal understanding of the body as a source of rights and freedoms, they convey the idea that this body should not be interfered with by the state, or other actors, without the consent of the individual (Locke 1980: 9). Such a strategy has its advantages. Human rights have proven to be a useful vehicle for making political claims intelligible to a wide audience (Munro 2007: 75, citing Smart 1989: 143). The strategy also responds to activist work that has been going on for some years. Principle 18 of the Yogyakarta Principles on the Application of International Human Rights Law in relation to Sexual Orientation and Gender Identity, originally agreed in 2006, states that 'a person's sexual orientation and gender identity are not, in and of themselves, medical conditions and are not to be treated, cured or suppressed'. Yet arguments in favour of a human right to depathologisation are still formulated in negative terms to some extent. They tell states what they need to stop doing, without clearly expressing what they ought actively to do instead. To ameliorate this, Theilen conceptualises the human right to depathologisation as part of a wider right to gender identity:

> the right to depathologisation […] is likewise a part of the right to gender identity, properly understood. The right to depathologisation of transgenderism may be both less accepted and less tangible than what is commonly understood to be part of the right to gender identity, that is, the right to have one's gender legally recognised; but the two issues are interrelated. (Theilen 2014: 342)

Theilen (2014) helps flesh out the content of this right by envisaging three prospective levels of obligation for state parties. The first level of obligation falls on states themselves: to ensure that gender recognition is available without pathologising pre-requisites (such as a requirement for psychiatric diagnosis). The second level of obligation falls upon sub-state institutions such as the medical profession, and civil society more widely: to treat trans people—and in the case of the medics, provide health care—without pathologising their identities. The third level of obligation applies to transnational bodies, such as the WHO, and would require diagnostic reform in order to allow states to acknowledge trans phenomena without understanding them as automatically constitutive of a mental illness.

The first and second levels of obligation are addressed by Argentina's LIG 2012, which was implemented following a successful campaign by transsexual and *travesti* activists working through organisations such as the Federación Argentina LGBT and the National Front for the Gender Identity Law (Rucovsky 2019). A key feature of the LIG 2012 is that legal recognition depends solely upon the request of the individual concerned (self-declaration), and not on any medical procedure or psychiatric diagnosis. The law also 'guarantees obligatory access to the medical system' (Rucovsky 2019: 230). This second key feature is implemented through Article 11 of the LIG 2012, which requires that all persons older than 18 years 'be able to access total and partial surgical interventions and/or comprehensive hormonal treatments to adjust their bodies, including their genitalia, to their self-perceived gender identity' (GATE 2012: 3). The right to free access to these medical interventions (including for migrants) through both public and private health providers is ensured through their explicit inclusion in Argentina's Compulsory Medical Plan (Arístegui et al. 2017). Moreover, as with legal recognition, this access to medical interventions is no longer reliant on psychiatric diagnosis: 'The only requirement will be [...] informed consent by the individual concerned' (GATE 2012: 3). Research indicates that this has resulted in increased access to specialist medical interventions for trans people, but this can be inconsistent in practice, depending on the attitude of local authorities and insurance providers and the availability of medical resources and relevant vocational training (Arístegui et al. 2017; Hollar 2018). Consequently, Rucovsky (2019: 233) observes that the recognition afforded by the LIG 2012 'marks a minimum departure point – not an arrival – with respect to the state of the law, which is to say, it does not pronounce itself on the effective mechanisms to resist inequality'.

Following the passage of the LIG 2012, several other states have met Theilen's first level of obligation, either partially or in full, by enacting laws which recognise gender on the basis of self-declaration (usually expected to take place through a statutory declaration or some other request to legal authorities). These include Belgium, Colombia, Denmark, Ireland, Malta,

Norway, Pakistan, Portugal, and Uruguay, plus several regions or states in Australia, Canada, Mexico, Spain, and the USA. Yet, in general, these laws do not explicitly require that trans people have access to appropriate health care. One exception is Uruguay's Comprehensive Law for Trans Persons 2018 (*Ley Integral Para Personas Trans*). Like the LIG 2012, this law ensures access to specialist medical interventions through public and private health care providers, on the basis of informed consent and a shared decision-making process. It also goes further, creating quotas for employment and access to education, and establishes reparations for trans people persecuted under Uruguay's 1973–1985 military dictatorship.

Developments at the third level of obligation—concerning international diagnostic categories—have also been forthcoming since the publication of Theilen's (2014) article. In June 2018, when the WHO updated its classification of diseases, 'transsexualism' was replaced with a new diagnosis of 'gender incongruence' in the *ICD-11*. This move followed extensive campaigning by trans human rights organisations, including GATE, that favour depathologisation. The location of the diagnosis shifted from Chapter V of the *ICD-10*, concerning 'mental and behavioural disorders' and 'disorders of adult personality and behaviour', to Chapter 17 of the *ICD-11*, which includes 'Conditions related to sexual health'. This shift in terminology has been welcomed by campaigners and researchers who support depathologisation (Moser 2017; Davy et al. 2018: 27). But it is too early for us to speculate as to exactly what effect the introduction of this new diagnosis will have in practice. Whether it will result in a genuine improvement in access to health care for trans people is something which must be assessed within future research. In the interim, questions can be asked as to how far the challenges raised by the depathologisation movement are likely to be resolved with reference to human rights language.

One approach would be to replicate legislation in Argentina and Uruguay. Another would be to explicitly understand requirements for sustained psychiatric diagnosis in order to be granted access to body modification technologies such as hormones and surgeries as a form of 'medical abuse', which human rights demand protection from (Davy et al. 2018: 15). However, even if more states are willing to remedy this by stepping into what has come to be regulated as a purely medical jurisdiction (Dietz 2020), human rights concepts such as personal autonomy and bodily integrity offer few pointers as to what active steps need to be put in place in order to ensure the consistent and universal provision of accessible health care. Moreover, while a significant body of human rights scholars and activists would point to international successes in gaining recognition of economic and social rights alongside civil and political rights in numerous areas, there have been few examples of this in the trans health context to date.[4]

Even more holistic gender recognition laws have been critiqued by the communities which supposedly stand to benefit, along with the wider language of human rights on which they are based. Rucovsky (2019: 232), citing *travesti* activist Marlene Wayar, observes that the LIG 2012's 'process of dispute and negotiation was hatched in the name of a markedly liberal trans model of citizenship [...] developed in the terms of individual, possessive and personal rights'. It requires trans people to become recognisable within a state framework built around the presumption of binary gender and mandatory surveillance. By focusing upon the individual, the law elides collective efforts to achieve trans liberation, both within and beyond trans communities—including through the concerted efforts of the coalition that successfully campaigned for the LIG 2012 itself. As Rucovsky (2015: 24) notes, the LIG 2012

> recognizes and guarantees access to certain rights, but it does not refer to the global networks that support life and make it proper to be lived – whether they involve education, employment, housing, nutrition, integral health, protection against police abuse, etc.

Similar arguments have been made by transfeminist activists based in the UK, including van der Drift (2019: 15), who critiques the turn to 'informed consent' in trans discourse, arguing that 'individualised consent will sign away those that need a changed institution and communal support [...]. Consent requires possibilities, timelines and support in ways that fit a person into a collective'. Similarly, Raha (2019: 17) insists that:

> The lack of resources for trans healthcare is linked to the neoliberal disinvestment in healthcare as a whole. They do not want us to live well. They do not believe in our futures: they only believe that we should join their future (assimilation). We know that this is a ruse, and that it won't end well (ecological collapse and new forms of climate colonialism) [...] Don't let them make this about 'Rights'. Don't make your slogans supporting us just about Rights.

In considering the potential limits of human rights language in the context of trans-related health care, we accept that rights claims are best judged in terms of their effect rather than their conceptual clarity or political coherence (Herman 1993). We also acknowledge that their political potential is not

[4] Even the Yogyakarta Principles constitute an example of non-binding, 'soft', law, as the UK Government Equalities Office (2016: 8–9) was keen to stress.

limited to existing formulations, which would underestimate the power of 'human rights to come' (McNeilly 2018: 4). As a 'malleable politico-legal language with widespread purchase' (ibid), human rights may continue to prove useful, strategically and rhetorically, for the depathologisation movement. We would be very happy if this proved to be the case. Certainly, the practical benefits of legislation such as the LIG 2012 should not be understated (Arístegui et al. 2017; Radi 2019; Rucovsky 2019). But even advocates of human rights have acknowledged that these are often inappropriately conceived as being property-based, autonomous, and protective, rather than contingent, interconnected, and dependent (Munro 2007: 75, citing Glendon 1991: 14). This might offer one explanation as to why, to date, human rights research has not been embedded well within health law (Brazier and Montgomery 2019: 24). If it is to be successful in articulating the importance of access to trans-related health care, facilitating the re-drawing of boundaries between health care systems, professional regulators, medical practitioners, and their trans patients, then the depathologisation movement will have to overcome various limitations in human rights language—including the libertarian posturing of individualised conceptions of autonomy—and focus instead upon contingency, interconnection, and dependency, among other factors. In what remains of this chapter, we suggest that vulnerability theory constitutes a useful ethical space which is more than capable of guiding this endeavour.

## 4 Acknowledging Vulnerability

Vulnerability has become an important concept for philosophical investigation of human bodies. In part, this is due to the scholarship of Butler (2006, 2016). Yet it is Fineman's work on vulnerability which has become most influential within feminist legal studies, and legal scholarship more generally. Unlike classical rights language (e.g. Locke 1980), vulnerability theory challenges any attempt to emphasise any individualised and atemporal approach to freedom or autonomy. Rather than centring an abstract and 'fully competent, capable individual adult' (Fineman 2017: 148), vulnerability theory asks researchers to shift their attention to the relational structures in which all humans are embedded. To avoid valorising independence and self-sufficiency, the vulnerable subject is understood to be both 'embodied' and 'embedded' (Fineman 2017: 143). This reflects the fact that humans are both physically and socially vulnerable. Physically, our skin is porous and subject to injury and lesion. We are also social beings embedded within social institutions and relationships, including those relations developed between health professionals and their trans patients.

Vulnerability theory develops Fineman's previous work on dependency (Fineman 2004). For, while people slip in and out of dependency over time, vulnerability is both constant and universal. Vulnerability should not be used to refer to individuals or groups—or 'vulnerable populations'—as somehow 'more or less' vulnerable than others (Fineman 2017: 142). Humans are all vulnerable, in that 'we are universally and individually constantly susceptible to change in our well being' (Fineman 2017: 142). If we accept that human vulnerability to injury is both constant and universal, then there is no completely safe and secure 'position of invulnerability':

> The term 'vulnerable', used to connote the continuous susceptibility to change in both our bodily and social well-being that all human beings experience, makes it clear that there is no position of invulnerability – no conclusive way to prevent or avoid change. (Fineman 2017: 142)

The insight 'that no individual can avoid vulnerability entirely' (Fineman 2008: 67) forces scholars to look beyond individual circumstances and onto societal institutions instead. As Fineman (2008: 67) admits, 'society cannot eradicate our vulnerability either'. Yet it can lessen our vulnerability through various institutions and structures:

> Undeniably universal, human vulnerability is also particular: it is experienced uniquely by each of us and this experience is greatly influenced by the quality and quantity of resources we possess or can command. Significantly, the realization that no individual can avoid vulnerability entirely spurs us to look to societal institutions for assistance. Of course, society cannot eradicate our vulnerability either. However, society can and does mediate, compensate, and lessen our vulnerability through programs, institutions, and structures. (Fineman 2008: 10)

Scholars are therefore encouraged to focus upon social and institutional contexts, without neglecting that the body is prone to injury and harm. Vulnerability theory acknowledges the importance of access to resources that will enable people 'to endure or prosper from change, even harm, throughout institutions and relationships across the life-course' (Fineman 2017: 149). From its point of conception, then, Fineman has moved her theory beyond its ontological concern with the material basis of the body, and onto the social policy that the result of this inquiry demands. She argues for an 'active' and 'responsive' state, which ought to be considered in 'non-authoritarian terms' (Fineman 2008: 19), adding:

> Orientating the state to be responsive to the Vulnerable Subject would require dedication to a different set of values than those that informed the state built on an image of the Liberal Subject. Vulnerability's values would be more egalitarian and collective in nature, preferring connection and interdependence rather than autonomy and independence in both political and personal visions. (Fineman 2013: 26)

How might this be applied in trans health law? In a context where trans people have been scrutinised by health professionals wielding significant power 'to determine what is considered sick or healthy, normal or pathological, sane or insane' (Stryker 2008: 36), it is unsurprising that the instinct of the depathologisation movement would be to claim rights to freedom and autonomy. It is possible then that calls for a shift towards vulnerability would be viewed with suspicion by activists and scholars, as in debates around disability (Clough 2017), sex work (Munro and Scoular 2012), and sexual assault (Munro 2017). Yet implicit acknowledgements of vulnerability have always been present in trans studies. Trans people and trans scholars have worked through their vulnerability via reflective biographies which address both difficult and affirmative aspects of life during transition (Raun 2016; Jacques 2016), autoethnographic accounts of sexual embodiment and gendering processes (Stryker 1994; Stewart 2017; cardenás 2016), and structural disempowerment in health care settings (Latham 2017; shuster 2018). Explicit conceptual engagement with vulnerability is also becoming more common in the trans studies literature (Horak 2018; Straube and Tainio 2019).

Even so, with trans people often patronised as a 'vulnerable population', and often one that is assumed to be 'more vulnerable' than other groups, it could seem counter-intuitive to foreground vulnerability. Understanding trans people as 'a particularly vulnerable group' is a theme of contemporary ECtHR jurisprudence (Cannoot 2019: 33–34).[5] And while attempts have been made to square such approaches with vulnerability theory (Peroni and Timmer 2013), individual responses to a particular group's apparent vulnerability are not likely to give rise to the universal policy responses favoured by Fineman. Labelling trans people as particularly vulnerable has also been used to justify what has become known as 'trans exceptionalism' (Heyes and Latham 2018: 174). This marks trans people out from their non-trans ('cis')

[5] We are grateful to the anonymous reviewer for raising this point.

peers,[6] justifying additional hurdles being placed in front of them—in order to access medical treatment, for example—as a direct consequence of being identified as trans. But if vulnerability is understood as constant and universal, and not merely as a descriptor of 'weak' and 'powerless' groups and 'populations' (Clough 2017: 469; Fineman 2008: 8), then trans people's health care needs could be understood as specific but still commensurate with the diverse health needs of populations.[7]

It is worth recalling that it is pathologisation, rather than health care as such, which has come under the scrutiny of the depathologisation movement (Theilen 2014: 335). Challenging a diagnosis does not mean neglecting the health care needs around which it was formulated (Davis 2010: 130). As Heyes and Latham (2018: 186) note, ensuring 'just and equitable treatment' does not require all trans patients to undergo 'identical regimes of interventions'. Vulnerability theory is well-equipped to mediate between seemingly conflicting issues of universality and particularity in this context. Vulnerability 'does not seek equality, but equity' in decision-making and social policy (Fineman 2017: 143). Rather than flattening out differences between subjects, vulnerability acknowledges the plasticity of the body by incorporating 'a life-course perspective' (Fineman 2017: 143). How to regulate the relationship between health professionals and their trans patients in a way that reflects this will be challenging. Historically, the adoption of a life-course perspective in trans health care has too often been used to justify sustained psychiatric investigation into a trans person's suitability for body modification, or indeed withholding access to hormones and surgeries altogether. This is something that the depathologisation movement is more than aware of. But this chequered history does not mean that a life-course perspective could not be used equitably in future, helping determine, supportively, what course of treatment would be best suited to the circumstances of an individual trans patient.

Theilen (2014: 336) suggests that while working towards a 'more genuine acceptance' of trans phenomena is 'bound to be difficult', it will be 'near impossible' while trans people continue to be pathologised. Parallels can be drawn with disability studies research into the social model of disability, which attempts to understand disabilities as arising from social structures and inequalities rather than individual pathologies (Lawson and Priestley 2017).

[6] 'Cis' is an adjective used to refer to people who do not identify as trans.

[7] The vast majority of trans-related body modification technologies were not originally developed for use on trans patients (Riggs et al. 2019). For example, phalloplasty was developed in the aftermath of the First World War to treat the victims of landmines (Schultheiss et al. 2005). The first total penis and scrotum transplant was recently performed on a veteran soldier who had suffered injury from an improvised explosive device while serving in Afghanistan (Nitkin 2018).

Again, a vulnerability perspective which is cognisant of relationality and attuned to structures which mediate between people and institutions appears better suited to this task than one which unrealistically and unhelpfully centres only on individual autonomy. As in the disability context, vulnerability theory could raise 'questions for how we can make law and policy responsive to particular individuals and how interventions or shifts in broader structures or institutions would impact on users of services' (Clough 2017: 479). The same could be said of the parallel drawn between trans activism and the reproductive rights movement (Theilen 2014), which also seeks to 'secure access to competent, legal, respectfully provided medical services for a nonpathological need' (Stryker 2008: 98).

Vulnerability theory demands 'a robust sense of state responsibility for social institutions and relationships' (Fineman 2017: 143). This should not be misinterpreted as implying that trans people are not the experts on their own identities. This is imperative in a context where family relationships have been exclusionary, and state regulation of trans people has been unresponsive at best, and authoritarian at worst (Stryker 2008; Monro and Van Der Ros 2018). While envisaging an active role for the state could be deemed paternalistic, state responsibility for trans health is an important element emphasised from a vulnerability perspective. Scholars and activists within the depathologisation movement will be all too aware that the role of the state remains imperative in increasing trans people's access to formal health care. Empirical research conducted in Argentina has identified a postcode lottery of unequal treatment depending upon the trans person's proximity to metropolitan clinics and pharmacies, plus a skills shortage in Argentinian hospitals when it comes to performing surgeries (Arístegui et al. 2017: 451–452). Moreover, the example of European countries such as Denmark has shown that if equity is to be achieved for trans people in their access to health care, it is not enough for the state to become more 'withdrawn' (Fineman 2008: 6), depathologising gender recognition in a way which permits access to health services only for those trans people who can either access pathologising public clinics or afford to travel overseas or turn to the black market for treatment. Instead, demanding accessible health care requires that questions be asked about how body modification technologies can be safely and equitably distributed. This, in turn, raises more challenging questions about how medical resources ought to be established and allocated.

As attention shifts from the micro to the macro—and the management of health resources—we would like to draw attention to a more recent development in the vulnerability theory literature. This turns attention slightly away from human vulnerability, and onto the vulnerability of institutions (Reiss

2010; Marvel 2015; Fineman 2015; Fineman et al. 2017; Dehaghani and Newman 2017; Travis 2019). While humans are vulnerable as a result of being physically embodied and socially embedded, Fineman has noted that institutions too can be understood as vulnerable:

> Of course, societal institutions themselves are not foolproof shelters, even in the short term. Metaphorically, they too can be conceptualized as vulnerable: They may fail in the wake of market fluctuations, changing international policies, institutional and political compromises, or human prejudices. Even the most established institutions viewed over time are potentially unstable and susceptible to challenges from both internal and external forces. (Fineman 2008: 12)

Though important research has been conducted into how bodies are affected by the norms promulgated by health and social welfare institutions (Garland and Travis 2018; Ries and Thomson 2019), it is also necessary to consider how those institutions resist or change their regulations in response to political pressure generated, at least in part, by the bodies that they regulate. In a trans health law context, this can be exemplified in various ways. In Argentina, the vulnerability felt by the psychiatric profession is demonstrated by their negative reaction to the enactment of the LIG 2012. As Hollar (2018: 464) observes, 'many doctors [in Argentina] have not been complying with the law—for example, requiring psychiatric evaluation before providing hormones'. In the UK, the vulnerability of the medical profession is exemplified by disciplinary investigations into practitioners including Helen Webberley, a private-sector physician who gained a reputation for providing more flexible treatment than the NHS gender clinics (Pearce 2018: 167–168). In Denmark, after evidence came to light of a series of failures to maintain professional treatment standards, the professional regulatory body responsible for authoring the medical guidelines which pathologised trans phenomena in Denmark was stripped of its supervisory duties and medicines licensing tasks.[8] Although this re-organisation of professional regulators could not be said to have resulted directly from trans activism,[9] it still serves to highlight how the

[8]The duties of the now defunct Danish Health and Medicines Authority (DHMA) have been devolved to the Danish Patient Safety Authority and the Danish Medicines Agency. The new Danish Health Authority website only alludes to these scandals, noting 'The purpose of the organisational change is to devote more attention to medicines licensing and to improve patient safety'; 'The history of the Danish Health Authority' Danish Health Authority, https://www.sst.dk/en/about-us/the-history-of-the-danish-health-authority

[9]Two other scandals attracted more controversy in Danish media: one involving two psychiatrists, who appeared to be implicated in the deaths of several patients in spite of the DHMA being aware that they had both been subject to numerous complaints; and another concerning the unauthorised use of the drug Misoprostol to induce births in hospitals, resulting in a number of tragic deaths.

institutions which might intimidate ordinary patients are themselves subject to existential political and economic pressures.

Insufficient attention has been paid to how these pressures factor into institutional judgements and decisions. To date, this form of vulnerability has not been explored as comprehensively as it might have been in the vulnerability literature. Unfortunately, we also do not have enough space to do justice to the concept of institutional vulnerability here. However, future research might productively explore the relationship between vulnerable humans and vulnerable institutions, particularly in the context of trans health and within health law more broadly. Such insights could give rise to a host of interesting questions for the depathologisation movement, including how best to work with professional medical regulators and health care institutions to allocate resources and develop treatment guidelines which are mutually acceptable to all actors and communities involved.

## 5 Conclusion

This chapter mounts a challenge to the way that the gendered body has been understood by health professionals. With a focus upon trans issues, which have arisen at the intersection of law and medicine, it has analysed recent developments in the literature on pathologisation. It acknowledged insights developed within the health sociology and human rights law literatures, before identifying a recent point of convergence around the importance of asserting a human right to depathologisation. Significant gains have been made in the regulation of trans people, not least in the area of legal gender recognition. At a time when self-declaration of legal gender status gains admiration from activists and scholars alike, it also draws attention from policymakers and legislators. In granting legal subjects the right to amend their legal gender status without pre-conditions, self-declaration might appear to be compatible with human rights concepts such as personal autonomy. However, its limitations—including not necessarily granting access to health care—have been criticised, particularly in instances where self-declaration does not stop states withdrawing from taking responsibility for the more complex issues which affect their subjects' embodiment.

As the trans depathologisation movement grows in stature and influence, more questions will be asked of its political strategy. Though it is perfectly possible that the increasing mobilisation of human rights language could lead to further political gains, this is by no means guaranteed. After discussing some potential drawbacks which may arise in the current human rights-oriented strategy in the first half of this chapter, we proposed an alternative in the second. With the aid of Fineman, we identified several areas in which the trans depathologisation movement could benefit from integrating vulnerability theory into its political strategy. Without shying away from potential limitations in engaging vulnerability, and without dismissing the potential of human rights language to further the demands of the trans depathologisation movement completely, we have made the case in this chapter for placing a greater emphasis on trans vulnerability. This applies to the trans depathologisation movement, as well as within trans health law and health law more widely. Beyond acknowledging the vulnerability of trans patients, this also offered us the opportunity to consider the vulnerability of institutions including professional medical regulators. Institutional vulnerabilities have been shown to have exerted an important influence on the regulation of trans bodies in UK, Danish, and Argentinian contexts and offered pause for thought for regulators, activists, and scholars in the future.

Vulnerability theory warns against indicating that trans people are somehow 'more vulnerable' (Peroni and Timmer 2013: 1060–1061) than cis others. Instead, the universal and constant vulnerability of all humans, and potentially also institutions, ought to be more widely acknowledged, and ameliorated through supportive policymaking. If it is applied in an engaged and universal register, vulnerability theory should be able to counter 'trans exceptionalism' and pathologisation, while offering an indication as to how trans issues could be better managed by states and institutions. Vulnerability theory's commitment to material and pragmatic concerns, alongside theoretical matters, is vital. As Radi (2019: 57) argues, with respect to criticisms of the LIG 2012 by non-Argentinian, non-trans, scholars such as Butler, 'the law was designed to ensure recognition of trans* people's gender identity, not to embody the emancipatory fantasies of cis theorists'. By reconsidering the role of the state, and not merely asking the state to withdraw from the management of trans health, vulnerability theory facilitates a move beyond straightforward calls for freedom and autonomy. It instead asks questions about how resources could be allocated to ensure that health care is accessible for all trans and cis bodies. Depending upon how these questions are answered, this could better reflect the needs and demands of trans people as they seek to access legal recognition and health care in practice.

## References


American Psychiatric Association. (2013). *Diagnostic and Statistical Manual of Mental Disorders* (5h ed.). Washington/London: American Psychiatric Publishing.

Arístegui, I., Radusky, P. D., Zalazar, V., Romero, M., Schwartz, J., & Sued, O. (2017). Impact of the Gender Identity Law in Argentinean Transgender Women. *International Journal of Transgenderism, 18*(4), 446–456.

Bartlett, P., & Sandland, R. (2014). *Mental Health Law: Policy and Practice* (4th ed.). Oxford: Oxford University Press.

Brazier, M., & Cave, E. (2016). *Medicine, Patients and the Law*. Manchester: Manchester University Press.

Brazier, M., & Montgomery, J. (2019). Whence and Whither 'Modern Medical Law'. *Northern Ireland Legal Quarterly, 70*(1), 5–30.

Butler, J. (1993). *Bodies That Matter: On the Discursive Limits of 'Sex'.* Abingdon/New York: Routledge.

Butler, J. (2006). *Precarious Life: The Power of Mourning and Violence*. London: Verso.

Butler, J. (2016). *Frames of War: When Is Life Grievable?* London: Verso.

Cabral, M., Suess, A., Ehrt, J., Seehole, T. J., & Wong, J. (2016). Removal of Gender Incongruence of Childhood Diagnostic Category: A Human Rights Perspective. *The Lancet Psychiatry, 3*(5), 405–406.

Cannoot, P. (2019). The Pathologisation of Trans* Persons in the ECtHR's Case Law on Legal Gender Recognition. *Netherlands Quarterly of Human Rights, 37*(1), 14–35.

cardenás, m. (2016). Pregnancy: Reproductive Futures in Trans of Color Feminism. *TSQ: Transgender Studies Quarterly, 3*(1–2), 48–57.

Castro-Peraza, M. E., García-Acosta, J. M., Delgado, N., Perdomo-Hernández, A. M., Sosa-Alvarez, M. I., Llabrés-Solé, R., & Lorenzo-Rocha, N. D. (2019). Gender Identity: The Human Right of Depathologization. *International Journal of Environmental Research and Public Health, 16*, 978.

Clough, B. (2017). Disability and Vulnerability: Challenging the Capacity/Incapacity Binary. *Social Policy & Society, 16*(3), 469–481.

Cowan, S. (2009). Looking Back (To)wards the Body: Medicalization and the GRA. *Social & Legal Studies, 18*(2), 247–252.

Davis, L. J. (2010). Obsession: Against Mental Health. In J. M. Metzl & A. Kirland (Eds.), *Against Health: How Health Became the New Morality* (p. 130). New York: New York University Press.

Davy, Z. (2010). Transsexual Agents: Negotiating Authenticity and Embodiment Within the UK's Medicolegal System. In S. Hines & T. Sanger (Eds.), *Transgender Identities: Towards a Social Analysis of Gender Diversity* (pp. 106–126). Oxon: Routledge.

Davy, Z. (2011). *Recognizing Transsexuals: Personal, Political and Medicolegal Embodiment*. Farnham: Ashgate.

Davy, Z., & Toze, M. (2018). What Is Gender Dysphoria? A Critical Systematic Narrative Review. *Transgender Health, 3*(1), 159–169.

Davy, Z., Sørlie, A., & Suess Schwend, A. (2018). Democratising Diagnoses? The Role of the Depathologisation Perspective in Constructing Corporeal Trans Citizenship. *Critical Social Policy, 38*(1), 13–34.

Dehaghani, R., & Newman, D. (2017). "We're Vulnerable Too": An (Alternative) Analysis of Vulnerability Within English Criminal Legal Aid and Police Custody. *Oñati Socio-Legal Series, 7*(6), 1199–1228.

Dietz, C. (2018). Governing Legal Embodiment: On the Limits of Self-Declaration. *Feminist Legal Studies, 26*(2), 185–204.

Dietz, C. (2020). Jurisdiction in Trans Health. *Journal of Law and Society, 47*(1), 60–86.

Dunne, P. (2015). Ten Years of Gender Recognition in the United Kingdom: Still a "Model for Reform"? *Public Law, 4*, 530–539.

Dunne, P. (2017). Transgender Sterilisation Requirements in Europe. *Medical Law Review*, 554–581.

Fineman, M. A. (2004). *The Autonomy Myth: A Theory of Dependency*. New York: The New Press.

Fineman, M. A. (2008). The Vulnerable Subject: Anchoring Equality in the Human Condition. *Yale Journal of Law and Feminism, 20*(1), 1–23.

Fineman, M. A. (2013). Equality, Autonomy, and the Vulnerable Subject in Law and Politics. In M. A. Fineman & A. Grear (Eds.), *Vulnerability: Reflections on a New Ethical Foundation for Law and Politics* (pp. 13–28). Farnham: Ashgate.

Fineman, M. A. (2015). Vulnerability and the Institution of Marriage. *The Emory Law Journal, 64*(6), 2089–2091.

Fineman, M. A. (2017). Vulnerability and Inevitable Inequality. *Oslo Law Review, 4*(3), 133–149.

Fineman, M. A., Mattsson, T., & Andersson, U. (Eds.). (2017). *Privatization, Vulnerability, and Social Responsibility: A Comparative Perspective*. London/New York: Routledge.

Garland, F., & Travis, M. (2018). Legislating Intersex Equality: Building the Resilience of Intersex People Through Law. *Legal Studies, 38*(4), 587–606.

GATE. (2012). *English Translation of the Argentinian Gender Identity Law as Approved by the Senate of Argentina on May 8, 2012*. Global Action for Trans∗ Equality. http://transactivists.org/wp-content/uploads/2012/05/argentina-gender-identity-law.pdf

Gill-Peterson, J. (2018). *Histories of the Transgender Child*. Minneapolis: University of Minnesota Press.

Glendon, M. A. (1991). *Rights Talk: The Impoverishment of Political Discourse*. New York: Free Press.

Gonzalez-Salzberg, D. A. (2019). *Sexuality and Transsexuality Under the European Convention on Human Rights: A Queer Reading of Human Rights Law*. Oxford: Hart.

Government Equalities Office. (2016). *Government Response to the Women and Equalities Committee Report on Transgender Equality*. https://www.gov.uk/government/uploads/system/uploads/attachment_data/file/535764/Government_Response_to_the_Women_and_Equalities_Committee_Report_on_Transgender_Equality.pdf. Accessed 7 Aug 2019.

Government Equalities Office. (2018). *Reform of the Gender Recognition Act – Government Consultation*. https://gov.uk/government/uploads/system/uploads/attachment_data/file/721725/GRA-Consultation-document.pdf. Accessed 20 July 2019.

Herman, D. (1993). Beyond the Rights Debate. *Social and Legal Studies, 2*, 25–43.

Herring, J. (2018). *Medical Law and Ethics* (7th ed.). Oxford: Oxford University Press.

Heyes, C. J., & Latham, J. R. (2018). Trans Surgeries and Cosmetic Surgeries: The Politics of Analogy. *TSQ: Transgender Studies Quarterly, 5*(2), 174–189.

Hines, S. (2010). Recognising Diversity? The Gender Recognition Act and Transgender Citizenship. In S. Hines & T. Sanger (Eds.), *Transgender Identities: Towards a Social Analysis of Gender Diversity* (pp. 87–105). Oxon: Routledge.

Hollar, J. (2018). The Political Mediation of Argentina's Gender Identity Law: LGBT Activism and Rights Innovation. *Journal of Human Rights, 17*(4), 453–469.

Honkasalo, J. (2020). In the Shadow of Eugenics: Transgender Sterilisation Legislation and the Struggle for Self-Determination. In R. Pearce, I. Moon, K. Gupta, & D. L. Steinberg (Eds.), *The Emergence of Trans: Cultures, Politics and Everyday Lives*. Abingdon: Routledge.

Horak, L. (2018). Visibility and Vulnerability: Negotiating Transgender Representation and Encounters with Translatina Worlds in *The Salt Mines* and *Wildness*. In A. Koivunen, K. Kyrölä, & I. Ryberg (Eds.), *The Power of Vulnerability: Mobilising Affect in Feminist, Queer and Anti-racist Media Cultures* (pp. 95–115). Manchester: Manchester University Press.

Jackson, E. (2016). *Medical Law: Text, Cases and Materials* (4th ed.). Oxford: Oxford University Press.

Jacques, J. (2016). *Trans: A Memoir*. London: Verso.

Kim, E. (2010). How Much Sex Is Healthy?: The Pleasures of Asexuality. In J. M. Metzl & A. Kirland (Eds.), *Against Health: How Health Became the New Morality*. New York: New York University Press.

Kramer, P. D. (1997). *Listening to Prozac: The Landmark Book about Antidepressants and the Remaking of the Self*. New York: Penguin.

Krieg, J. (2013). A Social Model of Trans and Crip Theory: Narratives and Strategies in the Redefinition of the Pathologized Trans Subject. *Lambda Nordica, 3–4*, 33–53.

Lane, C. (2010). The Strangely Passive-Aggressive History of Passive-Aggressive Personality Disorder. In J. M. Metzl & A. Kirland (Eds.), *Against Health: How Health Became the New Morality* (p. 105). New York: New York University Press.

Latham, J. R. (2017). (Re)making Sex: A Praxiography of the Gender Clinic. *Feminist Theory, 18*(2), 177–2014.

Lawson, A. (2008). *Disability and Equality Law in Britain: The Role of Reasonable Adjustment*. Oxford/Portland: Hart Publishing.

Lawson, A., & Priestley, M. (2017). The Social Model of Disability; Questions for Law and Legal Scholarship? In P. Blanck & E. Flynn (Eds.), *Routledge Handbook of Disability Law and Human Rights* (pp. 3–15). Oxon: Routledge.

Locke, J. (1980). *Second Treatise of Government (First Published 1690)*. Indianapolis/ Cambridge: Hackett.

Marvel, S. (2015). The Evolution of Plural Parentage: Applying Vulnerability Theory to Polygamy and Same-Sex Marriage. *The Emory Law Journal, 64*(6), 2047–2088.

McNeilly, K. (2018). *Human Rights and Radical Social Transformation: Futurity, Alterity, Power*. Oxford/New York: Routledge.

Meyerowitz, J. (2002). *How Sex Changed: A History of Transsexuality in the United States*. Cambridge, MA: Harvard University Press.

Monro, S., & Van Der Ros, J. (2018). Trans* and Gender Variant Citizenship and the State in Norway. *Critical Social Policy, 38*(1), 57–78.

Moser, C. (2017). ICD-11 and Gender Incongruence: Language Is Important. *Archives of Sexual Behavior, 46*(8), 2515–2516.

Munro, V. (2007). *Law and Politics at the Perimeter: Re-evaluating Key Debates in Feminist Theory*. Oxford/Portland: Hart.

Munro, V. (2017). Shifting Sands? Consent, Context and Vulnerability in Contemporary Sexual Offences Policy in England and Wales. *Social & Legal Studies, 26*(4), 417–440.

Munro, V., & Scoular, J. (2012). Abusing Vulnerability? Contemporary Law and Policy Responses to Sex Work in the UK. *Feminist Legal Studies, 20*, 189–206.

Nitkin, K. (2018). *First-Ever Penis and Scrotum Transplant Makes History at Johns Hopkins*. https://hopkinsmedicine.org/news/articles/first-ever-penis-and-scrotum-transplant-makes-history-at-johns-hopkins. Accessed 2 Sept 2019.

Pearce, R. (2018). *Understanding Trans Health: Discourse, Power and Possibility*. Bristol: Policy Press.

Peroni, L., & Timmer, A. (2013). Vulnerable Groups: The Promise of an Emerging Concept in European Human Rights Convention Law. *International Journal of Constitutional Law, 11*(4), 1056–1085.

Radi, B. (2019). On Trans* Epistemology: Critiques, Contributions, and Challenges. *TSQ: Transgender Studies Quarterly, 6*(1), 43–63.

Raha, N. (2019). Some Current Things.... In *Trans Reproductive Justice: A Radical Transfeminism Mini Zine*. Leith: Radical Transfeminist Collective.

Raun, T. (2016). *Out Online: Trans Self-Representation and Community Building on YouTube*. London/New York: Routledge.

Reiss, B. (2010). Madness After Virginia Tech: From Psychiatric Risk to Institutional Vulnerability. *Social Text, 28*(4), 25–44.

Ries, N. M., & Thomson, M. (2019). Bioethics & Universal Vulnerability: Exploring the Ethics and Practices of Research Participation. *Medical Law Review*. https://academic.oup.com/medlaw/advance-article/doi/10.1093/medlaw/fwz026/5571045

Riggs, D., Pearce, R., Pfeffer, C., Hines, S., White, F. R., & Ruspini, E. (2019). Transnormativity in the PSY Disciplines: Constructing Pathology in the Diagnostic and Statistical Manual and Standards of Care. *American Psychologist, 74*(8), 912–924.
Rose, N. (2019). *Our Psychiatric Future*. Cambridge: Polity Press.
Rucovsky, M. D. M. (2015). Trans∗ Necropolitics: Gender Identity Law in Argentina. *Sexualidad, Salud y Sociedad, 20*, 10–27.
Rucovsky, M. D. M. (2019). The *Travesti* Critique of the Gender Identity Law in Argentina. *TSQ: Transgender Studies Quarterly, 6*(2), 223–238.
Schultheiss, S., Gabouev, A. I., & Jonas, U. (2005). Nikolaj A. Bogoraz (1874–1952): Pioneer of Phalloplasty and Penile Implant Surgery. *The Journal of Sexual Medicine, 2*(1), 139–146.
Sharpe, A. (2009). Gender Recognition in the UK: A Great Leap Forward. *Social & Legal Studies, 18*, 241–245.
Sharpe, A. (2010). *Foucault's Monsters and the Challenge of Law*. Abingdon: Routledge.
Sharpe, A. (2018). *Sexual Intimacy and Gender Identity 'Fraud': Reframing the Legal and Ethical Debate*. Oxon: Routledge.
shuster, s. (2018). Passing as Experts in Transgender Medicine. In A. Jones, M. Yarbrough, & J. DeFilippis (Eds.), *The Unfinished Queer Agenda After Marriage*. New York: Routledge.
Sørlie, A. (2018). The Right to Trans-Specific Healthcare in Norway: Understanding the Health Needs of Transgender People. *Medical Law Review, 27*(2), 295–317.
Stewart, D.-L. (2017). Trans∗Versing the DMZ: A Non-Binary Autoethnographic Exploration of Gender and Masculinity. *International Journal of Qualitative Studies in Education, 30*(3), 285–304.
Straube, W., & Tainio, L. (2019). Book Review: The Power of Vulnerability: Mobilising Affect in Feminist, Queer and Anti-Racist Media Cultures. *NORA – Nordic Journal of Feminist and Gender Research, 27*(3), 210–212.
Stryker, S. (1994). My Words to Victor Frankenstein Above the Village of Chamounix: Performing Transgender Rage. *GLQ, 1*(3), 237–254.
Stryker, S. (2008). *Transgender History*. Berkeley: Seal Press.
Theilen, J. T. (2014). Depathologisation of Transgenderism and International Human Rights Law. *Human Rights Law Review, 14*, 327–342.
Travis, M. (2019). The Vulnerability of Heterosexuality: Consent, Gender Deception and Embodiment. *Social & Legal Studies, 28*(3), 303–326.
van der Drift, M. (2019). A Misplaced Headline in Times of Fascism. In *Trans Reproductive Justice: A Radical Transfeminism Mini Zine*. Leith: Radical Transfeminist Collective.
Vincent, B. (2020). *Non-Binary Genders: Navigating Communities, Identities, Healthcare*. Bristol: Policy Press.
Whittle, S. (2002). *Respect and Equality: Transsexual and Transgender Rights*. London: Cavendish.
World Health Organization. (1992). *The ICD-10 Classification of Mental and Behavioural Disorders: Clinical Descriptions and Diagnostic Guidelines*. Geneva: World Health Organization.

# 9

# Feminist Activism in the Context of Clinical Trials and Drug Roll-Out

Aziza Ahmed

## 1 Introduction

In 2006, the Food and Drug Administration (FDA) approved Gardasil, a Human Papilloma Virus (HPV) vaccine, for the purposes of stopping the spread of HPV, a primary cause of cervical cancer. While its development and approval were largely seen as necessary steps forward for women's health, feminist movements in both the United States and India took a critical posture toward the vaccine. Their reactions derived from a shared skepticism of how knowledge is produced and diffused by federal agencies and pharmaceutical companies about women's bodies.

In the United States, where the vaccine was quickly approved and rolled out, the feminist women's health movement joined other activists in raising key questions about how the drug was approved, the long-term effects of the drugs, and the influence of Merck Pharmaceuticals, the maker of the vaccine, in attempting to get state legislatures to adopt mandatory HPV vaccine laws. While feminists were critical of pharmaceutical companies, they also praised the vaccine as a symbol of progress in women's health. The Indian story was more complicated. In 2009, Merck began the process to roll out the vaccine in India. In India, however, the studies took a dark turn when seven participants in the studies died. Women's health activists in India decried the deaths of the young women, several who were members of scheduled tribes. Further,

A. Ahmed (✉)
Northeastern University School of Law, Boston, MA, USA
e-mail: Az.Ahmed@northeastern.edu



C. Dietz et al. (eds.), *A Jurisprudence of the Body*, Palgrave Socio-Legal Studies,
https://doi.org/10.1007/978-3-030-42200-4_9

activists raised concerns about the means in which the clinical trials took place: questioning the mode of obtaining consent, the information given to parents, and the capacity of the state health facilities to test and treat for cancer (Sarojini et al. 2010). The idea that Indian citizens were being treated as "guinea pigs" resulted in the Indian government halting all clinical trials of new chemical entities in 2013. The location of Indian feminists in the third world, where the many clinical trials for new drugs occur, placed the feminist critique inside a larger national discussion of how Indian citizens are exploited as experimental subjects. This was markedly distinct from the reaction of feminists in the United States in which broader political and economic issues played a minor role in advocacy, and there was no mention of exploitation in clinical trials despite ongoing advocacy for the inclusion of women as research subjects. Using the HPV vaccine as an example, this chapter examines the role of feminists in bioethical debates about the production of knowledge about women's bodies and the politics of vaccine roll-out. The chapter concludes by offering lessons gleaned from observing these two movements in relationship to one another.[1]

## 2 Women as Test Subjects

Prior to the 1980s, women were excluded from clinical trials largely due to fears of harm to the fetus of women who were pregnant or potentially pregnant. This had broad impact: little was known about disease or illness in women's bodies, gynecological illnesses, and pregnancy. In the 1980s and 1990s, feminist bioethicists, scientists, and advocates took up the cause for the greater inclusion of women in biomedical research. Feminists mobilized an identity-based frame on health advocacy to rectify the way "imbalances of power in the sex-gender system play themselves out in medical practice," medical research, and to demand greater inclusion in clinical trials (Lindemann 2000: 492). The Food and Drug Administration (FDA) and National Institutes for Health (NIH) became key targets for American feminists (Dresser 1992: 25). While the struggle against the FDA and NIH was largely domestic, their implications for women in the third world were vast as clinical trials began to relocate to the global south.

[1] In his book *Pharmocracy: Value, Politics, and Knowledge in Global Biomedicine*, Kaushik Sunder Rajan describes how "one can consider the gaze of Western biomedicine upon the Third World, tribal, female, minor body, and analyze how the construction of cervical cancer as an object of knowledge operates through the construction of these girls as subjects of experimentation" (Sunder Rajan 68–69).

The feminist fight for inclusion in clinical trials was game-changing and high-profile. Inspired by their belief that knowledge about the impact of drugs on women's bodies was lacking, they waged several successful campaigns against the National Institutes for Health (NIH) and the Food and Drug Administration (FDA). The most notable early victory came with a transformation in the National Institutes for Health. In 1984, the Task Force on Women's Health Issues, mandated by the then US Assistant Secretary for Health, issued a report which called for federal, state, local, and private research agencies to conduct more biomedical and behavioral research to "ensure emphasis on conditions and diseases unique to, or more prevalent in, women in all age groups" (Kirschstein and Merrittk 1985: 80). The report prompted the National Institutes of Health to announce a policy which *encouraged* the inclusion of women in study populations in all clinical research efforts. In July 1990, at the behest of the Congressional Caucus for Women's Issues, the Government Accountability Office (GAO) issued a report stating that the NIH had made little progress in bringing women into clinical research. The GAO report was utilized as a tool to motivate legal change. Inspired by feminist congresswomen and scientists, there was a new common sense: that it was "ludicrous, offensive, and unscientific" to exclude women from studies[2] (Epstein 2004: 187). Feminists mobilized clear examples to make this case including research on aspirin and estrogen on heart disease, a leading cause of death for women, with all-male study populations. Key congresswomen inserted language into the NIH reauthorization bill and provided testimony that women were being excluded from research. They also worked with lobbying agencies and women's health organizations to ensure that pressure came from both inside and outside of congress. In 1993, congress passed the NIH Revitalization Act, which mandated that women and minorities be included in clinical research with some exceptions (NIH Revitalization Act 1993).

The FDA also came under attack for a guideline issued in 1977 that barred women of childbearing potential from early phases of clinical trial research. Women's rights advocates argued that this exclusion produced deficits of knowledge about women and medications[3] (Epstein 2004). In 1993, the HIV

---

[2] Stephen Epstein argues that female scientists also played an important role in forging a new "common sense" which suggested that it was "ludicrous, offensive, and unscientific" that women were excluded from studies.

[3] See, also, Philip J. Hilts, "F.D.A. Ends Ban on Women in Drug Testing," The New York Times, March 25, 1993, https://www.nytimes.com/1993/03/25/us/fda-ends-ban-on-women-in-drug-testing.html?mcubz=0; Ruth B. Merkatz et al., "Women in Clinical Trials of New Drugs -- A Change in Food and Drug Administration Policy," *New England Journal of Medicine* 329, no. 4 (1993): 293–94.

Law Project, the NOW Legal Defense and Education Fund, and the American Civil Liberties Union AIDS Project filed a citizen's petition with the FDA. Later the same year, the FDA published new guidelines which allowed for women to be included in drug trials. The FDA also decided to request data concerning research on women from drug companies seeking FDA approval. Activists take credit for this transformation arguing that it was largely in response to the petition and activism. The FDA credits their shift to women's health advocacy groups as well as by internal reconsiderations of the role of informed consent and autonomy in the capacity of people to participate in studies.[4]

These victories led to an increase in women being included in clinical trials. And, while more was known about women, it also subjected women and girls to the broader range of harms that exist in the context of clinical trials and their roll-out. The story of the HPV vaccine describes the way knowledge production about women's bodies—and the management of their bodies through drug delivery—is implicated in the broader political economy of pharmaceutical development and roll-out. The remainder of the chapter turns to the case of the HPV vaccine trials, and their roll-out in the United States and India, to provide two examples of the struggles that feminists face after successfully advocating that women be included in clinical trials.

# 3 The Case of the HPV Vaccine

## 3.1 A Brief History of the HPV Vaccine

Data suggests that cervical cancer is a major contributor to women's morbidity and mortality globally. The majority of cervical cancer deaths occur in the third world. Most cases are associated with Human Papilloma Virus—a sexually transmitted infection (CDC 2019). In the early 2000s there was a breakthrough in cervical cancer research that led to a series of vaccines over the next decade that would prove to prevent the spread of HPV and thus lower the incidence of cervical cancer. In 2006, the FDA approved Gardasil, a drug manufactured by Merck Pharmaceuticals, which would prevent the transmission of specific strands of the HPV vaccine responsible for some forms of cervical cancer (FDA 2019). In 2009, the FDA approved a version of the HPV vaccine manufactured by GlaxoSmithKline called Cervarix and in 2014,

[4] In fact, in the United States, fight for women's inclusion was often a means to get poor women access to medicines.

a newer version of Gardasil by Merck. Each iteration of the drug protected against additional or different strains of the virus (FDA 2019). Of the vaccines, Gardasil was most heavily marketed and utilized. Following these approvals, the Centers for Disease Control (CDC) issued guidelines for the implementation of the vaccine that were adapted over time with the arrival of new data and approvals for the various vaccines.

In each country, feminist skepticism toward the vaccine took different forms but shared a critical posture toward a vaccine roll-out process dictated largely by pharmaceutical companies. This feminist skepticism derived from a broader feminist critique of the medical establishment. In the case of the HPV vaccine, as in the past, each feminist struggle took on the contours of the respective country and, at times, these national differences spoke to the structural positions of the advocates on the global stage. Below I describe the movement in the United States, which began in 2006, and in India, which began around 2009.

## 3.2 United States

The approval of the HPV vaccine in the United States was a cause for celebration—the spread of the virus known to cause cervical cancer could be substantially curbed having the potential to save lives. While feminist advocates celebrated the potential of an HPV vaccine, several organizations voiced concerns about the drug approval and roll-out process. The National Women's Health Network (NWHN) was among the first organizations that raised questions about the production of the vaccine. The organization had previously highlighted the abuses of women in drug development and testing outside of the HPV context[5] (Prescott 2010). In the case of the HPV vaccine, NWHN did not seek to challenge the approval of Gardasil by the FDA. Rather, as they testified before the FDA Vaccines and Related Products Advisory Committee Meeting, they had three goals, first, to ensure that there was follow-up research with the study population to learn more about safety and efficacy, second, to ensure a fair dispersal of the vaccine including to those most vulnerable to cervical cancer, and third, that the FDA mandate labeling that reminds providers and patients that it is necessary to continue to be screened for cervical cancer. Of these points, the latter had the most support

[5] National Women's Health Network was founded in 1975 and has a long history of challenging the FDA and pharmaceutical companies on behalf of women who were wronged. Five Colleges Women's Health Archive, Historical Note, available at http://asteria.fivecolleges.edu/findaids/sophiasmith/mnsss371_bioghist.html

with several organizations including the American Social Health Association and the American College of Obstetrics and Gynecologists also raising the concern that the vaccines do not derail efforts to increase cervical cancer screening (Prescott 2010).

A second set of feminist responses stemmed from the question of whether or not the vaccine should be mandatory for all girls. Beginning with Gardasil's approval, Merck engaged in a campaign to make the vaccine mandatory (Rosenthal 2008). Part of their strategy capitalized on feminist images and process. Much to the chagrin of many feminists (though not all), Merck engaged in a visible campaign that looked and sounded feminist. The campaign began with the "one less" TV campaign that mobilized ideas of "girl power" (Mamo et al. 2010: 125–126). In the ad, young women looked directly into the camera stating that they might be one less woman to get cervical cancer if they are given the HPV vaccine. Merck also took a more covert approach. With other pharmaceutical companies, Merck sponsored Women in Government—a network of progressive and conservative female legislators who meet regularly to discuss advocacy goals (Siers-Poisson 2007). The goals of Women in Government map the legislative changes desired by pharmaceutical companies. Unsurprisingly, they pushed for the roll-out of mandatory vaccines for Gardasil. In response to the Merck campaign,[6] feminists called for the need to remain critical (White 2014). Second, feminists took issue with the fact that state governments were only requiring girls to be vaccinated. Although boys carried HPV, and often developed related cancers, proposed legislation tended not to require boys to get the vaccine. Feminists thought of this as blatant gender discrimination.[7]

[6] "The vaccine has been controversial because some parents objected to state mandates to give it to young girls, preferring to encourage their daughters to abstain from sexual activity until marriage" (Ogilvie et al. 2007: 1204). See, also, Kevin Outterson, "Foreword—Will HPV Vaccines Prevent Cervical Cancers Among Poor Women of Color?: Global Health Policy at the Intersection of Human Rights and Intellectual Property Law," *American Journal of Law & Medicine* 35, no. 2–3 (2009): 247–252.

[7] The push for mandatory vaccines faced political backlash from political and religious conservatives who argued that vaccinating young women against a sexually transmitted infection would lead them to be promiscuous. Merck sought to influence conservative politicians with financial incentives. In at least one case they succeeded: initially resistant to the vaccine because he felt that abstinence and conservative values should come first, Texas Governor Rick Perry flipped his position when a lobbyist for Merck and Perry's former Chief-of-Staff as well as a founder of a SuperPac came in support of Perry's bid for president. Bypassing the legislature, Perry signed an executive order mandating that all 11- and 12-year-old girls in Texas get vaccinated, making it the first state to make the vaccine mandatory. Perry's support for a proposal that some associated with advancing women's health raised red flags and led to an unraveling of Merck's influence in shaping the regulatory environment around the HPV roll out. State of Texas, Office of the Governor, Rick Perry, *Executive Order Relating to the Immunization of Young Women from the Cancer Causing Human Papillomavirus*; Ralph Blumenthal, "Texas is First Require Cancer Shots for School Girls," *New York Times*, February 3, 2007, http://www.nytimes.com/2007/02/03/us/03texas.html; Sheila Krumholz and Michael Beckel, "HPV Vaccine, Merck, and Rick Perry's Money," *CNN*,

A third HPV vaccine-related issue cropped up in 2008 when the Centers for Disease Control and the Advisory Committee on Immunization Practices (ACIP) recommended that all immigrant girls and women aged 11–26 be vaccinated for HPV. The justification was a 1996 law mandating that vaccines recommended for US citizens be made mandatory for US green-card applicants (Peterson 2007). The mandate came at the same time that there was rising public perception that the vaccine was unsafe (Chitale 2009). The concern that young women would be forced to take an unsafe vaccine brought a range of feminist organizations with immigrant constituencies into the debate. Organizations including the National Asian Pacific American Women's Forum, California Latinas for Reproductive Justice, the National Latina Institute for Reproductive Health, and SisterSong waged a campaign to have the requirement removed (Yeung and Allen 2009). In a letter sent to Richard Besser, the Acting Director of the CDC, and in accompanying advocacy, the organizations demanded that the requirement that immigrant women be vaccinated be lifted. In the letter and in advocacy documents, feminist groups argued that the vaccine requirement was discriminatory along multiple lines. First (at the time the letter was written), no states required the vaccination for US citizens. Second, outside of the letter, organizations argued that the quick approval process (harkening to the broader critique of Merck's undue influence over the approval process) didn't yet fully explore the long-term consequences and efficacy of the vaccine (Yeung and Allen 2009). Third, in joining a broader chorus of advocacy groups for women of color, organizations highlighted the structural inequalities that led poor immigrant women, largely living outside of the United States, to pay the large fee required to access an HPV vaccine (Letter to Richard Besser 2009). Attention generated by feminists helped mobilize and bolster a nation-wide critique of Merck's undue influence by physicians and activists. Importantly for immigrant groups, the CDC and ACIP removed the mandatory requirement that immigrant girls and women receive the HPV vaccine before being granted entry.

Despite these numerous critiques arising in response to specific issues regarding the vaccine's roll-out, American feminists have largely gotten on board with the vaccine (Walden 2013). While often, although not always, acknowledging the political realities of drug approval and influence of pharmaceutical companies, women's health advocates celebrated and promoted

September 20, 2011, https://www.cnn.com/2011/09/15/opinion/krumholz-beckel-perry-pharmaceutical/index.html. The tide of legislation requiring mandating the vaccine began in 2006 with Michigan and quickly moved onto other states and is still being debated and adopted or rejected by state legislatures.

Gardasil as an advancement for women's health. They sought to pave the way for greater access to the vaccine and more attention to cervical cancer.[8]

## 3.3 India

While the American feminist mode of critical engagement (critiquing the conduct of pharmaceutical companies but celebrating the vaccine) continued in the United States, in 2009 Indian feminists began to pay close attention to the HPV vaccine when Merck launched Gardasil in two sites in India: Andhra Pradesh and Gujarat. In Andhra Pradesh, the study was the product of a joint initiative of the Andhra Pradesh Ministry for Health and Family Welfare, the Indian Council for Medical Research (ICMR), and the international non-profit organization PATH (Sunder Rajan 2017). In Gujarat, the research was jointly implemented by PATH and the Gujarat Ministry for Health and Family Welfare with other local partners. The Bill and Melinda Gates Foundation also funded the research.

Researchers designed the studies with three phases. Phase I assessed how potential patients would receive the vaccine. Phase II consisted of vaccine roll-out. The goal of Phase II was to vaccinate all eligible girls aged 10–14 in three areas of the two districts. Described as a post-licensure observational study, the goal was to detect adverse events to the vaccine. Phase III was an assessment of "coverage, acceptability, feasibility and cost of HPV vaccine delivery" (Government of India Report 2011: 7). The research population in Andhra Pradesh was largely members of scheduled tribes, a poor community whose main livelihood is agriculture and gathering local produce. The tribal population has been further sinking into poverty with large scale deforestation, continued loss of land rights, flooding, and ongoing conflict. In both Andhra Pradesh and Gujarat, the study population was young women.

In 2010, after approximately 24,000 girls received the vaccine in India, the Indian Council on Medical Research (ICMR) halted the studies—approximately seven girls enrolled in the trials had died. Five of these girls were from Andhra Pradesh, and the other two were from Gujarat. Women's health advocates, alongside other activists, raised questions and drew attention to the

[8] See also the push for women's health advocates but funded by Merck: "Young Scholars Join Project to Support Women's Health Advocates," *American Cancer Society MediaRoom*, March 8, 2017, http://pressroom.cancer.org/2017-03-08-American-Cancer-Society-Celebrates-Young-Scholars-Joining-All-of-Me-Projects-in-Latin-America-to-Support-a-New-Generation-of-Womens-Health-Advocates

potential unethical nature of the clinical trials. News of the deaths reached SAMA, a network of women's health advocates.

In 2010, SAMA conducted a field study to help understand the nature of the trials and the impact. According to the study, SAMA advocates interviewed individuals involved in the observational trial. The final report outlined a host of challenges in the study design and implementation. First, the report documented a complete failure on issues of consent. Research participants who had signed informed consent forms should have been able to articulate the potential consequences of the vaccine. In interviewing girls, SAMA researchers found that few could articulate the possible consequences of the vaccine. Second, many of the research participants lacked official documentation (e.g. birth certificates); thus, the individuals who enrolled the girls in clinical trials could not verify their age as between 10 and 14 potentially risking the health of the participant (Sarojini et al. 2010). Third, material given to the girls was often in English, a language the girls were not able to read, and documents bore the logos of the government. Further, informational cards about HPV given to the girls were not only in English, they were misleading—calling the trial an "HPV Vaccination Campaign by the Department of Health and Family Welfare, Government of Andhra Pradesh" (Sarojini et al. 2010: 8). Parents reported to SAMA that they believed that they were receiving a free vaccine from the government that would otherwise be very expensive (Sarojini et al. 2010). In other words, while the girls were participating in a study, they and their parents (when informed of the study) were led to believe that they were receiving a free vaccine. Finally, some of the trial participants resided in hostels (*ashram paathsalas*). In these situations, permission for participation in the study was given by the hostel administrators rather than by parents. SAMA argued that by choosing girls living in hostels "the authorities" were able to evade getting parental permission before administering the trial and questioned whether the caretakers of residences should be able to give permission for participation in clinical trials (Sarojini et al. 2010).

The SAMA investigation, media outcry, and word of the deaths inspired a government response. Shortly after SAMA released their report, the Indian Government also released findings from an investigation of the clinical trial sites. The government study found that the girls who died did not die due to their participation in the HPV vaccine study. The report concludes that two girls died due to consumption of poisoning (14 and 13 years old), one drowned in a well (12 years old), one from an "unrelated disease" (11 years old), two from severe malaria (10 and 13 years old), and, finally, the last girl died of a snake bite (15 years old). The investigation exculpated ICMR and PATH.

Women's health advocates continued to push for greater accountability for the deaths of the young trial participants. By 2013, they were not alone. Attention turned toward the large number of deaths occurring in clinical trials in India inspired by a related struggle led by a whistle blower in the Indian state of Madhya Pradesh. These activists highlighted that since 2003, the number of clinical trials in India increased from 50 over 1850. By the end of 2011, over 150,000 people in India were enrolled in clinical trials, and an international pharmaceutical industry was profiting from human research: clinical research outsourcing companies (CROs), third-party organizations that implement clinical trials, generated 485 million dollars in revenue between 2010 and 2011. India's popularity as a site of clinical trial research included cheaper costs, English-speaking physicians who could oversee trials, high-quality hospitals, many people with illnesses that needed be studied, and its genetically diverse population (Yee 2012: 397–98).

In keeping with this momentum, at the behest of women's health activists, the Parliamentary Standing Committee on Health and Family Welfare considered the issues arising with the Gardasil clinical trial research. In August of 2013, the Committee released its scathing assessment of the situation in a report titled "Alleged Irregularities in the Conduct of Studies Using Human Papilloma Virus (HPV) Vaccine" by PATH. Unlike the Ministry of Health, the Parliamentary Committee Report criticized the actions of the ICMR, the Drug Controller General of India (DCGI),[9] and PATH (Parliament of India 2013). The report makes several important interventions into the broader debate on the regulation of clinical trials. The report found that PATH misrepresented the nature of the research to the Indian government. PATH called the study an "observational" study, sometimes using the language of a "demonstration" study rather than a "clinical trial." Observational studies do not have the same level of regulatory oversight, and there is no such thing as a demonstration study in the regulatory framework. In utilizing this language, the report states that PATH was able to evade the regulatory oversight of conducting a clinical trial. The Parliamentary Committee reports also placed blame on various governmental agencies involved—stating that they should

[9] "The Committee noted that as per Rule122-DA and Schedule Y of the Drugs and Cosmetics Rules, 1945 made under the Drugs and Cosmetics Act, 1940, no clinical trial on a drug can be conducted except under, and in accordance with the permission in writing, of the Licensing Authority i.e. DCGI. All vaccines are deemed to be drugs. Clinical trials of pharmaceutical products are conducted on human subjects in the country to determine or verify safety and/or efficacy. Every permission for conducting clinical trials also, inter alia, includes a condition that in event of trial related injury or death, the sponsor will provide complete medical care as well as compensation. Statement to this effect needs to be incorporated in the Informed Consent Form. The details of compensation provided are to be intimated to the office of DCGI" (India 2013: 14).

have noticed and interrogated PATH's actions. If they had, PATH would have had additional regulatory oversight. Instead, the report notes that different arms of the Indian government understood the research differently. ICMR, for example, felt that since the study was "observational" rather than a "clinical trial"[10] that they did not need to follow "clinical trial rules" which included "reporting serious adverse effects within a particular time frame" (Parliament of India 2013). The committee states that this is "intriguing and fishy."

> The choice of countries and population groups, the monopolistic nature, at that point of time of the product being pushed, and the unlimited market potential and opportunities in the universal immunization programs of the respective countries are all pointers to a well-planned scheme to commercially exploit a situation. Had PATH been successful in getting the HPV vaccine included in the universal immunization program of concerned countries, this would have generated windfall profit for the manufacture(s) by way of automatic sale, year after year, without any promotional or marketing expenses. It is well known that once introduced into the immunization program, it becomes politically impossible to stop any vaccination. To achieve this end effortlessly without going through the arduous and strictly regulated route of clinical trials, PATH resorted to an element of subterfuge by calling the clinical trials "Observational Studies" or "Demonstration Project" and various such expressions. Thus, the interest, safety, and well-being of subjects were completely jeopardized by PATH by using self-determined and self-servicing nomenclature which is not only highly deplorable but a serious breach of the law of the land. (Parliament of India 2013: 6–7)

Following from this, the report also critiques the Indian Council on Medical Research. The report outlines that while there are ethical guidelines that the ICMR should follow to protect participants and, in turn, the ICMR betrayed their role in ensuring that ethical standards were met (Parliament of India 2013). This began with the meetings between PATH and ICMR in 2006 which resulted, the same year, in a Memorandum of Understanding (MOU) between PATH and ICMR to "to explore collaboration to support public sector decision regarding HPV vaccine introduction in India and…to generate necessary evidence to allow…the possible introduction of HPV vaccine into India's Universal Immunization Programme." Voicing deep suspect of American pharmaceutical countries, and noting that the MOU was signed

[10] The FDA defines a clinical trial as "clinical research designed to evaluate and test new interventions such as… medications" (FDA 2018).

prior to approval of the drugs, the Parliamentary Committee report finds that the work of the DCGI and ICMR was suspect:

> there was a serious dereliction of duty by many of the Institutions and individuals involved…the Committee observes that ICMR representatives, instead of ensuring the highest levels of ethical standards in research studies, apparently acted at the behest of the PATH in promoting the interests of manufactures of the HPV vaccine. (Rule 122-DA and Schedule Y of the Drugs and Cosmetics Rules 1945)
>
> the DHR/ICMR have completely failed to perform their mandated role and responsibility as the apex body for medical research in the Country.[11]

The Parliamentary Committee also investigated the thorny question of informed consent. Taking on the feminist position, the committee noted that a large number of the individuals who signed the informed consent statement provided by PATH were illiterate in both English and in their local language (Telugu or Gujarati). Echoing the findings of the SAMA report, the Parliamentary Committee notes that many of the informed consent forms were not signed or were signed by headmasters of schools rather than parents. Here they stated that "obtaining informed consent from study subjects is a fundamental requirement in the conduct of clinical trials to ensure that the human rights of the study subjects are ensured" (Parliamentary Committee Report 2013: 11). They concluded that "most, if not all consent forms, were carelessly filled-up and were incomplete and inaccurate. The full explanation, role, usefulness and pros and cos of the vaccination had not been properly communicated to the parents/guardians" (Parliamentary Committee Report 2013: 12). Importantly the Committee was unwilling to write off the deaths as unrelated to the vaccines. Instead they proposed mechanisms by which the vaccines could have resulted in the deaths including through suicidal ideation (Parliamentary Committee Report 2013).

[11] The Parliamentary Committee notes that PATH clearly had two goals and objectives based on PATH's own stated objectives of the study. (1) to generate evidence, data, and arguments to support inclusion of HPV vaccines into India's state-funded Universal Immunization Program (UIP) and (2) to collect data on serious and non-serious adverse effects. "Given that similar projects were launched in Peru, Uganda, and Vietnam, the entire exercise would have collected side effect profiles of HPV vaccines in all the ethnic groups that reside in developing countries. Such data would be invaluable to promote the two-branded, patented, single source HPV vaccines as safe all over the world." Also note, that the PC report highlights that "before approving any new drug (including vaccines), under Drugs and Cosmetics Rules, it is mandatory to conduct Phase III clinical trials in India to determine any differences in the safety and efficacy profiles." For a broader discussion on the use of racial categories in research design, see Dorothy Roberts, *Fatal Invention: How Science, Politics, and Big Business Re-Create Race in the Twenty-First Century* (New York: New Press, 2011).

While the response of the government dragged, the findings of the Parliamentary Committee were taken up by lawyers for the Human Rights Law Network and the Lawyers Committee based in New Delhi, India. In 2012, both organizations filed Public Interest Litigation through a writ petition, a mechanism by which individuals and organizations in India can petition the Supreme Court to hear violations of fundamental rights. The petition was filed on behalf of three women, each representative of health advocacy groups: the Saheli Women's Resource Center, the Voluntary Health Association of India, and the Gramya Resource Center for Women. The petition begins by acknowledging that women's groups and health groups brought the issue of the violations associated with the HPV trials to light. The litigation reflects the critical posture of the women's rights groups toward the HPV vaccine and, arguably, takes them further in suggesting that the HPV vaccine is both "unproven and hazardous" and that they were licensed in India "without sufficient clinical trials in appropriate age groups to determine their safety and efficacy" (in the United States, by 2012, the vaccine was widely in circulation) (Writ Petition 2012: 14). Further, the petition argues that:

> manufacturers, international NGOs, research organizations, government institutions and even so-called charitable institutions are involved in collusion and fraud which has nothing to do with charity or even public health and has everything to do with pushing for the introduction of a vaccine in the public health system which may come free in the first instance but which will bankrupt the public health system in the long run denying vitally needed funds for more critical sectors. All this is being done in the guise of charity to benefit private parties in the long run. (Writ Petition 2012: 14)

The petitioners made a series of demands which included legal experts and NGOs largely intended to increase accountability for drug trials and for the girls who died. Among other issues, they sought a study to better understand "the number of deaths and persons adversely impacted by the administration of the HPV vaccine"; medical examinations of the trial victims who died to better understand and determine the culpability of PATH, the State Governments of Gujarat and Andhra Pradesh, "in causing adverse reactions including death and to make a report to the Court in this regard and to make recommendations with regards to compensation and continuing medical treatment"; an order preventing the ICMR from entering into MOUs with pharmaceutical companies and multinational agencies and NGOs to conduct research into specific products, a plan of action to respond to the criticisms of the PSC and for further monitoring of clinical trials and drug marketing in

India, criminal liability for respondents that are found responsible for deaths, to prevent the sale of the HPV vaccine in India, and for the PATH findings to be declared null and void (Mehta v. Union of India 2012: 8). The brief also highlighted that current technologies, including pap smears, also had the capacity to effectively help in cancer prevention and raised the concern that the HPV vaccine could detract from the implementation of broader health systems solutions.

While awaiting a resolution to their case, in 2013 the Indian Supreme Court responded to a petition filed by another health activist group, Swasthya Adhikar Manch, in which SAMA provided an affidavit. The petition led the court to halt 162 trials of new chemical entities. Alongside new proposed regulations, the halting of the trials sent a clear signal that the Indian clinical trial landscape was on the potential precipice of change.

In 2014, in response to the writ petition filed on behalf of the HPV trial victims, the Court ordered that "government set up an agency" that links all agencies involved in processing requests for clinical trials (Supreme Court of India 2014: 4). The Court also stated that the act of PATH in conducting clinical trials as "demonstration trials" was a "serious breach of medical ethics" and a "clear cut violation of human rights" (Supreme Court of India 2014: 4). The Court highlights that the Committee report recommended that the National Human Rights Commission and National Commission for the Protection of Children should "take up" this issue from the point of view of human rights and child abuse and that the National Commission for Women should take cognizance of this case "as all the poor and hapless subjects are females" (Supreme Court of India 2014: 4). The Court also recommends that the Ministry of Health and Family Welfare should report the violations of PATH to "international bodies" like the WHO and UNICEF, "so as to ensure that appropriate remedial actions initiated by these agencies worldwide" (Supreme Court of India 2014: 4). The court also highlights a series of concerns and questions including asking what action had been taken after the Parliamentary Committee Report and further details on study design.

Since 2014, various branches of the government have made a series of conflicting moves with the end goal of deciding that the HPV vaccine should be introduced as part of India's universal vaccine program. Some cities have moved forward with implementing the HPV vaccine (Mehrotra et al. 2018). The Supreme Court has yet to decide the outcome of the 2012 case. For feminists, the contemporary moment represents both a victory and a loss. The SAMA report, and the ongoing advocacy of the organization, resulted in regulatory shifts[12] (Riles 2002). Yet the more specific fight, one for greater accountability for the victims of the HPV trials, and for the set of girls who participated in the study, remained to be decided.

## 4 Supply and Demand for Women's Bodies

The American and Indian feminist advocacy stories around HPV teach us at least two lessons about clinical trials and the production of knowledge about women's bodies that have been vastly underexplored in the academic literature.

First, although feminist activism may seem to be jurisdictionally bound, the broader political economy of clinical trials means that the global impact of national-level activism must be taken into account by advocates. When American feminists began their fight for inclusion into clinical trials, most trials were still being conducted in the United States. Over the last 40 years, as Adriana Petryna notes in her book *When Experiments Travel: Clinical Trials and the Global Search for Human Subjects*, almost all clinical trials have now been exported to the third world (Petryna 2009). This shift is largely attributable to the cheaper cost of carrying out clinical trials and weak regulatory oversight the latter demonstrated by the Indian example. While clinical trials and drug roll-out processes are subject to national-level regulation, the idea that representation matters often shapes how drugs trials occur. In other words, the demand for the inclusion of women in clinical trials in the United States has produced a need to find women to recruit within the existing political and economic landscape.

The death of the young girls in India, and the broader debate it engendered about ethics in clinical trials, however, seems to have had almost no impact on women's health advocacy on drugs research. To the contrary, in 2014, the FDA also released a new report, *the Action Plan to Enhance the Collection and Availability of Demographic Subgroup Data*. The report, which came at the encouragement of American women's health organizations and feminists, was celebrated as a long-awaited step in continuing to understand how sex impacts how bodies process drugs by encouraging greater use of women as research subjects. Little attention has been paid to how the call for greater diversity in clinical trial research has an uneven, and even exploitative, dimension when trials and drug roll-out move around the globe.

---

[12] The idea of feminist advocates as shaping and making institutions has been written about extensively. See, for example, Annelise Riles, "Rights Inside Out: The Case of the Women's Human Rights Campaign," *Leiden Journal of International Law* 15, no. 2 (2002): 285–305.

Second, as highlighted in the work of Kaushik Sunder Rajan in his book *Pharmocracy: Value, Politics, and Knowledge in Global Biomedicine*, and illustrated by the fall out of the HPV implementation in the Indian context in this chapter, it is clear that the expansion of clinical trials to the third world, and the politics of roll-out in both the United States and India, have resulted in an uneven impact on national populations. Although bioethicists highlight the importance of considering the needs of study populations in the testing and roll-out of pharmaceuticals, the reality is that context is frequently ignored. Instead, for many, access to experimental trials may be their only access to healthcare. This is particularly true for the groups impacted by the drug roll-out in India and those made subject to political battles—including immigrants—in the United States. This makes it necessary to not only consider the broader ecosystem of trials and drug roll-outs but the impact on specific communities.

## 5 Conclusion

National-level feminists organizing in response to clinical trials and drug roll-out are bound together through the broader political and economic drivers of pharmaceutical research and sales. The bodies of young women and girls are implicated in research and drug roll-out as the demand for research subjects continues. The experiences of India and the United States suggest feminists have had the ability to shape the regulatory environment for clinical trials and drug roll-out. Yet, these accounts also suggest that there is a greater need to think through the linkages between national-level activism and reorient some activist goals given the global political and economic landscape in which clinical trials and drug roll-out currently take place.

## References

"10 Years after HPV Vaccines' Approval, Where Do We Stand?," *National Women's Health Network* (blog), September 6, 2016., https://www.nwhn.org/10-years-hpv-vaccines-approval-stand/

"Cervarix," Food and Drug Administration, October 25, 2019., https://www.fda.gov/BiologicsBloodVaccines/Vaccines/ApprovedProducts/ucm186957.htm.

"Cervical Cancer Statistics," *Centers for Disease Control and Prevention*, May 28, 2019., https://www.cdc.gov/cancer/cervical/statistics/index.htm.

"Cervical Cancer," Cancer, *World Health Organization*, Accessed December 5, 2019., http://www.who.int/cancer/prevention/diagnosis-screening/cervical-cancer/en/.

"Gardasil Vaccine Safety," *U.S. Food and Drug Administration*, February 1, 2018., https://www.fda.gov/BiologicsBloodVaccines/SafetyAvailability/VaccineSafety/ucm179549.htm.

"Gardasil," *U.S. Food and Drug Administration*, October 24, 2019., https://www.fda.gov/vaccines-blood-biologics/vaccines/gardasil.

"Guard Us All? Immigrant Women and the HPV Vaccine (encore)," *Making Contact Radio* (blog), July 29, 2009., https://www.radioproject.org/2009/07/guard-us-all-immigrant-women-and-the-hpv-vaccine-encore/.

"Hold the Hype on HPV," *National Women's Health Network* (blog), March 1, 2007., https://www.nwhn.org/hold-the-hype-on-hpv/ vaccine takes away from structural concerns)

"SC Ruling on Clinical Trials," April 22, 2014., https://www.telegraphindia.com/india/sc-ruling-on-clinical-trials/cid/191579

"Statement from PATH: HPV Demonstration Project in India," *PATH*, May 11, 2011., https://www.path.org/media-center/statement-from-path-hpv-demonstration-project-in-india/.

Ogilvie, D., et al. (2007). Interventions to Promote Walking: Systematic Review. *BMJ, 334*(7605), 1204.

Petryna, A. (2009). *When Experiments Travel: Clinical Trials and the Global Search for Human Subjects* (Vol. 23). Princeton: Princeton University Press.

Advocates Letter to Richard Besser, Atlanta, GA, June 26, 2009. The National Latina Institute for Reproductive Health, *The National Latina Institute for Reproductive Health Advocates for Access to the HPV Vaccine*, http://latinainstitute.org/sites/default/files/NLIRHHPVStmt-31July07-final.pdf

Yee, A. (2012). Regulation Failing to Keep up with India's Trials Boom. *The Lancet, 379*(9814), 397–398.

Carpenter, L. M., & Casper, M. J. (2009, December). A Tale of Two Technologies: HPV Vaccination, Male Circumcision, and Sexual Health. *Gender & Society, 23*(6), 809.

Chamberlain, G. (2015, January 13). Judges Demand Answers After Children Die in Cancer Vaccine Trial, *Daily Mail Online*, https://www.dailymail.co.uk/news/article-2908963/Judges-demand-answers-children-die-controversial-cancer-vaccine-trial-India.html

Chitale, R. (2009, August 19). Parents Doubt Gardasil's Safety, *ABC News*, https://abcnews.go.com/Health/WellnessNews/story?id=8368062

Dresser, R. (1992). Wanted: Single, White Male for Medical Research. *The Hastings Center Report, 22*(1), 25.

Epstein, S. (2004). Bodily Differences and Collective Identities: The Politics of Gender and Race in Biomedical Research in the United States. *Body & Society, 10*(2–3), 183.

Epstein, S., & Science, I. (1996). *AIDS, Activism, and the Politics of Knowledge* (p. 298). Berkeley: University of California Press.

Final Report of the Committee Appointed by the Government of India, "Alleged Irregularities in the Conduct of Studies of the Human Papilloma Virus Vaccine" by PATH, https://www.icmr.nic.in/sites/default/files/reports/Cervix%20Cancer.pdf

Gonzalez-Rojas, J. (2009, November 13). CDC Removes Discriminatory HPV Vaccination Requirement for Immigrant Women and Girls: Victory for Reproductive Justice Advocates, *National Latina Institute for Reproductive Health*, https://latinainstitute.org/es/node/452

Government of India, Press Information Bureau, Ministry of Health and Family Welfare, *Drug Trial Policy*, (India, 2013).

Houppert, K. (2007, March 8). Who's Afraid of Gardasil? *The Nation.*

Kalpana Mehtha Supreme Court of India Record of Proceedings 558/2012, Kalpana Mehta and Ors v. Union of India 7 SCC 302 (2012).

Kirschstein, R. L., & Merrittk, D. H. (1985). Women's Health: Report of the Public Health Service Task Force on Women's Health Issues. *Public Health Reports, 100*(1), 80.

Knox, R.. (2011, September 19). HPV Vaccine: The Science Behind the Controversy, *NPR*, https://www.npr.org/2011/09/19/140543977/hpv-vaccine-the-science-behind-the-controversy

Lindemann Nelson, H. (2000). Feminist Bioethics: Where We've Been, Where We're Going. *Metaphilosophy, 31*(5), 492.

Lloyd-Roberts, S. (2012, November 1). Have India's Poor Become Human Guinea Pigs? *BBC News*, https://www.bbc.com/news/magazine-20136654

Mamo, L., et al. (2010). Producing and Protecting Risky Girlhoods. In K. Wailoo et al. (Eds.), *Three Shots at Prevention: The HPV Vaccine and the Politics of Medicine's Simple Solutions* (pp. 125–126). Baltimore: The Johns Hopkins University Press.

Marouf, F. E., & Esplin, B. S. (2015, June 4). Setting a Minimum Standard of Care in Clinical Trials: Human Rights and Bioethics as Complementary Frameworks, *Health and Human Rights Journal* (blog), https://www.hhrjournal.org/2015/06/setting-a-minimum-standard-of-care-in-clinical-trials-human-rights-and-bioethics-as-complementary-frameworks/

McGovern, T. (1997). Barriers to the Inclusion of Women in Research and Clinical Trials. In N. Goldstein & J. L. Manlowe (Eds.), *The Gender Politics of HIV/AIDs in Women: Perspectives on the Pandemic in the United States* (p. 46). New York: New York University Press.

Mehrotra, R., Hariprasad, R., Rajaraman, P., Mahajan, V., Grover, R., Kaur, P., & Swaminathan, S. (2018). Stemming the Wave of Cervical Cancer: Human Papillomavirus Vaccine Introduction in India. *Journal of Global Oncology, 4*, 1–4.

NIH Revitalization Act, 42 U.S.C. § 289a-2 (1993).

Parliament of India, Department of Health Research, Ministry of Health and Family Welfare, *Seventy-Second Report on Alleged Irregularities in the Conduct of Studies Using Human Papilloma Virus (HPV) Vaccine by PATH in India* (India, 2013).

Peterson, L. A. (2007, February 3). Texas Gov. Orders Anti-Cancer Vaccine, *The Washington Post*, https://www.washingtonpost.com/wpdyn/content/article/2007/02/03/AR2007020300276.html

Prescott, H. M. (2010). Safeguarding Girls: Morality, Risk, and Activism. In K. Wailoo et al. (Eds.), *Three Shots at Prevention: The HPV Vaccine and the Politics of Medicine's Simple Solutions* (p. 114). Baltimore: The Johns Hopkins University Press.

Riles, A. (2002). Rights Inside Out: The Case of the Women's Human Rights Campaign. *Leiden Journal of International Law, 15*(2), 285–305

Rosenthal, E. (2008, August 20). Drug Makers' Push Leads to Cancer Vaccines' Rise, *The New York Times*, https://www.nytimes.com/2008/08/20/health/policy/20vaccine.html

Rucke, K. (2013, November 22). India's High Court Rules To Protect People 'Used As Guinea Pigs' In Drug Trials, https://www.mintpressnews.com/indias-high-court-rules-to-protect-people-used-as-guinea-pigs-in-drug-trials/173223/

Rule 122-DA and Schedule Y of the Drugs and Cosmetics Rules, 1945.

Sarojini, N. et al. (2010). *Preliminary Findings of Visit to Bhadrachalam: HPV Vaccine 'Demonstration Project' Site in Andhra Pradesh*, SAMA, 7.

Siers-Poisson, J. (2007, July). Women in Government, Merck's Trojan Horse: Part Three in a Series on the Politics and PR of Cervical Cancer, *New Doctor* 87.

Strehkle, S. (2015, November 4). Can the HPV Vaccine Really Kill You?, *Teen Vogue*, https://www.teenvogue.com/story/gardasil-hpv-vaccine-safety

Sunder Rajan, K. (2017). *Pharmocracy: Value, Politics, and Knowledge in Global Biomedicine* (pp. 68–69). Durham: Duke University Press.

"What Are the Different Types of Clinical Research?" *FDA*, November 3, 2018., http://www.fda.gov/patients/clinical-trials-what-patients-need-know/what-are-different-types-clinical-research

Tomljenovic, L., & Shaw, C. A. (2012). Too Fast or Not Too Fast: The FDA's Approval of Merck's HPV Vaccine Gardasil. *The Journal of Law, Medicine & Ethics, 40*(3), 673–681.

Urooj, M., et al. (2017). Compensation to Clinical Trial Participants in India: A Gap Analysis. *International Journal of Pharmaceutical Investigation, 7*(2), 41–46.

Walden, R. (2013, July/August). What You Need to Know About the HPV Vaccine, *National Women's Health Network*, https://www.nwhn.org/what-you-need-to-know-about-the-hpv-vaccine/

White, M. D. (2014). Pros, Cons, and Ethics of HPV Vaccine in Teens—Why Such Controversy? *Translational Andrology and Urology, 3*(4), 429–434.

Writ Petition in the Supreme Court of India, Kalpana Mehta and Ors v. Union of India 7 SCC 302, 14 (2012).

Writ petition Kalpana Mehta, Kalpana Mehta and Ors v. Union of India 7 SCC 302 (2012).

Yeung, Miriam Amanda Allen. (2009, December 14). Eliminating HPV Vaccine Mandate For Immigrant Women: A Victory On the Road To Reproductive Justice, *Rewire News* (blog), https://rewire.news/article/2009/12/14/eliminating-hpv-vaccine-mandate-for-immigrant-women-a-victory-on-road-to-reproductive-justice/; Miriam Jordan, Gardasil Requirement for Immigrants Stirs Backlash, *Wall Street Journal*, October 1, 2008, https://www.wsj.com/articles/SB122282354408892791.

# Part III

## Reframing Health Law Through Bodies

# 10

# Establishing Boundaries for Speculation About Artificial Wombs, Ectogenesis, Gender, and the Gestating Body

Claire Horn and Elizabeth Chloe Romanis

## 1 Introduction

In 2017, a team of foetal scientists at the Philadelphia Children's Hospital first announced successful animal trials of "the biobag" (Partridge et al. 2017). The biobag is designed to mimic the uterus, and was able to sustain lamb foetuses on the current viability threshold for a lamb (the equivalent of 23–24 weeks for a human foetus) for a period of four weeks. Given that this technology is intended to replicate the human uterus, in this chapter, we are interested in drawing the growing literature on the artificial womb towards considerations of the way classed, raced, and gendered embodiment may shape its meaning and impact. The construction of an external structure to facilitate gestation invites an analysis of the lived realities that make human pregnancies distinct from automated gestation, yet we argue that such an analysis is rarely engaged in the literature.

The team behind the biobag has indicated that it might be ready for testing on human subjects within only a few years, sparking a new wave of speculation in bioethical and legal literature about the possibility of gestating an

C. Horn (✉)
School of Law, Birkbeck, University of London, London, UK
e-mail: chorn04@mail.bbk.ac.uk

E. C. Romanis
Department of Law, University of Manchester, Manchester, UK
e-mail: elizabeth.romanis@manchester.ac.uk



C. Dietz et al. (eds.), *A Jurisprudence of the Body*, Palgrave Socio-Legal Studies,
https://doi.org/10.1007/978-3-030-42200-4_10

embryo from conception to full term in an artificial womb (full ectogenesis). We have observed with growing concern that this literature often overstates the capacities of ectogenic technologies currently in development (Räsänen 2017; Mathison and Davis 2017). This has led to an echo-chamber effect in which debates about the impact of artificial wombs are structured around the claim that the end of human gestation is upon us (Romanis and Horn forthcoming). We hold that the dominant focus on full ectogenesis and the thought experiments that this focus generates come at the expense of considering ethico-legal matters more immediate to the development of this technology.

The introduction of the term 'ectogenesis' is often traced to a speech given in 1923 by geneticist J.B.S Haldane to the Cambridge Heretics society. In 'Daedalus; or, Science and the Future,' Haldane predicted that by the 1960s, ectogenesis would replace 'natural' gestation. Of the debates over ectogenesis that occurred in the next several years, culminating in Huxley's *Brave New World* (1932), Franklin writes, "these stories [...] typically wove together elements from the history of embryology with science fiction, even sometimes very accurately predicting the future" (2013, 245). As Franklin observes, the literary set that speculated on the impact of artificial wombs in the 1920s did so alongside the emergence of the independent, proto-feminist 'new woman' and the growing popularity of the eugenics movement in the United Kingdom. From the first iteration of 'ectogenesis,' then, in which Haldane blended his knowledge of embryo transfer and a whimsical interest in the future possibilities of science, artificial wombs were treated both as a legitimately achievable technology and as a fantasy through which to explore burgeoning cultural anxieties. In fiction and non-fiction alike, authors have continued to use ectogenesis as a tool for examining broader concerns about motherhood, femininity, eugenics, and sexuality (Franklin 2013).

Recent excitement from legal and bioethical scholars over the artificial womb is no exception to this entanglement of scientific practice and fantasy. In 2016, scientists at Rockefeller and Cambridge Universities succeeded in growing human embryos up to 13 days, ending the experiment only to respect the legal limit of 14 days. In 2017, two separate teams of paediatricians and foetal scientists in Philadelphia (Partridge et al) and Australia (Usuda et al. 2019) respectively succeeded in creating advanced incubation technology for gestating premature lamb foetuses at the equivalent of 22-week human gestation through to term in good health. While most of the existing social science literature on artificial wombs was written prior to 2016, much of the work anticipates this progress (Kendal 2015; Simonstein 2009; Alghrani 2008).

Examining the ways that bioethical and legal scholars have speculated about the impact of ectogenesis on law serves as a rich ground for assessing normative assumptions about what a desirable future looks like. As Travis argues, discourse on emerging technologies reflects a "triangulation between science fiction, law, and popular opinion" (2011, 255), through which conclusions about the possible meaning of these technologies are co-produced. In ethico-legal speculation about the ways ectogenesis could impact future frameworks for parenthood, the gendered body, and reproductive rights, whose perspectives are valued? And whose contemporary lived realities are left out?

In this chapter, we address the ways in which speculation has been used thus far in the ectogenesis literature. We first address the claim on which speculation about the future impact of artificial womb technology is built; namely, that the development of full ectogenesis is imminent or inevitable. The ethico-legal literature thus far has largely been directed towards the prospect of technology that could entirely replace gestation (growing babies from conception to complete gestation in artificial conditions) as opposed to technologies that might 'take over' gestation—effectively acting as a more advanced version of neonatal intensive care (Romanis 2018). In this section, we explore the value of speculating about technological prospects, and argue that such a literature is important, but should be carefully grounded in contemporary scientific, legal, and social context.

In keeping with the focus on embodiment that shapes this book, we then turn to one key speculative claim that arises repeatedly in the literature on full ectogenesis: that by removing gestation from the body, ectogenesis will improve equality between men and women, effectively redistributing the labour of child bearing and rearing. We contend that this hypothetical assumption is problematic for three reasons. First, it locates the problem of inequity in gendered care labour in the gestating body, rather than in the institutional structures that produce it. Second, it presents a limited view of contemporary issues in gendered (in)equality by narrowly focusing on heterosexual relationships. Finally, it inaccurately presumes the stability of reproductive autonomy for all women. Building on this final contention, we turn to considering the impact of the artificial womb within the context of contemporary issues in stratified reproduction: the persistence of inequity of access to reproductive care and technologies across "hierarchies of class, race, ethnicity, gender, place in a global economy, and migration status" (Colen 1995, 78).

Ultimately, we agree that there is a legitimate place for speculative ethico-legal scholarship. We recognize the radical potential of imagining a future with ectogenesis to orient society and jurisprudence in emancipatory directions. Claims made by Firestone (1970) and Lewis (2019) that artificial wombs might constitute a tool for creating societies committed to shared and collaborative care labour, for instance, are compelling calls to a feminist future. We propose, however, that grounding these thought experiments in the contemporary realities of stratified reproduction and attending to existing inequities of access to reproductive care and support for care labour will ultimately better serve us in realizing these goals.

## 2 The Contemporary Scientific Reality of Artificial Wombs

Two working research teams have now claimed to have established 'proof of principle' for artificial wombs capable of sustaining the continued gestation of human entities *ex utero*. In 2017, Partridge et al. made headlines by managing to sustain the continued gestation of lambs born prematurely, equivalent to a 24-week human foetus, for a 28-day period. Their design, the 'biobag,' mimics uterine conditions by sealing the subject in a single-use plastic sac containing artificial amniotic fluid, with catheters to imitate umbilical cord access. The most crucial feature of the design is that the device seeks to facilitate placental gas exchange, so that the subject does not need to draw breath to obtain oxygen. All the lamb subjects in the initial trial of the biobag emerged healthy, and it appeared they had continued to develop as all exhibited organ maturation and growth. Further research trials, using similar designs, have substantiated these results (Hornick et al. 2019; Usuda et al. 2019), with the biobag team concluding that their design could soon be ready for human testing. Dr Flake, leading the biobag study, confidently speculated in an interview that only 'a decade from now' artificial wombs will have replaced conventional neonatal intensive care (Children's Hospital of Philadelphia 2017).

Despite these conclusions, there are limitations to the current prototypes and there are significant hurdles yet to be overcome before they are ready for human testing. The devices have thus far only been tested for short durations and with small sample sizes. They have also only been tested on lamb foetuses, which have a significantly different physiology to the human foetus (Hornick et al. 2019). There were also instances of concerning complications in the EVE platform study, including brain damage. There are, crucially, also legal and ethical issues to be resolved before such testing is approved and artificial womb devices utilized outside of the context of a clinical trial (Romanis 2019b). Furthermore, these devices are being designed expressly as alternatives to neonatal intensive care. While it is hoped that they will be able to continue gestation of only partially developed human foetuses *ex utero*, there is no suggestion that they could or will be used to facilitate the complete development of a human *ex utero* (from conception to full-term). In fact, the biobag research team were explicit that this was not their intention or objective in developing the device. Thus, these prototype artificial wombs are potentially the beginning of partial ectogenesis, but they are unlikely to be used for complete ectogenesis in the foreseeable future. Developments in this field, seeking to create novel interventions for preterm neonates, are certainly fast-paced. However, it remains to be seen how long it will take for these designs to be translated into devices that might be ready for testing on humans, and eventually clinically useful. In spite of significant barriers to full ectogenesis becoming a reality in the near future, assumptions are made in much of the ethico-legal literature that the technology is imminent and inevitable. This constitutes the first recurring claim in the literature that we will analyse in this chapter.

## 3 The Assumption That Ectogenesis Is Inevitable

Fascination with artificial wombs has long been apparent in the ethico-legal literature, with significant doctrinal scholarship focusing on questions related to the impact of the technology on reproductive life. There has been significant scholarship probing matters ranging from changing requirements in pregnancy termination (Goldstein 1978; Dalzell 2019), changing gender roles in child rearing (Smajdor 2007), increasing equality in the workplace (Kendal 2015), and allowing for equity in the decision to reproduce itself (Räsänen 2017). Common to much of this work is the claim that artificial wombs are on the horizon or that they are already here and constantly improving. Claims that the artificial womb is inevitable have recurred since the first wave of debates about the technology in the 1920s (see Goldstein 1978; Singer and Wells 1984). One hundred years on, we have yet to develop an artificial womb capable of supporting the full gestation of a human entity.

In 1984, Singer and Wells suggested that artificial womb technology already existed in the form of incubators in neonatal intensive care (11). The conceptual difference between incubation and gestation explains why current neonatal intensive care technologies cannot be accurately described as early artificial wombs (Romanis 2018). The technology that the bioethical literature is interested in is that which can 'take over' the creation of a human being, as opposed to 'saving' one born premature. Despite scientists emphasizing that artificial womb prototypes are designed as an improvement on neonatal intensive care, these devices *are* conceptually distinct because they facilitate an environment in which birth is not complete (Romanis 2019a, 727). If the devices function as conceptually designed, the process of gestation is not ended, and thus there are meaningful physiological and behavioural differences between the 'gestateling' in the artificial womb and the neonate in intensive care. Primarily, these differences are that the gestateling does not exercise any capacity for independent life and does not interact with the external environment or persons in the external environment. Thus, even though the gestateling has been delivered from a pregnant person, it is not born because it has not undergone all the necessary biological state changes to demonstrate a complete birth (Romanis 2019a, 727–728). It is clear, therefore, that there are substantive differences between these technologies, and neonatal intensive care cannot thus be utilized as evidence that artificial wombs already exist.

Speculation that artificial wombs are imminent and/or inevitable, however, continues. Simonstein (2006) claims that "in some medical circles the development of a fully functioning artificial womb is considered to be just a matter of time" (361). Welin (2004) refers to the "therapeutic imperative" and suggests that the development of the artificial womb is inevitable because "whatever techniques that can be used to save life will be developed" (623). Alghrani (2008) posits that, "as scientists continually strive to perfect… technology and developments in neonatal care continues to reduce viability, the reality of ectogenesis may not be as far off as imagined" (303). Kendal (2017) refers to "several noteworthy technological advances" on the path to full ectogenesis and that "the science behind ectogenesis may soon cease to be a major limiting factor in its development" (186). These examples demonstrate just how pervasive claims about a future with ectogenesis are. Speculations about future technological possibilities are transformed into a set of probable facts that any reader is encouraged to understand as immediate.

Some scholars are silent as to the scientific realities that undergird the technology about which they speculate. This can be misleading, as without nuance, this approach equally has the potential to collapse future possibilities into the present, because it presupposes that the practical issues related to ectogenesis raised in the present tense are, thus, a 'present' issue. As just one example, Räsänen (2017), in arguing that ectogenesis will create an imperative against abortion resulting in foetal death, makes no statement about the prospects for ectogenesis, nor of his paper being based on a speculative reproductive technological aspiration. When taken as a whole, the literature, in not qualifying the practical realities of full artificial wombs with reference to contemporary science, implies that the development of ectogenesis is upon us.

To be clear, we agree that there is important value in speculation: but we contend that that speculation must be grounded in crucial scientific and social realities. We agree with Alghrani (2018) that it would be "imprudent to dismiss ectogenesis as being confined to the realms of science fiction because both directly and indirectly scientific endeavours continue to slowly make progress into what is needed for this advance" (142). Scientists are continuing to design and improve prototypes, and we have reason to believe they will continue to work towards this end, and will attempt to trial their technology on premature neonates. Because of the fast-paced and unpredictable nature of research, and the prospect that both teams will be seeking to create some clinical impact directly from their results, it is important that we anticipate some of the implications of the development of the technology. Speculative literature plays an important role in anticipating some of what will happen following medical developments, and how we should regulate such possibilities.

The law often lags behind scientific progress, and this can render some stakeholders susceptible to harm. As Tranter argues, speculative thinking about the future impact of new technologies on law requires "lawyer scholars [...] to sketch the technological future" (2011, 821) in order to anticipate possible outcomes. Lawmakers—both legislatures and courts—are often at a disadvantage when striving to understand and respond to legal, ethical, and social implications of new technologies. It is also often the case that such situations highlight gaps in the law that were not noticeable before the technological possibility made it so. Consider, for instance, the infamous *In re Baby M*, the first surrogacy dispute to be heard in an American court. In this case, William and Elizabeth Stern were intending parents who commissioned Mary Beth Whitehead for a surrogacy agreement.[1] Whitehead was inseminated with William's sperm, and was both the gestational and genetic mother of the resulting child, but not the social mother. Because no laws were yet in place to regulate how custody should be established in surrogacy cases, when Whitehead claimed custody of the child, a legal battle raged over whether surrogacy contracts should be upheld and who could be considered the rightful parents of the child. Similar instances of rapidly advancing research on reproductive technologies resulting in novel scenarios for which the law is underprepared have occurred in cases related to posthumous conception, in which family members or partners have fought to use the frozen gametes of a loved

[1] Re Baby M, 537 A.2d 1227 (N.j. 1998).

one after their death, as in the case of Diane Blood,[2] who ultimately won her battle to use the sperm of her deceased husband. Speculating on the legal impact of artificial wombs can act as a means of "highlighting possible futures [...] to consider different strategies for dealing with new events and scenarios" (Travis 2011, 248), an attempt to anticipate some of the fraught questions that could arise.

Novel questions are particularly difficult to address in the context of reproduction because, as Lemmens and Martin (2017) explain, "while all technology creates new possibilities, assisted reproductive technologies enable the creation of human life. In so doing, these technologies often harness the biology of existing humans.... [and] also raise[.] questions about the commodification and commercialisation of human life, in a way few medical advancements have done before" (7–8). Thus, there are many complicating societal factors, political, social, and legal rights, and conflicting legal principles to consider when making rules. It also raises more fundamental questions about the role of the law in this context: "are regulation and criminal law appropriate tools for imposing restraints on a technology that may offer boundless new applications?" (Lemmens and Martin 2017, 8). Without speculative literature, such questions are often missed, because lawmakers are tasked with issuing a response and do not often stop to question whether any interference in private life by the law is necessary. Speculative questioning, then, has the potential to consider how 'future-proof' the law is and highlight problems in need of re-examination.

Schick (2016) argues, however, that such practical examination of future technologies is damaging because considering future technology as "generating practical ethical issues that must be addressed well in advance of their arrival, [however]... bypasses the present as a site of moral agency and locates ethics within a simulation of the imagined future" (226). For the reasons outlined above, we do not agree that it is inherently damaging to speculate about the impact of future technology, but we agree that in order to ensure that exploring future possibilities does not do injustice to present-day ethical discourse, a kind of grounded speculation is needed. There are some aspects of the speculation in the ectogenesis literature, as it has been written as a body, that are thus far problematic because they have not been mindful of these realities.

We have already discussed the first of our concerns: a disproportionate focus on full ectogenesis as opposed to partial ectogenesis, and a consequent lack of attention to the many barriers: scientific, social, political, on the way

[2] R v Human Fertilisation and Embryology Authority, ex parte Blood [1997] 2 All ER 687.

there. The majority of literature about the ethico-legal implications of artificial wombs is based on accounts of ectogenesis coming to fruition as a meeting of advances in embryology and neonatology, such that we will eventually be able to gestate from conception to term entirely *in vitro* (Alghrani 2018). However, an exact prediction of how such technology will be developed is almost impossible. Partial ectogenesis offers us a more concrete vision about the potential development of the technology. There are important reasons to believe that full ectogenesis is some way from being developed due to legal restrictions on embryo research in many of the jurisdictions where this work is being done, and the present limits of knowledge in embryo science. Thus, ignoring the current experimentation that is actually being undertaken, and how it is anticipated it might be translated into a clinical solution, neglects an important source of information that can help ground speculative argumentation.

Moreover, assumptions about the inevitability of the technology are often written in such a way as to make a normative judgement about the desirability of artificial wombs. In exploring what we should do, or how we should regulate the use of technology once artificial wombs are available, the literature often fails to provide a justification for the development of the technology in the first place. Schick (2016) explains that focusing on the question of implications neglects asking, "what technologies we want to develop and why" (229). In the ectogenesis literature, there are often accounts as to the normative desirability of the technology in terms of their implications, for example liberating women from the physical turmoil innate to a pregnancy (Kendal 2015), but such accounts often bypass questions about the development of such technology. How might ectogenesis be developed, and what are the potential harms in that process? The biological realities of such a process are that the only way in which such technology can be developed is by experimenting on the bodies of pregnant persons, and on preterm neonates. Acknowledgement of such issues is noticeably absent from the literature, as few authors cite or make reference to these issues. Without these concerns acknowledged the reader is often left with the impression that if there are advantages to artificial wombs, then we must actively seek to develop the technology. This leaves the gestating body vulnerable to the assumption that experimentation is an acceptable means to benefit future individuals.

As we will argue in what follows, a focus on full artificial wombs has also prompted significant speculation about a different kind of future in which ectogenesis has 'solved' contemporary social issues of the present. Travis argues of the speculative feedback loop between science fiction that imagines the impact of new technologies on law, and law's respective construction of how those technologies may be used, that "our imaginations and the language we use are bound to, and are products of, current cultural and social paradigms" (2011, 251). Our concern with the trajectory of speculation in the literature on artificial wombs reflects a curious paradox: in order to escape 'current cultural and social paradigms,' the literature tends to leap to a future in which these paradigms have been erased. In so doing, it fails to address the contemporary limitations that make this future ungraspable. As we will argue, by neglecting existing social conditions, or selectively considering particular social concerns over others, much of this literature negates the structural, social, and legal barriers that currently limit the possible meaning and uses of the artificial womb. To illustrate our point here, we will turn to the way in which claims that full ectogenesis is inevitable have been mobilized to present the argument that this technology will bring gender equity in childbearing and rearing.

## 4 The Assumption That Ectogenesis Will Result in Gender Equity in Child Bearing and Rearing

After taking the position, either explicitly or implicitly, that full ectogenesis is inevitable, a number of scholars have speculated that by removing gestation from the body, artificial wombs will facilitate a 're-definition' of parenting roles. In this line of argument, scholars hold that "the continuing lack of equality between the sexes boils down to the fact that women (and only women) are expected to bear and rear children" (Takala 2009, 187). Because a pregnancy need no longer be tied to a gendered body, bioethical and legal scholars speculate that a male progenitor could take responsibility for a gestating foetus, and thus take on primary care duties well prior to their child's birth (Pence 2006; Brassington 2009; Welin 2004; Randall and Randall 2008). As a result, this argument concludes, the technology may allow the work of gestation to be shared, and ultimately produce greater equality between men and women.

In the literature, the possibility that ectogenesis will effectively 'de-gender' gestation produces speculative claims as to how decisional responsibility for a gestating foetus will be reorganized in law as a result. Brassington (2009) writes that in the context of existing law, attempts by fathers to intervene in an abortion decision are rightly considered unjust infringements on women's autonomy, but that with the introduction of ectogenesis, these attempts would "simply reflect the view that an abortion without authorisation would be impermissible, for the same reason that it would be impermissible for one of the partners in a business to close it without the authorisation of the other" (199). Schultz (2010) likewise claims that artificial wombs would mean "neither the genetic mother nor the genetic father has a greater legal right incidental to their bodily integrity" (883). These normative claims are all intended to influence the way the law is formulated. They suggest that the very basis of legal regulation on abortion being a pregnant person's bodily integrity, at least in England and Wales and the United States (US), is out-dated in light of artificial wombs.

While ultimately arriving at the same end: that the removal of gestation from the body will mean that responsibility for gestating may be equitably shared, there are nuances in the political meaning which scholars speculatively draw from this outcome. On one side is a feminist imaginary that takes seriously the physical, emotional, and social tolls pregnancy can have. Firestone (1970), Smajdor (2007), and Kendal (2015), among others, speculate that ectogenesis may be a worthy social goal primarily because it could fulfil "the desire of women to be able to reproduce as men do, without risking their physical and mental health, economic and social well-being, and crucially—their bodily integrity" (Smajdor 2007, 340).

By contrast, some scholars are primarily interested in how the removal of gestation from the body might facilitate an increase in rights for male progenitors. At present in England and Wales,[3] the US,[4] and Canada[5] legal precedents are clear that putative 'fathers' obtain no rights to make decisions for a foetus during gestation sustained by a pregnant person. A great importance is placed on the biological facts about gestation—that it takes place dependent on a pregnant person. Thus, scholars seeking to make arguments about *ex utero* gestation increasing rights for putative non-gestating parents, focus is placed on the possibility that fathers would have a new kind of access to the gestating foetus (that is not through a pregnant person). Brassington's claim that "the father would have to have a say in the future of the foetus if either parent did, because both would be 'fathers.' There would be no 'mother'" (2009, 204), as well as Welin's speculation that the shift "will mean reproductive empowerment of men and end the historically short monopoly of women in regard to deciding the fate of the embryo and fetus" (2004, 624), are particularly striking examples of this form of speculation.

[3] C v S [1987] QB 135.

[4] Planned Parenthood of Southeastern Pennsylvania v. Casey. 505 U.S. 833 (1992).

[5] Tremblay v Daigle (1989) 2 S.C.R. 530.

The political valence of these two claims—one which is focused on the potential of a technology in development to have emancipatory ends for women, the other which is focused on the potential of this same technology to grant men new forms of control over gestating foetuses—differs in important ways. While the first is an attempt to imagine something beyond the ways that gendered social roles have been prescribed based on the presumed limitations of reproductive bodies, the second imagines a future technology as a means of realizing a goal with old roots (the intervention of men in reproductive decisions). Yet with few exceptions (Woolfrey 2006; Firestone 1970), scholarship across these categories comes to the same end in not establishing how contemporary realities produce, limit, and shape the possibility that ectogenesis could 'de-gender' gestation, regardless of the political consequences of this effect. There are three concerns in particular that we have with the way that these speculative theories have departed from contemporary realities. First, we argue that they locate the problem of inequitable distribution of care labour in the gestating body. Second, we argue that they present a limited view of contemporary issues in gender equality by narrowly focusing on equity in heterosexual relationships. Finally, we argue that they presume the stability of reproductive autonomy amongst and for women and do not sufficiently account for contemporary issues in stratified reproduction.

## 4.1 The Realities of Inequity in Care Labour Are Not Reducible to the Gestating Body

While often presented with a view towards a radical reimagining of gender roles, speculative claims that the introduction of ectogenesis will produce parental equality problematize human gestation and the work of the gestating body, and in so doing, turn from more pressing contemporary questions of the devaluing of care labour and structural and social barriers to resources for sharing the work of child rearing. Speculative arguments that ectogenesis will produce greater equality are focused solely on the way the technology could impact responsibility taken for the foetus during gestation, yet use this speculation to draw conclusions about the impact on parental equality more broadly. Pence (2006) writes that "with extracorporeal gestation, a man could much more easily be the primary nurturer" (78), proposing that the removal of gestation from the gendered body would allow men to take primary care role throughout the entire period of child rearing. Takala (2009) similarly argues that "the possibility of ectogenesis would not only free women from pregnancy, but [...] as it would take away the biggest difference between the sexes, it would also take away the grounds for oppression and eventually, lead to true equality" (191). Claims such as these present the gestating body as a barrier to gender equality, suggesting that the social burden often placed on women as caretakers and gendered oppression in general can essentially be boiled down to the association of pregnancy with women's bodies. Not only are these claims reductive in frequently neglecting to acknowledge that under contemporary circumstances, there are indeed men who can and do get pregnant, and women who cannot gestate, the on-going 'problem' of gender imbalanced parenting is located in the gestating body (Limon 2016), rather than the social devaluing of care labour and structural and social barriers to resources for sharing the work of child rearing. Rather than addressing contemporary limitations, such as the absence of support for the work done by caregivers more broadly, or exploring why gestation, as something that historically has been done by women, may be socially devalued, these claims vest in a future in which ectogenesis has solved the problem of gendered inequality by 'solving' the problem of human pregnancy. The danger of this form of speculation in the legal literature is that rather than attending to contemporary limitations enforced or enabled by law, such as the lack of sufficient provision for statutory and de-gendered parental leave or the failure of the state to positively provide support for caretakers (West 2009), this thought experiment imagines these problems away in favour of presuming that they begin and end with the fact that (some) women can become pregnant.

Even where some scholars do acknowledge that the problem may have more to do with a lack of social and legal infrastructure to support equality in child rearing, they frequently arrive back at the claim that the barrier is too substantial, and "only by thus remedying the natural or physical injustices involved in the unequal gender roles of reproduction can we alleviate the social injustices that arise from them" (Smajdor 2007, 337).

Yet, such claims presume that ectogenesis would be produced and available in a way that it was sufficiently taken up electively by heterosexual couples as an alternative to human pregnancy, and that these couples would react to it in a way that would result in a substantive change to inequity in care labour. As Jackson rightfully notes, pregnancy is just one nine-month passage in raising a child, and "without equality in the distribution of household labour after birth, most notably in relation to childcare, it is of course true that eliminating pregnancy would not necessarily eliminate gender inequality" (359). There is some merit in claims that gestation has been situated in law as a means of constructing mothers as primary caregivers, for example the status of legal mother being afforded to the woman that gestated[6] and explicit references in the law to the relationship that is developed in gestation. In a recent case, *R on the Application of TT* (2019),[7] the court for the first time ruled decisively that a child's legal mother was the person that gestated. TT, a trans man who gave birth to his child, sought legal recognition of his status as the child's father. While acknowledging TT's legal gender, the court held that because he had gestated and given birth to the child, he was a mother in the eyes of the law. As a consequence, TT could be legally recognized as a male mother, but not as a father. In *Re G* (2006),[8] Baroness Hale claimed that the gestational mother being recognized as the legal mother recognizes a 'deeper truth' because the process of carrying a child and giving him birth results, in the majority of cases, in a 'very special relationship between child and mother that is like no other' (per Baroness Hale at para 34). In England and Wales, the continued treatment of the person who gives birth as the presumptive legal mother means that gestation has been given a privileged place in securing a parental, and now, explicitly maternal, role. There are also the practical realities of couples choosing the person that gestated to take the majority of parenting leave because they already have to take time from work to complete childbirth and may choose to breast-feed. But crucially, the issue here does not lie in the gestating body (a point made stark by the Court's willingness to acknowledge TT's male gender but refusal to attribute the act of gestation to a father). Instead, these are legal and social constructs, ones that seem very unlikely to be undone were ectogenesis to be dropped in their midst. It is hard to believe that just the potential removal of gestation from the body would automatically and necessarily challenge these assumptions that have become so socially engrained, and engrained into social memory, and are not reducible to physical gestation.

Perhaps the most pressing example of why, even if ectogenesis were to have the effect of changing the balance of responsibility for gestation, the legal limitations on equality in shared care labour must still be addressed is that even with the availability of ectogenesis people may still become and opt to sustain a human pregnancy. Consider that many go to great lengths to gestate: people seek out IVF treatments for this purpose, and contemporary efforts to develop uterus transplants too are directed towards allowing people who might otherwise be unable to experience pregnancy.

[6] Human Fertilisation and Embryology Act 2008, s.33 (United Kingdom).

[7] R on the Application of TT v. the Register General for England and Others [2019] EWHC 2384 (Fam).

[8] Re G [2006] UKHL 43.

There is also no guarantee that 'gestational work' becoming semi-automated would not still require a caring role played by an intended parent, and given current social circumstances, it should not be assumed that there would not be more pressures on women to take a more proactive role as 'mothers.' While we recognize that there may be ways of demonstrating changing social narratives about changing gendered roles in reproduction, we argue that authors who seek to make such claims need to provide a stronger account of how a meaningful change in societal norms might happen. If these changes in the distribution of care labour are to come to pass, we will need to commit to producing changes in social attitudes towards caregiving and laws governing parenthood ahead of the arrival of full ectogenesis, as opposed to projecting that these problems will be solved at a hitherto unknown date when the technology is perfected. On this point, focusing solely on issues of parenting in heterosexual relationships, these claims present a limited view of what constitutes equity or 'degendering' in parental rights more broadly.

## 4.2 'Degendering Gestation' Is Limited to Heterosexual Paradigms

In presenting the argument that ectogenesis will shift gendered responsibility for gestation, several scholars suggest that this shift will unsettle "conventional notions of family life" (Pence 2006). Yet, in an age of continually shifting and emerging family forms, in which the parenting rights of lesbian, gay, queer, and trans parents remain precarious, reflections on parenting that account only for heterosexual couples for whom the technology would allegedly be 'equalizing' are limiting. As we have already established, the possibility of artificial wombs being available for elective use early in pregnancy is, and will remain for the time being, speculative. Given that this is the case, if we are to engage a future technology to imagine what new ways it might allow us to build families, what impact it might have on gender, and where and for whom it could have emancipatory effects, continuing to presume that the greatest inequality in parenting is that which exists between heterosexual men and heterosexual women neglects to imagine the impact ectogenesis could have for those whom it might most benefit. We might consider, for instance, the continued legal limitations in many nations when it comes to the legal gender of parents. LGBTQ+ parents have struggled to benefit from IVF and surrogacy because of legal and social restrictions in multiple jurisdictions of many aspects of the process, for example, gamete donation,[9] recognition of parenthood,[10] restrictions on surrogacy contracts,[11] and welfare clauses in legislation related to conception.[12]

The idea that "the fact that women have to gestate and give birth in order to have children, whereas men do not, is a prima facie injustice that should be addressed by the development of ectogenesis" (Smajdor 2007, 338) emerges from a binary understanding of both biological sex and gender. The assumption that undergirds the claim that ectogenesis will produce "true equality" (Takala 2009, 191) is that there are two categories of person, 'men,' and 'women.' Women, and not men, are presumed to have the biological capacity to become pregnant, and thus it is only in creating an artificial womb that men will be able to share in pregnancy. This technology is then positioned as the tool that will disrupt what has henceforth been a rigid division between two roles in a family: a woman who is the genetic, gestational, and social mother of a child, and a man who is the genetic and social father of a child.

But it is already the case that many families exist wherein these relations are reordered or disrupted. And it is already the case that trans men, transmasculine, and non-binary people become pregnant and give birth. As Kararian argues, contemporary medical and legal institutions in many parts of the world have increasingly produced barriers to recognizing the healthcare needs and identities of non-binary and trans pregnant people, and in so doing, have demonstrated a resistance to the contemporary disruption of gendered relations to gestation. As Kararian writes, "pregnant men engender a critical re(conceive)ing of the idea that sex is biologically determined, that pregnancy is necessary sexed as female, and that one's sex, gender identity and identification as mother/father neatly align" (2013, 213). We agree that 'degendering'

---

[9] In Germany, whilst sperm donation is lawful and allows same-sex female couples to reproduce, the Embryo Protection Act 1990 (Germany) renders egg donation illegal. In other jurisdictions, egg donation is unlawful for the specific purpose of allowing same-sex couples to reproduce using fertility services. For example, in Italy, law 40/2004 Art 12 prohibits same-sex couples from accessing IVF treatment.

[10] See the agreed female parenthood conditions for lesbian couples in s.43 (b) (1) and s.44 (1) Human Fertilisation and Embryology Act 2008 (United Kingdom).

[11] At present, the law of England and Wales means that surrogacy arrangements are unenforceable under the Surrogacy Arrangements Act 1985 (United Kingdom), though a parental order can be sought by commissioning parents under the Human Fertilisation and Embryology Act 2008, s.54 (United Kingdom). However, s.54 specifies that either sperm, or eggs, or both come from the commissioning husband or wife, which to some extent assumes a heterosexual commissioning couple.

[12] In England and Wales, s.13 (5) of the Human Fertilisation and Embryology Act 2008 (United Kingdom) requires clinics, in deciding whether to give treatment to any particular treatment, to take account of the welfare of any child who might be born as a result of fertility treatment and the welfare of any other child who might be affected by the birth. S.14 proscribed the need for clinics to consider a child's need for 'supportive parenting' that amended previous provisions that emphasised a child's need for a 'father.'

gestation is a desirable goal (a goal that might ultimately result in the redistribution of care labour), but we argue that speculation about what this might look like and what role ectogenesis might ultimately play should be grounded in thinking that recognizes contemporary barriers to these goals beyond heterosexual paradigms. Speculation that is oriented towards a 'degendering' of gestational responsibility which acknowledges these barriers may be more likely to identify strategies for addressing legal and social challenges pertaining to the self-determination of trans, non-binary, and queer parents and reaching towards a more emancipatory vision for ectogenesis.

On this subject, there are two points to consider with reference to speculation and contemporary realities. Firstly, that speculation on the possible parental and care equity produced by this technology that uses relatively privileged heterosexual couples as its starting point will reveal limited possibilities for how the technology might impact familial paradigms. And secondly, that speculation that presumes that inequity of care labour can only be escaped with technology is grounded in a particular idea of the nuclear family and cannot account for the ways that kinship formations beyond this have survived and thrived. What kind of impact, for example, might become possible for ectogenesis if it emerged from a context in which multiple forms of kinship, and multiple gendered relations to gestation were acknowledged and protected?

Here, it is useful to turn to two scholars whose approach differs from the gender equality paradigm discussed above. Firestone, like other scholars discussed above, proceeds with a biological, binary understanding of sex and gender by presuming that "reproductive biology" (1970, 206) is a 'tyranny' that produces one's gender. But Firestone does not situate ectogenesis as something that could produce a shift in gendered relations to gestation in and of itself. Instead, artificial wombs are a possible means, after a socialist revolution, of reaching towards the "diffusion of childbearing and childrearing role[s] to the society as a whole" (206). Lewis too imagines a future that might include a "queer gestational commune in which 'bio-bags' of some kind enabled gestators to pause, share, transfer, redistribute, and walk away from pregnancies" (2019, np). Lewis begins with an understanding of both sex and gender as fluid, socially constructed categories. The place of artificial wombs in altering gendered relations to gestating then emerges from a position in which the pregnancies of gender queer, non-binary, and trans people are already recognized as realities that disrupt a binary understanding of human reproductive roles, and where multitudes of queer forms of kinship already exist outside of a nuclear norm. Consequently, in Lewis's writing, artificial wombs play a speculative role, but the dismantling of institutions that violently enforce gender must precede them. Before ectogenesis could allow us to 'diffuse' gestation, we would need to live in a world in which institutions and individuals had accepted these reconceptions of gender in pregnancy.

On this point, we want to turn to our final concern, which is the way in which speculation about ectogenesis producing equality between men and women presumes that women's reproductive autonomy is currently stable, an assumption that overlooks the fact that access to reproductive health care and reproductive rights remains widely disparate globally and across classed, raced, geographical, gender, and sexuality-based lines.

## 4.3 Women's Ability to Exercise Reproductive Autonomy Is Assumed Stable

In much of the literature that posits that ectogenesis is inevitable and that the technology may result in a newfound equality in gestational responsibility between men and women, scholars make the assumption that for women, contemporary reproductive autonomy can be taken as given. Kendal, for instance, argues that in spite of possible concerns about how ectogenesis could impact abortion access, or the dangers of the technology being used coercively, contemporary "respect for autonomy" (2015, 73) and the presumption of women's control over their reproductive bodies will guard against such challenges. Welin, in giving reference to the "historical monopoly" of women in reproductive decision-making, similarly presumes that women have consistent access to reproductive autonomy, and Bennett (2008) similarly refers to a "female prerogative model" (9) of reproductive choice.

In the literature that frames ectogenesis as removing gestation from the body and therefore equalizing care labour between men and women, artificial wombs tend to be represented as a turning point at which women will maintain their right to choice while men will correspondingly gain access to reproductive decision-making that has previously been denied to them. The alleged stability of women's reproductive rights and access to care is presented as an obstacle to male progenitors' rights to the foetus in debates about ectogenesis (Welin 2004, Brassington 2009). Yet, we argue that these claims fail to acknowledge that women's access to reproductive autonomy (including access to abortion, birth control, and antenatal care), and the ways in which new reproductive technologies have been experienced, remains widely disparate globally, and across classed, raced, gender identity, and sexuality-based lines. The assumption of the stability of women's reproductive autonomy comes from a particular situated position: that in which access to reproductive care is taken for granted, and reproductive technologies enabling more 'choice' are coded as inherently positive. Adams, writing about utopian speculation on artificial wombs in the 1990s, presents a critique of this positionality that is very much in line with the concerns we are raising here. Citing Spallone's argument that for black women, poor women, and disabled women in America, "'choice' was not the issue, which was rather how to resist sterilization abuse, eugenic abortion, and the lack of options in contraceptive practice'" (1993, 270). Adams suggests that literature imagining artificial wombs as utopian tends to draw from experiences of reproductive technologies specific to wealthier white women. Consider, for instance, that the popular introduction of birth control pills was preceded by non-consensual, unsafe trials on Puerto Rican women. The technology hailed for ushering in a new age of sexual liberation and ascertaining freedom for all women in fact was experienced in this way only by some (read: white and relatively wealthy) women, while for black women and women in the global South, birth control became a new form of targeted state sterilization (Ross 2017). This legacy of forced sterilization and inequitable access to reproductive care continues in the US, enabled by measures such as the continued existence of the Hyde Amendment, which bans federal funds from being used for abortions. Effectively, this statute prevents women dependent on Medicaid (disproportionately black women) as well as Indigenous women funded by the Indian Health Service from accessing abortions. The introduction of the full artificial womb, then, while perhaps having no effect for some women, needs to be considered for how it could impact women whose access to reproductive autonomy is not sufficiently protected even in the absence of ectogenesis. Inequality in both national access to abortion and to the right to refuse birth control and sterilization measures is by no means limited to the US, but we cite these striking examples here to emphasize that the presumption of the stability of women's experiences of reproductive autonomy emerges from a particular subject position.

As Romanis has argued elsewhere (2018), the biobag has the capacity to drastically improve patterns of mortality and morbidity among preterm infants. It also may have uses, as Kendal (2015) and Smajdor (2007) suggest, in situations in which continuing a wanted pregnancy poses a danger to the pregnant person's health and well-being. We argue that before imagining the end of human gestation, it is beneficial to unpack the possible uses of partially ectogenic technologies like the biobag against the extraordinary contemporary disparities in access to both advanced neonatal intensive care and to reproductive health care. In addition, we argue that consideration of how the *partial* use of artificial wombs will be legally regulated is a key point that must be taken up before we can begin truly speculating on the impact of full ectogenesis for the distribution of care labour. Focusing on these issues in the present may contribute to considerations in the development of such technologies, such as the cost of the materials to produce them, how their design might be adaptable to different environments, and who might be trained in their use.

With regard to both the development of this technology and its application, we argue that there needs to be more discussion about ectogenesis and stratified reproduction. Stratified reproduction is a term coined by Colen (1995) to refer to the persistence of inequity of access to reproductive care and technologies across "hierarchies of class, race, ethnicity, gender, place in a global economy, and migration status" (78). This praxis, in going beyond the sweepingly broad and presumptive categories of 'men' and 'women,' can reveal the ways that, in order for ectogenesis to have the beneficial effects that many hope it will, we must first attend to the vast disparities in access to reproductive care.

## 5 The Realities of How Artificial Wombs Could Impact Stratification

Given the potential importance of the biobag as neonatal intensive care or as a form of relief for pregnant persons experiencing dangerous pregnancies, we must consider when, where, and to whom these benefits would be accessible. There are two important issues we will consider: first, issues of access in the development of the technology, and second, access to the 'perfected' technology.

It is likely that given that significant resources are invested into improving outcomes for neonates, the imminent push to trial this technology will be on preterm babies on the threshold of viability. There is also noteworthy public support for medical developments to aid the parent(s) of these preterms. In the UK, considerable public sympathy has been displayed towards high-profile cases in which parents wanted to optimize experimental technology in order to aid their disabled neonates (in particular Charlie Gard and Alfie Evans). Moreover, both working research teams have been explicit that their intention is to improve neonatal intensive care and the prospects for preterms. The EVE team are explicit about their technology being used to emulate a pregnancy, but they discuss the utility of this approach in the context of improving neonatal care as opposed to replacing natural pregnancy altogether

(Usuda et al. 2019). The biobag group also explicitly identify their clinical target population in these terms (preterms between 22 and 24 weeks). There are thus good reasons to believe that if artificial wombs are developed, it is likely to be as a tool to aid the neonatologist. There are, therefore, unique issues in this context in terms of the development of the technology that must be explored.

We are concerned that pregnant persons and their preterms will have to shoulder the risks and burdens in the development of this technology and there are several ways in which certain groups are likely to be more precarious. There is an emerging and significant body of empirical work that demonstrates the relationship of maternal stress and preterm birth (Matoba and Collins 2017). Factors that exacerbate maternal stress include structural racism, and financial strain produced by socio-economic inequality. These factors are interrelated with inequality of care, which particularly impacts black women in both the United States and the United Kingdom who are far more likely to die, or lose their newborn, in childbirth than white women regardless of socio-economic status or educational background (Matoba and Collins 2017; Novoa and Taylor 2018). Therefore, there are reasons to believe that pregnant people already marginalized in the treatment they receive are more likely to be those who give birth prematurely and therefore to be those persons encouraged to submit their preterm neonate to clinical trials of these technologies. There is likely to be trial and error in the development of artificial wombs (because of the limitations noted earlier in this chapter) both for the pregnant person and their neonate. There are compelling reasons to believe that complications in the initial clinical translation of experimental artificial wombs may be unlikely to benefit those preterms who it is initially trialled on. It is often the case that new technologies and therapies in this context are unsuccessful at first, because there is a delicate balance in establishing the correct conditions for their success, and animal studies provide little help due to significant differences in physiology (Romanis 2019b). Consequently, there are pressing considerations here about how to ensure that pregnant people who are already harmed by contemporary inequity and discrimination are not placed at further risk during these trials. If and when artificial wombs are introduced as an alternative form of neonatal care, there are also significant questions to be explored about the nature of informed consent to their use (Romanis 2019b).

Once the trial period has passed and artificial wombs are confirmed as safe for pregnant people and neonates, we also have concerns about access as an alternative to an incubator. Access to equal healthcare is a problem in both public and private health-care systems, especially in the context of reproductive health. There is, for example, a huge disparity in access to family planning (Kaposy 2010) and fertility treatments (Mladovsky and Sorenson 2010) in most high-income economies. Even if only seen as a neonatal intensive care replacement, rather than a reproductive technology, artificial wombs are still likely to have issues of disparate access, as is already the case in both obstetric care and neonatal care provisions (Bauer et al. 2017). Many NHS hospitals do not have neonatal intensive care units, or do not have neonatal intensive care for complex needs. It was an express NHS policy to concentrate complex neonatal intensive care into few centres in order to concentrate expertise and maximize the use of expensive resources (NHS England 2015). This can often result in families travelling for access to treatment, or poor outcomes at or immediately after birth because of a lack of expertise in immediate management. It is likely that artificial wombs, as an expensive resource, would be treated in the same way.

There should be concerns that if the artificial womb is framed as an alternative to neonatal intensive care (if the conceptual differences between the two technologies, highlighted earlier in this chapter, are ignored) that there is the potential for it to be considered a 'luxury' healthcare resource accessible only for those in private health systems with insurance or those with premium health insurance, or those able to pay. Health insurance coverage varies widely even in developed nations with inequalities in insurance coverage observably often correlating with other disadvantages. For example, in the US, racial minorities (both individuals of African-American or Hispanic origin) have much lower insurance coverage rates (Ross 2017). Even for those who access the public health insurance for children accessing this 'state of the art' treatment would be limited to those lucky enough to reside in an area with or have access to hospitals accepting this insurance plan and that have artificial womb devices. Furthermore, evidence from the United States suggests that there is disparity in care based on race in neonatal intensive care units (Profit et al. 2017).

Such problems may be likely even in public health systems that are free at the point of access, there is likely to be travel involved for individuals to have access to hospitals with neonatal intensive care units with these enhanced technological capacities. Additionally, in both private and public health systems, insurance companies or clinical commissioning groups (CCGs) are frequently able to demand that patients receive cheaper alternatives to 'state-of-the-art' treatments. They have incentives to do this in order to save funds, and to prevent the normalization of expensive treatments in certain contexts. If these sorts of factors become an impediment to accessing artificial womb technologies, it is likely the greatest impact will be felt by those from lower-socio economic backgrounds who are giving birth prematurely more often and are least empowered to demand healthcare resources. If this is the case, it makes our concerns about those from lower socio-economic backgrounds and potentially racial minorities shouldering the burden of developing the technologies all the more concerning. There are, then, two intersecting concerns that need to be addressed. Firstly, ensuring informed consent and safeguarding against potential coercion or pressure directed towards already marginalized groups in the trial stage when the technology is inevitably experimental, and addressing inequity of access if and when the technology improves health outcomes for pregnant people and neonates.

Moreover, we argue that concerns over how artificial wombs might interact with ongoing practices of surveillance and control over pregnant people's bodies should be taken seriously. We have already seen in the United States attempts for legislatures and courts to seize more control over the process of gestation even when it had been located inside a person's body with foetal homicide laws or attempts to take custody of pregnant women using the artificial womb in order to closely regulate their behaviour. There are legitimate concerns about limited access resulting in increased discrimination, for example at work, for women who choose to opt for (or cannot afford the alternative to) natural pregnancy. There are also legitimate concerns about women from lower socio-economic backgrounds losing even greater degrees of privacy and bodily control as the process of gestation is seen as more publicly owned (irrespective of location because there is at least the possibility of it being *ex utero*). When it comes to taking steps to ensure that these outcomes do not occur, it is important for legal scholars to identify and inform regulatory measures at each stage of the artificial womb's development as to under what circumstances, and with what forms of consent, the technology may be used. As Tranter argues, giving reference to Octavia Butler's speculative writings, "it is not so much a concern that scientists can 'make test tube babies,' but rather who decides, what process, whose bodies are involved, who gets to use this technology" (2011, 841). In other words, as with so many technologies before and alongside it, it is through asking these questions about artificial wombs, rather than imagining that the technology might negate such questions, that we might reach towards emancipatory possibilities for ectogenesis.

## 6 Conclusion: Whose Future/Whose Ideals Are Represented When We Speculate About Ectogenesis?

Ultimately, we agree that speculative ethics and legal scholarship has an important role. We recognize the radical potential of the ways in which imagining the possibilities raised by ectogenesis might orient us in emancipatory directions. Claims made by Firestone (1970) and Lewis (2018) that artificial wombs might constitute a tool for creating societies committed to shared and collaborative care labour, for instance, are compelling calls to a feminist future. We propose, however, that grounding these thought experiments in contemporary scientific and social realities, in particular the existing extent of reproductive stratification and inequity of access to reproductive care and support for care labour, will ultimately better serve us in realizing these goals.

There are significant social barriers to women in particular accessing the emancipatory benefits of this technology. It is frequently the case, however, that arguments claiming emancipation do not consider the nuances in social conditions that underlie their entire argument. For example, Kendal's arguments are dependent on a society that is accepting of artificial gestation, but we might have good reasons to be sceptical of this. These arguments are also assuming that gestation *ex utero* is widely utilized as an alternative to gestation, and often neglect to consider the impact on the way gestation is conceptualized as a private or public process. We believe that it is odd how frequently claims are made about emancipatory change in the literature without an account of the necessary accompanying societal change in attitudes towards the body, gender, and gestation. This is a concern that is not limited to artificial wombs but is instead a much broader contention pertaining to the relationship between technologies, speculation, and the law. Imagining future technologies can be a means of dreaming of a better world, or of anticipating novel and recurring dangers. In law, it opens us to considering "different strategies for dealing with new events and scenarios" (Travis 2011, 248). But it is through grounding these forms of speculation in contemporary, embodied realities (in this case, in the realities of the gendered, raced, classed bodies that are too often subsumed in the literature on ectogenesis) that we may enable them. The law has been recognized as an amazing vehicle for social change in some contexts, and it is likely that if we are to see a positive future with ectogenesis, the law will have a crucial role to play in formulating the conditions in which that emancipation becomes possible. But so too is it necessary to look at the historical and contemporary ways that law has acted as a tool that sometimes violently limits or endangers some forms of social change. It is through grappling with these tensions that we might find a generative path forward.

Firestone, whose uncompromising text *The Dialectic of Sex* is often cited by scholars arguing for the emancipatory nature of ectogenesis, was in fact very clear that artificial wombs could be used as one *tool* after a full feminist revolution. Firestone was clear that ectogenesis on its own, without requisite social change, would solve nothing, and could only be dangerous for those whom, under the right circumstances, it would most stand to benefit. We reiterate Firestone's call: speculation on ectogenesis can be a useful tool for directing us towards a better future, but we need to first acknowledge and address the limitations of the places from which we speculate.

## References

Adams, A. (1993). Out of the Womb: The Future of the Uterine Metaphor. *Feminist Studies, 19*(2), 269–289.

Alghrani, A. (2008). Regulating the Reproductive Revolution: Ectogenesis – A Regulatory Minefield? In M. Freeman (Ed.), *Law and Bioethics: Volume 11* (pp. 303–329). Oxford: Oxford University Press.

Alghrani, A. (2018). *Regulating Assisted Reproductive Technologies*. Cambridge: Cambridge University Press.

Bauer, J., Groneberg, D., Maier, W., Manek, R., Louwen, F., & Brüggman, D. (2017). Accessibility of General and Specialized Obstetric Care Providers in Germany and England: An Analysis of Location and Neonatal Outcome. *International Journal of Health Geographics, 16*, 44.

Bennett, R. (2008). Is Reproduction Women's Business? *Studies in Ethics, Law, Gender, and Technology, 2*(1).

Brassington, I. (2009). The Glass Womb. In F. Simonstein (Ed.), *Reprogen-Ethics and the Future of Gender* (pp. 197–209). Dordrecht: Springer.

Children's Hospital of Philadelphia. (2017). *Unique Womb-Like Device Could Reduce Mortality and Disability for Extremely Premature Babies*. https://medicalxpress.com/news/2017-04-unique-womb-like-device-mortalitydisability.html?utm_source=TrendMD&utm_medium=cpc&utm_campaign=MedicalXpress_TrendMD_1. Accessed 14 Aug 2019.

Colen, S. (1995). Like a Mother to Them': Stratified Reproduction and the West Indian Childcare Workers and Employers in New York. In F. Ginsburg & R. Rapp (Eds.), *Conceiving the New World Order: The Global Politics of Reproduction* (pp. 78–102). Berkeley: University of California Press.

Dalzell, J. (2019). The Impact of Artificial Womb Technology on Abortion Jurisprudence. *William & Mary Journal of Race, Gender, and Social Justice, 25*(2), 327–350.
Deglincerti, A., Croft, G. F., Pietila, L. N., et al. (2016). Self-Organisation of the In Vitro Attached Human Embryo. *Nature, 533*, 251–254.
Firestone, S. (1970). *The Dialectic of Sex: The Case for Feminist Revolution*. New York: William Morrow and Company.
Franklin, S. (2013). *Biological Relatives: IVF, Stem Cells, and the Future of Kinship*. Durham: Duke University Press.
Goldstein, M. (1978). Choice Rights and Abortion: The Begetting Choice Right and State Obstacles to Choice in Light of Artificial Womb Technology. *Southern California Law Review, 51*(5), 877–921.
Hornick, M., Mejaddam, A., McGovern, P., et al. (2019). Technical Feasibility of Umbilical Cannulation in Midgestation Lambs Supported by the EXTra-Uterine Environment for Neonatal Development (EXTEND). *Artificial Organs*. https://doi.org/10.1111/aor.13524.
Jackson, E. (2008). Degendering Reproduction? *Medical Law Review, 16*(3), 346–368.
Kaposy, C. (2010). Improving Abortion Access in Canada. *Health Care Analysis, 18*(1), 17–34.
Karaian, L. (2013). Pregnant Men: Repronormativity, Critical Trans Theory and the Re(conceive)ing of Sex, Gender and Pregnancy in Anti-Discrimination Law. *Social and Legal Studies, 22*(2), 211–230.
Kendal, E. (2015). *Equal Opportunity and the Case for State-Sponsored Ectogenesis*. Basingstoke: Palgrave Macmillan.
Kendal, E. (2017). The Perfect Womb: Promoting Equality of (Fetal) Opportunity. *Journal of Bioethical Inquiry, 14*(2), 185–195.
Lemmens, T., & Martin, A. (2017). Introduction. In T. Lemmens, A. Martin, C. Milne, & I. Lee (Eds)., *Regulating Creation* (pp. 1–20). Toronto: University of Toronto Press.
Lewis, S. (2018). Cyborg Uterine Geography: Complicating 'Care' and Social Reproduction. *Dialogues in Human Geography, 8*(3), 300–316.
Lewis, S. (2019). Do Electric Sheep Dream of Water Babies? *Logic Magazine*, 8.
Limon, C. (2016). From Surrogacy to Ectogenesis: Reproductive Justice and Equal Opportunity in Neoliberal Times. *Australian Feminist Studies, 31*(88), 203–219.
Mathison, E., & Davis, J. (2017). Is There a Right to the Death of the Foetus? *Bioethics* 31(4), np. https://doi.org/10.1111/bioe.12331.
Matoba, N., & Collins, J. W. (2017). Racial Disparity in Infant Mortality. *Seminars in Perinatology, 4*(6), 354–359.
Mladovsky, P., & Sorenson, C. (2010). Public Financing of IVF: A Review of Policy Rationales. *Health Care Analysis, 18*(2), 113–128.
NHS England. (2015). *NHS Commissioning E08/S/a Neonatal Critical Care (Intensive Care, HDU and Special Care)*. https://www.england.nhs.uk/commissioning/wp-

content/uploads/sites/12/2015/01/e08-serv-spec-neonatal-critical.pdf. Accessed 20 July 2019.

Novoa, C., & Taylor J. (2018). *Exploring African Americans' High Maternal and Infant Death Rates.* Resource document, Center for American Progress. https://www.americanprogress.org/issues/early-childhood/reports/2018/02/01/445576/exploring-african-americans-high-maternal-infant-death-rates/. Accessed 10 July 2019.

Partridge, E. A., Davey, M. G., Hornick, M. A., McGovern, P. E., Mejaddam, A. Y., Vrecenak, J. D., et al. (2017). An Extrauterine System to Physiologically Support the Extreme Premature Lamb. *Nature Communications, 8*, 1–15.

Pence, G. (2006). What's So Good About Natural Motherhood? In S. Gefland & J. Shook (Eds.), *Ectogenesis: Artificial Womb Technology and the Future of Human Reproduction* (pp. 77–87). New York: Rodopi.

Profit, J., Gould, J. B., Bennett, M., Goldstein, B. A., Draper, D., Phibbs, C. S., et al. (2017). Racial/Ethnic Disparity in NICU Quality of Care Delivery. *Pediatrics, 140*(3), e20170918.

Randall, V. R., & Randall, T. C. (2008). Built in Obsolescence: The Coming End to the Abortion Debate. *Journal of Health and Biomedical Law, 4*, 291–310.

Räsänen, J. (2017). Ectogenesis, Abortion and a Right to the Death of the Fetus. *Bioethics, 31*(9), 697–702.

Romanis, E. C. (2018). Artificial Womb Technology and the Frontiers of Human Reproduction: Conceptual Differences and Potential Implications. *Journal of Medical Ethics, 44*(11), 751–755.

Romanis, E. C. (2019a). Artificial Womb Technology and the Significance of Birth: Why Gestatelings Are Not Newborns (or Foetuses). *Journal of Medical Ethics, 45*(11), 727–729.

Romanis, E. C. (2019b). Artificial Womb Technology and Clinical Translation: Innovative Treatment or Medical Research? *Bioethics* (online first). https://doi.org/10.1111/bioe.12701

Romanis, E. C., & Horn, C. (Forthcoming). Artificial Wombs and the Ectogenesis Conversation: A Misplaced Focus? Technology, Abortion and Reproductive Freedom. *International Journal of Feminist Approaches to Bioethics.*

Ross, L. (2017). *Reproductive Justice: An Introduction.* Oakland: University of California Press.

Schick, A. (2016). Whereto Speculative Bioethics? Technological Visions and Future Simulations in a Science Fictional Culture. *Medical Humanities, 42*(4), 225–231.

Schultz, J. H. (2010). Development of Ectogenesis: How Will Artificial Wombs Affect the Legal Status of a Fetus or Embryo. *Chicago-Kent Law Review, 84*(3), 877–906.

Simonstein, F. (2006). Artificial Reproduction Technologies (RTs) - all the Way to the Artificial Womb? *Medicine, Healthcare and Philosophy, 9*(3): 359–363.

Simonstein, F. (2009). Artificial Rerproductive Technologies and the Advent of the Artificial Womb. In F. Simonstein (Ed.), *Reprogen-ethics and the Future of Gender*. (pp. 177–186) London: Springer Dordecht.

Singer, P., & Wells, D. (1984). *The Reproductive Revolution: New Ways of Making Babies*. Oxford: Oxford University Press.

Smajdor, A. (2007). The Moral Imperative for Ectogenesis. *The Cambridge Quarterly of Healthcare Ethics, 16*, 336–345.

Takala, T. (2009). Human Before Sex? Ectogenesis as a Way to Equality. In F. Simonstein (Ed.), *Reprogen-ethics and the Future of Gender* (pp. 197–196). London: Springer Dordecht.

Tranter, K. (2011). The Speculative Jurisdiction: The Science Fictionality of Law and Technology. *Griffith Law Review, 20*(4), 817–850.

Travis, M. (2011). Making Space: Law and Science Fiction. *Law and Literature, 23*(2), 241–261.

Usuda, H., Watanabe, S., Masatoshi, S., et al. (2019). Successful Use of an Artificial Placenta to Support Ovine Fetuses at the Border of Viability. *American Journal of Obstetrics and Gynecology, 221*(1), 69e.1–69e.17.

Welin, S. (2004). Reproductive Ectogenesis: The Third Era of Human Reproduction and Some Moral Consequences. *Science and Engineering Ethics, 10*, 615–626.

West, R. (2009). From Choice to Reproductive Justice: De-constitutionalizing Abortion Rights. *Yale Law Journal, 118*, 1394.

Woolfrey, J. (2006). Ectogenesis: Liberation, Technological Tyranny, or Just More of the Same? In S. Gefland & J. R. Shook (Eds.), *Ectogenesis: Artificial Womb Technology and the Future of Human Reproduction* (pp. 129–138). New York: Rodopi.

# 11

# A Relational Responsibilities Framework for Children's Healthcare Law

Jo Bridgeman

## 1 Relational Responsibilities: A Response to the Current Legal Framework

In the first cases concerned with the medical treatment of children, in the 1980s, medical paternalism and parental authority were challenged by the involvement of the court, which established its protective role through independent determination by a judge of the best interests of the child.[1] Judgments that followed expanded upon the scope of the protective best interests principle such that judgments now explain that it is considered 'in the widest sense and to include every kind of consideration capable of impacting on the decision. These include, non-exhaustively, medical, emotional, sensory (pleasure, pain and suffering) and instinctive (the human instinct to survive) considerations' (*An NHS Trust v A* 2007, [40]). The recent cases concerning

I thank the editors and an anonymous reviewer for their helpful comments on an earlier draft and in particular for encouraging me to develop more fully consideration of social and institutional responsibilities.

[1] *Re D (a minor) (wardship: sterilisation)* (1976) concerned with the legality of sterilisation of a child with learning difficulties; *Re B (a minor) (wardship: medical treatment)* (1981) on the question whether it was in the best interests of a baby with Downs Syndrome to have surgery to remove an intestinal blockage.

J. Bridgeman (✉)
University of Sussex, Brighton, UK
e-mail: j.c.bridgeman@sussex.ac.uk



C. Dietz et al. (eds.), *A Jurisprudence of the Body*, Palgrave Socio-Legal Studies,
https://doi.org/10.1007/978-3-030-42200-4_11

the future medical treatment of Charlie Gard[2] and Alfie Evans[3] involved an unsuccessful challenge to the best interests principle through an assertion of parental rights grounded in their knowledge of their child and affirmation of the principle by the highest courts.

When disagreements about a child's medical treatment are referred to court,[4] cases are decided by the judges of the Family Division of the High Court and, like cases concerning disputes between parents over their child's upbringing and local authority applications for child protection, adjudication involves a particularistic, fact-based assessment of the best interests of the child. However, whilst the judge may feel that he or she has weighed up the available evidence to arrive at the best outcome for the child, parents often continue to object to the outcome and to the process which resulted in it. To give just one example, following a court order that C should be tested to determine her HIV status, her parents, who rejected mainstream medical explanations of HIV and hence its treatment, removed her from the UK and lived with her in Australia (*In re C (A Child) (HIV Testing)* 2000, 275; further examples are given in Bridgeman 2017). The mother, who had herself tested HIV positive but chose to manage her health through a holistic lifestyle, objected to such state intervention into family life, expressing the view that parents should make decisions on behalf of their child until the child is old enough to make her own decisions (Levin 1999). C and her father eventually returned to the UK, following her mother's death, at which time she was made a ward of court which as a consequence had responsibility for future decisions about her medical treatment (Duckworth 2002).

In *Parental Responsibility, Young Children and Healthcare Law* (Bridgeman 2007), I offered a critique of the legal framework for children's medical treatment decision-making and presented the case for a legal framework for determination of the best interests of the child underpinned by a moral framework of relational responsibilities. The critique of the law was that the particularistic analysis of best interests is being applied to a child who is legally

[2] The declarations made by Francis J, in *GOSH v Yates & Gard* (April 2017), that it was in Charlie's best interests and lawful for him not to be provided with a trial of nucleoside therapy and for ventilation to be withdrawn and palliative care provided were upheld through the appeal courts.

[3] The declarations made by Hayden J in *Alder Hey Children's NHS Foundation Trust v Evans* (February 2018) that it was in Alfie's best interests and lawful for ventilation to be withdrawn and palliative care provided were upheld by the appeal courts.

[4] This chapter focuses upon court determination of disagreements between parents and professionals with respect to the medical treatment of children who lack the capacity to make decisions about their own medical treatment, and it does not consider disagreements between parents over medical treatment, cases which have been referred to court because the local authority also has parental responsibility of a child in care or cases concerning older children who may have capacity to decide for themselves.

constructed as a separate, isolated, vulnerable individual whose physical, emotional and personal boundaries are in need of protection from invasion by others including from his or her own parents who are pursuing their own self-interest and asserting their rights. As with vulnerability scholarship (e.g., Fineman 2008; Mackenzie et al. 2014; Herring and Wallbank 2013), a relational responsibilities approach seeks to reveal the effects of liberal legalism's understanding of the legal subject. Rather than employing the concept of vulnerability, the relational responsibilities approach I developed drew upon the feminist ethic of care. To take one foundational example from Carol Gilligan's research on moral reasoning, Carol Gilligan contrasted the approach of 11 year-olds Amy and Jake to the Heinz dilemma—whether Heinz should steal from the chemist the drug needed to save his dying wife which he could not afford to buy (Gilligan 1982, 25–32). Jake approached the problem as a simple prioritisation of conflicting moral values of life and property and with the assumption that there is societal consensus on prioritisation of the former. Amy, 'seeing a world comprised of relationships rather than of people standing alone, a world that coheres through human connection rather than through systems of rules, … finds the puzzle in the dilemma to lie in the failure of the druggist to respond to the wife', so that the solution lay in changing the terms of the dilemma by providing the chemist with more information about the wife's condition or identifying others who could help (Gilligan 1982, 29). As Carol Gilligan explained, Amy's approach was premised upon connections between people which give rise to an awareness of responsibility for the other and the need for a response, with communication enabling a better understanding and leading to resolution. The particular relevance to the law is that if the legal process takes the people involved, their needs and relationships and re-constructs them as abstract ideals, it will not provide an adequate solution to the human issue which concerns them. Whilst of the opinion that best interests is the appropriate principle by which to determine disputes over a child's future medical treatment, given that all involved, parents, clinicians and judges are seeking to secure what is best for the child,[5] I argued that the approach to determination of the best interests of the child failed to recognise or support relational responsibilities in the provision of care to children.

[5] Others have argued for a threshold of significant harm, Diekema (2004), Gillam (2016), Auckland and Goold (2019).

Inspired by the feminist ethic of care,[6] this approach recognises that the child is cared for within relevant relationships of responsibility. As I presented it, there were three elements to the moral orientation of relational responsibilities which I argued should underpin the legal framework for decision-making about a child's medical treatment.[7] The first, in contrast to the understanding of the child as an abstract ideal, was recognition of the child as an individual. The second, rather than seeing the child as endangered by parental pursuit of their own interests, was recognition of the knowledge and experience of parents gained as they cared for their child but who were in turn dependent upon the expertise of professionals. Third, rather than isolating the decision before the court, the treatment decision should be placed within the wider context of the provision of care recognising that there are external constraints upon the ability to care which cannot be ignored when reaching decisions about a child's best interests. Whilst I initially considered responsibilities as an alternative to rights, I have subsequently developed this framework to incorporate recognition of the rights of the child (Bridgeman 2008). Appreciation of the individuality of the child as well as their rights recognises that care and justice are complementary, not alternatives. Originally stressing the need for recognition of the different roles and expertise of parents and clinicians arising from their relationships with the child, I have subsequently also addressed the dependency of parents upon professionals for the care of their child and of the state upon parental care (Bridgeman 2008). In this chapter, I develop this conceptual framework further in light of the body of case law concerned with the medical treatment of a child. Whilst some of the leading cases in the jurisprudence concerning children's medical law had been decided when I wrote in 2007, for example, *Re J* (1991),[8] *R v Cambridge Health Authority ex parte Bowen* (1995),[9] *Re T* (1997),[10] *Re A (Conjoined Twins)* (2000)[11] and *Wyatt* (2003–2006),[12] despite the applicable law being

[6] Key pieces included Gilligan (1982), Tronto (1993), Urban Walker (1998), Smart and Neale (1999), Bartlett (1988) and Lindeman Nelson (1999).

[7] Kirsty Moreton has developed this framework in relation to children in mid-childhood, between the years of 9 and 15, see Moreton (2019). I think it would work equally well with older children, but their ability to state their own experiences, the range of relationships material to them and the contextual factors affecting their care are deserving of separate consideration.

[8] Whether it was lawful to withhold ventilation from J who had severe brain damage due to his premature birth.

[9] Judicial review of the decision of the health authority not to fund an extra-contractual referral for experimental treatment following relapse of cancer.

[10] Whether a liver transplant refused by T's parents was in his best interests.

[11] Whether surgical separation of conjoined twins resulting in the immediate death of one twin was lawful.

[12] There were a number of judgments given by Hedley J, concerning the legality of withholding of mechanical ventilation from Charlotte Wyatt who had mental and physical disabilities resulting from her premature birth, the first of which was *Portsmouth NHS Trust v Wyatt & Wyatt* (2004). The leading Court of Appeal judgement is *Re Wyatt (a child) (medical treatment: continuation of order)* (2005).

clear, the courts have increasingly been asked to resolve disputes between parents and professionals, so in this chapter I am able to develop the elements of the framework in light of the increased body of case law. The framework developed here is informed by the extensive body of academic literature over the past decade on medical law, care, responsibilities and re-writing judgments. In particular, I have sought to draw out the complex web of relationships of care in the provision of medical treatment to a seriously ill child which needs to be recognised in deciding these cases. Furthermore, decisions about a child's future medical treatment have to be embedded within social responsibilities of public services and institutions to support caring responsibilities and hence within the social, historical, cultural and political context for decisions about the provision of medical treatment. I conclude by applying this framework to a hypothetical case which draws upon the facts of a number of decided cases to demonstrate how it would work and, I argue, result in more careful judgments which reflect the lived realities, inherent relationality and embedded lives of those directly affected.

## 2 The Child: An Individual Situated Within Relationships

A relational responsibilities framework for determination of the best interests of a child with respect to a child's medical treatment would recognise that the child is an individual with specific needs, experiences, preferences and interests and entitled to protection of his or her moral and legal rights. Rather than abstract ideas of a seriously ill child, it would ensure that the child as an individual is at the centre of decision-making. The focus would be upon the lived experience of the child, with a chronic or acute illness or life-limiting condition, resulting in embodied rather than disembodied decision-making. In many of the earlier judgments, the child appeared as an abstract object of concern: a body upon which surgery needed to be performed; a potentially diseased body; or in terms of lack of capacities and, consequently, lacking the ordinary qualities of life (e.g., *Re J* 1991, 1992). More recently, judgments have recognised to a greater extent the particular child, perhaps following a visit to hospital by the judge,[13] or evidence from the Guardian or parents. A recent example of a more situated judgment which gives some sense of the child about whose life the judge was making decisions, and which could be

[13] For example, Hayden J visited Alfie Evans and his family in Alder Hey, *Alder Hey Children's NHS Foundation Trust v Evans* (February 2018), [54]–[56].

developed further, is the judgment of MacDonald J in the case of five-year-old Tafida Raqeeb. Tafida had suffered a bleed on her brain which caused catastrophic brain damage rendering her in a minimally conscious state. Her parents refused consent to the withdrawal of ventilation and wanted to transfer her to Italy for continued ventilation. MacDonald J observed that her parents had described, and provided videos which showed that she had been, a 'happy, joyful little girl':

> She was the helping hand monitor in her class, her favourite film was 'Frozen', she attended ballet lessons and she was always running everywhere. She was bilingual in English and Bengali, had learnt some verses from the Quran and was due to attend Arabic classes in September 2019. She had already, at her young age, travelled widely across the world. (*Tafida Raqeeb v Barts NHS Foundation Trust* 2019, [9])

In her evidence as to Tafida's wishes and feelings, her mother said that,

> Tafida demonstrated herself to greatly value all life, reiterating a story of Tafida becoming upset at the death of a ladybird and of a goldfish, and of Tafida's gentle, accepting and non-judgmental approach to another child with serious disabilities. (*Tafida Raqeeb v Barts NHS Foundation Trust* 2019, [41])

Although she was too young to have a developed understanding of the issues before the court, Tafida had begun to follow Islamic practices, such as prayer, and had understood that '"if you kill or do harm you will be in trouble with Allah" and her mother's view was that Tafida would wish to live whatever life is left to her notwithstanding her current condition' (*Tafida Raqeeb v Barts NHS Foundation Trust* 2019, [42]).

MacDonald J had also recognised personhood, the pleasure of human interaction and the development of the self through relationships with others, although in the context of their absence, in his conclusions in the case of Isaiah Haastrup capturing something of the human life that Isaiah's condition had deprived him of. The evidence was that Isaiah's condition meant that he would never be able to engage in meaningful interaction, to see, to move independently, he may have some hearing but there was no evidence that he could make sense of anything he might hear, no evidence that he was aware of what was going on around him, or of an ability to experience enjoyment or comfort or to experience pleasure from interaction with his family or to develop emotional attachment to them, to benefit from the experiences of love, human connection or a sense of identity and belonging (*King's College*

*NHS Trust v Thomas & Haastrup* 2018, [107]). In comparison, the possibility of awareness of connected others, albeit minimal, and the provision of loving care at home as experienced by children in similar conditions, recognising the importance of caring relationships to the development of the self and to the maximisation of capacities, led MacDonald J to the conclusion that it was not in Tafida's best interests for ventilation to be withdrawn (*Tafida Raqeeb v Barts NHS Foundation Trust* 2019, [168] [173]).

It could be argued that Tafida had years to develop her personality, whereas children in other cases, such as Isaiah Haastrup who was born with his life-limiting condition and had never left hospital or Charlie Gard and Alfie Evans, hospitalised at six weeks-old and seven months-old respectively, had not formed their individual personalities. However, the study by Priscilla Alderson et al. clearly demonstrated, what anyone who has spent any time with children knows, that even very young children (in their study premature newborn babies in the neonatal intensive care unit) demonstrate character and express themselves through sounds, facial expressions and movements to which those caring for them can attend, interpret and respond (Alderson et al. 2005). As Joan Tronto has argued, rather than drawing upon adult impressions of life for a child in a given situation, attentiveness to the individual child is required in order to recognise the child's specific needs, experiences, preferences and interests and identify what, at the current time, is best for the child.[14] Even if the child's capacities have now been diminished by their condition, what is required to respect their personal integrity is consideration of the personality, the character, the spirit of the child and attentiveness to their ability to cope with their condition and with the pain caused by it and its treatment.

Within the current legal framework, the independent interests of the child are, in cases concerning future medical treatment, represented by the Guardian. Appointed by the state to represent the 'voice of the child', the Guardian will form an independent view of best interests by visiting the child in hospital, speaking to his or her parents, doctors and nurses, and considering the oral evidence presented at the hearing. Where the Guardian, whose relationship with the child cannot be as intimate as that with his or her parents, reaches the same conclusion as to best interests as the child's clinicians, the parents are then positioned in opposition to their child's interests. For example, the parents of Charlie Gard, diagnosed with an extremely rare, inherited, progressive condition, mitochondrial depletion syndrome, RRM2B,

[14] Joan Tronto (1993) identified the values of the ethic of care as attentiveness, responsibility, competence and responsiveness, 127–36.

which affected his ability to move, breathe, neurological functioning and hearing, wanted him to have a trial of nucleoside therapy which they believed offered him the chance of an improved quality of life. When they appealed the decision of Francis J that it was lawful for ventilation to be withdrawn and palliative care provided, they appeared in court as appellants against Great Ormond Street Hospital and Charlie, represented by his Guardian, as respondents (*In the Matter of Charles Gard* 2017). Baroness Hale, in her speech rejecting the parents' application for permission to appeal to the Supreme Court, stated that in significant disputes over a child's best interests, the child 'must have an independent voice in that dispute', but that this was provided through representation by his Guardian not by his parents (*In the matter of Charlie Gard (Permission to Appeal Hearing)* 2017). Baroness Hale further observed that there were questions, which the Supreme Court did not need to resolve, about the ability of his parents to apply to the European Court of Human Rights (ECtHR), in their attempt to protect his interests, on the grounds that the interests of Charlie and his parents conflicted.[15] Whilst, as both the Supreme Court and European Court of Human Rights stressed, it is important that the child is independently represented, as the Guardian had reached the same conclusion as his doctors as to Charlie's best interests (*GOSH v Yates & Gard* (April 2017), [116]–[122]), it is understandable that Charlie's parents felt that the Guardian was supporting the position of his doctors leaving them to defend their child's right to life. Rather than independently representing the voice of the child ensuring the interests of the child were separately identified, the Guardian appeared as a distanced adult making an independent assessment of the available evidence and deciding which of the two opposed positions to support. Instead, we could expect the Guardian to bring independent evidence to the court of the child as an individual. Appointed by the state, fulfilment by the Guardian of the responsibility to give a voice to the child in this way would serve to address concerns that Marie Fox and Michael Thomson have raised that relational approaches risk doing nothing more than recognising the importance of family relationships and '[i]n so doing, they risk continuing to prioritize family integrity over the child's interests and rights, thus reinforcing the parental power'.[16]

Dominated by the welfare principle, judgments concerning a child's future medical treatment may reference the rights of the child under Articles 2 or 8

[15] These questions were left unresolved as the ECtHR considered it sufficient to address the parents' complaints under Articles 2 and 5.

[16] Fox and Thomson (2017), 531, in which they developed the concept of embodied integrity as a 'useful supplement to the current vogue for relational approaches', 31.

of the European Convention on Human Rights,[17] or Articles 5, 6 or 24 of the United Nations Convention on the Rights of the Child (e.g., *In Re C (A Child) (HIV Testing)* 2000, 282), understood within the current legal framework to confirm rather than 'alter or add to established principles of English domestic law' (*In Re A (Children) (Conjoined Twins: Surgical Separation)* 2001, 257; *An NHS Trust v A* 2007, [44]; *Portsmouth NHS Trust v Wyatt* 2004, [25]). Whilst this is one view of the judgments of the ECtHR in *Glass v United Kingdom* (2004)[18] and, more recently, *Gard* (*Charles Gard and Others v United Kingdom* 2017), these cases themselves merely served to confirm the established domestic legal framework which fails to engage with the rights of the child. The feminist judgment in *Glass* sought to demonstrate the potential for a more rigorous engagement with the rights of the child to recognise the child as an individual situated in caring relationships (Bridgeman 2010). The children's rights judgment in *Re A* examined the rights of the children and those of the parents in depth and viewed the welfare of the twins from the perspective of their connectedness (Alghrani 2017), and Jonathan Herring's commentary upon it reflected further on a relational understanding of rights (Herring 2017). Warning against the dangers of conflating the interests of the child and his or her parents, in his children's rights judgment on *Re T,* Michael Freeman respected the participation rights of young children, with reference to the research of Priscilla Alderson et al. noted above, emphasising the ability of even the youngest child to express their feelings which can be understood by attentive adults in caring relationships (Freeman 2017).

## 3 Caring Relationships

Despite the concern of both parents and clinicians to ensure that the child receives the treatment that is in his or her best interests, it is the differences between the adult decision-makers, rather than their common purpose or common ground, that becomes the focus in court proceedings, formulated as a dispute through which opposing positions have become entrenched. As Carrie Menkel-Meadow has observed, whilst as people they may have empathy for the position of the other, the legal process discourages expression of concern for those positioned on the other side (Menkel-Meadow 1985, 52).

[17] For example, *In the Matter of Ashya King (a Child)* (2014), [30], in which Baker J in wardship proceedings authorised the administration of Proton Beam Therapy in a Prague clinic as post-operative treatment following the removal of a malignant brain tumour.

[18] Provision of diamorphine to 12-year-old David Glass contrary to the refusal of his mother was a breach of Article 8 ECHR.

The legal process creates or cements separation between those previously working in partnership and widens the distance between them when they most need to come together, depending as they do upon the other to secure what each considers to be in the child's best interests. Rather than understanding persons to be primarily separate, self-interested, rational individuals whose principal concern is to protect themselves from invasion by others but who form relations by agreement, feminist theories of care and responsibility understand individuals to be primarily connected through relationships. The self is conceived of as relational with interests which are inevitably tied to those of others. Dependency and vulnerability are universal experiences not the exception to the liberal male ideal. If the law chooses to ignore the relationality of persons, it ignores a crucial aspect of the reality of the persons it is regulating. As Jonathan Herring has argued legal norms are required which understand and respond to people in interdependent relationships, with entwined interests and responsibilities to each other (Herring 2010, 254). A relational responsibilities approach would place the individual child at the centre of care and the provision of his or her medical treatment within the context of caring relationships and recognise both the experience of parents and the expertise of professionals. Its application requires consideration to the attentiveness to the cared-for and, in the context of medical treatment where both parents and professionals have responsibilities to the child, consideration of the care taken of the other in these relationships.

As Joan Tronto has argued, whilst parents have obligations to their children simply by virtue of having them, responsibilities arise out of relationships, shaped by the particular needs of the child, rather than choices or promises (Tronto 1993, 133). Parents generally take responsibility for meeting the needs of their dependent child in order to preserve this valued relationship. The feminist judgment in *Re A* observed that the parental objection to separation surgery of their conjoined twins was reinforced by their growing relationship of love and protection for both girls (Hastings 2010). The responsibilities of parenthood are both general, those which arise from the relationship of parent and child, and specific, shaped by the particular needs of the child. Working out what ought to be done in the provision of care requires attentiveness to the requirements of institutions such as the law and to societal expectations and to the specific context and individual needs. Upon diagnosis of a child's serious illness, parents are immediately required to make important decisions about their child's medical treatment often to subject the child to invasive and painful interventions with unpleasant side effects and risks to future quality of life in the attempt to save life and improve health. Whilst the ordinary rhythms of family life will be disrupted by a child's minor illness, everything changes with the diagnosis of a child's serious illness: family life is disrupted; careers put on hold; responsibilities to other family members—parents, other children, siblings—accommodate to focus upon the needs and interests of the seriously ill child.[19] Not only do parents have specific knowledge of their own child as an individual material to the child's medical treatment (Anderzen-Carlsson et al. 2007, 243), they are usually focused upon their child's needs and consequently develop expertise in the individual child's ability to cope with their condition and the pain and distress which results from it and its treatment, necessary to respect the child's personal integrity. As Carol Glass said of her relationship with her son David,

> I have known David all his life. I know when he is happy, when he is sad or when he is in pain. ... I was angry for David because I knew him best and I needed to stick up for him. I needed to give him a voice. (Day 2004, quoting Carol Glass)

In their judgments, it is usual for judges to note the weight they give to parental views of the child's best interests as the persons who know the child 'immeasurably better than anybody else does, professional or otherwise' (*GOSH v Yates & Gard* (April 2017), [107]). Yet, decisions are explained largely in terms of the benefits and burdens of treatment and its effect upon quality of life, rather than the interests of the child as a person in relationship. The short paragraphs detailing parental views are set alongside the much more lengthy account of the medical evidence of the child's treating clinicians and second opinions. For example, in the case of Charlie Gard, the parental evidence is set out in 6 paragraphs noting the number of hours they had spent with their son, how they thought he reacted to their presence, toys and to medical interventions, that he liked to be stroked on his head and to be tickled but not on his feet and the parental belief that, contrary to the views of his clinicians, he did have a wake/sleep cycle indicating that his brain damage was not as bad as his doctors thought. Their wishes for him to be given the chance to improve his quality of life which they believed nucleoside therapy offered were noted (*GOSH v Yates & Gard* (April 2017), [107]–[112]). Of course, these are decisions about the provision of medical treatment to a child, but whilst the parental experiences of their son's reactions were noted, as evidence relevant to determination of whether continued ventilation for the trial of a therapy

[19] This is quite a big claim and, of course, as is recognised below, the circumstances of individual families and how they respond will be different. However, this view is supported by the accounts of parents of children who underwent heart surgery at Bristol Royal Infirmary considered in Bridgeman (2003); of studies of parents caring for a child with cancer, explored in Bridgeman (2017); and of personal accounts of parents whose child is born with severe disabilities, for example, Raca (2012), Wright (2015) and Melville-Ross (2016).

administered via his feed, they were not tested. Neither were the views of the parents of 18-month-old T who had decided to refuse further surgery given the pain and distress caused to him by surgery he had undergone when a few weeks old (*Re T (a minor) (wardship: medical treatment)* 1997). Neither was the expertise recognised of the mother of 12-year-old David Glass, a child with mental and physical disabilities, who had cared for him at home with the help of family and community professionals with occasional periods of hospitalisation and who, contrary to the views of the clinicians caring for him, was adamant that he was not dying. As Judge Casadevall observed, giving a separate opinion in the ECtHR six years later when David was still alive, the facts showed that 'in the particular circumstances of the present case, maternal instinct has had more weight than medical opinion' (*Glass v United Kingdom* 2004). Whilst parental knowledge and expertise needs to be taken into consideration in determination of a child's best interests so too must the experience of other carers where it is they rather than the child's parents who have gained knowledge and expertise of the individual child through their day-to-day care of the child. For example, where parents have removed themselves from involvement in their child's care (e.g., *Bolton NHS Foundation Trust v C and LB and PT* 2015) or been unable to meet their child's needs (e.g., *Re B* 2008) so that the child has been taken into the care of the state and the day-to-day care of the child is provided by foster carers, it is they who will have gained the knowledge and expertise relevant to determination of the child's best interests.

The parent/child relationship is 'generally but one configuration in a cluster of overlapping relationships of partiality, each of which gives rise to its own set of responsibilities' (Lindeman Nelson 1999). Children with serious illnesses or complex health needs usually receive care from a range of professionals who will as a consequence gain particular knowledge of the child which needs to be given full recognition in the legal process. Nineteen-month-old ID, who had severe, chronic and irreversible lung disease, was cared for at home by his parents with the assistance of community healthcare professionals and occasional hospital treatment. The parental view of his best interests was supported by the evidence of his paediatric therapist, occupational therapist, home visitor, lead nurse in neo-natal home care and speech and language therapist on the developmental progress ID had made and his current state of health. His speech and language therapist gave evidence of

> ID becoming more alert and responsive to the environment around him and that he greeted familiar people with recognition. He follows with his eyes people and toys which interest him. He is beginning to show signs of some vocabulary with a hand and arm movement to indicate "bye bye". He has a delightful smile

> and can indicate pleasure and displeasure. (*A National Health Service Trust v D* 2000, 684)

Yet Cazalet J, who authorised clinicians to withhold mechanical ventilation in the event of a respiratory or cardiac failure or arrest, seemed to give more weight to the medical evidence of Dr P, consultant in paediatric intensive care, based upon a review of the hospital records and clinical notes and a clinical examination of ID conducted four days after he was admitted to hospital with a fever. Dr P noted that the

> *family's* description of ID's development appears at odds with what has been documented by the medical staff, saying that he could find no record of DI having head control, visual fixation and following, sitting, speaking words or reaching for an object. (*A National Health Service Trust v D* 2000, 683)

Judgments sometimes, but not always, consider evidence from the nursing staff, but if they do so, it is only brief. Yet, it is the nurses rather than clinicians who will spend a lot of time with the child providing nursing care and thus have views material to the evidence as to child's interests in the wider sense beyond medical interests. As Jonathan Herring has observed, after quoting from an anonymous healthcare professional who had cared for Charlie Gard, 'the mask of professional detachment … means that arguments based on their emotional attachment and the dedication of their care work get underplayed in the legal system'. As Jonathan Herring argued, 'the depth of their caring relationship with the children gives them a legitimate voice in the legal decision-making process' (Jonathan Herring 2019, 204). Relational perspectives, as Marie Fox and Thérèse Murphy have suggested, challenge 'traditional legal understandings of authority, status and power'. However, they expressed concern that they can also 'valorize' the views of parents when they differ from healthcare professionals (Fox and Murphy 2013, 254). This can be avoided by ensuring that an approach which gives insufficient consideration to parental experience is not replaced by one which uncritically accepts their views. What it requires is a critical assessment of and appropriate weight given to the evidence all in the web of caring relationships who gain experience and knowledge through the provision of care to a seriously ill child.

In her commentary, reflecting upon the ethical judgment of Richard Huxtable in *Re A*, (Huxtable 2017), Jackie Leach Scully argued that his conclusion that the finely balanced welfare arguments meant that the decision should have been left to the parents reached in good conscience, was 'pragmatic and compassionate' but was 'theoretically rather thin'. In her view, an 'ethically satisfying basis may be found in *a relationally grounded ethics of* care' (Leach Scully 2017, 32). In addition to the twins' dependency on each other which would be recognised in any ethical analysis, she argued that an ethic of care approach would ensure fuller consideration of the importance to the parents of providing the best kind of care to that dependency through consideration of existing and future relationships amongst all involved, the children, their parents and the healthcare professionals (Leach Scully 2017, 33). To examine critically the evidence provided by those in the wider web of care is not to suggest that clinical evidence and professional judgement are not important. To the contrary, in the context of a seriously ill child, relationships with healthcare professionals take on particular significance for the child's future, but it must be emphasised that these are *professional relationships of care*. The provision of medical treatment to a seriously ill child is a process of judgement-making in the delivery of individualised medicine involving complex judgements of diagnosis, identification of treatment options and modification of treatment in response to the reaction of the individual child (Downie and Macnaughton 2013). It involves the interaction of a team of experts, exercising professional judgement, responding to uncertainty and changing information with regard to the child. As professionals subjecting a seriously ill child to tests, monitoring, medication and invasive procedures, they have, as Hilde Lindemann and Alisa Carse have argued, to be true to their conscience[20] and to accept responsibility for their moral judgements (Lindemann and Carse 1996, 25). Where professionals and parents disagree about the future medical treatment of a child, professional judgement has to be supported by second opinions and reached in accordance with professional guidance.

As Tove Pettersen has identified, an ethic of care seeks to avoid moral conflicts, prevent harm and promote flourishing by reconciling different interests (Pettersen 2008, 76). This requires attentiveness also to the relationship between those with responsibility to care. To counter the tendency in medical ethics to focus upon the responsibilities of doctors, Heather Draper and Tom Sorrell have examined the responsibilities which adult patients owe to their doctors. The first obligations they identified, owed by adult patients to their doctors but equally applicable to the relationship between parents and their child's clinicians are grounded in the general responsibility to treat others with the respect that is owed to anyone, that is not to be abusive or disrespectful (Draper and Sorrell 2002, 341). But further, the responsibilities which parents have towards their child's doctors, parallel to those owed by the

[20] Lindemann and Carse (1996), 25. For consideration of professional conscience in relation to the provision of medical treatment to children, see Bridgeman (2019).

autonomous individual arising from duties to take care of the self, arise from the legal and moral responsibilities that parents owe to their child. The law imposes the legal duty upon parents, as those with primary responsibility for care of the child, to seek medical advice, but once they have done so they have a duty to listen to that advice even if there may be circumstances, such as when different values are placed upon quality and quantity of life, when they are justified in not following that advice (Draper and Sorrell 2002, 343).

The clinical duty of care to the child and parental responsibilities to their child require both to take care to maintain an effective partnership of care each respectful of the interests, expertise, views and concerns of the other. The question to consider is whether the parties have worked to achieve what Tove Pettersen refered to as mature care (Pettersen 2008, 4), balancing the respective interests of the self and others. In the provision of medical treatment to a child, this requires both parents and professionals to seek to respond to needs, to be concerned to maintain trust and to be concerned for the emotional and physical well-being of all others. Mature care, Tove Pettersen has argued, requires reflection on well-being, on the relationship, and on the social, moral and intellectual issues (Pettersen 2008, 57). It requires those in the relationship to attend to the relationship, not only reflecting upon how to understand and respond to the other but also upon the way in which, and how well, one responds to the other (Pettersen 2008, 73–4). It requires all to be true to their conscience without, as Hilde Lindemann and Alisa Carse have argued, becoming self-interested, by 'being responsible for one's own moral judgements' (Lindemann and Carse 1996). Where interests of self and other diverge and seem incompatible, rather than follow the conflict pathway (Forbat et al. 2015), what is required is careful listening to the different perspective to attempt better to understand and to respond to the other (Pettersen 2008, 94). As Tove Pettersen has suggested, solutions will not be found through entrenched positions, but more contextualised knowledge may present a way forward (Pettersen 2008, 94).

## 4 The Context for Care

A relational autonomy approach challenges the isolated individualism of traditional approaches to autonomy, as Jennifer Nedelsky has argued, understanding our autonomous decisions or actions, our 'own laws' as constituted and nurtured by our relationships with others and by the 'shared social norms, values, and concepts' of the societies in which we live.[21] A relational responsibilities approach, in contrast, recognises that the ability of parents and professionals to care for a seriously ill child is not a matter of individual choice, however constituted, but that in addition to informing choices, the social, cultural and political context affects abilities to ensure the best possible care is provided.

With respect to the medical treatment of children, the obvious contextual factors are advancements in medicine and medical technology which now mean that diseases once invariably fatal, such as leukaemia,[22] are more often survived so that children live with their experiences and effects of illness and its treatment. Advances in medical technology enable lives to be sustained even when there are no further treatment options to try. Children who are, for example, reliant upon ventilation can be assisted to live with life-sustaining technology at home in the care of their parents, as was the hope with both Alfie Evans and Tafida Raqeeb.

Decisions about NHS funding are political decisions. Provisions of facilities, equipment, resources, medicines and services—locally and nationally—affect the ability to care. There are examples in the case law from early in the jurisprudence of parents undertaking research to find innovative treatment, beyond that offered by the child's clinicians through the NHS, for their child with the aim of saving his or her life (*R v Cambridge District Health Authority, ex parte B* 1995) or improving his or her condition (*Donald Simms and Jonathan Simms v An NHS Trust and Secretary of State for Health; PA and JA v An NHS Trust and Secretary of State for Health* 2002).[23] But, parents no longer have to use the library of the Royal Society of Medicine as did the father of Jaymee Bowen in his search for treatment options for his daughter, who relapsed after a period in remission from acute myeloid leukaemia. Information is now easily accessible via the internet, if no easier to assess. Where the treatment is not currently available in the UK, parents are confronted with examples of parents of other children raising money through crowdfunding,[24] or selling their most valuable asset, their home (Strange 2014a, b), to raise money to travel abroad, framing societal norms of parenting expectations in the con-

---

[21] Nedelsky (1989), 10, 11. However, what relational autonomy shares with traditional accounts is the starting point of a separated, isolated individual.

[22] In the 1960s, the most common form of childhood cancer, acute lymphoblastic leukaemia, was invariably fatal, Dixon-Woods et al. (2008), 62. Treatment now offers a five-year survival rate of about 80%, Cancer Research UK (2019) http://www.cancerresearchuk.org/about-cancer/type/rare-cancers/rare-cancers-name/childrens-cancers#cure

[23] In which Butler-Sloss P determined that the administration of experimental treatment was in the best interests of two teenagers both of whom had vCJD.

[24] Dressler and Kelly (2018) noted that health-related issues are GoFundMe's largest category of fundraising for personal use.

text of the care of a seriously ill child. The responsibilities of parents are in part constituted by the minimum expectations set by the law but also by social norms, given individual interpretation. This was part of the context to the court determination of the future medical treatment of Ashya King whose parents removed him from hospital to take him to Spain with the intention of selling their house there to pay for his treatment in Prague (*In the Matter of Ashya King* 2014). Concerned about the effects upon Ashya of the surgery to remove the malignant brain tumour which left him unable to move his limbs, head or eyes and with difficulties swallowing so that he required nasogastric feeding, his parents were concerned about the effects of radiotherapy, the risks of which include intellectual and cognitive impairment, effects upon growth, thyroid (which may cause lethargy or weight gain) and sub-, or in-, fertility, and risks secondary cancers in later life. His parents thought that Proton Beam Therapy, which they had discovered from a search of the internet, presented risks of fewer side-effects. As Baker J observed in his judgment, '[a]ny parents in the position of Mr and Mrs King would do whatever they could to explore all options, some would follow the advice of the responsible clinicians, others the 'relatively untested option of proton therapy… in the hope that the toxic effects of radiation will be reduced' (*In the Matter of Ashya King* 2014, [34]). The concern of parents to do all they can to secure the best possible treatment for their child, 'leaving no stone unturned' (Bridgeman 2017), is framed by searching out alternative treatment options offered outside the NHS, finding facilities for privately funded treatment abroad, raising funds, leaving home and travelling overseas. Ashya King's parents are not alone in risking prosecution and imprisonment in their efforts to secure what they believe to be the best possible treatment for their child. For example, Charlotte Caldwell brought cannabis oil from abroad where its use is legal to administer to her son, Billy, with the aim of stopping his life-threatening and damaging epileptic fits.[25] This is not to suggest that all parents would, or should, take these steps, but that these examples form part of understandings of the expected norms.

But the ability of parents of a seriously ill child to be involved in their child's care will be affected by their financial situation, such as the need to work to provide for themselves and other children. Decisions about care will be affected by their family situation, for example having other children to care for whilst, because families no longer live in close proximity, they may lack support with childcare. Although made within the context of their study of families caring for a child with disabilities, the argument made by Janice

[25] Gilligan (2018). The home secretary subsequently issued a licence permitting its administration.

McLaughlin et al. that where the provision of care is perceived as primarily a private and individualised responsibility which parents, and more specifically mothers, are expected to fulfil questions about rights to care, state responsibility and the requirement for a caring society are avoided (McLaughlin et al. 2008, 182), is of wider significance. Decisions about the provision of treatment have to be approached within the context of societal decisions about the provision of institutional and public support for parents caring for children with additional needs, including those which result from life-saving treatment. As a society we need to recognise caring responsibilities and ensure they are properly supported by communities, public institutions and services so that once children are discharged from hospital, families are not abandoned to their caring responsibilities. Caring needs to be fully understood not solely as a private, individualised, responsibility but that the care provided within families is embedded within the care and support of a range of public services and institutions.

I now turn to consider a hypothetical example the facts of which are drawn from a number of recent cases. Although I am not seeking to re-write the judgment in a specific case, the methodology is inspired by the turn in academic work to re-writing judgments. The primary goal of the academic practice of re-writing judgments is to explore the extent to which the critical perspectives employed in academic critique of judgments, whether that be from a feminist, ethical or children's rights perspective, can be applied in the writing of judgments which remain faithful to judicial conventions. The purpose of applying the relational responsibilities framework to a hypothetical constructed from the facts of recent cases is to demonstrate that a relational responsibilities perspective for the resolution of children's medical treatment decisions is not a purely theoretical academic enterprise but one of practical application.

## 5 Application of a Relational Responsibilities Approach: A Hypothetical Case

Seven-year-old Samuel James first underwent surgery, radiotherapy and chemotherapy in the treatment of a malignant brain tumour when he was 18 months old. After a period in remission, Samuel relapsed. After further invasive treatment, his treating doctors formed the view that all medical and surgical options had been exhausted. The position of the tumour meant that further surgery was not possible and the radiotherapy and chemotherapy which had been administered had not stopped the tumour from growing. His clinicians considered that his condition was now deteriorating quickly. His parents, whose religious beliefs meant that they believed in the sanctity of life and that life should be sustained through all means possible, had searched the internet, identified a novel therapy which had been used by an expert abroad in the treatment of adults with a similar form of brain cancer and who had advised them that he considered that there was a theoretical chance it could work in Samuel's case. His parents claimed that Samuel was a brave fighter who had a right to be given this chance of life. They had raised half of the costs of treatment abroad by cashing in life insurance policies and re-mortgaging the family home. A children's cancer charity had offered to pay the balance. The Trust applied to court for authority to withhold further invasive treatment and to provide palliative care to ease the pain and suffering in the remainder of Samuel's life. His parents considered that it was in his best interests to travel abroad for a trial of the innovative therapy and that the risks involved in doing so were not the same as in other cases, such as that of Charlie Gard, given that he was not dependent upon a ventilator.

A relational responsibilities approach to determination of Samuel's best interests would ensure that the child was at the centre of decision-making. To ensure that the focus is upon him as an individual, the court would require evidence from his parents, family members and others who know him well about his interests, his character and his developing views on relevant issues such as quality and sanctity of life. In contrast to the similar aged boys, Ashya King (*In the Matter of Ashya King* 2014) and Neon Roberts (*An NHS Trust v SR* 2012), both of whom were shadowy presences in the background to the disputes between adults, videos could also be used to bring the child to life for the judge. In the same way that Samuel would have received support, such as play therapy, in preparation for his treatment, the same kind of support could be made available to gain a better understanding of how he is currently feeling, to inform the Guardian's independent representation of him and give effect to his participation rights to ascertain as far as possible his attitude to further treatment aimed at giving him a chance of life.

In addition to the clinical judgement of those responsible for his treatment and their professional judgement informed by second opinions and professional guidance, a relational responsibilities approach would require evidence from Samuel's parents, other family members and those involved in his daily life of how he had coped with the previous treatment he had received, the attitude he demonstrated to the pain of medical intervention and the side-effects of treatment and how the treatment he had received had affected him in the years he was in remission. As the question for the judge to determine relates to the future medical treatment of Samuel, evidence should be secured from a range of health professionals such as his GP and nurses and other community health professionals as to the effect of the treatment he has received upon his quality of life. The court would seek substance to the claims that he was a 'brave fighter' in his experience of his illness and its treatment and how that bears upon decisions about his future treatment.

The judge would need to be satisfied as to the nature of the professional relationship of care between Samuel and the doctor who was offering the innovative therapy abroad. The judge would need evidence that the doctor had examined Samuel, his medical records and consulted with his clinicians and been informed of the second opinions (as Francis J stated in *Re Gard* 2017, [12]). Whilst, as Butler-Sloss P observed in *Simms*, the *Bolam* test (*Bolam v Friern Hospital Management Committee* 1957) should not 'inhibit medical progress' (*Donald Simms and Jonathan Simms v An NHS Trust and Secretary of State for Health; PA and JA v An NHS Trust and Secretary of State for Health* 2002, [48]), but before the administration of the therapy could be considered in Samuel's best interests, the judge would have to be satisfied that there was a responsible body of professional opinion capable of withstanding logical analysis supporting its administration. It would not be in Samuel's best interests to be subjected to further treatment which had no reasonable prospect, and an assessment would have to be made of the side-effects and short-, medium- and long-term risks of the therapy. Samuel and his parents would depend upon the doctor offering treatment fulfilling his legal and moral duties to take care, including consideration of why the therapy was not available to him. There would need to be evidence as to why it had not been approved for use in children, whether that was due to resources or to judgements about its efficacy or standards of care to protect children from being subjected to experimental treatment. The social, political and cultural context for decisions about the care being offered would have to be understood.

As is apparent, a relational responsibilities approach, more attentive to the particular and contextual, seeks to identify a way forward either through gaining more information to bring greater clarity to the best interests determination, or through a more detailed exploration of the relevant issues to find an alternative solution to the two separate routes currently favoured by those primarily responsible for the care of the child. For example, the additional information may lead the caring professionals to the conclusion that they should try the medication, lead the parents to understand why this is not a possibility or enable them to arrive at a different solution. By responding to each other they may find 'shareable interpretations of their responsibilities, and/or bearable resolutions to their moral binds' (Urban Walker 1989, 20).

## 6 Judging with Care

The current legal framework polarises the positions of those confronted with making decisions about the medical treatment of children in their care, condensing the views of parent and professional as oppositional, one of which must prevail. It creates a clash of conflicting assessments of what is best, a conflict in which there is a winner and a loser, and in doing so contributes further to the breakdown in trust between those seeking to do the best for the child. As Katherine Bartlett has identified, when disputes arise, the law forces the parties to present their positions and the court to decide through individualised, abstract, conflicting claims when the reality is of connections and interdependencies (Bartlett 1988, 295).

As Leslie Bender has observed, the ethic of justice,

> closely parallels the dominant rationality and methodology of Anglo-American law. This justice ethic is based on a rights model, where problem-solving consists of the application of abstract, generalized principles to arbitrate rights disputes between separate individuals (conflicting rights-holders) and to privilege one over another. The justice-oriented problem-solver seeks a distanced stance from which to make objective decisions by applying formal rules of equality and other general principles of justice. (Bender 1990–1991, 37)

Once the decisions of parents and professionals are subject to determination by the court, within the existing legal framework, justice prevails at the expense of care. A legal framework of abstract prioritisation of the competing rights of the unconnected other will not reflect the reality of those with responsibilities and determined to take responsibility for the care of a seriously ill child. In contrast the ethic of care, the principles of which inform the relational responsibilities approach, as Leslie Bender has observed,

> focuses attention on the unique context of the dispute and the parties' on-going relationships and interdependencies. The care-oriented problem-solver examines the connections between and among people, looking at their interpersonal responsibilities and needs. Preventing hurt, preserving relationships, and developing cooperative solutions rooted in the concrete particulars of the conflict are objectives of a care-oriented ethical analysis. A care-based problem-solver … gather[s] more relevant information in order to better understand the full scope

> of the problem and the practical, material consequences of any decision. By considering the specific needs of all the parties, as articulated from those parties' own perspectives, and by attending to particularized contexts rather than abstract rights and universalizable rules, care-oriented problem-solvers frequently design creative, alternative solutions that may never occur to their justice-oriented counterparts. (Bender 1990–1991, 37)

The legal framework should not just be content to protect the interests of individuals but should also encourage those involved to take more care of each other with consideration of the consequences for others, as well as themselves, of their actions and decisions. As Margaret Urban Walker stated,

> If the others I need to understand really are actual others in a particular case at hand, and not repeatable instances or replaceable occupants of a general status, they will require of me an understanding of their/our story and its concrete detail. Without this I really cannot know how it is with others towards whom I will act, or what the meaning and consequence of any acts will be. (Urban Walker 1989, 18)

I argue that a conceptual framework of relational responsibilities would better achieve child-centred care through recognition of the lived realities of caring responsibilities and inherent relationality of the child, parents and professions; it would situate decisions about a child's future medical treatment in the context of social responsibilities of public services and institutions to support caring responsibilities. Reframing welfare around relational responsibilities would ensure recognition of both justice and care.

## Case List

*Alder Hey Children's NHS Foundation Trust v Evans* [2018] EWHC 308 (February 2018)
*A National Health Service Trust v D* [2000] 2 FLR 677
*An NHS Trust v A* [2007] EWHC 1696
*An NHS Trust v SR* [2012] EWHC 3842
*Bolam v Friern Hospital Management Committee* [1957] 1 WLR 582
*Bolton NHS Foundation Trust v C and LB and PT* [2015] EWHC 2920
*Charles Gard and Others v United Kingdom. Application no. 39793/it 17, 28 June 2017,* http://hudoc.echr.coe.int/eng#{"documentcollectionid2":["DECGRANDCHAMBER","ADMISSIBILITY","ADMISSIBILITYCOM"],"itemid":["001-175359"]}

*Donald Simms and Jonathan Simms v An NHS Trust and Secretary of State for Health; PA and JA v An NHS Trust and Secretary of State for Health* [2002] EWHC 2734
*Glass v United Kingdom* (2004) 39 EHRR 15
*GOSH v Yates & Gard* [2017] EWHC 972 (April 2017)
*In the Matter of Ashya King (a Child)* [2014] EWHC 2964
*In the Matter of Charles Gard* [2017] EWCA Civ 410
*In the matter of Charlie Gard (Permission to Appeal Hearing), 8 June 2017,* https://www.supremecourt.uk/news/permission-to-appeal-hearing-in-the-matter-of-charlie-gard.html
*Portsmouth NHS Trust v Wyatt & Wyatt* [2004] EWHC 2247
*Re A (Children) (Conjoined Twins: Surgical Separation)* [2001] Fam 147
*Re B (a minor) (wardship: medical treatment)* [1981] 1 WLR 1421
*Re B* [2008] EWHC 1996
*Re C (A Child) (HIV Testing)* [2000] 2 WLR 270
*Re D (a minor) (wardship: sterilisation)* [1976] 1 All ER 326
*Re Gard (A Child)* [2017] EWHC 1909 (July 2017)
*Re J (A Minor) (Wardship: Medical Treatment)* [1991] 2 WLR 140
*Re J (A Minor) (Child in Care: Medical Treatment)* [1992] 3 WLR 507
*Re T (a minor) (wardship: medical treatment)* [1997] 1 WLR 242
*Re Wyatt (a child) (medical treatment: continuation of order)* [2005] EWCA Civ 1181
*R v Cambridge District Health Authority, ex parte B* [1995] 1 FLR 1055
*Tafida Raqeeb v Barts NHS FoundationTrust* [2019] EWHC 2531 *& Barts NHS Foundation Trust v Shalina Begum and Muhhamed Raqeeb & Tafida Raqeeb* [2019] EWHC 2530

## References


Alderson, P., Hawthorn, J., & Killen, M. (2005). The Participation Rights of Premature Babies. *The International Journal of Children's Rights, 13*, 31–50.

Alghrani, A. (2017). Judgment in *Re A (Conjoined Twins)*. In H. Stalford, K. Hollingsworth, & S. Gilmore (Eds.), *Rewriting Children's Rights Judgments: From Academic Vision to New Practice* (pp. 264–272). Oxford: Bloomsbury Publishing.

Anderzen-Carlsson, A., Kihlgren, M., Svantesson, M., & Sorlie, V. (2007). Children's Fear as Experienced by the Parents of Children with Cancer. *Journal of Pediatric Nursing, 22*, 233–244.

Auckland, C., & Goold, I. (2019). Parental Rights, Best Interests and Significant Harms: Who Should Have the Final Say Over a Child's Medical Care? *Cambridge Law Journal, 78*, 287–323.

Bartlett, K. (1988). Re-expressing Parenthood. *Yale Law Journal, 98*, 293–304.

Bender, L. (1990–1991). From Gender Difference to Feminist Solidarity: Using Carol Gilligan and an Ethic of Care in Law. *Vermont Law Review, 15*, 1–48.

Bridgeman, J. (2003). After Bristol: The Healthcare of Young Children and the Law. *Legal Studies, 23*, 229–250.
Bridgeman, J. (2007). *Parental Responsibility, Young Children and Healthcare Law,1.* Cambridge: Cambridge University Press.
Bridgeman, J. (2008). Children with Severe Disabilities and Their Families: Re-examining Private Responsibilities and Public Obligations from a Caring Perspective. In M. D. A. Freeman (Ed.), *Law and Bioethics: Current Legal Issues 2008* (pp. 358–375). Oxford: OUP.
Bridgeman, J. (2010). Judgment in *R v Portsmouth Hospitals NHS Trust, ex parte Glass* [1999] 2 FLR 905. In R. Hunter, C. McGlynn, & E. Rackley (Eds.), *Feminist Judgments: From Theory to Practice* (pp. 369–378). Oxford: Hart.
Bridgeman, J. (2017). Leaving No Stone Unturned': Contesting the Medical Care of a Seriously Ill Child. *Child and Family Law Quarterly, 1*, 63–84.
Bridgeman, J. (2019). Beyond Best Interests: A Question of Professional Conscience? In I. Goold, J. Herring, & C. Auckland (Eds.), *Parental Rights, Best Interests and Significant Harms: Medical Decision-Making on Behalf of Children Post-Great Ormond Street Hospital v Gard* (pp. 137–152). Oxford: Hart.
Cancer Research UK. (2019). http://www.cancerresearchuk.org/about-cancer/type/rare-cancers/rare-cancers-name/childrens-cancers#cure. Accessed 30 July 2019.
Day, E. (2004, March 14). Do Not Resuscitate – And Don't Bother Consulting the Family. *The Sunday Telegraph.*
Diekema, D. (2004). Parental Refusals of Medical Treatment: The Harm Principle as Threshold for State Intervention. *Theoretical Medicine, 25*, 243–264.
Dixon-Woods, M., Wilson, D., Jackson, C., Cavers, D., & Pritchard-Jones, K. (2008). Human Tissue and "The Public": The Case of Childhood Cancer Tumour Banking. *BioSocieties, 3*, 57–80.
Downie, R., & Macnaughton, M. (2013). In Defence of Professional Judgement. *Advances in Psychiatric Treatment, 15*, 322–327.
Draper, H., & Sorrell, T. (2002). Patients' Responsibilities in Medical Ethics. *Bioethics, 16*, 335–352.
Dressler, G., & Kelly, S. (2018). Ethical Implications of Medical Crowdfunding: The Case of Charlie Gard. *Journal of Medical Ethics, 44*, 453–457.
Duckworth, L. (2002, May 9). Girl Denied HIV Therapy by Father Is Put into Care. *The Independent*, p. 5.
Fineman, M. (2008). The Vulnerable Subject: Anchoring Equality in the Human Condition. *Yale Journal of Law & Feminism, 20*(1), 1–23.
Forbat, L., Teuten, B., & Barclay, S. (2015). Conflict Escalation in Paediatric Services: Findings from a Qualitative Study. *Archives of Diseases in Childhood.* https://doi.org/10.1136/archdischild-2014-307780.
Fox, M., & Murphy, T. (2013). The Body, Bodies, Embodiment: Feminist Legal Engagement with Health. In M. Davies & V. Munro (Eds.), *The Ashgate Research Companion to Feminist Legal Theory* (pp. 249–265). Farnham: Ashgate Publisher.

Fox, M., & Thomson, M. (2017). Bodily Integrity, Embodiment, and the Regulation of Parental Choice. *Journal of Law and Society, 44*, 501–531.

Freeman, M. (2017). Judgment in *Re T (A Minor) (Wardship: Medical Treatment)*. In H. Stalford, K. Hollingsworth, & S. Gilmore (Eds.), *Rewriting Children's Rights Judgments: From Academic Vision to New Practice* (pp. 252–256). Oxford: Bloomsbury Publishing.

Gillam, L. (2016). The Zone of Parental Discretion: An Ethical Tool for Dealing with Disagreement between Parents and Doctors about Medical Treatment for a Child. *Clinical Ethics, 11*, 1–8.

Gilligan, C. (1982). *In a Different Voice: Psychological Theory and Women's Development*. Cambridge, MA: Harvard University Press.

Gilligan, A. (2018, July 30). Cannabis Ban Is a Death Sentence for My Son. *The Times*. Last Accessed 30 July 19.

Hastings, G. (2010). Judgment in *Re A (Children) (Conjoined Twins: Surgical Separation)* [2000] EWCA Civ 254. In R. Hunter, C. McGlynn, & E. Rackley (Eds.), *Feminist Judgments: From Theory to Practice* (pp. 139–146). Oxford: Hart.

Herring, J. (2010). The Legal Duties of Carers. *Medical Law Review, 18*, 248–255.

Herring, J. (2017). Commentary on *Re A (Conjoined Twins)*. In H. Stalford, K. Hollingsworth, & S. Gilmore (Eds.), *Rewriting Children's Rights Judgments: From Academic Vision to New Practice* (pp. 257–263). Oxford: Bloomsbury Publishing.

Herring, J. (2019). Vulnerability and Medical Decisions Concerning Children. In I. Goold, J. Herring, & C. Auckland (Eds.), *Parental Rights, Best Interests and Significant Harms: Medical Decision-Making on Behalf of Children Post-Great Ormond Street Hospital v Gard* (pp. 191–206). Oxford: Hart.

Herring, J., & Wallbank, J. (Eds.). (2013). *Vulnerabilities, Care and Family Law*. Abingdon: Routledge.

Huxtable, R. (2017). Judgment in *Re A (Conjoined Twins)*. In S. Smith, J. Coggon, C. Hobson, R. Huxtable, S. McGuiness, J. Miola, & M. Neal (Eds.), *Ethical Judgments: Re-writing Medical Law* (pp. 18–23). Oxford: Hart.

Leach Scully, J. (2017). Ethical Commentary – Conjoineds, Care and the Question of Identity: Some Reflections on the Ethics of *Re A*. In S. Smith, J. Coggon, C. Hobson, R. Huxtable, S. McGuiness, J. Miola, & M. Neal (Eds.), *Ethical Judgments: Re-writing Medical Law* (pp. 31–37). Oxford: Hart.

Levin, A. (1999, September 18). HIV-Test Couple Flee Abroad with Daughter. *Daily Mail*, p. 19.

Lindeman Nelson, H. (1999). Always Connect: Towards a Parental Ethics of Divorce. In J. E. Hanigsberg & S. Ruddick (Eds.), *Mother Troubles: Rethinking Contemporary Maternal Dilemmas* (pp. 117–135). Boston: Beacon Press.

Lindemann, H., & Carse, A. (1996). Rehabilitating Care. *Kennedy Institute of Ethics Journal, 6*, 19–35.

Mackenzie, C., Rogers, W., & Dodds, S. (Eds.). (2014). *Vulnerability: New Essays in Ethics and Feminist Philosophy*. New York: Oxford University Press.

McLaughlin, J., Goodley, D., Clavering, E., & Fisher, P. (2008). *Families Raising Disabled Children: Enabling Care and Social Justice*. Hampshire: Palgrave.

Melville-Ross, J. (2016). *Two for Joy*. London: John Blake.

Menkel-Meadow, C. (1985). Portia in a Different Voice: Speculations on a Women's Lawyering Process. *Berkeley Journal of Gender, Law & Justice, 1*, 39–63.

Moreton, K. L. (2019). Reflecting on "Hannah's Choice": Using the Ethics of Care to Justify Child Participation in End of Life Decision-Making. *Medical Law Review*. https://doi.org/10.1093/medlaw/fwz011.

Nedelsky, J. (1989). Reconceiving Autonomy: Sources, Thoughts and Possibilities. *Yale Journal of Law and Feminism, 1*, 7–36.

Pettersen, T. (2008). *Comprehending Care: Problems and Possibilities in the Ethics of Care*. Lanham: Lexington Books.

Raca, J. (2012). *Standing Up for James*. London: Clarendon.

Smart, C., & Neale, B. (1999). *Family Fragments?* Cambridge: Polity Press.

Strange, K. (2014a, November 14). Couple in Desperate Race to Sell Family Home to Fund Daughter's Cancer Treatment After Doctors Say She Won't Live Until Christmas Without It. *MailOnline*. Last Accessed 31 July 19.

Strange, K. (2014b, November 17). "Overwhelmed" Family of Little Girl Battling Cancer Will No Longer Have to Sell Their Home After Strangers Donate £176,000 in One Weekend to Fund Life-Saving Treatment. *MailOnline*. Last Accessed 31 July 19.

Tronto, J. (1993). *Moral Boundaries: The Political Argument for an Ethic of Care*. London: Routledge.

Urban Walker, M. (1989). Moral Understandings: Alternative "Epistemology" for a Feminist Ethics. *Hypatia, 4*, 16–28.

Urban Walker, M. (1998). *Moral Understandings: A Feminist Study in Ethics*. New York: Routledge.

Wright, R. (2015). *The Skies I'm Under*. Born at the Right Time Publishing.

# 12

# Embodied Integrity, Shaping Surgeries and the Profoundly Disabled Child

Marie Fox, Michael Thomson, and Joshua Warburton

## 1 Introduction

In this chapter we seek to develop a model of embodied integrity that we have proposed elsewhere (Fox and Thomson 2017; Fox et al. 2019) by applying it to the context of profoundly disabled children. We explore the role that embodied integrity might play in protecting such children from irreversible non-therapeutic bodily interventions. Bodily integrity is a key foundational value in the jurisprudence of the body and is increasingly understood as underpinning fundamental human rights (Brazier 2009). However, building on our earlier framework, we suggest that this value is not fully recognised in the lives of disabled people. Bringing together concerns with embodiment, care and disability, our more specific focus is on children such as Ashley X, whose condition was described by her parents as follows:

M. Fox (✉)
School of Law & Social Justice, University of Liverpool, Liverpool, UK
e-mail: Marie.Fox@liverpool.ac.uk

M. Thomson
Faculty of Law, University of Technology Sydney, Sydney, NSW, Australia

School of Law, University of Leeds, Leeds, UK
e-mail: Michael.Thomson@uts.edu.au

J. Warburton
School of Law, University of Leeds, Leeds, UK
e-mail: J.Warburton1@leeds.ac.uk



C. Dietz et al. (eds.), *A Jurisprudence of the Body*, Palgrave Socio-Legal Studies,
https://doi.org/10.1007/978-3-030-42200-4_12

> Our daughter Ashley had a normal birth, but her mental and motor faculties did not develop. Over the years, neurologists, geneticists, and other specialists conducted every known traditional and experimental test, but still could not determine a diagnosis or a cause. Doctors call her condition "static encephalopathy of unknown etiology", which means an insult to the brain of unknown origin or cause, and one that will not improve. Now nine years old, Ashley cannot keep her head up, roll or change her sleeping position, hold a toy, or sit up by herself, let alone walk or talk. She is tube fed and depends on her caregivers in every way. We call her our Pillow Angel since she is so sweet and stays right where we place her—usually on a pillow. (http://pillowangel.org)

In responding to the question of how such severely disabled children can 'have a life' (Latimer 2019, 274) as they grow older and develop physically, we suggest that our embodied integrity model can help in framing an appropriate ethico-legal response to their care. Our vision builds on more conventional accounts of bodily integrity which, notwithstanding their increasing prominence in bioethics, socio-legal and health law scholarship, were strikingly absent from much of the extensive academic and popular commentary that the Ashley X case generated. As we will demonstrate, although conventional accounts of bodily integrity may play a role in protecting children such as Ashley from interventions designed to manage their bodies, they are nevertheless problematic. In this context it is their tendency to treat the bodies of profoundly disabled children as fixed, asocial and reducible to their material or corporeal bodies that is especially troubling.

Embodied integrity, by contrast, provides a more complex understanding of corporeality which acknowledges that the body is inseparable from the social and institutional context within which it exists. It is better equipped than conventional accounts to accommodate corporeal change and to situate these children as entangled (Latimer and López Gómez 2019) in the medical discourses and practices that surround them. Similarly, they are intimately entangled in the lives of their families—a reality exacerbated by the privatisation of caring responsibilities. Paying attention to these social dimensions of bodies allows us to problematise surgical procedures on these children and to contextualise them in a long history of interventions on bodies constructed as improper or wrong (Sullivan 2008)—notably, coercive sterilisation of disabled children and adults. Indeed, as Read and Clements remind us, only a generation ago it was 'common practice to bring about the deaths of some children with learning disabilities or physical impairments' (Read and Clements 2004, 482). Since then, although UK law has increasingly called the medical profession to account, as the sterilisation jurisprudence we outline below demonstrates, law continues to have a chequered record in protecting such disabled children and adults from invasive, irreversible procedures.

In contesting such interventions, recourse to the value of bodily integrity has become increasingly prevalent (e.g. Savell 2003–4), including in legal studies (Ludbrook 1995–6; Miller 2007; Brazier 2009; Grabham 2012; Ammaturo 2016; Fox and Thomson 2017; Herring and Wall 2017). Bodily integrity has also generated an extensive ethics literature (Fabre 2006; Viens 2017; Mazor 2019). However, below we will argue that judicial decision-making, certainly in the UK, has yet to fully recognise the value of bodily integrity, reflecting the inconsistent way in which the bodily integrity principle is mobilised in law (Fox and Thomson 2017). Furthermore, notwithstanding what we might characterise as a *corporeal turn* in health law (Fox and Murphy 2013), when the language of bodily integrity is deployed, it is often done with scant interrogation of how the concept is interpreted or how it might operate in practice. In this chapter, our aim is to offer a more compelling justification for our embodied integrity model in medico-legal decision-making. We developed this model through a consideration of non-therapeutic interventions on the bodies of children who were not yet competent, but who were likely to acquire the capabilities to reason and choose that characterise the classical legal subject (Naffine 2003). Focusing on genital cutting, we argued that protecting the embodied integrity of children from non-therapeutic and non-consensual surgical interventions is essential to protecting their rights to self-determination and to an open future (Feinberg 1992). This requires that embodied integrity should be the primary factor in any assessment of the best interests of children by health decision-makers, and we argued that this will generally entail deferring decisions until the child is in a position to decide for herself about irreversible body modifications. In this chapter we seek to develop our model by applying it to the 'harder' case of managing the bodies of profoundly disabled children. Turning our attention to the particular body of children like Ashley X complicates our earlier reasoning by raising challenging questions about deferring decisions until a child is competent to decide, and how such competence is defined and recognised. While our focus is bodily interventions on children, it is important to acknowledge that they will grow to be disabled adults who, as we trace below using the jurisprudence on sterilisation, will likely continue to have decisions made for them and to have their bodily integrity disregarded.

As far as children are concerned, Read and Clements have traced how the formative legal cases which addressed withdrawal of treatment from disabled children (see further Bridgeman in this volume) have generated other socio-legal challenges. A legacy of this jurisprudence has been that a greater number of families now live with disability, while 'communities and municipalities hav[e] to cater for and accommodate disability' (Read and Clements 2004, 484). One response to caring for these children in the home has been to medicalise their bodies by resort to surgery and other interventions designed to make the body more manageable. In this chapter we suggest that, too often, decision-makers have sanctioned such interventions on the assumption that these children lack any agency to contribute to decision-making about their lives. We caution against assumptions that a profoundly disabled child will remain fixed in time (on the question of temporality in the legal construction of bodies, see Garland and Travis, this volume) as well as a tendency to homogenise disability. We argue that our model of embodied integrity is broadly congruent with the social model of disability (Oliver 1996, 2013), or at least those variants that take into account the importance of corporeality (Hughes and Paterson 1997; Freund 2001; Shakespeare 2013; Barnes 2016). We also hope that it can have particular purchase in protecting the interests of the most marginalised legal subjects, and as underlining obligations to support decision-making by disabled people, as required by the UN Convention on the Rights of Persons with Disabilities (CRPD) (Flynn and Arstein-Kerlake 2014; Harris 2016). Currently we see decision-making for profoundly disabled children as partly dictated by social responses to their (non-normative) corporeality and assumptions about their (lack of) agency. Often this centres on a 'wrong body' narrative which privileges medical management or normalisation (Sullivan 2008; Dietz 2018). Embodied integrity can contest such narratives by rendering visible the social meanings ascribed to bodily impairments and understanding the body as an emancipatory concept (Hughes and Paterson 1997). It also directs us, in line with approaches underpinning the CRPD, to seek to identify the 'will and preference' of the disabled child (or adult) and helps with the thorny issue of disentangling their interests from those of the families on whom they depend, thus problematising requests for non-consensual and irreversible interventions by family members.

We begin by outlining the case of Ashley X, the public responses it generated and the subsequent afterlife of the 'Ashley treatment'. Notwithstanding its international ramifications, the case failed to attract sustained legal analysis, while the ethics literature often relegated it to the status of a (sensationalised) one-off case study, in which bodily integrity received scant attention. We seek to contest the notion that such cases are exceptional, first by tracing media reports of global demand for this 'treatment' and then locating such practices in a genealogy of attempts to modify, contain and render 'non-reproductive' the bodies of disabled children and adults (Trombley 1988). To contest these interventions we invoke the bodily integrity principle outlining how it is conventionally conceived before arguing that our embodied understanding better captures and promotes the immediate and future interests of children, including those who are profoundly disabled. We conclude by considering the role of law, and the need to challenge the privatisation of care that dramatically impacts those who care for disabled family members (Sakellariou and Rotarou 2017, 200). More generally, we argue for a legal conception of the child as emergent (Fox and Thomson 2017) and, following Read and Clements, for 'the authenticity of impaired modes of being' (Read and Clements 2004, 507). To realise such ends we suggest that law must 'avoid colluding with and adding to the power and dominance of an order of the normal' (Moser 2005, 668).

## 2 The Legacy of Ashley X

In 2004 Seattle's Children's Hospital Ethics Committee considered an application by Ashley's parents. Having consulted hospital doctors when she began to develop pubic hair and breast buds, they requested that high doses of oestrogen be administered to permanently stunt her growth, and that she undergo a hysterectomy and mastectomy. Her condition was described by her doctors as follows:

> At the age of 6 years, she cannot sit up, ambulate, or use language. She is gastrostomy-tube dependent for nutrition… [S]he clearly responds to others – vocalizing and smiling in response to care and affection. The combined opinion of the specialists involved in her care is that there will be no significant future improvement in her cognitive or neurological baseline. (Gunther and Diekema 2006, 1004)

The Committee approved the interventions in Ashley's best interests. It would render her body more manageable by allowing her to be more easily carried and cared for, thus facilitating her participation in family life (Diekema and Fost 2010):

> It was the consensus of the committee members that the potential long-term benefit to Ashley herself outweighed the risks; and that the procedures/interventions would improve her quality of life, facilitate home care, and avoid institutionalisation in the foreseeable future. (p. 3, minutes)

Having justified these procedures within a cost-benefit framework, doctors also removed her appendix in the course of surgery, asserting that so doing presented no additional risk. In 2006 the doctors, at her parents' request, published an account that attracted international media attention (Gunther and Diekema 2006).

Subsequently, the Washington Protection and Advocacy System (now Disability Rights Washington) concluded that the hospital had acted unlawfully by performing the hysterectomy without a court order, and that a court order *should* also have been sought for a mastectomy or administration of growth attenuation (Carlson and Dorfman 2007). The hospital has not since performed growth attenuation on a child with a developmental disability (Field 2016). Given the concerns generated by the case, the Seattle Growth Attenuation and Ethics Working Group was established to provide practical guidance for health professionals. Reporting in 2010, the 20-person Working Group identified growth attenuation as the 'particularly interesting' intervention. It thus failed to consider the mastectomy (since to do so would only add 'a layer of complexity') and deemed it unnecessary to discuss the hysterectomy 'because there is an established literature and a general consensus on policy, including the issue of judicial review' (Wilford et al. 2010). Below we suggest that the failure to address the interventions as a suite of procedures was highly problematic, and allowed Ashley's case to be read as exceptional and distinguishable from past interventions on disabled bodies that have increasingly been challenged for violating human rights. The Working Group ultimately concluded that growth attenuation could be a legitimate intervention for the most profoundly intellectually impaired children (defined as those with an IQ below 25).

Since the first account of Ashley's treatment (Gunther and Diekema 2006), her case has attracted extensive international commentary, demonstrating a global uncertainty about the legitimacy of the practice (Vallis 2005; Ayres 2007; Cook 2007; Tanner 2007). The clinicians' account generated reactions ranging from condemnation (Prigg 2007), through acquiescence (Lewis 2007), to approval (Singer 2007) from media outlets worldwide (Saletan 2007). Subsequently, the debate has resurfaced periodically across jurisdictions, as families have sought this 'treatment'. Media reports are populated with these children's pseudonyms, often accompanied by parental narratives of battles to care for their disabled children. For instance, in 2007 a mother in England sought a hysterectomy for her daughter, Katie (Bowcott 2007). It was reported that if the 'Ashley treatment' had been available five years earlier, she would have pursued those interventions instead (Ainsworth 2007). Media reaction to this case was relatively positive (Anonymous Daily Telegraph

2007; Anonymous Brentwood Gazette 2007), although disability rights groups disputed the need for a hysterectomy (Smock 2007). The debate was reignited in 2012 (Anonymous 2012) with news of Erica and Tom, the first boy recorded as having had aspects of the 'Ashley treatment' (McVeigh 2012b). In 2015, having become aware of the treatment, the parents of Charley Hooper spent two years finding a doctor willing to perform it in New Zealand (Tsvirko 2015). The *New York Times Magazine* ran an extended feature in 2016 on nine-year-old Ricky Preslar who had been subjected to high levels of oestrogen from the age of three until his seventh birthday (Field 2016). In 2017, the Portland Tribute reported on Blue, who was given growth attenuation at the age of nine after her mother publicised the family's desire for the procedure (Anonymous Portland Tribune 2017). While focused on individual children, these various reports are typically accompanied by claims of a growing demand for the treatment.

The controversial nature of the Ashley treatment, coupled with the lack of transparency surrounding the activities of doctors, ethics committees and hospitals, means that it is unclear how many children, in any jurisdiction, have been subject to these interventions. Yet, the popular accounts above indicate that the publicity attracted by Ashley's case has generated a sizeable demand in the US, UK and elsewhere (e.g. Pilkington 2007; McVeigh 2012a, b; Field 2016; Wrigley et al. 2018). In 2012 media reports suggested that at least 12 other instances of the treatment had occurred, with numbers potentially as high as 100 globally (Pilkington 2012). Philip Zeitler, chair of the Endocrinology Department of Children's Hospital Colorado in Aurora, told *The Times* that since 2001 he had been approached on an annual basis by parents wishing to obtain growth attenuation treatment for their children (Pavia 2016) and was reported as having overseen growth attenuation in approximately 20 cases (Field 2016). A 2015 US survey of paediatric endocrinologists indicated that 65 children had undergone growth attenuation. Since only 26 per cent of surveyed doctors responded, the number of actual interventions is likely to have been substantially higher (McGhee 2016). A 2016–2017 study evidenced demand in New Zealand (Wrigley et al. 2018), with 5 paediatricians having prescribed it and a further 15 referring children elsewhere, including one to a clinician in the UK. More broadly, Curt Decker, director of the National Disability Rights Network (NDRN), suggested that thousands of families were actively exploring the possibility of the 'Ashley treatment' for their children (Bates 2012). Finally, in 2018 the blog established by Ashley's parents claimed that 'hundreds of children [had been] through growth attenuation therapy. Parents of about 50 of them are members of a private support group that we host' (www.pillowangel.org).

We argue that the precedent set by Ashley X in legitimising such interventions, coupled with the subsequent growth in interest and acceptance of ethical justifications (Edwards 2008, 343), raises significant concerns. These are heightened given that 4000 children (equivalent to 1 in 1000 births) are born each year in the US with the level of impairment that was deemed a threshold for intervention by the Working Group (Wilford et al. 2010, 30). Hence a significant population of children are potentially subject to the same suite of procedures. Given that evidence suggests that the intellectual abilities of people with severe motor impairments are grossly under estimated (Serna et al. 1997), it is essential that developmental specialists are involved in decision-making. However, it appears that this does not happen (Field 2016), while the secrecy surrounding all aspects of the 'Ashley treatment' militates against accountability or compliance.

## 3 Fragmenting the Person

As noted above, the Seattle Ethics Committee decision and the Working Party were primarily concerned with growth attenuation. This partial focus is highly problematic given the overall attack on Ashley's embodied integrity (Lantos 2010; Wrigley et al. 2018). Yet, even within this narrow remit, the failure to consider the very contested history of growth attenuation is striking. Academic reports dating from the 1930s document emerging experimentation (Shimon and Barkan 2012, 193). The ability to isolate oestrogen (Lee and Howell 2006) offered the prospect of new treatment for children with acromegaly—a disorder resulting from excessive growth hormone once the growth plates have closed (Shiman and Barkan 2012)—and gigantism (Lee and Howell 2006). However, oestrogen was soon more widely deployed to treat girls for 'excess' growth, rather than specific conditions. Indeed, to warrant growth attenuation, they needed only to have a predicted height of 5′9″ (Goldzieher 1956), and during the twentieth century, it became a 'standard treatment' for tall girls (Lee and Howell 2006). This practice did not attract serious criticism within the medical community until the mid-1970s, when a gradual consensus emerged that it was overused (Marshall 1975). More recently, growth attenuation has been linked to breast and uterine cancer, and other common side effects have emerged, including leg cramps and headaches, with some patients developing migraines to the point of requiring the treatment to be halted (Rask et al. 2008, 345). Nausea, weight gain, mild hypertension, benign breast disease and ovarian cysts have all been reported in growth attenuation treatments that took place through the 1960s and 1970s. Additionally, oestrogen treatment may reduce antithrombin levels, leading to a hypercoagulable state and possibly decreasing Protein S levels (Rask et al. 2008). These are risk factors for thrombosis. Ricky Preslar's oestrogen treatment was stopped early when his toes turned blue, indicating thrombosis (Field 2016). While reports of its use continued (Lipsett 1977; Rask et al. 2008), over time these documented risks, coupled with a greater social acceptability of tall women and absence of a clear ethical justification for the widespread use of growth attenuation, contributed to a drastic decline in popularity (Barnard et al. 2002, 25; Clark and Vasta 2006, 3). Against this backdrop of documented risks, we would suggest that the repurposing of growth attenuation to 'treat' profoundly disabled children is ethically and legally troubling. It becomes still more problematic as one of a suite of invasive modifications, particularly since known side effects of the procedure are in turn used to justify performing mastectomies and hysterectomies (Field 2016).

Ashley's bilateral mastectomy, sanitised in some accounts as 'breast bud removal' (Frader 2007) or removal of 'breast nodules' (Field 2016), was initially omitted from Gunther and Diekema's report. Later they justified it due to the side effects of high-dose oestrogen, including 'heavy menstrual bleeding and rapid advancement of breast development' (Diekema and Fost 2010, 31). Complications of mastectomies include short-term pain and swelling and normal surgical scarring. Seromas (fluid collecting under the skin) and lymphoedema are further possible outcomes (NHS Choices 2017). Studies suggest that, for 60 per cent of mastectomy patients, the short-term pain is 'severe'; while 10 per cent claim severe pain lasts for more than six months (Sobsey 2009, 76). Chronic pain is believed to last over a year in many patients (Gartner et al. 2009, 1991). Still more problematically, mastectomies on these children have been justified for non-therapeutic reasons. For instance, Ashley's mother was not alone in seeking the mastectomy to avert the risk of sexual abuse (Field 2016).

The other main procedure in Ashley's case was the hysterectomy which, in the narratives of parents who subsequently sought such treatment, was cast as central to the treatment. By discounting the hysterectomy, her clinicians distinguished the Ashley intervention from a long and contested history of non-consensual modification of disabled bodies. Indeed, notwithstanding the power of discourses of reproductive autonomy and choice (Alghrani 2018) that are also at stake in sterilisation decisions, law's past ineffectiveness at constraining non-therapeutic sterilisation clearly demonstrates the fragility of reproductive and other rights in the lives of disabled people. Thus, as Lee and Morgan observed back in 1989, analysing the landmark House of Lords decision in *Re B*, 'the effect… (and perhaps the intention)' was 'to treat mentally handicapped [sic] young women in a manner quite distinct from other young women' (Lee and Morgan 1988, 134). Contesting Margaret Shone's controversial view that to refuse non-therapeutic sterilisation of a disabled woman was 'to fragment the person' (Shone 1987, 639), Lee and Morgan asserted that '[o]n the contrary, to view the person as a whole, rather than atomised bits, mandates a wider view of what is at issue than simply reproductive organs'. Below we take up the potential of embodied integrity discourse to contest such fragmentation, but for now it is worth noting that, just as growth attenuation fell into decline but was repurposed for this treatment, Ashley's sterilisation suggests that the issue of non-consensual sterilisation continues to be a legal and political concern.

As with mastectomies, hysterectomies—whether abdominal, vaginal or laparoscopic—carry side effects that must be balanced against intended benefits. Infectious complications following hysterectomy vary dependant on the procedure, but typically occur in 9–13 per cent of all cases. Common infections include vaginal cuff cellulitis, infected haematoma or abscess, wound infection, urinary tract infection, postoperative haemorrhage, respiratory infection and febrile morbidity (Clarke-Pearson and Geller 2013, 655). Around 25.9 per cent of hysterectomy patients report at least one post-surgical complication in a two-year period after the surgery (Kjerulff et al. 2000, 1445). As with growth attenuation, hysterectomies can lead to venous thromboembolic complications (Clarke-Pearson and Geller 2013, 659). They too cause significant levels of post-surgical pain, with chronic pain reported in 5 to 32 per cent of all patients (Sobsey 2009, 97). Residual ovary syndrome, which is often very painful, is a common side effect of the type of hysterectomy utilised in the 'Ashley treatment', which causes the ovaries to enlarge (Rane and Ohizua 1998). For profoundly disabled children, a key concern is their ability to communicate such pain and the impact of these complications on their quality of life. Significantly, these very concerns were raised to justify the appendectomy, an aspect of the interventions on Ashley's body that has attracted no commentary in the ethics literature.

To demonstrate the inadequate attention paid in health law jurisprudence both to the complications of sterilisation and to the role of bodily integrity, it is worth briefly revisiting the early sterilisation cases before the English courts. Aside from the first reported case of *Re D* in 1976, where Heilbron J refused an application to sterilise an 11-year-old girl because the procedure would involve 'the deprivation of a basic human right, namely the right of a woman to reproduce' (Heilbron J, *Re D* [1976] 1 All ER 326) in rulings over the final quarter of the twentieth century judges eschewed any form of rights analysis (Lee 1988). This series of cases were read as pertaining to sex and pregnancy, with the twofold imperative of preventing pregnancy and restraining sexual behaviour of disabled adolescents and adults. Pregnancy was universally presented as a catastrophic outcome for a woman or girl with a mental disability or learning difficulties (Lee and Morgan 1988; Freeman 1988; Hegginbotham 1989; Brazier 1990). As Lord Bridge opined in *Re B (a Minor)* [1988] 1 AC 199, 'It is clear beyond argument that for her pregnancy would be an unmitigated disaster. The *only question* is how she may best be protected against it' (emphasis added, 205). Judges were similarly preoccupied with containing sexuality, casting disabled people as either 'out of control' or 'vulnerable to seduction' (Savell 2003–2004; Keywood 1995). As Sandland notes, this fits with a general legal tendency to construct the sexuality of disabled people as monstrous (Sandland 2013) rendering it easier to limit their rights. In contrast, over the same period, jurisdictions which placed a higher premium on bodily integrity reached different outcomes. In Canada, La Forest J in *Re Eve* [1986] 2 SCR 388 highlighted the 'grave intrusion on a person's rights and the certain physical damage' (86) that would necessarily result. Similarly, Brennan J in the leading Australian case followed *Re Eve,* and explicitly couched the issue as one of bodily integrity rather than a right to reproduce, thus eschewing the possibility of trading this off against the interests of others: 'the rule must give priority to the right to physical integrity and the human dignity it protected even though such a rule imposes burden[s]' (*Department of Health and Community Services (NT) V JWB and SMB* (1992) 175 CLR 218, at 24).

Decades later, UK judges have yet to exhibit such a clear commitment to protecting the disabled child's bodily integrity. Certainly, as Kennedy and Grubb predicted, the higher profile accorded 'rights talk' following enactment of the Human Rights Act 1998 has prompted English courts to re-evaluate *Re B* and its progeny (Kennedy and Grubb 2000, 909), heralding an approach better attuned to the rights of incapacitated children and adults. In the sterilisation context this has entailed a more detailed cost-benefit framework for assessing best interests, which means weighing the:

> advantages and disadvantages of the various treatment and management options, the viability of each such option and the likely effect each would have on the patient's best interests and, I would add, his enjoyment of life... (per Dame Butler-Sloss in *Re A* Hospital NHS Trust v S and Others [2003] Lloyds Rep Med 137, at 47)

In such assessments, case law has stressed that account must be taken of a broad range of factors which extend far beyond medical considerations (per

Thorpe LJ in *Re S (Adult Patient)* (*Sterilisation:* [2000] 2 F.L.R. 389 at 560). Consequently, judges have demonstrated a willingness to explore less restrictive and invasive alternatives to sterilisation, which were notably absent from earlier decisions (*Re S (Adult Patient: Sterilisation Patient's Best Interests)* [2000] 2 F.L.R. 389). Moreover, since 2005, the Mental Capacity Act requires applications for non-consensual and non-therapeutic sterilisation to be referred to the Court of Protection (2007, para 8.18), signalling their problematic nature. At the supranational level, the European Court of Human Rights (ECrtHR) has been clear (albeit in a case concerning a young woman found to be competent) that non-consensual sterilisation breaches various provisions of the European Convention on Human Rights (ECHR). Indeed, and notwithstanding the high threshold that needs to be satisfied for the Court to find a breach of the Article 3 prohibition on torture or inhuman and degrading treatment,[1] it ruled, in a case involving Slovakia, that sterilising a woman during a caesarean breached her Article 3 as well as Article 8 rights (*Case of V.C. v Slovakia* (Application No 18968/07). This ruling, as with the Australian and Canadian sterilisation cases, underlines the power of bodily integrity discourse. The absence of a similarly strong tradition in the UK means that protections are correspondingly weaker. The current approach is perhaps best summed up by the 2015 decision in *DD*, where Cobb J stipulated that:

> Any proposal for significant, life-changing surgery, in respect of a person who lacks capacity will inevitably be (as it has been in this case) extremely carefully scrutinised, and only authorised where is clearly demonstrated to be necessary, proportionate and 'best' for the individual involved. (*Re DD (No4) (Sterilisation)* (2015) EWCOP 4)

Yet, ongoing paternalistic attitudes to those with disabilities (*A NHS Trust v DE* [2013] EWHC 2562 (Fam)) mean that such procedures are unlikely to be definitively ruled out in the UK. Thus, in *DD* the sterilisation was authorised, notwithstanding Cobb J's acknowledgement that:

> The ethical, legal and medical issues arising here are self-evidently of the utmost gravity, engaging and profoundly impacting upon DD's personal autonomy, privacy, bodily integrity, and reproductive rights. (para 5)

He justified this outcome given DD's obstetric history, which had resulted in six children being removed, medical evidence regarding the threat to life that

[1] See, for example, in the matter of an Application by the Northern Ireland Human Rights Commission for Judicial Review [2018] UKSC 27.

a further Caesarean section would pose to her and the strong likelihood that she would not comply with medical advice. Consequently the 'predominant purpose' of the sterilisation was to preserve DD's life (at 130). It is noteworthy that, having considered an IUD/IUS as a less restrictive option, Cobb J invoked bodily integrity discourse to authorise the hysterectomy, since it would be a one-off procedure:

> [DD] has been consistent in maintaining a wish to be left alone, and to assert her personal autonomy in relation to her body... she is reported to have said that "if I cannot work my body and be who I am there is no point in being on this planet..." As her recent letter to Ms Y makes clear... "my body is mine", and she asserts "human rights" in relation to it. She abhors social work or other professional involvement in her life...

This case thus illustrates how deploying conventional bodily integrity discourse will not necessarily rule out non-consensual and irreversible surgical interventions.[2] Similarly, another recent decision, by Williams J, authorised a hysterectomy on 'Anne'—a young woman with autism, a severe learning disability, and endometriosis (*University Hospitals of Derby and Burton NHS Foundation Trust v J (by her litigation friend, the Official Solicitor) (Medical Treatment: Best Interests)* [2019] EWCOP 16.). Other contraceptive options had been tried in her case, but expert evidence indicated that long-term use of monthly injections of Decapeptyl, as well as being distressing for Anne, carried an 'almost inevitable' risk of osteoporosis and other side effects. This led Williams J to concur with the Official Solicitor's view:

> that this is significant life changing surgery which will impact profoundly upon Anne's personal autonomy, bodily integrity and reproductive rights. Nevertheless he supports the gynaecological intervention (and other interventions) as being in her best interests and thus lawful. They are necessary and proportionate interferences with her rights. (at para 23)

As in the Ashley case, this intervention was cast as therapeutic (at para 35), and it was stressed that a key benefit was that 'likely improvements in Anne's behaviour as a result of not having to deal with her menstrual cycle or 3 monthly injections is likely to mean that her devoted parents will be able to care for her for longer than might be the case otherwise' (at para 40). Interestingly, similar objections had also been raised in Ashley's case about the

[2] See also *A Local Authority v P (by her litigation friend, the Official Solicitor) The NHS Trust, A Family Member* [2018] EWCOP 10.

likely distress that menstruation would occasion. Significantly, and again echoing Ashley's case, Anne's consultant psychiatrist testified that:

> an effective intervention to minimise the monthly fluctuation in her mood and resolution of the abdominal pain she is experiencing will certainly make her behaviour more manageable and thus improve the quality of her life'. (at para 22)

William J's ruling illustrates well the continuities in how decision-making for profoundly disabled children carries over into their adult lives. It also evidences a preoccupation with menstruation which exemplifies Shildrick's contention that disabled people are defined 'as excessive, as contaminatory, as at once malign and helpless' (Shildrick 2005, 756). We explore in more detail below how these slippages between the interests of the disabled adult or child and their carers, and the rendering of disabled bodies as more 'manageable', are interpreted as improving the lives of children and adults. In authorising interventions, an implicit notion of *family integrity* is mobilised to trump the bodily integrity of individual family members (Fox and Thomson 2017). For now, however, the key point is that, notwithstanding Cobb J's pronouncement that 'it will be a rare case... in which the more radical alternative of sterilisation will be found to be in the best interest of an incapacitous woman of child bearing age' (para 11), sterilisation continues to be sanctioned in several recent Court of Protection cases. This suggests that English courts have, at best, paid only lip service to the value of bodily integrity.

## 4 The Limits of Bodily Integrity

In cases such as Ashley and Anne, as well as the broader jurisprudence on sterilisation and the limited discussions of growth attenuation, the body is clearly central (Savell 2003–2004). And, as we noted above, legal scholars are increasingly turning to bodily integrity and asserting its psychological and jurisprudential primacy. Typically, such scholars rely on conventional understandings of bodily integrity, given the doctrine's powerful message to others to keep off our bodies. As Elizabeth Shaw contends, violating bodily integrity:

> invades a particularly intimate sphere. The individual's body and mind are constitutive of the person and invading the mind and body therefore amounts to a fundamental attack on the person. (Shaw 2016, 9)

Thus, the right to bodily integrity as conventionally understood is a right to be free from physical interference. In Herring and Wall's words, 'it is the right not to have your body touched or your body interfered with without your consent' (Herring and Wall 2017, 571). Similarly, in a landmark children's case, Walker L.J. defined it as 'the right to have one's own body whole and intact and (on reaching an age of understanding) to take decisions about one's own body' (per Walker L.J. in *Re A (Conjoined Twins)* at 258). Law thus responds to the idea of sovereign control over the body by conceiving it as space which the individual is empowered to defend. Consequently, Kristen Savell argues that an 'invasion narrative' underpins consent provisions preventing unwarranted medical interference with the body (Savell 2003–2004, 1124). Such constructions of the body as bounded defensible space resonate with dominant understandings of the classical autonomous legal subject—what Ngaire Naffine terms the 'man of law' (Naffine 1998). Yet, while bodily integrity is thus inextricably linked with the right to make autonomous decisions, Herring and Wall argue persuasively that it is not reducible to autonomy, nor a mere subset of autonomy. In health law, bodily integrity comes into play when a patient refuses or withdraws consent to treatment and direct interference with the body is entailed (Herring and Wall 2017, 570). It is partly for this reason that Brazier deems bodily integrity to be 'the core value' in contemporary health law (Brazier 2009, 7). In its power to exclude others, it 'literally and figuratively provide[s] the necessary walls' to separate oneself from others (Herring and Wall 2017, 580). As Mary Koll has compellingly argued, its value lies in protecting profoundly developmentally impaired children from unnecessary bodily invasion 'even though self-determination is not possible' (Koll 2010, 240).

Conventional integrity then has many important benefits. For instance, its value in revealing harms that are otherwise downplayed can be traced in differential legal approaches to male and female genital cutting. Cutting of boys has traditionally been cast as a non-issue which is legally tolerated, whereas positioning female cutting as a breach of a woman's bodily integrity has resulted in it being constituted as mutilation and regulated by criminal law (Fox and Thomson 2017). This is because, to be justifiable, infringements of bodily integrity require 'the competing value to have considerable moral weight and practicable urgency' (Herring and Wall 2017 583). As a result, the most serious criminal offences constitute invasions of bodily integrity, and are cast as more serious than property and other offences which do not entail bodily invasion. Again, this can be seen in the genital cutting context, notably in the ruling by the Cologne District court that bodily integrity trumped benefits seen to derive from protection of cultural and religious traditions

(Landgericht Koln (Cologne District Court), Judgment on May 7 (2012) No. 151 Ns 169/11). This case, like the law governing FGM, offers a powerful instance of the legal force of the invasion narrative, which, in the case of children, serves to limit parental powers to make irreversible decisions to modify their bodies. Conventional notions of integrity, therefore, have important revealing and protective effects, and had they been applied in the Ashley X case it would have been difficult for the ethics committee to have found as it did. Yet, although the 'Ashley treatment' seems a particularly clear violation of bodily integrity, this discourse and the considerable risks of the 'treatment' were consistently absent from or downplayed in the ethics committee decision and subsequent commentary (with notable exceptions, e.g. Koll 2010; Kittay 2011; Epstein and Rosenbaum 2019). As Alicia Ouellette remarks of the Committee which unanimously sanctioned the procedures in a sitting that lasted for a single hour:

> [It] appears to have discounted entirely the physical harm the procedures would necessarily involve. It is as though the loss of a uterus, the removal of breasts, and the intentional disabling of normal growth had no significance or value. But these physical losses were in no way inconsequential. In any other context … [it] would be considered abusive. (Ouellette 2008, 236)

Clearly this resonates with other instances of how disabled people are subject to abuse under the guise of treatment.[3] Invoking bodily integrity doctrine would, as a minimum, have served to highlight such harms, and the significant risks of these experimental procedures documented above. Yet, even when commentators have acknowledged the principle, it has at times been summarily dismissed as inapplicable to disabled children. For instance, Steven Edwards concedes that: 'Ashley's "physical integrity" has plainly been violated. Her body has been radically changed, as has her future "trajectory" as a naturally developing being' (Edwards 2008, 342).

Yet, for him this objection 'does not seem compelling' since breaches of integrity may be legitimate. He invokes the analogy of an incompetent, severely physically disabled child trapped under rubble who requires a leg amputation to save her, which he states would clearly be permissible, especially if the quality of the disabled person's life would be no worse than before. This logic is puzzling, but Edward's analogy highlights a problematic strand of mainstream bioethics discourse. Such reasoning, dominated by individual ethical principles and technological developments, typically fails to attend to

[3] See e.g. *Hercegfalvy v Austria* (1992) 15 EHRR 437.

the social context of bodies and embodiment (Thomson 2018). In our context, this failure is compounded by how children or adults with mental impairments are often afforded fewer rights and less consideration than those with physical disabilities. Edwards' analogy problematically equates Ashley's healthy body with a physically disabled body that has undergone devastating injury and is in need of life-saving intervention. For as long as such hierarchies are maintained, both physically and mentally impaired bodies will inevitably 'fail', or be rendered deficient in comparison to the idealised 'normal' or able body (Barnes 2016).

Thus, notwithstanding its potential power, conventional bodily integrity discourse has clear limitations. Moreover, as we saw in the case of *DD*, bodily integrity arguments can be invoked to *justify* sterilisation if alternative procedures also compromise bodily integrity. In consequence, we argue that a richer formulation of integrity is necessary to overcome at least four problems with the conventional conception that we have addressed previously. We have argued that conventional integrity defines the body as owned property, thereby replicating a problematic mind/body split, that boundary metaphors associated with integrity exclude many forms of non-normative embodiment, that it opens up all bodies (but especially those of children) to excessive surveillance and that it can mandate punitive responses which potentially criminalise the actions of caring parents (Fox and Thomson 2017, 517–8). Additionally, we have traced in this chapter how the ill-defined scope of bodily integrity allows it to be mobilised in partial, often contradictory, ways or even wholly neglected, as the deliberations of the ethics committee, the sterilisation case law and much bioethical commentary demonstrate. Furthermore, conventional approaches grounded in defending bodily boundaries remain ill-equipped to cope with anomalous or disabled embodiment, while the static nature of property-based conceptions of the body struggles to accommodate bodily change and development.

## 5 Towards Embodied Integrity

Complementing the approach we develop in this chapter, Alan Hyde has highlighted the limitations of conventional integrity. While acknowledging its value, he suggests that what is needed is not a new or expanded right to bodily integrity, but rather:

> a bringing into consciousness of the multiple constructions already immanent in law, including alternatives to the body as property or privacy right or machine,

> alternatives that always treat people as embodied, that do not shy away from pain, sex or other embodied experiences, that replace the metaphors of property, machine or privacy right with a language of bodily presence. (Hyde 1997, 6)

In advocating a similarly embodied approach, we build upon the turn within feminist and other critical theories from bodies to embodiment as the object and subject of analysis (Fletcher et al. 2008; Thomson 2010). This shift addresses the limitations of the conventional body integrity approach, which as we have seen splits the body from the mind and conceives it as static, a feature which proves particularly problematic in freezing in time the body of the disabled child (see further Garland and Travis, this volume). Embodied approaches, in contrast, recognise the contingent, relational and biographical nature of bodies. They acknowledge that we experience our bodies in the context of discourses and institutional domains which shape our being in the world and mediate our relationship with it. Embodied understandings conceptualise bodies as more than instrumentally valuable, since they represent 'a constitutive part of who we are' (Kittay 2011, 617) and, importantly, who we may become. Thus, Chris Dietz has argued for embodiment to be understood as an ontological and epistemological process of becoming (Dietz 2018, see also Morland 2008). This feature, which contrasts with the static nature of conventional integrity approaches, renders embodiment an especially useful principle when medical interventions on children are proposed, since the child's body is a 'biologically and socially "unfinished" entity' (Williams and Bendelow 1998, 20) in a constant state of emergence. Embodied integrity therefore accommodates the mutability, contingency and plasticity of bodies (Fox and Thomson 2017, 519). Equally important, whilst conventional integrity is premised on the injunction to refrain from interfering with the bounded singular body, embodied integrity more readily encompasses a range of bodily states, including the 'improper' (Sullivan 2008, 112) bodies of disabled children. It 'shift[s] attention from the singular body or even multiple bodies as objects of analysis by mandating a broader focus on lived experience and the question of how we inhabit and experience the world through our bodies' (Fox and Murphy 2013, 256). Like conventional integrity, the importance of being able to transcend our bodies, to take the body for granted in a way that can be denied when actions—violent or otherwise—compromise our physical being in the world, is acknowledged (Priaulx 2008). Indeed, for disabled subjects, as for other marginalised legal subjects, the prospect of forgetting one's body and simply *being* embodied (Dietz 2018,199) may be especially hard to achieve (Garland-Thomson 1997, Koll 2010). Moreover, in the context of the

Ashley treatment, a focus on embodiment facilitates attempts to unpack the specificity of the threats to her integrity that this suite of interventions entails.

Our embodied integrity model is indebted to the theories of Joel Feinberg and Drucilla Cornell. Specifically, we have drawn on the potential of Cornell's conception of bodily integrity (Cornell 1995, Chap. 2) to substantiate and enrich Feinberg's argument that children have a right to an open future (Fox and Thomson 2017). To recap briefly, Feinberg proposes that children have autonomy rights that are held in trust for the adult that the child will become (Feinberg 1992). He argues that parents and others should refrain from actions that limit or deny options that the child should have when she reaches adulthood. This resonates with Cornell's vision of bodily integrity, which casts it as an open-ended process that must be protected if a person is to be accorded equal citizenship. Guaranteeing bodily integrity creates a zone within which individuals may 'transform themselves into political citizens' (Cornell 2002, 431). Our model brings these strands of argument together in the claim that protecting a child's embodied integrity is necessary to realising an open future where she can make the embodied choices that are the hallmark of the sovereign person. Although infringements of bodily integrity can have the negative biographical implications that conventional integrity flags up, embodied integrity also engages more positive biographical dimensions of the body as a feature of future change and development, as well as a vehicle for self-expression. Embodied integrity therefore both protects the body from encroachment and secures the right to make future embodied choices, as our bodies develop and are impacted by their environment and other entanglements. As Grosz notes:

> There is no bodily integrity in the sense of an unchanging continuity over time, only mixtures, ideas encountering each other and bodies affecting each other, each transforming and being transformed by its engagement (Grosz 2018, 79).

As outlined above, our model was formulated in the context of decision-making for children who will ultimately possess the capacities for independent decision-making in later life. By contrast, a focus on decision-making with mentally disabled children requires us to take account of the problematic feature of current legal understandings of capacity (Donnelly 2010; Clough 2018) and to strengthen the relational framing within which we reach decisions and which require support (Flynn and Arstein-Kerlake 2014; Arstein-Kerlake and Flynn 2016; Harris 2016). While Feinberg's model of a child's right to an open future remains central to our conception of embodied integrity, the fact that children like Ashley or young women like Anne may never obtain levels of competence required by legal tests embedded in the *Gillick* ruling (*Gillick v West Norfolk and Wisbech Area Health Authority* [1986] AC 112) or the Mental Capacity Act point to the need for greater support in decision-making (Donnelly 2017), which must respect the individual's 'will and preference' as required by the CRPD (Bantekas et al. 2018).

In seeking tentatively to bring our model into conversation with the social model of disability and the legal requirements of the CRPD, we suggest that four aspects have particular purchase in the lives of children with profound disabilities. First, and in line with our claim that bodily integrity discourse renders harms visible, we contend that an embodied integrity approach highlights how disabled embodiment is cast as inherently problematic, improper or wrong. Secondly, it mandates that we reason *from* the body and lived embodied experience, rather than reason *about* bodies in a detached and disembodied way (Williams and Bendelow 1998). Thirdly, our model recognises that humans are inevitably relational. Yet, importantly, and notwithstanding the dependency of the disabled child upon her family, it stresses the necessity of disentangling her rights from those of her parents, thereby contesting notions of family integrity which often underpin these discussions. Consequently, valuing the child's embodied integrity recognises her as a rights holder, and obligates us to support her to articulate or assert those rights. Finally, our focus on the child's right to an open future as a key aspect of her embodied integrity holds notwithstanding the reality that impairment may mean that future life is non-normative. Accordingly, and as raised particularly acutely by the case of the profoundly disabled child, the question is what is open to that particular child. We now consider these features of embodied integrity in turn, before summarising the implications for legal responses and suggesting how law can play a more productive role in the lives of profoundly disabled children.

## 5.1 Challenging the Negation of Disability

Disability theorists have long contested the 'negation of disabled embodiment' (Overboe 1999, 17) and the manner in which the lived experiences of disabled people are routinely discounted, with their bodies understood as medical lack or absence (Leder 1990). This is counterposed to the 'explicit privileging of wholeness, independence and integrity demanded of the able bodied subject' (Shildrick 2005, 757). As Overboe notes, one consequence is that the physical body of the disabled person is constituted as an object, rather than 'a lived body with an embodied self that lives and breathes, perceives and acts, speaks and reasons' (Overboe 1999, 18). Not only is the disabled body objectified, but it is coded as problematic or improper in line with Garland-Thomson's contention that disability is constituted as a 'state of corporeal inferiority' (Garland-Thomson 2002, 4–5). Relatedly, as we noted above, disabled people are rendered 'forever visible and problematic, never able to disappear into the background because of their body particularities' (Moser 2005, 677) or to be 'left alone' (Koll 2010). This tension between visibility and negation has very tangible consequences in reasoning about disabled bodies, as the Committee that unanimously sanctioned the Ashley procedures demonstrates.

Questions of reproductive autonomy or even sexual pleasure, which are simply assumed to play no part in the lives of the intellectually and physically disabled child, are similarly absent. Thus, Eve Feder Kittay, herself the parent of a child with severe impairments, observes of one prominent commentary:

> Diekema and Fost take an... instrumental stance toward sexual organs. Surmising that the removal of the breast buds might reduce sexually pleasurable sensations, they promptly dismiss the worry since Ashley would never "experience sexual pleasure without being exploited or sexually abused". Asking "what is it about becoming a woman that would be of interest to Ashley", they write: "Most of the usual features that distinguish a woman from a girl – the opportunity to marry, procreate, work, lead an autonomous life – would not have been available to Ashley with or without a uterus, fully developed breasts, or normal stature". (Kittay 2011, 260)

Relatedly, Sullivan highlights how disabilities generate narratives of the 'wrong body' which are cast as central to demands to medically modify or normalise bodies. While her work concerns such narratives in the case of transsexuals or self-demand amputees, similar imperatives underpin Ashley's case. In her parents' claim for corrective 'treatment', Ashley's body is rendered 'im-proper' as she grows too big and heavy to be transported easily and displays disruptive signs of 'precocious' puberty while being unable to value her reproductive capacity. Similarly, as we traced above, the bodies of women and girls in the sterilisation case law are constructed as messy or excessive, while girls in the past have been cast as excessively tall. These unruly bodies are then positioned as requiring medical management or discipline, and in extreme cases surgical correction. As Sullivan argues:

> this narrativization of wrong embodiment posits a distention between mind and body, and...constitute[s] the body as im-proper, that is, as *not* the property of

> the subject, and conceive[s] of surgery as the means by which to overcome somatic non-ownership, to achieve integrity. (Sullivan 2008, 107)

In this process, it becomes apparent how Ashley's lived body is reduced to 'thinghood'—an object separate from the self (Sullivan 2008, 113). Similar processes of objectification can be traced in cases of the disabled subjects of the early English sterilisation decisions. Such rulings allowed the surgical shaping of disabled people to accommodate the needs of others, including their carers. As with Ashley X, these decisions exemplify how, under the guise of best interests, disabled children and adults are the subject of decisions which in other contexts would undoubtedly be deemed abusive and legally impermissible. Indeed, it is difficult to identify another scenario in which law or medical ethics would sanction such radical interventions. By negating disabled embodiment, the discursive technologies at play in these decisions skew the cost-benefit assessments that are said to underpin decision-making. Thus, as Ouellette and Kittay note, the harms we have outlined in relation to growth attenuation are largely ignored. In bringing together 'disabled people's presences, bodies and their flesh' (Overboe 1999, 21), an embodied integrity approach helps challenge this negation and objectification of disabled bodes and the accompanying valorisation of liberal individualistic embodiment. It makes embodied experience central to decision-making and, while rendering disabled bodies visible, contests the view that they can be fragmented and separated from the person in ways that conventional bodily integrity discourse can allow.

## 5.2 Reasoning from the Body

In opposition to bodily negation, embodied integrity demands that we reason from the body and assert its embodied presence (Hyde 1997) rather than absence. This challenges the 'wrong body' narrative by valuing what Read and Clements term 'the authenticity of impaired modes of being' (Read and Clements 2004, 507). Such an approach contrasts starkly with much of the literature addressing Ashley X, and with reports of subsequent cases, which make limited attempts to understand the lived reality of such lives. Rather, Ashley is constituted as existing in and trapped in a state of perpetual childhood, understood in much of the academic literature and popular accounts as rendering her more manageable—a 'pillow angel'; 'forever small'—with prospects of development effectively frozen (see further Garland and Travis, this volume). As Koll observes, standard rationales and justifications for medical interventions 'rely on a very incomplete, and perhaps incorrect, understanding of the profoundly impaired child's quality of life as experienced by the child' (Koll 2010, 259–60). She demonstrates how, in practice, carers and health professionals consistently underestimate the quality of life of those living with disabilities and chronic conditions. Discussions of Ashley's case echoed earlier sterilisation cases in being replete with accounts of what she lacked (Lee and Morgan 1988)—a recurrent trope in discussions of disabled persons (Moser 2005, 675). Ashley was estimated to have the cognitive ability of a 3-month-old child, notwithstanding compelling critiques of the concept of 'mental age' (Koll 2010). In line with our embodied approach, Koll stresses the importance of reasoning instead from lived bodily experience and focusing on developmental and relational aspects of the child's life, including her potential to develop emotionally and sexually and to form relationships. Again, this resonates with scholarship in disability studies highlighting the discrimination inherent in excluding disabled persons from decisions about their lives and assessments of what they value (Fricker 2007; Series and Nilsson 2018). As Epstein and Rosenbaum note, it 'renders [children like Ashley] powerless over the fate of their own bodies' (Epstein and Rosenbaum 2019, 108). In this regard, it is noteworthy that the pleasure that Ashley is capable of deriving was downplayed or erased in many accounts. In contrast, Edwards comments that:

> she is said to enjoy changes of scenery, listening to music and family affection. She makes sounds when music plays and also moves her arms. She is said to smile and to show some recognition of her parents. (Edwards 2011, 41)

Still more tellingly, at nine years old, two years after conclusion of his growth attenuation, it was reported that Ricky Preslar was demonstrating increased purposeful movement (a key developmental milestone) and could move through the family home with a gait trainer (Field 2016).

Recognising the lived experience of those who are profoundly impaired is undoubtedly challenging, and raises difficult questions about who is best placed to interpret the 'lived reality' of the disabled child if s/he is unable to communicate it. In our view, approaches grounded in embodiment are best placed to capture these realities since they recognise our place in the world as 'relational, experiential, and contingent' (Garland-Thomson 1997, 596) susceptible to change and capable of being enhanced and supported. As Garland-Thomson argues, we must attend to the 'particularity of varying lived embodiments' (Garland-Thomson 1997, 592) while acknowledging the social politics of physical difference (Kuusisto 2012).

## 5.3 Children as Rights Holders Distinct from their Families

Margit Shildrick has observed how the status and meanings of disabled embodiment 'are from the start relational, rather than having autonomous standing' (Shildrick 2005, 756). Disabled peoples' lives are clearly enhanced by networks of care, and in Ashley's case, her family is evidently central to her everyday life. Stories of her life depict her as a deeply loved family member and show that her family functions as a collective which sustains her. Yet, in our view a crucial explanation for the erasure or downplaying of significant harms and risks inherent in the experimental interventions to which she was subject was how they functioned to maintain a sense of *family integrity*. Significantly, Edwards describes how Ashley is a 'bonding factor' in the family (Edwards 2008, 342), so that a central reason for seeking the procedures was to prevent her from becoming so burdensome that she could not be cared for at home. Stunting her growth ensured she remained easily portable and shielded her from being unduly distressed by menstruation. Arguably, by underlining these considerations, her parents and the ethics committee were both concerned primarily with the best interests or integrity of the family unit. This imperative to keep Ashley within the family, and the family intact, results in scant attention to arguments addressing *her* human rights, particularly those rooted in bodily integrity. In seeking to make her fit with her family, the procedures she underwent entailed that, in a literal sense, her experience of 'bodily being is constituted by [her] dwelling in a world of others' (Sullivan 2008, 126). In contrast, we argue that it is crucial to recognise that the interests of dependent family members may conflict with those of their families requiring limits to be placed on parental power to decide for children (Lyons 2010; Fox and Thomson 2017). This is why the child's right to embodied integrity must be the starting point for best interests assessments regarding medical treatment. At this juncture in our argument we encounter an obvious tension between individual and relational interests and rights. Our response is that in order to counter the construction of disabled people as objects—akin to pet animals to be spayed or surgically shaped for the convenience of their owners—it is necessary to prioritise the child's rights or interests in this way. Otherwise, their rights risk being subsumed into those of the family or other carers (Fox and Thomson 2017). However, in recognition of the importance of sustaining the entanglement of profoundly disabled children in their family networks, and in line with the social model of disability which makes us attentive to the relationships, networks and structures in which they are situated, we shall conclude by arguing for greater state support for families caring for disabled children and adults.

## 5.4 Child's Right to an Open Future

Alicia Ouellette has argued that a child's right to an open future is underpinned by the right to bodily integrity, as well as self-determination. Building on this, we have argued elsewhere that dicta in recent English cases tentatively acknowledge this point by recognising the importance of protecting a child's bodily integrity and therefore deferring irreversible non-therapeutic surgical interventions until the child can decide for herself (Fox and Thomson 2017). In order to participate in decisions, children and adults with mental impairments will need fuller support in decision-making in order to reflect their 'will and preference' (Szmukler 2019). In this regard, we would argue that embodied integrity is crucial in their lives, since their more pronounced dependency renders them particularly susceptible to becoming submerged in parental projects, and even of being surgically shaped to better fit with their parents' needs and lives. Moreover, as commentators including Bridgeman (2005), Kittay (2011) and Peace and Roy (2014) highlight, it is important to simultaneously recognise limitations to what children with severe cognitive impairments may intellectually achieve, while appreciating that their interactions and experiences can develop. Interests in, and responses to, the outside world may change, just as they do for those who are not cognitively impaired. We saw above that Ashley was able to derive demonstrable pleasure from interactions and sensations. Relevant changes in her life may include preferences for and reactions to music, activities and persons, as Peace and Roy argue:

> Most importantly, however, is the simple fact that children just like Ashley change over their lifespan. Their minds "progress" and change though not necessarily in a typical fashion. For example, Sophie [Roy's daughter], at 19, while eating lunch at a mall food court, expressed her significant interest in a young man walking past by gaping and dropping her fork in admiration. This is not the behaviour of a little girl or remotely like infant behaviour. Many other parents of children even more compromised than Roy's daughter report similar growth. (Peace and Roy 2014, 43)

Kittay similarly talks of her daughter 'ogling' attractive men her own age (Kittay 2011). Acknowledging such potential leads us to advocate that an embodied integrity model can advance a child's interests by protecting her right to an open future, however atypical it might be. Recognising her embodied integrity, and positioning it as a central consideration in best interests assessments, in turn enhances her capacity for intimate entanglements and for change and development, while according her body a central place in these experiences. Importantly, in our view, it would rule out surgical attempts to infantilise disabled children by sterilising them and freezing them in time as 'forever small'.

## 6 Concluding Thoughts

Shildrick has claimed that, 'the construction of physical difference as a failing, incomplete and inferior marks disabled embodiment as deeply devalued, not so much for what it is, but for what it fails to be' (Shildrick 2005, 756). In our view, the Ashley case and the earlier sterilisation cases with which we would align it exemplify the ongoing power of such constructions. The sustained attention which Ashley X has attracted is partly attributable to the radical nature of the intervention, which was shrouded in secrecy and cast in earlier commentary as 'exceptional'. In this chapter we have sought to contest its exceptionality. We suggest that significant demand exists for this controversial suite of procedures, which we locate within the long history of modifying the bodies of disabled adults, adolescents and children. In our view, this suggests the need for a broader legal response to govern interventions on the bodies and in the lives of profoundly disabled children, which as for all children should be grounded in the protection of their embodied integrity.

As regards Ashley specifically, we concur with Ouellette that 'the law failed Ashley'. It allowed her parents to alter her body profoundly and permanently for social, not medical, reasons without adequate process or oversight' (Ouellette 2008, 209) and it failed to understand her as emergent. In a UK context, Court of Protection authorisation would be required for such procedures on over 16s, suggesting that High Court authorisation should be required in the case of children. Yet, recent cases such as the *University Hospitals of Derby and Burton NHS Foundation Trust v J (Medical Treatment: Best Interests)* [2019] EWCOP 16 indicate that judicial oversight remains an imperfect vehicle for protecting the integrity of the disabled body. Notwithstanding the legal and cultural shifts heralded by the Human Rights Act and Mental Capacity Act, the protection of bodily integrity in UK law remains partial and incomplete. Case law contains scant reference to the CPRD, and disabled adults and children continue to be subject to controversial interventions. The history of legal responses to non-consensual sterilisation suggests that interventions akin to those in the Ashley case are unlikely to be definitively ruled out in the UK.

There are, however, encouraging signs in the emerging empirical literature (Wrigley et al. 2018) that such debates are increasingly couched in the language of bodily integrity. Yet, for the reasons articulated in this chapter, such discourse needs to be reformulated to adequately accommodate the complexity of disabled embodiment. As Dietz has argued, legal embodiment should be reconceptualised as an ongoing process which produces normative bodies and behaviours, and shapes the conditions and possibilities for embodied resistance (Dietz 2018, 186–7). In similar vein, James Overboe has argued for the validation of both a disabled embodiment and sensibility:

> Our physical, mental and emotional manifestations of disability as well as the social, political, moral and physical environment will continue to have an impact upon us. But shifting the notion of an identity which is devalued to lived experience that is valued causes a change in approach. (Overboe 1999, 23)

We see our model of embodied integrity as contributing to such a change in approach, as well as fitting within the broader turn within the humanities and social sciences to the role of embodiment in new models of social justice. Our focus on Ashley's embodied integrity and the importance of how she is supported in society direct us to the obligations of the state. Following Epstein and Rosenbaum (2019), we would stress the importance of equipping her family with the assets or resources to care for her, so that recourse to an experimental suite of medical interventions designed to 'remake' their daughter and sister is unnecessary. Rather than prioritising family integrity, as we argue happened in the Ashley case, the focus should be on state obligations to provide for the family in the face of the significant caring responsibilities entailed by living with children and adults like Ashley and Anne. We see this as consonant with the vulnerability framework set out in this collection and elsewhere by Martha Fineman (e.g. 2010, 2011, 2013) but which we cannot elaborate on here.

Crucially, in endorsing an experimental chemical and surgical solution, standard bioethical accounts of the case omit discussion of embodiment, of social attitudes to disability (Oliver 1990; Shakespeare 2006) and of the need for a broader social strategy. In the rare instances where these issues are raised within bioethics, they dismissed as irrelevant to Ashley's case (Edwards 2011). We believe that our embodied integrity model has an important role to play in ensuring health professionals can less readily sanction interventions on children that will reduce their material bodies to legal objects to be fragmented and medically managed, since they will be called to account legally if they acquiesce in such requests. This should, in our view, be seen as a first step towards a broader social justice approach that fully values embodied difference and supports families to realise and respect such difference.

## References

— (2007, October 8). Let the Mother Decide, *The Daily Telegraph.*

— (2007, October 10). Mother's plea to Remove Disabled Katie's Womb, *Brentwood Gazette.*

— (2007, January 9). Ashley X and the Perils of Morality, *The New Zealand Herald*, New Zealand.

— (2007, January 2007). Welcome to Ashley's Blog, Dedicated for the Wellbeing of Pillow Angels, Prepared by her Parents., *PillowAngel.org*

— (2012, March 17). Tom Becomes First Boy to Receive Ashley Treatment *Topnews*, UAE.

— (2017, January 5). Where are they Now? *Portland Tribune*, Portland.

Ainsworth, D. (2007, January 10). Don't Judge Us, *Brentwood Gazette.*

Alghrani, A. (2018). *Regulating Assisted Reproductive Technologies*. Cambridge: CUP. New Horizons.

Ammaturo, F. (2016). Intersexuality and the "Right to Bodily Integrity": Critical Reflections on Female Genital Cutting, Circumcision and Intersex "Normalising" Surgeries in Europe. *Social & Legal Studies, 25*, 591–610.

Arstein-Kerlake, A., & Flynn, E. (2016). The General Comment on Article 12 of the Convention on the Rights of Persons with Disabilities: A Roadmap for Equality Before the Law. 20 *International Journal of Human Rights* 471.

Ayres, C. (2007, January 4). Parents Defend Decision to Keep Girl a Child. *The Times*, London, 9.

Bantekas, I., Stein, M. A., & Anastasiou, D. (Eds.). (2018). *The UN Convention on the Rights of Persons with Disabilities: A Commentary*. New York: OUP.

Barnard, N. D., Scialli, R. A., & Bobela, S. (2002). The Current Use of Estrogens for Growth Suppressant Therapy in Adolescent Girls. *Journal of Pediatric and Adolescent Gynecology, 15*, 23–26.

Barnes, E. (2016). *The Minority Body: A Theory of Disability*. Oxford University Press.

Bates, C. (2012, March 16). Should Parents Stop their Very Disabled Children from Growing up? Father Sparks Debate about Treatment that Could Spread to UK. *MailOnline.*

Bowcott, O. (2007, October 8). Mother Defends Hysterectomy for Disabled Daughter: Campaigners Say Surgery Raises Ethical Issues. Removal of Womb 'in Best Interests' of Girl, 15. *The Guardian.*

Brazier, M. (1990). Down the Slippery Slope. *Professional Negligence, 6*, 25–28.

Brazier, M. (2009). Introduction: Being Human: Of Liberty and Privilege. In S. Smith & R. Deazley (Eds.), *The Legal, Medical and Cultural Regulation of the Body: Transformation and Transgression*. London: Routledge.

Bridgeman, J. (2005). Caring for Children with Severe Disabilities: Boundaried and Relational Rights. *International Journal of Children's Rights, 13*(1–2), 99–120. ISSN 0927-5568.

Carlson, D., & Dorfman, D. (2007). Investigative Report Regarding the "Ashley Treatment". *Disability Rights Education and Defense Fund*, 8 May <http://dredf.org/public-policy/ethics/investigative-report-regarding-the-ashley-treatment/≥ Accessed 16 June 2018.

Clark, P., & Vasta, L. (2006). The Ashley Treatment: An Ethical Analysis. *The Internet Journal of Law, Healthcare and Ethics, 5*(1), 1.

Clarke-Pearson, D. L., & Geller, E. J. (2013). Complications of Hysterectomy. *Obstetrics and Gynecology, 121*(3), 654.

Clough, B. A. (2018). New Legal Landscapes: (Re)Constructing the Boundaries of Mental Capacity Law. *Medical Law Review, 26*, 246–275.

Cook, M. (2007, January 15). The Ashley Experiment Should Never Be Repeated. *Sydney Morning Herald*, Australia, 11.

Cornell, D. (1995). *The Imaginary Domain: Abortion, Pornography and Sexual Harassment*. Routledge.

Cornell, D. (2002). Anti-Racism, Multiculturalism and the Ethics of Identification. *Philosophy and Social Criticism, 28*(4), 419–449.

Diekema, D. S., & Fost, N. (2010). Ashleigh Revisited: A Response to the Peer Commentaries. *American Journal of Bioethics, 10*, 4–6.

Dietz, C. (2018). Governing Legal Embodiment: On the Limits of Self Declaration. *Feminist Legal Studies, 26*, 185–204.

Donnelly, M. (2010). *Healthcare Decision-Making and the Law: Autonomy, Capacity and the Limits of Liberalism*. Cambridge University Press.

Donnelly, M. (2017). Changing Values and Growing Expectations: The Evolution of Capacity Law. *Current Legal Problems, 70*.

Edwards, S. D. (2008). The Ashley Treatment: A Step Too Far or Not Far Enough? *Journal of Medical Ethics, 34*, 341–343.

Edwards, S. D. (2011). The Case of Ashley X. *Clinical Ethics, 6*, 39–44.

Epstein, J., & Rosenbaum, S. A. (2019). Revisiting Ashley X: An Essay on Disabled Bodily Integrity, Sexuality, Dignity and Family Caregiving. *Touro Law Review, 35*(2019), 101–138.

Fabre, C. (2006). *Whose Body is it Anyway? Justice and the Integrity of the Person*. Oxford University Press.

Feinberg, J. (1992). The Child's Right to an Open Future. In *Freedom and Fulfilment: Philosophical Essays* (pp. 76–89). Princeton.

Field, G (2016, March 22). Should Parents of Children with Severe Disabilities be Allowed to Stop Their Growth? *NYTimes.com*.

Fineman, M. (2010). The Vulnerable Subject and the Responsive State. *Emory Law Journal, 60*, 251.

Fineman, M. (2011). "Elderly" as Vulnerable: Rethinking the Nature of Individual and Societal Responsibility. *Elder Law Journal, 20*(1), 71–111.

Fineman, M. A. (2013). Equality, Autonomy, and the Vulnerable Subject in Law and Politics. In M.A. Fineman & A. Grear (Eds.) *Vulnerability: Reflections on a New Ethical Foundation for Law and Politics* (pp. 13–28). Ashgate.

Fletcher, R., Fox, M., & McCandless, J. (2008). Legal Embodiment: Analysing the Body of Healthcare Law. *Medical Law Review, 16*, 321–345.

Flynn, E., & Arstein-Kerlake, A. (2014). Legislating Personhood: Realizing the Right to Support in Exercising Legal Capacity. *International Journal of Law in Context, 10*, 81.

Fox, M., & Murphy, T. (2013). The Body, Bodies, Embodiment: Feminist, Legal Engagement with Health. In M. Davies & V. Munro (Eds.), *The Ashgate Research Companion to Feminist Legal Theory* (pp. 249–267). Ashgate.

Fox, M., & Thomson, M. (2017). Bodily Integrity, Embodiment and the Regulation of Parental Choice. *Journal of Law & Society, 44*(4), 501–530.

Fox, M., Thomson, M., & Warburton, J. (2019). Non-therapeutic Male Genital Cutting & Harm: Law, Policy, & Evidence from UK Hospitals. *Bioethics, 33*(4), 467–474.

Frader, J. E. (2007). Ashley's Case. *Paediatric Research, 61*, 517–517.

Freeman, M. (1988). Sterilising the Mentally Handicapped. In Freeman (Ed.), *Medicine Ethics and the Law*. Sweet and Maxwell.

Freund, P. (2001). Bodies, Disability and Spaces: The Social Model and Disabling Spatial Organisations. *Disability & Society, 16*, 689–706.

Fricker, M. (2007). *Epistemic Injustice*. Oxford: Oxford University Press.

Garland-Thomson, R. (1997). Feminist Theory, the Body, and the Disabled Figure. In J. L. Davis (Ed.), *The Disability Studies Reader*. London: Routledge.

Garland-Thomson, R. (2002). Integrating Disability, Transforming Feminist Theory. *National Women's Studies Association Journal, 14*(2), 1–32.

Gartner, R., Jensen, M. B., Nielsen, J., Ewertz, M., Kroman, N., & Kehlet, H. (2009). Prevalence of and Factors Associated with Persistent Pain Following Breast Cancer Surgery. *JAMA, 302*(18), 1985–1992

Goldzieher, M. A. (1956). Treatment of Excessive Growth in the Adolescent Female. *The Journal of Clinical Endocrinology and Metabolism, 16*(2), 249.

Grabham, E. (2012). Bodily Integrity and the Surgical Management of Intersex. *Body & Society, 18*, 1–26.

Grosz, E. (2018). *The Incorporeal: Ontology, Ethics and the Limits of Materialism*. Columbia University Press.

Gunther, D. F., & Diekema, D. S. (2006). Attenuating Growth in Children with Profound Developmental Disability: A New Approach to an Old Dilemma. *Archives of Pediatrics and Adolescent Medicine, 160*, 1013–1017.

Harris, J. (2016). The Role of Support in Sexual Decision-Making for People with Intellectual and Developmental Disabilities. *Ohio State Law Journal, 77*, 83.

Hegginbotham, C. (1989). Sterilising People with Mental Handicaps. In S. Mc Lean (Ed.), *Legal Issues in Human Reproduction*. Dartmouth: Aldershot.

Herring, J., & Wall, J. (2017). The Nature and Significance of the Right to Bodily Integrity. *Cambridge Law Journal, 76*, 566–588.

Hughes, B., & Paterson, K. (1997). The Social Model of Disability and the Disappearing Body: Towards a Sociology of Impairment. *Disability & Society, 12*, 325–340.

Hyde, A. (1997). *Bodies of Law*. Princeton: Princeton University Press.

Kennedy, I., & Grubb, A. (2000). *Kennedy and Grubb Medical Law* (3rd ed.). London: Butterworths.

Keywood, K. (1995). Sterilising the Woman with Learning Difficulties – In her Best Interests? In J. Bridgeman & S. Millns (Eds.), *Law and Body Politics*. Aldershot: Dartmouth.

Kittay, E. F. (2011). Forever Small: The Strange Case of Ashley X. *Hypatia, 26*, 610–631.

Koll, M. (2010). Growth Interrupted: Nontherapeutic Growth Attenuation, Parental Medical Decision Making and the Profoundly Developmentally Disabled Child's Right to Bodily Integrity. *University of Illinois Law Review, 2010*(1), 225–264.

Kjerulff, K. H., Rhodes, J. C., Langenberg, P. W., & Harvey, L. A. (2000). Patient Satisfaction with Results of Hysterectomy. *American Journal of Obstetrics and Gynaecology, 183*(6), 1440.

Kuusisto, S. (2012). When Is a Failure of Imagination Dangerous? *Hastings Centre Report*.

Lantos, J. (2010). It's Not the Growth Attenuation, It's the Sterilization! *American Journal of Bioethics, 10*, 45.

Latimer, J. (2019). Science under Siege? Being alongside the Life Sciences, Giving Science Life. *The Sociological Review Monographs, 67*(2), 264–268.

Latimer, J., & Lopez Gomez, D. (2019). *Intimate Entanglements*: Affects, More-than-Human Intimacies and the Politics of Relations in Science and Technology. *The Sociological Review Monographs, 67*(2), 246–263.

Leder, D. (1990). *The Absent Body*. University of Chicago Press.

Lee, S. (1988). From D. to B. to T.: Sterilising Mentally Handicapped Teenagers., 15–17.

Lee, J. M., & Howell, J. D. (2006). Tall Girls: The Shaping of a Medical Therapy. *Archives of Pediatrics & Adolescent Medicine, 160*, 1035–1039.

Lee, R., & Morgan, D. (1988). Sterilisation and Mental Handicap: Sapping the Strength of the State. *Journal of Law and Society, 15*, 229–246.

Lewis, J. (2007, January 6). The Moral Line in Medicine Shifts Once Again *The Independent*, London, 36.

Lipsett, M. B. (1977). Estrogen Use and Cancer Risk. *JAMA, 237*, 1112–1115.

Lyons, B. (2010). The Limits of Parental Authority. *American Journal of Bioethics, 10*, 50.

Ludbook, R. (1995–6). The Child's Right to Bodily Integrity. *Current Issues in Criminal Justice* 7: 123–132.
Marshall, W. A. (1975). What Can We Do About Tall Girls? *Arch Dis Child, 50*, 671.
Mazor, J. (2019). 'On the Strength of Children's Right to Bodily Integrity: The Case of Circumcision? *Journal of Applied Philosophy, 36*(1), 1–16.
McGhee, T. (2016, May 24). Controversial Procedure. *The Denver Post*, 1A.
McVeigh, K. (2012a, March 16). The "Ashley Treatment": Erica's' story. *The Guardian.*
McVeigh, K. (2012b, March 16). Growth Attenuation Treatment: Tom, the First Boy to Undergo Procedure. *The Guardian*, Accessed 6 June 2019. https://www.theguardian.com/society/2012/mar/16/growth-attenuation-treatment-toms-story
Miller, R. A. (2007). *The Limits of Bodily Integrity: Abortion, Adultery and Rape Legislation in Comparative Perspective* (1st ed.). Routledge.
Morland, I. (2008). Intimate Violations: Intersex and the Ethics of Bodily Integrity. *Feminism & Psychology, 18*(3), 425–430.
Moser, I. (2005). On Becoming Disabled and Articulating Alternatives. The Multiple Modes of Ordering Disability and their Interferences. *Cultural Studies, 19*(6), 667–700.
Naffine, N. (1998). The Legal Structure of Self-Ownership: Or the Self-Possessed Man and the Woman Possessed. *Journal of Law & Society, 25*(2), 193–212.
Naffine, N. (2003). Who Are Law's Persons? From Cheshire Cats to Responsible Subjects. *Modern Law Review., 66*(3), 346–367.
NHS Choices. (2017, May 14). Mastectomy – Complications. *NHS Choices*, http://www.nhs.uk/Conditions/Mastectomy/Pages/Complications.aspx
Oliver, M. (1990). *The Politics of Disablement: A Sociological Approach*. London: St Martin's Press.
Oliver, M. (1996). *Understanding Disability: From Theory to Practice*. Palgrave Macmillan: London.
Oliver, M. (2013). The Social Model of Disability: Thirty Years on. *Disability & Society, 28*, 1024.
Ouellette, A. R. (2008). Growth Attenuation, Parental Choice, and the Rights of Disabled Children: Lessons from the Ashley X Case. *Houston Journal of Health Law and Policy, 8*, 207–244.
Overboe, J. (1999). Difference in Itself': Validating Disabled People's Lived Experience. *Body & Society, 5*(4), 17–29.
Pavia, W. (2016, March 24). Parents Drug their Disabled Children to Stunt Growth. *The Times.*
Peace, W. J., & Roy, C. (2014). Scrutinizing Ashley X: Presumed Medical "Solutions" vs Real Social Adaptation. *Journal of Philosophy, Science and Law, 14*, 33–52.
Pilkington, E. (2007, January 8). Parents of Disabled Children Ask Doctors for "Ashley Treatment". *The Guardian.*
Pilkington E. (2012, March 15). Ashley Treatment on the Rise Amid Concerns from Disability Rights Groups. *The Guardian*, Accessed 6 June 2019. https://www.theguardian.com/society/2012/mar/15/ashley-treatment-rise-amid-concerns.

Priaulx, N. (2008). Rethinking Progenitive Conflict: Why Reproductive Autonomy Matters. *Medical Law Review, 16*(2), 169–200.

Prigg, M. (2007, January 5). How Can they Mutilate Ashley? *The Evening Standard*. London, 9.

Rane, A., & Ohizua, O. (1998). "Acute" Residual Ovary Syndrome. *Journal of Obstetrics and Gynaecology, 38*, 447–448.

Rask, O., Nilsson, K. O., & Berntorp, E. (2008). Oestrogen Treatment of Constitutional Tall Stature in Girls: Is there a Risk of Thrombosis or Bleeding? *Acta Pediatrica, 97*(3), 342–347.

Read, J., & Clements, L. (2004). Demonstrably Awful: The Right to Life and the Selective Non-Treatment of Disabled Babies and Children. *Journal of Law and Society, 31*(4), 482–509.

Saletan, W. (2007, January 20). Girl, Interrupted *Slate Magazine*.

Sandland, R. (2013). Sex and capacity: the management of monsters? *Modern Law Review, 76*(6), 981–1009.

Savell, K. (2003–4). Sex and the Sacred: Sterilization and Bodily Integrity in English and Canadian Law. *McGill LJ, 49*, 1093–1141.

Sekellariou, D., & Rotarou, E. S. (2017). The Effects of Neoliberal Policies on Access to Healthcare for People with Disabilities. *International Journal for Equity in Health, 16*, 199–207.

Series, L., & Nilsson, A. (2018). Article 12 CRPD: Equal Recognition before the Law. In I. Bantekas, M. A. Stein, & D. Anastasiou (Eds.), *The UN Convention on the Rights of Persons with Disabilities: A Commentary* (pp. 339–382). Oxford: Oxford University Press.

Serna et al., (1997). Assessing Same/Different Judgements in Individuals with Severe Intellectual Disabilities: A Status Report. *Research in Developmental Disabilities 18*(5), 343–368

Shakespeare, T. (2006). *Disability Rights and Wrongs*. Routledge.

Shakespeare, T. (2013). The Social Model of Disability. In L. J. Davis (Ed.), *The Disability Studies Reader* (4th ed., pp. 214–221). London: Routledge.

Shaw, E. (2016). Against the Mandatory Use of Neurointerventions in Criminal Sentencing. In D. Birks & T. Douglas (Eds.), *Treatment for Crime: Philosophical Essays on Neuro- Interventions in Criminal Justice*. Oxford: Oxford University Press.

Shone, M. (1987). Mental Health – Sterilization of Mentally Retarded Persons – Parens Patriae Power: Re Eve. *The Canadian Bar Review, 66*, 635.

Shildrick, M. (2005). The Disabled Body, Genealogy and Undecidability. *Cultural Studies, 9*(6), 755–770.

Shimon, I., & Barkan, A. (2012). Estrogen Treatment for Acromegaly. *Pituitary, 15*, 601–607.

Singer, P. (2007, January 26). A Convenient Truth, *The New York Times*, Accessed 1 Sep 2019. https://www.nytimes.com/2007/01/26/opinion/26singer.html

Smock, A. (2007, October 9). Americans with Disabilities Affirm Katie Thorpe's Right to Bodily Integrity, *Feminist Response in Disability Activism*, Accessed 10

Aug 2019. http://fridanow.blogspot.co.uk/2007/10/americans-with-disabilities-affirm.html

Sobsey, D. (2009). Cutting Edge Treatment: Pain and Surgery in the Ashley X Case. *Developmental Disabilities Bulletin, 37*(1–2), 63–90.

Sullivan, N. (2008). The Role of Medicine in the (Trans)Formation of 'Wrong' Bodies. *Body & Society, 14*(1), 105–116.

Szmukler, G. (2019). "Capacity", "Best Interests", "Will and Preferences" and the UN Convention on the Rights of Persons with Disabilities. *World Psychiatry, 18*(1), 34–41.

Tanner, L. (2007, January 4). Surgery to Stunt Disabled girl's Growth Raises Ethical Questions; some Decry "Eugenics". *The Associated Press*, Chicago.

Thomson, M. (2010). A Tale of Two Bodies: The Male Body in Feminist Legal Theory. In M. Fineman (Ed.), *Transcending the Boundaries of Law* (pp. 143–155). London: Routledge.

Thomson, M. (2018). Bioethics and Vulnerability: Recasting the Objects of Ethical Concern. *Emory Law Journal, 67*(6), 1207–1233.

Trombley, S. (1988). *The Right to Reproduce: A History of Coercive Sterilization.* Weidenfeld and Nicolson: London.

Tsvirko, N. (2015, 29 October). Severely Disabled New Zealand Girl, 10, Will Never Become a Woman after Parents Give her Controversial Hormone Therapy to Stunt her Growth. *MailOnline*, Australia.

Vallis, M. (2005, January 5). "What Is Best for this Child?": Disabled Rights Case: Parents Stunt the Growth of their "Pillow Angel". *National Post (f/k/a The Financial Post)*, Canada, A3.

Viens, A. M. (2017). *The Right to Bodily Integrity.* Routledge.

Wilford, B. S., et al. (2010). Navigating Growth Attenuation in Children with Profound Disabilities: Children's Interests, Family Decision-Making, and Community Concerns. *Hastings Center Report, 40*(6), 27–40. Seattle Growth Attenuation and Ethics Working Group http://www.jstor.org/stable/pdf/40928341.pdf?_=1467368052302.

Williams, S. J., & Bendelow, G. (1998). *The Lived Body: Sociological Themes, Embodied Issues.* London: Routledge.

Wrigley R (et al) (2018) Growth Attenuation Therapy for Children with Severe Physical and Cognitive Disability: Practice and Perspectives of New Zealand Paediatricians Journal of Paediatrics and Child Health 53(12): 1180–1185.

# Correction to: Healthcare, Well-being, and the Regulation of Diversity in Healing

Emilie Cloatre and Nayeli Urquiza-Haas

## Correction to:

**Chapter 5 in: C. Dietz et al. (eds.), *A Jurisprudence of the Body*, Palgrave Socio-Legal Studies, https://doi.org/10.1007/978-3-030-42200-4_5**

Chapter 5 was previously published non-open access. It has now been changed to open access under a CC BY 4.0 license and the copyright holder updated to 'The Author(s)'. The book has also been updated with this change.

The updated version of this chapter can be found at
https://doi.org/10.1007/978-3-030-42200-4_5



C. Dietz et al. (eds.), *A Jurisprudence of the Body*, Palgrave Socio-Legal Studies,
https://doi.org/10.1007/978-3-030-42200-4_13

# Index[1]



[1] Note: Page numbers followed by 'n' refer to notes.



C. Dietz et al. (eds.), *A Jurisprudence of the Body*, Palgrave Socio-Legal Studies,
https://doi.org/10.1007/978-3-030-42200-4

The manufacturer's authorised representative in the EU is Springer Nature Customer Service Centre GmbH, Europaplatz 3, 69115 Heidelberg, Germany. If you have any concerns regarding our products, please contact ProductSafety@springernature.com

Printed and bound by CPI Group (UK) Ltd, Croydon, CR0 4YY
25/09/2026
02222902-0018